Czechoslovakia

WORLD BIBLIOGRAPHICAL SERIES

General Editors:
Robert L. Collison (Editor-in-chief)
Sheila R. Herstein
Louis J. Reith
Hans H. Wellisch

VOLUMES IN THE SERIES

VOLUME 68

Czechoslovakia

David Short

Compiler

CLIO PRESS

OXFORD, ENGLAND · SANTA BARBARA, CALIFORNIA
DENVER, COLORADO

016.9437
S 559

British Library Cataloguing in Publication Data

Short, David
Czechoslovakia.– (World bibliographical series;
v. 68)
1. Czechoslovakia – Bibliography
I. Title   II. Series
016.9437   ZZ136

ISBN 1–85109–011–8

Clio Press Ltd.,
55 St. Thomas' Street,
Oxford OX1 1JG, England.

ABC-Clio Information Services,
Riviera Campus, 2040 Alameda Padre Serra,
Santa Barbara, Ca. 93103, USA

Designed by Bernard Crossland
Typeset by Columns Design and Production Services, Reading, England
Printed and bound in Great Britain by
Billing and Sons Ltd., Worcester

THE WORLD BIBLIOGRAPHICAL SERIES

This series will eventually cover every country in the world, each in a separate volume comprising annotated entries on works dealing with its history, geography, economy and politics; and with its people, their culture, customs, religion and social organization. Attention will also be paid to current living conditions – housing, education, newspapers, clothing, etc. – that are all too often ignored in standard bibliographies; and to those particular aspects relevant to individual countries. Each volume seeks to achieve, by use of careful selectivity and critical assessment of the literature, an expression of the country and an appreciation of its nature and national aspirations, to guide the reader towards an understanding of its importance. The keynote of the series is to provide, in a uniform format, an interpretation of each country that will express its culture, its place in the world, and the qualities and background that make it unique.

SERIES EDITORS

Robert L. Collison (Editor-in-chief) is Professor Emeritus, Library and Information Studies, University of California, Los Angeles, and is currently the President of the Society of Indexers. Following the war, he served as Reference Librarian for the City of Westminster and later became Librarian to the BBC. During his fifty years as a professional librarian in England and the USA, he has written more than twenty works on bibliography, librarianship, indexing and related subjects.

Sheila R. Herstein is Reference Librarian and Library Instruction Coordinator at the City College of the City University of New York. She has extensive bibliographic experience and has described her innovations in the field of bibliographic instruction in 'Team teaching and bibliographic instruction', *The Bookmark*, Autumn 1979. In addition, Doctor Herstein co-authored a basic annotated bibliography in history for Funk & Wagnalls *New encyclopedia*, and for several years reviewed books for *Library Journal*.

Louis J. Reith is librarian with the Franciscan Institute, St. Bonaventure University, New York. He received his PhD from Stanford University, California, and later studied at Eberhard-Karls-Universität, Tübingen. In addition to his activities as a librarian, Dr. Reith is a specialist on 16th-century German history and the Reformation and has published many articles and papers in both German and English. He was also editor of the *American Society for Reformation Research Newsletter*.

Hans H. Wellisch is a Professor at the College of Library and Information Services, University of Maryland, and a member of the American Society of Indexers and the International Federation for Documentation. He is the author of numerous articles and several books on indexing and abstracting, and has also published *Indexing and abstracting: an international bibliography*. He also contributes frequently to *Journal of the American Society for Information Science, Library Quarterly*, and *The Indexer*.

Contents

Contents

Contents

Preface

The preparation of the present bibliography has been a source of some satisfaction, but also some tribulation. The satisfaction has come from the continuing discovery of so much material in English on a country for which I have no small affection, material the existence of which was, in one sense, previously irrelevant to me. The tribulation is the natural by-product of the awareness that the final outcome may, despite the size, contain omissions which this or that user might deem indefensible. Such omissions will be a consequence in part of the semi-random pattern by which I found material surfacing, and in part of the need to pare down one or two of the sections which were covered by large numbers of publications.

Most of the materials listed are in English; the exceptions relate to titles in the other major West European languages, and some works with Czech or Slovak titles and either a relevant section, or at least summary in English. Furthermore, book titles have been preferred in general to periodical works, chiefly in the belief that, on the whole, books are probably easier to run to earth. Some subjects are, however, better covered by periodical publications. In most areas a great number of other articles may well be traced, often from the bibliographies in the volumes listed or, where no bibliography is mentioned, in the usual footnotes which in many works take the place of a formal organized bibliography. It is a rare work that has neither bibliography nor references. Within the sections items are generally ordered approximately chronologically, where there is an historical dimension, or regionally from West to East (Bohemia, Moravia, Slovakia, Ruthenia, other), where there is a geographical spread. In some sections ordering represents a gradation downwards from the more to the less significant (e.g. the daily press), though relative degrees of significance could be weighed on various scales. In one or two cases, where no other system is warranted, titles are

Preface

ordered alphabetically by authors' surnames.

It goes without saying that no book of this scope and complexity could be produced without a great deal of assistance, which, in this author's case was given generously and willingly by many institutions and countless individuals. It is my first duty to thank the British Academy for sponsoring me on a trip to Prague where, as guest of the Czechoslovak Academy of Sciences, I was enabled to visit a number of institutes to explore their libraries and consult their staffs on some of the English-language resources available in spheres with which I was, at the time, completely non-conversant. My thanks are also due therefore to the members of those various institutes in Prague and České Budějovice who gave willingly of their time and advice. Next, I am recurrently indebted to the British Council for having sponsored me on various occasions in the past, most recently to the Slovak Summer School in Bratislava, an occasion which I was able to use, though less intensively, for similar purposes. At my place of work, the School of Slavonic and East European Studies of the University of London, I was singularly fortunate in having immediate access to a vast amount of material in the Library and many colleagues who could provide useful pointers in various directions. My unbounded gratitude goes to all the staff of the Library, but especially to Mrs Vlasta Gyenes, who personally traced so much material for me, and to all the others who either found me semi-permanently under their feet or found themselves with yards of re-shelving to do on my account. Of my colleagues I must particularly thank Dr. Robert Pynsent and Dr. Frank Carter who have been unstinting in their assistance. Others who have helped me at various stages are simply too numerous to mention individually, though my gratitude is no less for all that. I make an exception, however, for Miss Joanna Fox of Orbis Books, London, and Dr. Elizabeth Robson, then Editorial Secretary to the *Slavonic and East European Review*, both of whom alerted me and gave me access to many new books as they appeared, i.e., before they found their way into libraries, and for Dr. Robert G. Neville of Clio Press, who not only edited the bibliography with great care and understanding, taking particular trouble over the most suitable location for many titles, but also indexed the volume and showed great patience when this author was being 'difficult'. The typesetters must also be thanked and congratulated on making, even at the proof stage, an excellent job of a difficult typescript.

My final debt of gratitude is due to my wife and family for their forbearance throughout the book's long gestation; may their hopes for a 'proper' holiday and the secondary double glazing be at last fulfilled, now that I am back in circulation. To them the book is dedicated.

David Short
Windsor, Berkshire
January, 1986

Introduction

It is a cliché to refer to Czechoslovakia as a fairly remote country about which we (the British in particular) know little or nothing, yet one which continues to contain more than a grain of truth. The country's first misfortune is perhaps its very name, alien and complex in form and, for some, too readily confused with the equally alien 'Yugoslavia'. It is also a relatively young name, having come into being along with the country only after the First World War, thus there is no common school experience of it from general history courses. Moreover, the one area, Bohemia, which cannot fail to feature in the general history of Europe, seems to pass in and out of the school-age mind without enquiry as to where it is now. Other reasons for the general low level of awareness of the country are the obvious fact of genuine distance from England, i.e., it lies beyond all the nearest neighbours, coupled with the more likely factor of its lack of a seaboard, hence it has never constituted a competitor or threat on the high seas. Add to all this the relatively low total population of the country (just under 15.4 million) and the low numbers of Czech and Slovak immigrants in Britain (contrast the position with the Poles), and the general ignorance of the country and its people becomes explicable, though not excusable. The position in the United States and Canada is rather different: not only are there much larger and more cohesive Czech and Slovak communities there, but in countries where almost everyone is an immigrant, or is at least aware that his fairly recent ancestors were, the tendency to carry a bit of 'the old country' with one is perhaps stronger. I say nothing here of the non-Anglo-Saxon world beyond the fact that there are isolated pockets, or even quite large communities, of Czechs and Slovaks in many countries of the world, but especially in Europe and the Americas. There have been several waves of emigration, for religious, economic or political reasons right through modern history, and starting

Introduction

centuries before the modern country was born. Notwithstanding this, although emigration has affected both nations, it must be remembered that in this, as in any other context, there are *two peoples*, with different histories, and so the pressures to emigrate, and even the countries to which migrants have turned, have varied not only in time but also across the Czech/Slovak divide.

Czechoslovakia lies at the heart of Europe (reference to its position at the cross-roads of Europe is another common cliché). Prague, the capital, lies only fractionally north of the 50th parallel, level with the Lizard Peninsular in Cornwall, and a line drawn due south of Prague will just miss Naples; the same line taken northwards cuts up the middle of Sweden. Prague is about 645 miles from London, less than half-way to the Black Sea.

Czechoslovakia is a smallish country at 46,360 square miles, only the fourteenth largest in Europe by its own reckoning. It is now a federal republic consisting of the Czech Socialist Republic, where the Czechs dominate and which is more or less co-extensive with the historic Lands of the Bohemian Crown (Bohemia, Moravia and part of Silesia), and the Slovak Socialist Republic, where the Slovaks dominate and which was previously Upper Hungary. During the period known as the First Republic, i.e., between the wars, the province known variously as Subcarpathian Ruthenia, Carpatho-Ukraine, Transcarpathian Ukraine, or, in this book, simply Ruthenia, also belonged to Czechoslovakia as its eastern-most province. This was inhabited chiefly by Ruthenians, or Rusyns, closely related to the Ukrainians, and it passed to the Soviet Union after the Second World War. A number of entries in this bibliography refer to this province because it was a part of the country, and to the Ruthenians, because a sizeable minority are still in Czechoslovakia, mostly in Eastern Slovakia.

During the last war the country ceased to exist. The Czech Lands were first reduced in size by cession of a quite large fringe to Germany, in consequence of the Munich Agreement between Hitler and the French and British, and ultimately overrun and occupied by Germany for the duration of the war as the Protectorate of Bohemia and Moravia. Slovakia had declared autonomy and then lived through the war as a quasi-independent ally of Germany, the Slovak State, though also reduced in size thanks to territorial concessions to Hungary. Ruthenia had also declared independence, but enjoyed it for only a matter of hours before being overrun by Hungary. After the war, the country was re-established within the traditional frontiers, but without Ruthenia.

Introduction

Since the war, and especially since 1948 when the communists gained power (Victorious February), Czechoslovakia has been firmly in the Soviet sphere of influence and is fully integrated into the socialist trading bloc, Comecon, or the Council for Mutual Economic Assistance (CMEA), and the defence bloc, the Warsaw Pact. These two factors explain why so many of the titles in the bibliography which follows, especially those to do with economics, politics, trade or foreign relations, relate to the bloc as a whole, out of which it is often difficult, if not pointless, to extricate the data or practices of any given member. There are of course certain country-specific features, and it is to be hoped that most of these have been picked up under one title or another.

For the period before the country was born, any uniform historiography is a difficult undertaking, the fates of the Czechs being tied essentially to those of Austria, while the Slovaks evolved alongside, or under, the Hungarians. It is largely coincidental that they eventually became just two of many nations within the ultimately united Austro-Hungarian Empire. Nevertheless, joint histories have been written. On the whole, however, separate histories have dominated, chiefly on national- ist grounds among the Slovaks, whose nationhood in the modern sense is of relatively recent date (though they can claim the first state entity on Czechoslovak territory, the shortlived, 7th century Empire of Samo) and on more traditional national grounds among the Czechs, whose Kingdom of Bohemia was for many centuries the main power in Central Europe and whose kings became Holy Roman Emperors. Even after the Thirty Years' War (1618-48), which brought the Czechs under Habsburg control (after the Battle of the White Mountain, near Prague, in 1620) the Czechs did not simply disappear from history, though the traditional Czech label for the period which ensued, the Age of Darkness, indicates the sense of hiatus that lasted up to the National Revival at the end of the 18th and the beginning of the 19th centuries.

The Czech National Revival really marks the beginning of modern Czech history. Initially it is connected with a recodifi- cation of the literary language (in fact based on an already obsolete model) and the deliberate provision of a corpus of original and translated literature in the language. This is the domain of such figures as Dobrovský and Jungmann. Then follow efforts to equip the language with the vocabulary to cope with the modern arts and sciences, and a new generation of national historians is born and the nation's history written (Palacký). New

xvii

Introduction

national music is written (Smetana, and later Dvořák), heavily
coloured by the folk idiom and rather unfairly ignoring the many
earlier composers of Czech origin, contemporaries of Mozart,
Beethoven and Schubert, who had been in the forefront of
European mainstream music (Mysliveček, Stamic, Dušek,
Tomášek, Voříšek and others, who are only now coming back
into their own). Similar national trends showed themselves in
painting and sculpture. Through the course of the 19th century,
though in fits and starts, and some retreats, Czech schools
became firmly established and a major event was the division in
1882 of the Prague University into separate Czech and German
institutions. The first large national encyclopaedia was Rieger's
Slovník naučný (1859-74, 10 vols. with later supplements),
followed by the larger *Ottův slovník naučný* (1888-1909, 28 vols.,
also with supplements).

The Slovaks also had a national revival, slightly later than the
Czechs, and there the issue of language and literature was even
more dominant. By the middle of the 19th century a codified
Slovak literary language, based on the Central Slovak dialect
(previous attempts had been based on West Slovak), had been
brought into existence, the work of Ľudovít Štúr and his
followers. A major contrast with the Czech position is that the
new standard, eventually adopted throughout Slovakia against
competing claims from other regional dialects and Czech, is that
it was rooted in living speech, not a 300-year-old model full of
obsolete features. By the time the Czechoslovak Republic came
into being in 1918 the Slovaks did have their own language and
literature, but one of the weaknesses of the First Republic was its
ideological insistence on a single Czechoslovak nation and
language, but with concessions to local variation in the latter.
This, and certain other manifestations of government from
Prague (a mixture of benevolent domination and unavoidable
expedient), led many Slovaks to feel that having shed Magyar
overlordship they had merely fallen prey to the Czechs. Not all
shared this view, but the nationalist mood was strong enough to
bring about the break-up of the country just before World War II
burst upon Europe. The Slovak State was led by the Catholic
People's Party, and it is symptomatic that so recently, as well as
for six centuries before, religion was a major factor in Czech and
Slovak history and politics, whether on the reform side going
back to the Hussites, whose tradition still contains considerable
national appeal to the Czechs, or on the conservative Catholic
side, from when Austria controlled Bohemian affairs, and among

the Slovaks. (There are still, or course, Catholic Czechs and Protestant Slovaks, the latter associated as much with the Hungarian as with the Czech Protestant tradition).

The country's presidency has always been of significance. The first president, Tomáš Garrigue Masaryk, was largely instrumental in bringing the country into being. He was a somewhat Victorian liberal philosopher-politician who enjoyed immense personal prestige, almost reverence, even being referred to as 'tatíček' ('daddy' is the literal, but totally inadequate translation). He was followed by Edvard Beneš, who had the unenviable task of coping with the onset, duration and aftermath of the last war. In the eyes of many he failed in the end by not preventing the post-war squabbling which let the communists in. Moreover, in the eyes of others he failed at the beginning by bowing to pressure from the appeasers instead of forcing their hand by offering armed resistance to Germany. Beneš died soon after the communist take-over in 1948, to be followed by the first worker-president, Klement Gottwald. His career was marked by the huge changes that followed upon closer alliance to the Soviet Union and the adoption of socialism. Nationalization had already proceeded a long way between 1945 and 1948. Now came collectivization of non-collectivized land-holdings and more centralized control of the previously existing, traditional collectives. Non-communist parties either merged with the Communist Party or hung on, without distinctive policies or the ability to constitute a real opposition, under the umbrella of the National Front. This was also the period of the notorious trials of the 1950s. Gottwald was followed by the milder Antonín Zápotocký (1953-57) and by Antonín Novotný (1957-68), the man under whom, though no thanks to whom, the 'thaw' set in. He is remembered for his moves to stem the thaw, his failure to understand the Slovaks, and as the man under whom the pre-1968 reformist trend eventually got under way. The economic and social reforms put forward in the mid to late 1960s culminated in his removal from both the First-Secretaryship of the Communist Party and the presidency, to be replaced by Alexander Dubček, a Slovak, and General Ludvík Svoboda. In this configuration the presidency lost much of its importance, though President Svoboda himself was a popular figurehead and overseer of the reforms that continued beneath him. The period 1967-69, otherwise known as the 'Prague Spring' (after the annual Prague music festival) but especially the years 1968-69, have been so extensively written about that nothing more need

Introduction

be said here, beyond the reminder that in August of 1968 things came to an abrupt halt when Warsaw Pact troops intervened, Dubček was soon ousted to be replaced by Gustáv Husák, President Svoboda served on until 1975, though a very sick man in his last years, and Husák has since worn the double mantle of First Secretary and President. Under Husák the country has been largely 'normalized', in the East European sense of the word, the economy has stabilized though there are plenty of problems attendant on the oil crisis (apart from the traditional problems of absenteeism and a generally cavalier attitude to work in many areas), and opposition has been all but silenced. Only Charter 77, remains vociferous, but its following is limited; there is still also an underground literature and some underground intellectual and religious activity, but it does not appear to impinge on the daily life of the silent majority. The other feature of Husák's régime is a much increased role of Slovaks in federal, as well as Slovak government, and the more extensive use of Slovak as a nation-wide language, particularly in broadcasting. Husák, himself the second Slovak First Secretary and first Slovak President (if we ignore Masaryk's mixed background), speaks both Slovak and Czech, according to the requirements of the moment, an appropriate recognition of the current, federal, constitution's provision whereby both nations and both languages enjoy equal status (this is not to overlook the feelings of some Czechs that the pendulum is swinging too far the other way, making Slovak 'more equal' than Czech for the first time).

Finally, a word on Czechoslovak publishing. The country possesses quite large printing facilities, great, though diminishing forests, and a comprehensive paper industry including a major recycling branch. A number of things follow from this. One is the national pride at being at, or near, the top of the international league table in the number of books published per head. The most important fact, however, is that printing has evolved into a major hard-currency earner. A number of foreign, including British publishers have over the years had many of their titles printed in Czechoslovakia. Following on from this, two Czechoslovak concerns, Artia for the Czech half and Slovart for the Slovak half of the country, have developed quite a successful book-publishing (i.e., as well as printing) industry on behalf of foreign publishers. Quite large numbers of popular works in the arts and sciences, already existing in domestic Czech or Slovak editions, are offered to foreign publishers, and if an offer is taken up the work is then translated, printed and bound in Czechoslovakia before being marketed by the purchasing company on the foreign side. Many find their way into specialist bookshops, while many appear among the popular book sections of more general stores and stationers'. Although masquerading in the end product as English publications, a number of these books retain sufficient of their Czechoslovak origin to warrant inclusion herein, as representative of one or other aspect of the country (see in particular the section on Flora and Fauna). Publishing abroad about Czechoslovakia is fairly widespread, but with more transatlantic than British publishers regularly interested, which is a reflection in part of the greater number of academic institutions and in part of the presence on North American soil of large immigrant communities.

A Note on the Languages of Czechoslovakia

The Czechoslovak Socialist Republic has been a federal state since 1969, and one of the consequences of this was that Czech and Slovak acquired constitutionally equal standing as joint official languages. Prior to that both languages had indeed been in use, but the position of Slovak had been less secure, being confined to the Slovak half of the country. During the First Republic (1918-38) the official view was that there was one Czechoslovak language, in two regional variants, just as there was one Czechoslovak nation.

Together with Polish and Upper and Lower Lusatian (Sorbian, Wendish), minority languages spoken in the German Democratic Republic on territory more or less contiguous with Czech and Polish, Czech and Slovak are members of the western branch of the Slavonic family of languages. In the average neutral literary or conversational styles they are mutually intelligible to a very high degree, so that it is possible to find texts which show a minimum of contrast, usually confined to word-endings (Czech and Slovak are inflecting languages). In more highly refined styles, or in styles with a higher dependency on peripheral elements (for example dialect and slang) the discrepancies are more conspicuous, and in the extreme case a Czech may actually not understand whole chunks of a Slovak text and vice versa (though on the whole Slovaks have less trouble with Czech). Thanks, however, to the effects of radio and television the problems are probably declining, each language becoming more familiar to more speakers of the other, and it is also the case that the differences in some areas are in any case declining through convergence, despite bouts of purism on either side.

Czech has been well established as a vehicle of literature since the 10th century, and there is a vast corpus of Old Czech literature, much of it still republished from time to time, and not just in scholarly editions. At different times in the nation's

A Note on the Languages of Czechoslovakia

history it has competed with Latin and German. At the time of the National Revival (late 18th and 19th centuries) one of the major concerns was to standardize the language and then to demonstrate that it was a viable instrument for the expression of any kind of literary mode and to equip it with the vocabulary for any kind of scholarly writing. The standard literary language of today owes most of its forms and rules to the grammars of the early 19th century, especially Dobrovský's. The trouble is that Dobrovský and others had taken as their model the Czech of the 'Golden Age', the 16th century. This overlooked at least two and a half centuries of changes through which the language had evolved quite naturally, so that with additional developments over the last century and a half there exists, side by side with the standard literary language, another Czech, usually known as Common Czech, which is, in many respects, as distinct from literary Czech as the latter is from Slovak. This is a gross oversimplification of both the present situation and its origins, but it does mean that there are, in widespread use, two distinct forms of Czech. Less distinct are the divisions between some of the intermediate varieties of the language. The foreign learner is generally taught standard literary Czech in its written and spoken form, but in the streets he is more likely to hear, and begin to imitate, Common Czech.

Slovak, as a fully fledged literary language in its present form, is a rather younger formation. It was codified only in the middle of last century and is based on the Central Slovak dialects. Bratislava, the capital of Slovakia, lies in the West Slovak dialect area, but is, or has been, a very cosmopolitan city—a stone's throw from Vienna (few Germans survive), capital of Hungary in the 16th century when the Turks held most of that country, with a fairly large Jewish population and more recently a small body of urban gypsies. Since it was consolidated in recent times, Slovak contains far fewer morphological archaisms than Czech; on the other hand, in the lexical area it contains certain items known in Old Czech but now extinct in Czech, in addition to the Hungarian, German and Romanian loan-words which add to its distinctiveness. Before the codification of Slovak, the local vernacular was in use in various regionally distinct forms, but the extent of its use was restricted to administrative, religious and private needs, with little 'true' literature. The description of the various versions of pre-literary Slovak ('cultured West/Central/East Slovak') is a major preoccupation of contemporary Slovak philology.

A Note on the Languages of Czechoslovakia

Czech and Slovak have never been widely studied by foreigners. In the English-speaking world it is really only a 20th-century study, starting basically with Morfill's *Grammar of the Bohemian or Čech Language* of 1899. Slovak grammars in English have come in the main from North America, where there are large concentrations of Slovaks, originating from the 19th-century migrant families. Only in recent years has Slovakia itself sought to make the language more accessible to English speakers through a string of text-book and descriptive works. Generally, however, despite the efforts of scholars and the availability of more and more materials, the two languages—even the fact of there being two, not one—remain exotic unknowns. When Trnava, a Slovak team, are playing an international football match, the commentator persists in calling them 'the Czechs'; when a well-known beer, renowned for its capacity to reach parts other beers cannot, needs testing for its ability to penetrate a mystery language and render it accessible, the mystery language selected is Czech; and when Hana Mandlíková's father is recorded at Wimbledon watching his daughter's performance, he is automatically assumed to have the same surname (though here the commentator may perhaps be forgiven for not knowing that male and female forms of Czech and Slovak surnames differ). Recurrent mispronunciation of any number of names of Czechs or Slovaks prominent especially in sport is a constant irritant to the initiated, and these are not just minor adjustments made to suit the phonetics of English.

So much for the official languages of Czechoslovakia. Other languages spoken are obviously associated with the minority populations, hence the areas or pockets where German, Hungarian, Polish or Ukrainian can be heard. The surviving Jews use the language of the group to which they are most closely assimilated, i.e., Czech or Slovak according more or less to residence, but also German or Hungarian. Many itinerant gypsies still speak a local version of Romany, with a strong admixture of Slovak or Hungarian lexical features. Of the many languages that may be heard from short-term residents (especially Third-World students, aid-programme trainees or people akin to, but not the same as Gastarbeiter—chiefly Cubans and Vietnamese) only one, Greek, represents a population settled for some time (since the Greek communists lost the civil war in the late 1940s) and likely to stay. It is perhaps worth adding that the Esperanto movement has many adherents among both Czechs and Slovaks with a tradition that goes back to the 1880s.

The Country and Its People

1 **The Soviet Union and Eastern Europe: a handbook.**
Edited by George Schöpflin. London: Anthony Blond, 1970. 614p.
maps. bibliog.
This compendium includes a whole range of papers dealing exclusively or
inclusively with Czechoslovakia. Those seeking information on statistics,
nationalism, national minorities, economic planning, trade with the European
Economic Community (EEC), trade unions, agriculture, transport, energy, law,
education, housing, religion, the arts, the media and literature will be well
rewarded with a substantial amount of information, some of it summarized in
tables. Much else can be elicited from the detailed index and each contribution
has its own bibliography.

2 **Eastern Europe in the 1980s.**
Edited by Stephen Fischer-Galati. Boulder, Colorado: West View
Press; London: Croom Helm, 1981. 291p. bibliog.
The essays in this collection concern various aspects of the life of the region and
cover: agriculture; industry; trade; politics; relations with the rest of the
Communist and non-Communist world; education; and culture. Czechoslovakia
features throughout, although each essay has to be read in its entirety to find the
relevant passages. References to constitutional reform, ethnic friction, nationalism
and dissent are indexed separately because these subject areas are not inferable
from the essay titles. Each section has its own bibliography and the texts are
supported by tables of statistics.

3 **Czechoslovakia.**
M. J. Burke. London: Batsford, 1976. 237p. (Batsford Travel
Books).
This is one of the best general works available on Czechoslovakia. It is partly
historical and partly geographical and contains a mass of information on many

1

aspects of the day-to-day life and management of the country. A work of interest to the general or academic reader as well as the intending tourist which is designed more to attract than guide.

4 **Czechoslovakia. A country study.**
Edited by Richard F. Nyrop. Washington, DC: The American University, Foreign Area Studies. Distributed by the United States Government Printing Office, 1982. 356p. bibliog. (Area Handbook Series).

This is an official handbook and therefore reflects the range of interests of the intended readership. Separate essays deal with history, society, the economy, government and politics, national security, Comecon, the Warsaw Pact, and Charter 77. The information is correct up to April 1981. Similar works have been produced earlier, or for different US departments, by E. K. Keefe.

5 **Czechoslovakia: profile of a socialist republic at the crossroads of Europe.**
David W. Paul. Boulder, Colorado: Westview Press, 1981. 196p. map. bibliog. (Nations of Contemporary Eastern Europe).

Provides good background information, two-thirds of which concerns contemporary government, politics, economics, society, culture and education. Each topic is further subdivided into other subjects including national groups, religion and folk-art. The first third of the volume serves as an introductory, general and geopolitical history, and the work includes a useful thematic bibliography, statistical tables, and photographs.

6 **Czechoslovakia: Lloyds Bank Group economic report.**
[London]: Lloyds Bank Group, 1985. 23p.

Despite its title and brevity, this is in many respects an ideal introductory text to the country as a whole, with sections on statistics, population, geography, politics, as well as all the main areas of the economy (prices and incomes, fiscal policy, the structure of industry and agriculture, mining, energy, housing, transport, tourism, imports and exports and investment). A final section deals with the structure of trade between Czechoslovakia and the United Kingdom.

7 **Czechoslovakia: the heritage of ages past; essays in memory of Josef Korbel.**
Edited by Hans Brisch, Ivan Volgyes. New York; Boulder, Colorado: East European Quarterly. Distributed by Columbia University Press, New York, 1979. 239p. bibliog.

The late Josef Korbel was one of the most highly respected Czech émigré writers on history and political science, though his work was by no means confined to Czechoslovakia. This collection of papers in his memory, which includes a bibliography, provides the student and general reader with a wide range of facts about Czechoslovakia. In addition to historical articles on, for example, Hus, the First Republic, World War II and three papers on the 'Prague Spring' period, there are essays on the economy, politics and justice, as well as 'the Czechoslovak

2

tradition'. The last named, by Bruce Garver, considers the relations and similarities between the Czechs and Slovaks and their history and also provides a brief historical account of arts and letters, religion, agriculture and industry, science and technology, education and scholarship, and politics.

8 **Socialist Czechoslovakia.**
Vít Calta (et al.), translated by Libor Trejdl.   Prague: Orbis Press Agency, 1983. 152p. maps.

A typical 'portrait of the country' publication which updates earlier works with similar titles. It summarizes the basic history and geography of the country, and provides an account of contemporary life and institutions, the economy (this in greatest detail), social policy, culture and sport. Published by a state press and publicity agency, much of the contents reflects official opinion.

9 **The land and people of Czechoslovakia.**
Kay Bernard.   London: A. & C. Black; New York: Macmillan, 1969. 95p. map. (Land and Peoples Series).

Although this book manages to provide a superficial introduction to the life of the people in present-day Czechoslovakia, and also outlines the country's economy and geographical features, it is marred by a number of factual errors, ambiguities and linguistic distortions. When a chamois becomes an ibis (presumably via an intermediate confusion with ibex), and the composer Smetana is consistently called 'Smetena', one is forced to advise caution in the use of the book. It is sounder on legend than on history. The appendix, apart from having dated slightly, is proportionately no more reliable than the text. One saving grace are the twenty-three well-chosen photographic illustrations.

10 **Československo.** (Czechoslovakia.)
Compiled and arranged by Ludvík Uhlíř, František Mikloš, with an introduction by Lubomír Štrougal, Russian translation by Margarita Rogačova, German translation by Helena Krausová, English translation by Joy Kadečková, French translation by Svatopluk Pacejka, and Spanish translation by Enrique Roldán.   Prague: Olympia; Bratislava: Šport, 1982. 2nd ed. 288p.

This is a beautifully produced 'coffee-table' book which seeks, through its text and excellent coloured photographs, to provide a picture of the outward appearance of the country including: its features of natural beauty; some of its cultural and historical monuments; and some of the aspects of modern society and culture. Its mission is frankly 'representative' and the range of languages into which the text has been translated, as well as the size of the print run (33,000), suggests an advertising motive.

11 **The Czechoslovak contribution to world culture.**
Edited by Miloslav Rechcígl, Jr.   The Hague, London, Paris: Mouton, 1964. 682p. bibliog.

There is something of a tradition attached to this kind of publication, ascribed by some to the need to counteract the national inferiority complex, the 'malý český

The Country and Its People

člověk' syndrome, made much of by some Czechs. Some of the fifty-six essays
recount what Czechs or Slovaks have done for this or that discipline while others
are directly relevant to the country, the people, individual writers or scholars.
Some of these essays will be listed selectively in the relevant sections of this
bibliography. The bibliography included in Rechcígl's (ed.) volume consists of
1,318 titles in various Western languages, the range of topics covered is broad and
the volume also includes a bibliography of bibliographies. The whole work was
published on behalf of the Czechoslovak Society of Arts and Sciences in America,
the 'academy in exile', known widely as SVU, from its Czech name.

12 **Czechoslovakia past and present.**
Edited by Miloslav Rechcígl, Jr.   The Hague, Paris: Mouton, 1968.
2 vols.

The numerous articles in these two volumes offer a microcosmic view of émigré
Czech and Slovak scholarly (and less scholarly) writing on many aspects of the
country's history, culture, economics, society, arts and sciences. They are the
product of the second congress of the Czechoslovak Society of Arts and Sciences
in America, elsewhere referred to as the 'émigré academy' or SVU. The sections
cover: Czechoslovakia up to the Second World War (seven papers); social and
economic aspects of the First Republic (eight papers); the Second World War
(five papers); political aspects of contemporary Czechoslovakia (seven papers);
social and economic aspects (nine papers); cultural aspects (seven papers);
Czechoslovakia and its neighbours (eight papers, including separate papers on
Czechoslovakia's relations with Austria, Hungary, Poland, Romania, and
Yugoslavia); Czechoslovakia's relations with the Great Powers (four papers;
separate attention being given to Germany, Britain and France); Czechs and
Slovaks abroad (four papers, most on literature and journalism); literature
(thirteen papers); linguistics (five papers); history (thirteen papers); music (four
papers); fine arts (five papers); social sciences (ten papers); physical, biological
and behavioural sciences (nine papers); and a 1,384-entry bibliography of
bibliographies and similar works pertaining completely, or partly, to Czechoslovakia. The sectional division is only a partial guide to what the collection
includes, and the enquirer is advised to consult the entire contents pages for items
that might well have appeared in more than one section.

13 **Town and Country development in Czechoslovakia.**
Otakar Nový, translated by Jiří Šmíd.   Prague: Orbis Press
Agency, 1983. 80p.

This book was published as a publicity document and was distributed through
embassies, travel agencies (Čedok) and the like. Approximately one quarter of
the work is taken up by a summary history of Czech and Slovak statehood,
settlement, demographic change and the growth of towns and industry. The bulk
of the volume consists of an account of the aims and achievements of the post-war
programme of urban and rural construction, stressing the even distribution of
industry and the transition to large-scale agriculture through state and collective
farms. Unusually, it emphasizes the private contribution to the contemporary fruit
and vegetable market. There is also a summary account of modern development
plans and the associated legislation, the status of different types of centres,
second-home ownership, housing, conservation and reconstruction. The whole
book is admirably illustrated by colour photographs illustrating different
architectural periods, typical regional centres and recent construction projects.

14 **The Tatra Mountains.**
    V. A. Firsoff. London: Lindsay Drummond, 1942. 128p. map.
More recent books in English on the Tatras produced in Slovakia provide a good
pictorial record of the undoubted beauty and majesty of the mountains but
nevertheless remain close to the coffee-table class of publication. This early work,
unsophisticated and slightly sentimental though it be, gives in addition a good
verbal description of the region, on the Polish and the Slovak side of the frontier,
and goes on to describe: the people; customs; buildings; the important occupation
of sheep-farming; and the flora and fauna above and below the tree-line. While
there have been undoubted changes since the war, the bulk of the factual
information contained here still applies. The mountains are also the premier
climbing area in Czechoslovakia, cf. Sir John Hunt's 'Climbers in the Tatras of
Czechoslovakia and Poland', *Geographical Magazine*, vol. 39, no. 8 (Dec. 1966),
p. 639-650.

15 **The towns and cities of Czechoslovakia.**
    Dobroslav Líbal, translated from Czech by Joy Turner-Kadečková.
    Prague: Artia, 1970. 99p.
This is more than just a pictorial record of some of the more (and less) well
known towns. It contains a potted social and political history of the regions and
outlines the artistic and architectural development of the towns.

16 **Portrait of Prague.**
    Emanuel Poche, photographs by Karel Neubert, Antonín Srch,
    translated from Czech by John Eisler.   London, New York,
    Sydney, Toronto: Hamlyn, 1969. 23p.
This book takes in the whole of the city, ancient and modern, and, though dated,
offers a good balance and reasonable overall picture of the city. It relies more on
its eighty-seven colour plates than the brief text, which provides a thumbnail
cultural and political history. The pictures are suitably annotated.

17 **The Prague ghetto: the story and legend of the Jewish quarter in
    Prague through its one thousand year history.**
    Jindřich Lion, with photographs by Jan Lukas.   London: Spring
    Books, 1959. 96p.
Prague's Jewish ghetto, one of the oldest in Europe, though now much changed in
character through population decline and 19th-century rebuilding, has a rich
history which is retold here in word and picture (36 plates). The author includes
the story of the legendary Rabbi Jehúdá Löw and his Golem [see also Byron L.
Sherwin's *Mystical theology and social dissent: the life and works of Judah Loew
of Prague* (q.v.) and Isaac B. Singer's *The Golem* (q.v.)] and an account of the
life of Franz Kafka.

The Country and Its People

18 **Prague Castle.**
Jiří Burian, Antonín Hartmann, photographs by Karel Neubert,
translated by Jan Eisler. London, New York, Sydney, Toronto:
Hamlyn, 1975. 175p.
There have been countless volumes of photographs of Prague Castle, among
which those by Karel Plicka are the best-known. Very few, however, bear a non-
Czechoslovak imprint. This particular large-format book, is in the coffee-table
mould, but with much substance to it for all that. It provides a portrait of Prague
Castle, Hradčany, as an architectural monument of considerable size, complexity
and beauty. The volume also depicts the castle as a symbol of Czech history,
Czech identity, and the seat of the Czechoslovak head of state. It does not seek to
be a consistent history, choosing instead certain core events and periods, with
quotations from contemporary sources 'to put flesh on the dry bones of history'.
The 150 photographs range from the most ancient to the most recent elements of
the architecture and from panoramas to the easily overlooked detail, and pictures
taken from inside and outside the castle are included.

19 **Vyšehrad.**
Bořivoj Nechvátal. Prague: Odeon, 1976. 427p. maps. bibliog.
A generously illustrated history of Prague's 'other' castle, Vyšehrad, which is
situated to the south of Hradčany and on the opposite bank of the Vltava. The
foreign language résumés (including English, p. 404-410) cannot do justice to the
work as a whole, but they do include the major points, some of the familiar
legends, and the main archaeological finds. They also introduce the reader to the
Slavín, or national cemetery, established in the 19th century as the final resting-
place for the nation's best-loved writers, poets, musicians, and also scientists.

20 **The castle of Bratislava.**
Štefan Holčík, Tatiana Štefanovičová, translated by Oľga
Horská. Bratislava: Obzor, 1982. 128p.
Less famous than its Prague sister, Bratislava Castle, which has recently been
completely renovated, is of great cultural and political historical significance, not
least of all because Bratislava itself, or Pozsony as it used to be known, was for a
time capital of Hungary. This book outlines the cultural history of the castle,
including the major events to which it has been witness, and provides a
chronology of the stages in its excavation. The numerous illustrations show
exhibits relating to each period and reproduce prints of the castle. The collection
of photographs at the end, many in colour, show various archaeological sites and
finds, architectural details and more engravings of the castle and city.

21 **Fishponds of Bohemia.**
N. B. Hodgson. *Country Life* vol. 157, no. 4,057 (3 April 1975),
p. 848-50.
The South-Bohemian fishponds are a striking feature of the landscape and some
of them are so vast as to make the name 'pond' in English a misnomer. They are
in fact huge man-made lakes, many of considerable antiquity, used primarily for
breeding and storing carp, and to a lesser degree trout. Carp is the main fish eaten
in this land-locked country and the central item in the traditional Christmas

dinner. The article provides a useful, if brief, introduction to a major geographical feature and economic asset to the country.

22 The Slovak way of life.
Sister M. Martina Tybor. *Furdek*, vol. 22 (Jan. 1983), p. 159-167. Describes some of the folk-customs of the Slovaks, especially where there is a link to the Christian calendar, and outlines the Slovak character as seen by the Slovaks themselves – including a coy acknowledgement of, and apologia for, the Slovaks' widespread alcoholism. The article closes with a summary of the rise of Slovakia's universities and of the work of some quite renowned Slovaks who made good in the world at large, or who made a major contribution to Slovak learning.

23 Komárov: a Czech farming village.
Zdenek Salzmann, Vladimír Scheufler.   New York: Holt, Rinehart & Winston, 1974. 150p. maps. bibliog. (Case Studies in Cultural Anthropology).
This is the first major study on a topic for which literature in English is virtually non-existent. As such, it has a variety of roles to fill, apart from its primary objective of providing a full account in cultural anthropological terms of this one village in the Blata area of South Bohemia. The first chapter places the subject in its Bohemian and Czechoslovak historical and geographical context, and sets out some generalizations. Particularly useful here is the glossary of English equivalents to, and exact definitions of, all the categories of peasants and farmers (there is another very mixed glossary of terms on p. 146-49). The main body of the book describes the buildings and their inhabitants, the traditional and modern ways of life and common practices connected with birth, marriage, death and the calendar. Local arts and crafts are described and an appendix provides a proper musicological analysis of folk-music and dance. The work is illustrated.

24 Bohemian section at the Austrian exhibition, Earl's Court, London, 1906: guide to the Bohemian section and to the Kingdom of Bohemia.
Anon.   Prague: Alois Wiesner, 1906. 224p. map. bibliog.
This book is obviously available only in very few libraries, nevertheless it merits inclusion here, not just as a guide to what the country was exhibiting in the way of arts, crafts and sciences, but as a kind of Czech 'Baedecker' of the day. It includes descriptions of people and places as well as a readable, if patriotic, general history and a collection of suggested excursions. The volume also has very good sections on cottage industries, some no longer pursued, a bibliography of books in English on Bohemia, and information about countless trade, cultural and industrial organizations of the time.

Geography

General, physical and regional

25   **Eastern Europe: a geography of the Comecon countries.**
Roy H. E. Mellor.   London; Basingstoke, England: Macmillan,
1975. 358p. maps. bibliog.

Part 1, 'Physical environment and political geography', and part 2, 'The
demographic and economic framework', are general in that the entire area is
covered simultaneously, with separate chapters on landscape, climate, flora,
fauna, periods of history, population, towns and villages, agriculture, industry and
transport; some sections being further sub-divided. Part 3, 'Comecon and the
national economies', opens with a description of the birth of Comecon and how
the division of labour works within it, and then briefly outlines the economic
geography of each country, Czechoslovakia being covered on p. 273-284. The
work is one of the standard geography textbooks of the area.

26   **Eastern Europe.**
N. J. G. Pounds.   London: Longmans, Green, 1969. 912p. maps.
bibliog.

Czechoslovakia's geography is described on p. 393-472 and the subjects covered
include historical, political, physical and economic geography and population.
The work is probably most valuable for its bibliography.

27   **Central Europe: a regional and human geography.**
A. F. A. Mutton.   London: Longmans, 1968. 2nd ed. 488p.

The relevant section in this dated, but still useful volume, is 'The Czechoslovak
Lands' (p. 185-222) but other useful information will also be found elsewhere.

Geography. General, physical and regional

28 **Geography of Czechoslovakia.**
Jaromír Demek, Miroslav Střída.   Prague: Academia, 1971. 330p.
maps. bibliog.

Widely held to be the best authoritative general geography of the country, this
comprehensive volume is not always easy to obtain outside specialist libraries.
Relatively little in its separate chapters on structure and relief, climate,
hydrology, soils, biogeography, economy, population and settlements, agriculture,
transport and tourism cannot be taken as a reliable guide even today, though
there have naturally been some changes of a statistical nature in certain areas. A
useful supplement to this work is the collection of papers edited by Miroslav
Blažek *Present-day Czech geography* (Brno, Czechoslovakia: Czechoslovak
Academy of Sciences, Institute of Geography, 1971. 197p. maps). This latter
work covers some topics not covered in Demek and Střída's book, or deals more
extensively with particular subjects such as cartography, for example. Linguistically
the book is less accessible, but the papers do have English résumés.

29 **Czechoslovakia.**
Harriet G. Wanklyn.   New York: Praeger, 1954. 445p. maps.
bibliog.

In its day this was the main geography of Czechoslovakia in English, and although
it has been superseded by some of the later works quoted elsewhere in this
section, it remains a useful source for the period up to the Second World War.
The book is based mostly on pre-war sources, with some material being derived
from a period of field-work in 1947. Each chapter in this descriptive and historical
study has its own list of references.

30 **Largest cave system of the Czech Socialist Republic in the Moravský
Kras (Moravian Karst).**
Edited by Jan Přibyl.   Brno, Czechoslovakia: Czechoslovak
Academy of Sciences, Institute of Geography, 1973. 83p. map.
bibliog. (Studia Geographica, no. 35).

This is a detailed description of one of the major features of Moravian geography,
the wild and beautiful system of limestone cliffs and caves near the town of
Blansko. The system includes the famous Macocha chasm and caves, wrapped in
local legend and the underground River Punkva, equally popular with tourists.
Přibyl is also the author of *Paleohydrography of the caves in the Moravský Kras*
which is no. 28 in this same series.

31 **The ice cave of Dobšiná – Czechoslovakia.**
G. V. Dojcsak.   *Canadian Geographical Journal*, vol. 84, no. 1
(Jan. 1972), p. 32-35. maps.

The Dobšiná cave is one of a number of extremely impressive ice caverns in
Slovakia of great importance not merely as a major geographical and geological
curiosity, but as a tourist attraction. This and the country's other caves are the
subject of considerable research; see, for example, the early report by Anton
Droppa: 'Cave research work in Slovakia', *National Speleological Society News*,
vol. 25, no. 6 (June 1967), p. 110-114, which is accompanied by maps.

9

Geography. General, physical and regional

32 **Československý kras.** (Czechoslovak karst.)
Prague: Academia.
Czechoslovakia has some large karst regions and their detailed study is one of the major preoccupations of geographers and geologists. This series of occasional collections of papers (no. 33 appeared in 1982) contains theoretical articles as well as descriptions of individual formations and reports on recent researches and the activities of the speleological societies. Each issue is generously illustrated, and for the foreign consumer résumés are provided in English.

33 **Czechoslovakia's North Moravian region: a geographical appraisal.**
Francis W. Carter. *Revue Géographique de l'Est*, vol. 10, no. 1-2 (1970), p. 65-86. maps. bibliog.
The author offers a complete geography of the region, from geological and physical features, through industry and agriculture, to population. Economically, the region is one of the most important in Czechoslovakia. It has large deposits of black coal and the coal and metallurgical industries, as well as agriculture, are of major significance. The actual location of various industries and branches of agriculture are described town by town, and district by district, and a separate sub-section deals with road and rail transport in the region. The article includes much statistical information, which is partly of an historical nature, for example, the population growth of Ostrava, the main industrial city, over the century to 1970. A brief outline of future developments is also provided.

34 **Czechoslovak mineral springs.**
Jan Šilar. *Geotimes*, vol. 13, no. 5 (May-June 1968), p. 10-13.
Describes the country's mineral springs, which are a major feature of Czechoslovakia's geography and its health service, since the spa cult is alive and well and the bottling of water from the springs has a longstanding tradition. A related article is A. Porubský's 'The mineral and thermal waters of Slovakia', *Geografický Časopis*, vol. 24, no. 2 (1972), p. 114-119.

35 **Soils of Czechoslovakia.**
J. Pelíšek. *Soil Science*, vol. 111, no. 3 (March 1971), p. 163-69.
A study of the country's soils is a vital prerequisite to an understanding of the quite significant regional differences in patterns of agriculture. Over a relatively small area there is great variety of terrain, from fairly extensive lowlands to high alps, the underlying fragmented geology giving rise to a considerable mixture of soil types.

36 **Geografický potenciál průmyslu v ČSR.** (The geographical potential of industry in the Czech Socialist Republic.)
J. Mareš. Brno, Czechoslovakia: Czechoslovak Academy of Sciences, Institute of Geography, 1969. 71p. map. bibliog. (Studia Geographica, no. 69).
This short monograph seeks to evaluate the Czech republic's industrial potential against the background of the natural and economic environment. It contains the elements of a discussion document because it analyses arguably feasible patterns

of regionalization and recommendations for possible future developments. An English résumé is included.

Maps and atlases

37 **Five centuries of Czech geography, exploration and cartography: comments on major trends and present status.**
Miloš Šebor. In: *The Czechoslovak contribution to world culture.*
Edited by Miloslav Rechcígl, Jr. The Hague, London, Paris:
Mouton, 1964, p. 482-89. bibliog.

Although this is a brief history of how geography has been studied and what it has achieved, the author does provide some background information on the early geographic and cartographic treatment of Bohemia itself, notably on the earliest maps.

38 **Rail Map of Europe 83-84.**
Peterborough, England: Thomas Cook. Six revisions annually.

Covers all the railways of Europe, including Czechoslovakia, noting such factors as narrow gauges and electrification. It includes a detailed map of the lines serving Prague.

39 **Europe leisure map: featuring places of tourist and historic interest for holiday planning.**
Tenterden, England: Estate Publications, 1983. Scale 1:3,100,000.

This general map indicates the major sites, in Czechoslovakia as elsewhere, suggested by its sub-title. In addition to individual monuments, or historic localities, it also shows areas of outstanding natural beauty, including national parks, and the main wine-growing centres. Prague is given separate treatment in the key with a list of the chief items of interest which are too numerous to be marked on the map proper.

40 **RDA – Pologne – Tchécoslovaquie.** (GDR – Poland – Czechoslovakia.)
Bern: Kümmerly & Frey, 1980. Scale 1:1,000,000.

A good touring map which marks the main sites of interest to the tourist, though the seasoned traveller may find some of his favourite places missing.

41 **Hungary, Czechoslovakia, Poland.**
Bern: Hallwag, 1984-85 ed. Scale 1:1,000,000.

One of the high-quality, standard folding tourist road-maps, with a wealth of detail.

42 **Czechoslovakia.**
    London: Geographia, 1980. Scale 1:600,000.
The standard folding map of the country and an English permutation of the
Ravenstein Verlag (Frankfurt, GFR) publication. Indicating relief by colour
shading, it provides a good cartographic representation of the country, including
roads, rivers and railways. A smaller-scale version of the same provenance in
Geographia's Pocket Map Series (1:800,000) is also available.

43 **Autoatlas ČSSR.** (Road atlas of Czechoslovakia.)
    Prague: GKP, 1984. 17th updated ed. 142p. Scale 1:400,000.
This is the standard, frequently republished road atlas of Czechoslovakia. In
addition to sectional maps it includes street plans of a number of town centres,
showing the through routes. The maps are followed by a mass of other
information of value to the driver from the location of petrol stations and garages
to camp sites, hotels and items of interest to the tourist all listed under the
respective towns. Unfortunately, only the sectional headings are reproduced in
English and other languages. A folding road map, *Automapa ČSSR* (Prague:
GKP, 1985. 9th Czech ed.) with a scale of 1:800,000 is also frequently re-issued.

44 **Automapa ČSSR – vybrané služby motoristom.** (Road map of
    Czechoslovakia – selected services for motorists.)
    Bratislava: Slovenská kartografia, 1982. Scale 1:1,000,000.
This is similar in nature to the folding road map referred to in the preceding
item, but on a smaller scale and including on the reverse side textual information
about accommodation.

45 **Autokempinky ČSSR.** (Camp sites for motorists in Czechoslovakia.)
    Prague: GKP, 1985. 6th ed. Scale 1:1,000,000.
This is a folding map, with some illustrative material, of all the approved camp
sites in the country.

46 **Atlas SSR.** (Atlas of the Slovak Socialist Republic.)
    Edited by Emil Mazúr (et al.).   Bratislava: Slovenská kartografia,
    1980. 1,136p. maps.
This is the first complete Slovak atlas and covers every aspect of the country's
geography, physical and political, as well as: geology; hydrology; meteorology;
archaeology; demography; agriculture; industry and trade; transport; and
'services' – public health, welfare, education, science and culture. An historical
account of earlier Slovak cartography is also included with reproductions, and a
description of the gradual settlement and regional organization of the country:
four maps record the distribution of population from the 10th century up to 1250
and others indicate the situation in 1598, 1720 and 1869. An unusual feature of
the atlas is the inclusion of maps dealing with the environment and the potential
of the Slovak landscape. Map titles, the general key to the atlas as a whole, and
the texts in the appendix are given in Russian and English, in addition to Slovak.
The 161 contributors and their forty-three home institutes are to be congratulated
on a magnificent work.

47 **Praha – plán města.** (Prague – city plan.)
Prague: GKP, 1985. 4th ed. 62p. maps.
This is Prague's equivalent to the familiar A-Z map of London. The map section proper (81p.) to a scale of 1:20,000, is preceded by a 'map for motorists' showing the city in relation to the network of main roads and indicating, for example, the ring road and restricted parking zone. The text (62p.) contains basic information on everything including: the emergency services; the Samaritans' telephone number; banks and lost-property offices; the location of the police car-pound; and the addresses and telephone numbers of embassies, airlines, travel agencies, hotels, camp sites, restaurants, department stores, specialist shops, health care and sports facilities, theatres, cinemas, concert halls, museums, galleries, and libraries, monuments and other places of interest. This is followed by the street gazetteer.

48 **Brno – plán města.** (Brno – city plan.)
Prague: GKP, 1985. 3rd ed. Scale 1:15,000.
A standard folding map of the capital of Moravia.

49 **Bratislava.**
Bratislava: Slovenská kartografia, 1984. 3rd ed.
This is the most up-to-date street-plan of Bratislava, and despite the date cited above, it actually appeared in mid-August 1985. A folding *Orientačný plán* is also frequently republished with a key in five languages, including English.

50 **Chráněná území přírody ČSSR.** (Nature conservation areas of Czechoslovakia.)
Prague: Kartografia, 1982. Scale 1:750,000.
This is an extremely well-produced map of the country which not only shows the National Parks, but also the larger and smaller areas of protected landscape and local sites of particular ecological interest. Despite opposing pressures from the parts of local and national administration with different views of land use, protection of the rural environment is making progress. Abuses continue, but one success of the conservationists is that since the publication of this map other areas have become listed in one or other category, so that, in law or on paper at least, the trend, as elsewhere in Europe, is for the better.

51 **Přehledná geologická mapa ČSSR.** (General geological map of Czechoslovakia.)
Prague: Ústřední ústav geodesie, 1982. 6th ed. Scale 1:1,500,000.

Travellers' Accounts

52   A July holiday in Saxony, Bohemia and Silesia.
Walter White.   London: Chapman & Hall, 1857. 305p.

This delightfully antiquated, charmingly informal travelogue takes the reader across the country, with fulsome comments on everything there was to see and hear, touch and smell, and especially, or so it sometimes seems, eat and drink. In consequence there is much on the insides and outsides of houses and hostelries and the food to be had, many a telling description of historic buildings or towns, or geological curiosities, and notes about the people and their dress, manners and language. The author's wanderings also led him to offer snippets, or whole chunks, of the country's religious history. Typical of the narrative are comparisons with the England of the day: Carlsbad – 'a Matlocky sort of place' the Moravians (i.e. Moravian Brethren) – 'wiser than the Quakers (for they) do not cheat their hearts and souls of music'.

53   A lady's glimpse of the late war in Bohemia.
Lizzie Selina Eden.   London: Hurst & Blackett, 1867. 305p.

A splendidly Victorian travelogue, which was the offshoot of the said lady's trip to Nice to her sister's wedding and which saw her caught up in the Austro-Prussian War. The relevant part of the journey took her through Vienna to Pressburg (Bratislava), Brno and Prague, Děčín to Dresden. She is clearly disturbed by some of the atrocities of the war (or indeed of past wars, where she refers to how the French knocked Devín Castle to pieces in 1810), but she is also a bemused observer of all else around ('In Bohemia our comfort is never disturbed by the intrusion of cows into our bedrooms'; 'We had a visit one day from a party of fourteen bears of all sizes. They were led by a party of Slovaks or Sclaves, such a ragged set of vagabonds . . .'), and she is very apt to make comparisons with England.

54 **From a terrace in Prague.**
   B. Granville Baker. London: George Allen & Unwin, 1923. 262p.
   map.

A distinctly idiosyncratic portrait of Prague, its past and present, full of romantic musings by one who has fallen in love with the city and would gladly have the rest of the English-speaking world besotted in like manner. More than on Prague itself, this deals with the whole of Czech history to the 17th century, told in a jocular style and bearing the marks of the amateur enthusiast, but still a good read. Passing allusion is made to some of the odd Britons who figure in the city's and country's history.

55 **Over the hills of Ruthenia.**
   Henry Baerlein. London: Leonard Parsons, 1923. 245p.

An interesting travelogue, which appreciates the uniqueness of the area and its people and clearly has misgivings for its future. Much of the narrative is taken up by the accounts of Ruthenians themselves of the country's history and current problems. A recurrent theme is the nature and effects of the Czech-inspired land reform of the time and the ambiguity of the advantages and disadvantages of the Czech presence. Passing references to the nationality of officials, waggoners and other wayfarers show just how mixed an area this was and still is. The book cannot avoid recurrent references to religion, education and agricultural practices.

56 **East of Prague.**
   C. J. C. Street, with a preface by Vojtěch Mastný. London:
   Geoffrey Bles, 1924. 288p.

There were undoubtedly 'beaten tracks' followed by the majority of early visitors to Czechoslovakia, but Street chose, for his traveller's portrait of the country, to explore some of the less well known areas. In particular he wished to fill the gap left by the absence of any writings in English on Slovakia and Ruthenia, but there are also accounts of Pilsen, Prague and other towns on the way. The book makes enjoyable reading and is full of descriptions of people and places. It is largely free of political bias beyond the acceptance of the almost ideal democracy of the young republic, but the author mentions, where relevant, some of the political attitudes he encountered. Like every decent travelogue it has its whimsical anecdotes.

57 **A wayfarer in Czecho-Slovakia.**
   E. I. Robson, with pencil drawings by J. R. E. Howard. London:
   Methuen, 1925. 211p.

This is a superficial, somewhat condescending travelogue through parts of Bohemia and Moravia. Beneath the condescension it offers a reasonable picture of many aspects of the daily life in the still young Czechoslovak Republic, as well as noting certain features of food, custom and outward appearances ('everything is being rebuilt; you must not be deterred by piles of fallen masonry, clouds of dust and impenetrable forests of scaffolding poles') which have not changed. In addition the author offers liberal doses of layman's history. From the not unknown premise that Czechoslovakia is rather remote and unknown, the author nevertheless points to many instances of contact between England and Bohemia.

Travellers' Accounts

The subjects of the good pencil drawings are a well-chosen selection of traditional views, but often from a slightly unusual angle.

58 **Czechoslovakia: the land of an unconquerable ideal.**
Jessie Mothersole.   London: John Lane, The Bodley Head; New York: Dodd, Mead, 1926. 296p. map. bibliog.

With a book like this only twelve years old in 1938 it is amazing that Neville Chamberlain could have claimed that Czechoslovakia was a 'far-away country . . . of [whose people] we know nothing'. Add to it the various travelogues that pre-date this one, and Elizabeth Wiskemann's *Czechs and Germans* (q.v.), and the assertion arguably puts the speaker in a poor light. From an account of the legends of Czech pre-history, through a kings-and-battles historical sketch of the early period, the authoress gives a very readable general history of the country, with particularly extended passages on major periods and individuals (Charles IV, the Hussite wars, Rudolph II, and Comenius, for example). She then moves on to a description of modern constitutional problems, Slovak aspirations, religion, education, 'finance and food', before considering contemporary art, the Sokol movement, folk costumes, the police, industry and many other subjects. The work evolves into a readable and intelligent travelogue, describing many of the better known, and some less well known, tourist areas. The work is well indexed and is beautifully illustrated by the authoress's own drawings and paintings. It is worth noting that she also devotes sections here and there to the position of women in society, particularly during the Hussite period and in her own times. Clearly, it is now out-of-date in many respects, but remains a valuable item in any Czechoslovak bibliography.

59 **In the heart of Europe: life in Czechoslovakia.**
Gerald Druce.   London: George Allen & Unwin, 1936. 228p. maps.

An account of every aspect of life in pre-war Czechoslovakia aimed at tourists and visitors by an enthusiastic one of their number. Druce notes the growing numbers of Britons visiting trade fairs, the industrial centres and sporting events. It contains a good cross-section of topics, from essentials like shopping, transport and eating out to education, religion, science, art and amusements. The author also discusses the many spas, including the complaints treated, which are still a major component in the country's health services. Many aspects of city life as well as industry and the trade unions, and life in the country (agriculture, hiking – still a major pastime) are also described. There are useful sections on Slovakia, Ruthenia and the various minorities, including the Romanians in Ruthenia. Finally there is a section on sport in general, and one on the Sokol movement in particular. It is much to be regretted that no similar book, essentially free of any political dimension, does not exist for the present. Druce is the author of another travel book, *Wanderings in Czechoslovakia* (London: Williams & Norgate, 1930. 103p. maps), which is more descriptive than advisory and takes in far more of the tourist areas. Both works are illustrated.

60 **In Czechoslovakia's hinterland.**
Henry Baerlein. London: Hutchinson, 1938. 287p.

Another generous travelogue from pre-war Czechoslovakia's easternmost province with many a well-observed detail of people of all nationalities and confessions, and places touched and untouched by man.

61 **Eastern Europe in the socialist world.**
Hewlett Johnson. London: Lawrence & Wishart, 1955. 279p.

Not quite a travelogue, this book does nevertheless provide a foreign visitor's account of what he saw and learnt. The Dean of Canterbury gives not only his own impressions, but also a most favourable interpretation of all that he saw, was told, or read concerning the country's new socialist posture. He is clearly convinced of the justice of all that was happening and accepts at face value all the constitutional guarantees and other positive statements about how the country was managed, and shares fully the government's justifications for the trials, especially those of churchmen, in the 1950's. Czechoslovakia is treated to a separate section (p. 113-149) and is well represented in the more general chapters. The socialist republic could not have wished for a better propagandist.

62 **Czechoslovakia: from the New World.**
Kevin Hartshorne. London: MacGibbon & Kee, 1964. 207p.

The author's aim is 'to present modern Czechoslovakia as the living, restless whole that it is, giving all life-situations and points of view'. He uses as his vehicle a quasi-autobiography of the period 1959-61, stringing together as fiction a mass of scenes and events that either did, or could, happen to him during his stay in the country. A strict chronology is not observed and few characters appear under their real names. Family life, the work-place, recreation, in fact the whole daily and yearly round are described, in a manner which seeks to portray things as objective reminiscence without commentary. The reports of the narrator's friends' attitudes to current affairs are quite revealing.

63 **The serpent and the nightingale.**
Cecil Parrott. London: Faber & Faber, 1977. 224p.

This is the second part of Sir Cecil Parrott's autobiography, the half in which Czechoslovakia plays a part in his life. It concerns the years 1945-48 (i.e., the crucial period between the Liberation and the months after the Communist take-over) and 1960-66 when he was British ambassador in Prague, as well as his post-retirement research visits in 1967-69 and 1975. The author is strongly pro-Czechoslovak (except in any political sense), and has great sympathy for all its nationalities' positive strivings and contributions to the arts (especially music and literature, to which he continually refers). He also reveals a diplomat's stiff reserve towards communist misdemeanours which occasionally twists into wry humour. The book amounts to a personal political and cultural history of the country, especially for the periods when Parrott was most intimately involved with it.

Tourism and
Travel Guides

64   **Europe 1985-86.**

Edited by Stephen Birnbaum.   Harmondsworth, England:

Penguin, in association with Houghton Mifflin, 1985. 1,220p. maps.

Separate sections deal with the country as a whole and with Prague in particular
(p. 524-533) and for the tourist who wishes to dispense with planning a trip
through unknown territory, a number of selected routes are set out (p. 664-670).

65   **Fodor's Europe 1985.**

London, Sydney, Auckland: Hodder & Stoughton, 1985. 838p.

map.

Czechoslovakia does not benefit from a current Fodor single-country guide,
though these have been published in the past. This all-Europe guide suffers, like
all such compendia, from restrictions of space, but Czechoslovakia is covered, in
some depth, at least for the short-term tourist interested in the main sights, on
p. 137-154.

66   **Czechoslovakia.**

Geneva, Paris, Munich: Nagel, 1983. 480p. maps. (Nagel's

Encyclopaedia-Guides).

This is perhaps the best all-round work on the country and meets the needs of
practically any kind of informal enquirer, tourist, businessman or idle reader. The
information covers not only hotels, embassies and other types of addresses
essential to the visitor, but also a wealth of other subjects including the country's
history, geography, literature, industry, culture, commerce and food. The maps
and plans cater for both motorist and foot-tourist and in the main obviate the
need for buying locally produced maps.

18

67 **Czechoslovakia.**
    Ctibor Rybár. Prague: Olympia, 1982. 194p.

A standard current guidebook which has in mind the tourist with little prior knowledge of the country, hence it includes a highly condensed history of the country and brief statements on, for example, the political system, industry, trade, education, public health, culture and sport. This is followed by a wide range of travel information: conditions for entry into the country; motoring regulations; insurance; a list of camp sites and other accommodation facilities; and such essentials as where to buy, and how to use, tram tickets. The bulk of the book is taken up with descriptions of all places of any interest to the tourist, arranged alphabetically and separately for the two republics. Necessarily superficial in places, the book nevertheless contains a great deal of essential information and much else besides.

68 **Czechoslovakia: land and nature.**
    Dušan Tomášek. Prague: Orbis, 1973. 4th ed. 62p. map.

An insubstantial and patriotic introduction to various areas of the country of interest to the foreign tourist, supported by a section of well-chosen photographs. There is a useful appendix of geographical, meteorological, demographic, industrial and economic statistics from official sources, and an introductory survey of the state administration. An orthodox piece of self-advertising.

69 **Mapa kulturních památek ČSSR.** (Atlas of cultural monuments in Czechoslovakia.)
    Prague: Kartografické nakladatelství, 1972. 187p.

The thirty-four map pages, twelve pages of black-and-white photographs and the alphabetical index of places marked on the maps, together with thumb-nail descriptions of the monuments involved, make this the simplest and most comprehensive reference-work for the tourist and others with a taste for Czech history. The text is in Czech only, but the key to the symbols and simple colour coding used is in Czech, Russian, English, French and German. Until re-issued, this useful work is regrettably hard to obtain.

70 **Le tourisme en Tchécoslovaquie.** (Tourism in Czechoslovakia.)
    Pul Veyset. *Revue Géographique de l'Est*, vol. 3, no. 2 (Apr.-June 1963), p. 131-36.

A useful description of foreign tourism in the country and of the main sites and sights, with little analysis of either a statistical or economic nature.

71 **Czechoslovakia camping 1983.**
    Committee for Tourism of the Czech and Slovak Socialist Republics. Prague: Merkur, 1983. 80p. maps.

Despite its date, this guide to all the country's scheduled camp sites is still being distributed (summer 1985). The sites are listed by region with a full description, by standardized symbols, of all the facilities available, and the proximity to rail and bus connections and petrol stations. The book is available through Čedok, the national travel and tourism agency.

72 **Through Czechoslovakia by Highway E85.**
[Prague]: Made in (Publicity), for the Government Committee for
Tourism, [n.d.] 32p.

This publication, together with *The E12 route through Czechoslovakia* (Prague:
Merkur, for the Government Committee for Tourism, 1975. unpaginated [32p.]),
and other, similar publications, are available chiefly through branches of Čedok,
the national travel agency. They both provide an excellent opportunity for the
transit tourist to gain at least something from his passage. Sectional maps guide
the traveller from entry to exit, west to east the whole length of the country on
the E85, and southwest to northeast through Bohemia on the E12, while the
accompanying text describes the points of historical or cultural interest in the
towns and villages en route. Both booklets indicate, on the maps, relevant tourist
information, such as the location of hotels, camp sites, petrol and service stations,
and the distances in kilometres between key points. In addition to the description
of the through routes both also contain similar accounts of various worthwhile
detours.

73 **Prague: an intimate guide to Czechoslovakia's thousand-year-old
capital, its beauties, its art-historical monuments, its sights, ancient
and modern, its romantic nooks and corners, with their historical
and literary associations.**
Alois Svoboda.   Prague: Sportovní a turistické nakladatelství,
1965. 299p. maps.

With a title like this, no further commentary is really necessary. Suffice it to say
that, though undoubtedly difficult to come by, this beautifully illustrated book is
one of the most imaginative guides any town could wish to be served by, although
its slightly sentimental tone may not suit every reader. More conventional guides
to the city exist but those are best sought out on arrival in the country. Otherwise
consult the relevant pages in the guides to the country mentioned above.

74 **Jízdní řád ČSD/Cestovný poriadok ČSD.** (Time-table of the
Czechoslovak State Railways.)
Prague: Nakladatelství dopravy a spojů. annual.

The standard time-table of the Czechoslovak railways which contains details of
domestic and international services, information concerning fares and distances
and a map of the network.

75 **Jízdní řád autobusových linek/Cestovný poriadok autobusových
liniek.** (Time-table of bus services.)
Regional capitals: ČSAD. 10 vols. annual

The standard time-table of the state road-transport undertaking (ČSAD). Each
volume is published by ČSAD at its regional headquarters.

76 **Letový řád.** (Airline time-table.)
    Prague: Czechoslovak Airlines (ČSA). biannual.

The full domestic and international time-table of Czechoslovak Airlines, complete
with a list of agencies, advertisements for other bodies involved in tourism, with
their addresses, and the usual range of air-travel information. Published in
summer and winter editions with complete bilingual, Czech and English, text.

77 **Seznam hotelů v ČSSR.** (List of hotels in Czechoslovakia.)
    Compiled by Vladimír Picka.   Prague: Merkur, 1975. 2nd ed. 225p.

Arranged by regions, this book offers an alphabetical list of towns with cross-
references to the tables in which the hotels are listed, with information on their
capacity and essential facilities (the number of single/double rooms with/without
shower/bathroom etc.), as well as such other non-universal facilities as parking,
on-site hairdresser, car-servicing and the availability of petrol. The text is only in
Czech, but the volume has the virtue of completeness and of pointing to a far
broader range of hotels than those to which the foreign tourist will be guided if he
seeks to arrange accommodation in advance of arriving in the country.

Flora and Fauna

78 **Forests of Czechoslovakia.**
L. Hružik (et al.). Prague: Ministerstvo lesního a vodního
hospodářství, 1960. 223p. maps.

An important primary source on the state of afforestation of the country before
the more recent much-discussed upswing in environmental damage that has
affected many forests so badly. This volume describes not only the distribution of
forests, but also Czechoslovak forest-management practices and the research
projects of the day.

79 **Farebný atlas rastlín.** (A coloured atlas of plants.)
Dušan Randuška, Ladislav Šomšák, Izabela Háberová. Bratislava:
Obzor, 1984. 639p.

There is no shortage of books on Czechoslovakia's flora and new works appear
fairly regularly. This is the latest, and the authors cover 1,035 wild plants and
examine their incidence and ecological significance. The work is fully illustrated
with accompanying notes, and is in Slovak only. The work appeared simultaneously in Czech translation under the title *Barevný atlas rostlin* (translation by
Bohumil Šula) in a printing double the size of the source edition.

80 **Horské rostliny ve fotografii.** (Mountain plants in photographs.)
Jiří Čihař, Miroslav Kovanda. Prague: Státní zemědělské
nakladatelství, 1983. 352p.

The core of this work is the collection of 150 colour photographs of many of the
mountain species represented in Czechoslovakia. The accompanying Czech text
describes the species illustrated and explains the influences which have given rise
to the present composition and distribution of the country's mountain flora.

81 Ecological and vegetational differentiation of a solitary conic hill.
Jiřina Slavíková (et al.).   Prague: Academia, 1983. 244p. bibliog.

This is a systematic study of the ecology and vegetation of one specific locality, an isolated conical hill in the relatively dry area of the Central Bohemian Massif, North-West Bohemia. It relates the different habitats, composition, structure and function of plant communities to the different biotypes arising under exposure to the elements at different points of the compass. The work is formulated in terms of the interests of ecologists, botanists, environmentalists and land-users engaged in both forestry and agriculture.

82 Mushrooms and other fungi.
Aurel Dermek, translated by Darina Reguliová.   Leicester, England: Galley Press (W. H. Smith), 1982. 223p.

This is one of a series of popular handbooks emanating from Slovakia. The general mycological sections are not specific in any sense to Czechoslovakia and the range of fungi described can be found in both Britain and Czechoslovakia. Although it is nowhere stated as such, Czechoslovakia, like much of Central Europe is very fungi-conscious, and mushrooming is a widespread pastime. Consequently, much of the people's expertise in processing fungi has gone into the recipe section, which includes many Czech recipes and involves far more species than just the field mushroom trusted by the English.

83 The Hamlyn encyclopedia of plants.
J. Tříska, edited by Helen L. Pursey.   London, New York, Sydney, Toronto: Hamlyn, 1975. 300p.

Like many Hamlyn publications this was printed in Czechoslovakia, and like some, it was also designed and produced there. Accordingly, although produced essentially for the British market, hence the editing into the texts of references to the incidence or non-incidence of individual species in Britain, the book gives a fair representation of Czechoslovak flora. Only one section, on plants of the seashore, and a tiny handful of unillustrated species refer to plants not occurring in Czechoslovakia. That it is actually very Czechoslovak and essentially un-British in its coverage is evidenced by the omission of such typical English species as the primrose and bluebell and the inclusion of such typical Czechoslovak species as wild hepatica or soldanella. Another very Czechoslovak aspect is the wealth of information on the past and present uses to which many plants have been put in folk-medicine, or the modern pharmaceutical industry. In Czechoslovakia books on the medicinal properties of native plants are published with relative frequency. In this book, wherever a plant is described as protected in certain countries, it is invariably the case that it is on the list of species protected in Czechoslovakia, though not all plants protected there carry the relevant note. It is worth mentioning that the illustrations are by some of the country's best artists specializing in nature subjects.

84 Birds of prey in Europe.
Maarten Bijleveld.   London: Macmillan, 1974. 263p.

This is a history of the massive decline in the populations of birds of prey and their losing battle for survival against man's land use and sometimes direct

Flora and Fauna

persecution. Czechoslovakia, along with a number of other countries, is singled out for particular criticism.

85 **Songbirds.**
   Karel Šťastný. London, New York, Sydney, Toronto: Hamlyn, 1980. 216p. maps.

The English mutation of a basic Czech handbook, with little concession to the English market. The volume at least serves to show that the basic range of Czechoslovak birds is essentially similar to that of the British Isles. Far more interesting of course is the area in which the two ranges differ. For current accounts of the specific peculiarities of Czechoslovak bird-life, especially new species or rare occurrences of otherwise known species, see Šťastný's regular contributions to the 'European News' sections, which are published two or three times annually, in *British Birds* (Royal Society for the Protection of Birds).

86 **Ptáci-aves.** (Birds.)
   Karel Hudec (et al.). Prague: Academia, 1972-83. 3 vols. maps. bibliog. (Fauna ČSSR).

A comprehensive work concerning Czechoslovakia's birdlife. It provides not only the various names for each species, but a full account of distribution, sub-species, all manner of statistical data, the means of recognition, the significance to man, relevant legislation and the incidence of avian parasites. Although in Czech, the volumes are accessible for comparative purposes through the maps and statistical data and the numerous illustrations; there are also synopses in German. It goes without saying that with such scope (vol. 3 is itself divided into 3/1 and 3/2, with 592 and 688 pages, and 320 and 325 illustrations respectively) this is a scientific, not a popular work.

87 **Primary succession and species diversity of avian communities on spoil banks after surface mining of lignite in the Most Basin (North-Western Bohemia).**
   Vladimír Bejček, Pavel Tyrner. *Folia Zoologica*, vol. 29, no. 1 (1980), p. 67-77.

Describes a long-term study of the growth of numbers of bird species and absolute numbers of birds occurring on the spoil heaps of North-West Bohemia at four different stages of their development between recently completed extraction and well-established re-afforestation. This is not the place to re-list all the species involved; suffice it to say that the first three species to appear in any density were the wheatear, tawny pipit and skylark. As a detailed ecological study, the article describes such constants as geology and climate and the variables of the changing vegetational cover and different local biotopes. An extension of the study, using six successional stages in the life of spoil heaps is Vladimír Bejček and Karel Šťastný's 'The succession of bird communities on spoil banks after surface brown coal mining', *Ekologia Polska*, vol. 32, no. 2 (1984), p. 245-59, which also takes in developments of vegetational cover.

88   **Bird communities of spruce forests affected by industrial emissions in the Krušné hory (Ore Mountains). Karel Šťastný, Vladimír Bejček.** In: *Bird census and atlas studies: proceedings of the VIII International Conference on Bird Census and Atlas work. Newland Park, Chalfont St. Giles, Buckinghamshire, England, 5th-9th September 1983.* Edited by K. Taylor, R. J. Fuller and P. C. Lack on behalf of the International Bird Census Committee and the European Ornithological Atlas Committee. [n.p.]: British Trust for Ornithology, 1983, p. 243-53.

Although nominally concerned with the qualitative and quantitative changes in the bird population of the unstable ecosystems represented by the huge spruce forests planted by man and currently suffering monumental damage from industrial emissions, the paper also gives a good account of the native beech forest of the area. The study is based on nine separate plots, which are described primarily from the point of view of the bird populations, but the authors also provide much detail on the grasses, shrubs and other vegetation occurring, with even passing references to other, non-industrial, noxious factors such as bark beetles and moths. There is some comparison with nearby mountain areas in Poland and East Germany.

89   **Conservation of wildfowl in fishpond regions.**
      K. Hudec, Karel Šťastný. *Ecological Studies,* vol. 28 (1978), p. 434-38.

A theoretical article which examines, for example, the required structures of reedbeds and sedge stands for certain groups of birds to be able to live and breed. The work is directly related to the case of such areas in the vicinity of some of the major fishponds of South Bohemia and South Moravia. The full range of birds visiting several of the lakes of the Třeboň Basin and the Lednice fishponds is given, including not just the ducks, swans, waders, reed-dwellers and other 'true' aquatic species, but also wet grassland species such as corncrake or meadow pipit, or the pygmy owls of the swampy woodlands. The fishponds are important sites both as resting-places for migrating species and for over-wintering. A number of the region's unique ornithological occurrences are mentioned, adding weight to the argument for continuing protection of the reserves named.

90   **Animal populations in fishpond littorals.**
      J. Pelikán, K. Hudec, Karel Šťastný. *Ecological Studies,* vol. 28 (1978), p. 74-79, 93-95.

A detailed statistical study of the complete fauna repertoire of the fishpond littorals of Southern Bohemia, in particular around the ponds of the Třeboň Basin, from thrips to muskrat, and including therefore insects, reptiles, birds, fish and mammals. The article contains numerous valuable references, including a number of further titles in English.

Flora and Fauna

91 **Freshwater fishes.**
J. Vostradovský, with illustrations by Jakub Malý, and translated by
D. Coxon. New York, London, Sydney, Toronto: Hamlyn, 1978.
5th reprint. 252p.

Although purporting to be more wide-ranging, this is in fact a permutation of a
native Czechoslovak publication and consequently includes at least as good a
representation of that country's fish world as of any other.

92 **A field guide in colour to butterflies and moths.**
Ivo Novák, translated by Marie Hejlová. London: Octopus Books,
1980. Reprinted 1982. 352p. bibliog.

More completely converted to British use and needs than many of the natural
history works emanating from Czechoslovakia, this one nevertheless allows the
reader to infer from explicit or implicit pointers in the text whether a given
species is also at home in Czechoslovakia. However, a knowledge of the
geography and climate of Central Europe would make such inferences easier. The
bibliography includes two earlier books about butterflies, of Czechoslovak origin,
but with the Octopus (London) imprint, namely J. Moucha's *A colour guide to
familiar butterflies, caterpillars and chrysalids* (1974) and V. J. Staněk's *Illustrated
encyclopedia of butterflies and moths* (1977).

Prehistory and Archaeology

93 **Czechoslovakia before the Slavs.**
Evžen Neustupný and Jiří Neustupný, translated by Lewis
Ducke.   London: Thames & Hudson, 1961. 225p. maps. bibliog.
(Ancient Peoples and Places).

This lavishly illustrated and fully annotated introduction to the prehistory of the
country manages to strike a happy balance between the popular and the
academic. It describes the old routes of migration (though these are still a topic of
some debate), the general topographical background, climate and the historical
and archaeological evidence then available. Evidence is presented relating to the
period from the lower Palaeolithic right up to the appearance of the Slavs, and
some cultures (Hallstatt, La Tène, Celtic, Teuton and Roman) are shown to be of
considerable importance. There is a tentative chronology of early finds, and a
good periodized bibliography containing many references in West European
languages in sources that are more accessible than in many other bibliographies.

94 **Středopaleolitické osídlení Čech.** (Middle palaeolithic settlement of
Bohemia.)
Jan Fridrich.   Prague: Archaeological Institute, 1982. 151p. maps.
bibliog.

One virtue of this account is its English résumé (p. 131-34) and the repetition in
English of the captions to the figures in the text and the plates in the appendix
(not paginated). Many different sites are described but much of the most recent
evidence comes from sites near Most in North Bohemia.

95 **Die paläolithische und mesolithische Höhlenbesiedlung des böhmischen Karstes.** (The palaeolithic and mesolithic cave settlements in the Bohemian Karst.)
Jan Fridrich, Karel Sklenář. Prague: National Museum, 1976. 124p. maps. bibliog. (Fontes Archaeologici Pragenses, no. 16).

With its thirty-two end-pages of photographic plates this work gives a complete archaeological description of the many limestone caves and the finds that have been made. It also includes a review of other contemporaneous discoveries outside caves and a general summary of Old and Middle Stone Age settlement of the region.

96 **Hunters, fishers and farmers of Eastern Europe, 6000-3000 B.C.**
Ruth Tringham. London: Hutchinson University Library, 1981. 240p. maps. bibliog.

Modern state boundaries are an obvious nonsense when it comes to prehistory, so this and many of the works quoted in the valuable bibliography are inevitably area-based. Remarks and findings specifically relevant to what is now Czechoslovakia can readily be traced through the index. These include descriptions of sites, classifications of pottery types, burial practices, and the early use of metals. The volume includes many photographs and line-drawn illustrations.

97 **Dolní Věstonice: tábořiště lovců mamutů.** (Dolní Věstonice: a mammoth-hunters' encampment.)
Bohuslav Klíma. Prague: Academia, 1983. 178p. bibliog.

Undoubtedly one of the major archaeological discoveries of the century, Dolní Věstonice north of Mikulov in South Moravia has produced a mass of evidence on the sheer scale of mammoth hunting and a large number of artefacts, including the famous Věstonice madonna, an early female figure. Many samples of mammoth-bone, flint and terracotta artefacts are illustrated. The reader is referred not only to the illustrations, but also to the German résumé.

98 **Analysis of the Czech neolithic pottery: morphological and chronological structure of projections.**
I. Pavlů, M. Zápotocká. Prague: Archaeological Institute, 1978. 217p. bibliog.

A highly specialized work which presents external descriptions of the various types of surface projections on a large corpus of neolithic finds. The text proper is supported by appendixes listing all the linear and stroked pottery finds, statistical and other relevant tables and many illustrations.

99 **Homolka, an eneolithic site in Bohemia.**
Robert W. Ehrich, Emilie Pleslová-Štíková, edited by Hugh O'Neill Hencken, Jan Filip. Prague: Academia; Cambridge, Massachusetts: Peabody Museum, 1968. 499p. maps. bibliog.

This very detailed description of one well-known site is a rare item in that it was produced simultaneously in the West. It presents a full account of the material culture, a chronology, some comparison with other local cultures and some useful appendixes on the non-artefact remains including human bones, burned burial fragments and mammalian bones. The work is the product of longstanding contacts between Prague and the Peabody Museum. It is well illustrated and contains full statistical documentation, diagrams and reproductions of the various types of artefacts.

100   **Osada z doby bronzovej v Pobedime.** (A Bronze Age settlement at Pobedim.)
Etela Studeníková, Jozef Paulík.   Bratislava: Osveta, 1983. 298p. 2 maps. (Museum Nationale Slovacum. Institutum Archeologicum, Fontes, vol. 6).

A detailed description of past and present investigations carried out at one especially striking Bronze Age site near Trenčín. All part-features and the various types of artefacts (tools and pottery dominate) unearthed in them are described and well-illustrated by plan and line drawings, and some photographs. A German résumé is provided (p. 193-209.)

101   **Westböhmen in der späten Bronzezeit.** (Western Bohemia in the late Bronze Age.)
V. Šaldová.   Prague: Archaeological Institute, 1981. 119p. maps. bibliog.

This specialist work describes the location of, and archaeological finds made at, the dozen or so fortified hilltop settlements in Western Bohemia. However, the main body of the book is a detailed account of Okrouhlé Hradiště, near Tachov, the largest and the only one to have revealed also post-Bronze Age occupation. The appendixes include photographs of the various sites, pottery finds, aerial and cross-sectional diagrams of the Okrouhlé Hradiště site, and statistical tables. (The appendixes follow the text proper and are not paginated.)

102   **Březno: osada z mladší doby kamenné v severozápadních Čechách.** (Březno: a late Stone Age settlement in Northwest Bohemia.)
Ivana Pleinerová, Ivan Pavlů.   Ústí nad Labem, Czechoslovakia: Severočeské nakladatelství, on behalf of the Louny District Museum, 1979. 143p. maps. bibliog.

A complete description of one site, together with many illustrations showing the range of linear pottery excavated and details of the structure of individual dwellings. Access to the core of the work for the foreign reader is through the German résumé (p. 129-40).

103   **Celtic civilization and its heritage.**
Jan Filip.   Prague: Academia, 1976. 2nd rev. ed. 232p. maps. bibliog. (New Horizons).

The very name of Bohemia derives from that of the Celtic tribe known as the Boii, and the Czechs are well aware that as Slavs they were not the original inhabitants of the Czech Lands. The present volume is a general history of Celtic society and culture, but the main emphasis is on the particular evidence to be

Prehistory and Archaeology

found in Czechoslovakia, of which there is no shortage. The book also contains forty black-and-white plates (unpaginated) and numerous illustrations in the text. A detailed account of one Central Bohemian Celtic oppidum, also illustrated and with a German résumé, is *Závist* by Karla Motyková, Petr Drda and Alena Rybová (Prague: Academia, 1978. 219p. bibliog.).

104 **Třísov, a Celtic oppidum in South Bohemia.**
Jiří Břeň, preface by Jiří Neustupný.   Prague: National Museum,
1966. 158p. maps. bibliog. (Guides to Prehistory, no. 2).
This entry exemplifies the type of archaeological 'current research' publication emanating from Prague in English. It is a full account of the topography of the site and a detailed description of finds, local as well as imported. The text is supplemented by a good set of maps, diagrams and photographic plates, with one in colour for the glass items. A great wealth of artefacts, in both quantity and variety, is described and illustrated. Other series covering Czech archaeology are *Fontes Archaeologici Pragenses* and *Acta Musei Nationalis Pragae, Series A – History*.

105 **The chemical identification of Baltic amber at the Celtic oppidum Staré Hradisko in Moravia.**
C. W. Beck (et al.).   *Journal of Archaeological Science*, vol. 5,
no. 4 (1978), p. 343-54.
This specialized paper deals with just one aspect of the many important finds at the large oppidum near Prostějov, a site with stone ramparts, workshops and paved tracks. The amber and other imported finds indicate that it was once an important trading centre.

106 **Roman imports in Bohemia.**
Vladimír Sakař.   Prague: National Museum, 1970. 72p. map.
bibliog. (Fontes Archaeologici Pragenses, no. 14).
An illustrated archaeological catalogue in the standard mould covering all the localities where Roman finds have been made. The finds are shown on the map and are described in detail. The conclusion covers the duration and intensity of the flow in Roman imports into Bohemia with a brief conjecture as to the likely trade routes.

107 **Roman bronze vessels from Slovakia.**
Ľudmila Kraskovská, translated from Slovak by Hana
Schuck.   Oxford: British Archaeological Reports, 1978. 81p. map.
bibliog. (International Series [supplementary], no. 44.)
Of great importance to the early history of Slovakia was contact with the Roman Empire. The Roman army was here for some time and recorded its victory over the Markomanni in 179 AD in an inscription on a rockface near the castle at Trenčín. The present work is a detailed catalogue of finds and the map locates twenty-nine different important sites.

108   **The Roman cemetery at Gerulata Rusovce.**
L'udmila Kraskovská, translated by Hana Schuck.   Oxford: British
Archaeological Reports, Series 10, 1976. 114p. maps. bibliog.
This is a standard account, in keeping with the series, of work carried out at this
important site at Rusovce (since 1971 part of Bratislava) which, as Gerulata, was
a major Roman station in the province of Pannonia from the 1st to the 4th
centuries. The finds are described in detail and well illustrated and include coins,
glassware, pottery, ornaments and iron objects.

109   **Römische und germanische Kunst in der Slowakei.** (Roman and
Germanic art in Slovakia.)
T. Kolník.   Bratislava: Tatran, 1984. 224p.
This is a lavishly illustrated volume, a mutation of a larger work in Slovak,
recording the major archaeological finds which reflect the ancient patterns of
trading and the military movement of the Germanic tribes and Roman legions
through the territory of modern Slovakia.

110   **Ars slovaca antiqua.** (Ancient Slovak art.)
Bratislava: Tatran. irregular.
This is a series of popular, exquisitely produced monographs on various aspects of
prehistoric art, decorative and applied, from household pottery to Roman coins.
The series has the rare attribute of carrying résumés (also indices and annotations
where relevant) in English.

111   **Morava na sklonku antiky.** (Moravia at the end of antiquity.)
Jaroslav Tejral.   Prague: Academia, 1982. 253p. bibliog.
This is a large-format volume on the late Roman era, with the Roman Empire
collapsing under the pressure of large tribal movements which ultimately led to
the formation of the early pre-feudal 'states'. The work tries to fill in some of the
historical and ethnographical blanks in the prehistory of the area north of the
Danube, especially Moravia. Some of the work also has a relevance to Slovakia.
It includes countless illustrations of artefacts and a German résumé.

112   **Grundzüge der Völkerwanderungszeit in Mähren.** (Outline of the
period of the migration of peoples in Moravia.)
Jaroslav Tejral.   Prague: Academia, 1976. 121p. maps. bibliog.
(Studie Archeologického ústavu ČSAV v Brně).
A useful summary account of the different periods of the prehistory of Moravia,
with a description of individual archaeological sites and the finds therefrom, many
illustrated by photographs and line drawings.

Prehistory and Archaeology

113 **Moravia Magna: the Great Moravian Empire, its art and times.**
Ján Dekan, with an introduction by Josef Poulík, and translated by
Heather Trebatická. Minneapolis, Minnesota: Control Data Arts,
1979. 166p.

This work, by a prominent Slovak archaeologist, is the country's own celebration
of the eleven-hundredth anniversary of the Great Moravian Empire, which was
marked by many exhibitions and other publications from 1963 onwards. The text
takes us from the earliest known prehistory of the region, through the fall of the
Roman Empire, the misty realm of Samo (7th century, the first state on Slovak
territory), to Great Moravia itself, providing an account of the cultural, spiritual
and economic life of the most highly developed state of 9th-century Central
Europe. The work is illustrated by countless superbly reproduced colour
photographs (unpaginated) and other illustrative material from the whole period,
representing all the major archaeological sites, some quite far from the centre of
the Empire (modern Moravia and West Slovakia). The book appeared
simultaneously in Czech, Slovak, German, Polish, Hungarian and Russian
editions.

114 **Great Moravia: the archaeology of ninth-century Czechoslovakia.**
Susan Beeby, David Buckton, Zdeněk Klanica. London: British
Museum Publications, 1982. 37p. map.

In 1982 London had the good fortune to see, at the British Museum, a collection
of artefacts found at numerous sites in Czechoslovakia and dating from the period
of the first more or less consolidated western Slav state, called Great Moravia by
the Byzantine emperor Constantine Porphyrogenitus. This guide to the exhibition
provides a useful insight to the historical background, although the textual
sections are regrettably brief. Nevertheless, it remains a valuable recent
introduction in English to a very early period of Czech and Slovak social history
(9th-10th centuries). Eight pages of appended black-and-white photographic
plates ensure a good, if limited, surviving visual record of the collection's visit to
London.

115 **Die Prager Burg zur Zeit der Přemyslidenfürsten.** (Prague Castle at
the time of the Přemyslide princes.)
Ivan Borkovský. Prague: Academia, 1972. 190p. maps.

In addition to rehearsing the overall history of the Přemyslide period, relating it
in particular to archaeological finds, this volume provides the histories of
individual buildings on, and around, the Hradčany hill past and present. The
book is illustrated by line drawings and a set of (unpaginated) black-and-white
plates. For many more illustrations and background on the Basilica of St. George
see the same author's *Svatojiřská bazilika a klášter na Pražském hradě* (The
basilica and monastery of St. George at Prague Castle) (Prague: Academia, 1975,
162p.) which contains 234 unpaginated plates and a German résumé).

116 **Archaeological news in the Czech Socialist Republic.**
Edited by Jiří Hrala. Prague; Brno, Czechoslovakia:
Archaeological Institute, 1981. 238p. bibliog.

Although published essentially for the internal needs of the institute, the contents
of this volume were intended as the Czech contribution to the 10th International
Congress of Prehistoric and Protohistoric Sciences held in Mexico in 1981. Some
seventy-six papers are included, all relating to the latest finds in various parts of
the country, and though brief, they cover a wide range of recent finds, many of
which are illustrated.

117 **Rapports du IIIᵉ Congrès Internationale d'Archéologie Slave,
Bratislava 7-14 septembre 1975.** (Proceedings of the 3rd
International Conference on Slav Archaeology, Bratislava, 7-14
September 1975.)
Edited by Bohuslav Chropovský. Bratislava: Veda, 1979. 2 vols.

A useful collection of papers, a number of which have a direct bearing on the pre-
and early history of what is now Czechoslovakia. These include: Veronika
Gervers-Molnár on Romanesque rotundas of which there are a number of well-
preserved examples in Bohemia and Moravia (in English, p. 307-12); Alojz
Habovštiak on 9th-10th-century castle fortifications in Slovakia (in German,
p. 359-66); Jaroslav Kudrnáč on early fortifications in Bohemia (German, p. 447-
51); Květa Reichertová on the Sázava monastery (French, p. 647-50); Zlata
Čilinská on Samo's Empire, the first state entity on Czechoslovak soil (German,
vol. 2, p. 79–84, with ensuing discussion; the paper proper contains a number of
references on this fascinating and little-known period); and Taťana Kučerovská
on the currencies in circulation in 9th-10th-century Moravia (German, vol. 2,
p. 211-21).

118 **Praehistorica.** (Prehistory.)
Prague: Univerzita Karlova, irregular.

A series consisting of monographs of miscellanea on aspects of current research
and excavations being conducted in Czechoslovakia and abroad. Many titles are
in German, and others contain German or English résumés.

119 **Studie archeologického ústavu Československé akademie věd
v Brně.** (Studies of the Archaeological Institute of the Czechoslovak
Academy of Sciences in Brno.)
Prague: Academia, 1973-. biannual or three times per year.

A series of major works giving the latest results of field work throughout the
Czech Socialist Republic. Each volume contains complete documentation – maps,
plans, illustrations (photographic and other), bibliographies and foreign-language
summaries, usually in German. Isolated volumes may be published completely in
a foreign language. Another series, published in Brno by the Archaeological
Institute itself, is *Fontes Archaeologiae Moravicae* (volumes have appeared
irregularly since 1959), again mostly in Czech, with German as the preferred
language for résumés.

Prehistory and Archaeology

120 **West- und südböhmische Funde in Wien.** (West and South
Bohemian finds in Vienna.)
Jan Michálek. Prague: Archaeological Institute, 1979. 2 vols.
4 maps. bibliog. (Výzkumy v Čechách – Supplementum).

The Vienna Museum of Natural History has, in its prehistoric section, one of the
largest collections of finds from Bohemia, Moravia and Slovakia. Of the two
present volumes, one contains over one hundred plates consisting of illustrations
of all the major exhibits, the other being a detailed catalogue providing
information on, for example, the date and nature of each find, some
measurements, and other literature on the particular find. In the same edition
other volumes are to follow, dealing with finds in other areas of the country. It
should be noted that the Archaeological Institute regularly publishes its current
research in the same general series, though the majority of volumes are in Czech.

121 **Archeologické výzkumy v severozápadních Čechách v letech 1953-
1972.** (Archaeological investigations in Northwest Bohemia, 1953-
72.)
D. Koutecký (et al.). Prague: Archaeological Institute, 1980.
202p. bibliog. (Archeologické Studijní Materiály, 13/1.)

This volume includes a substantial German résumé. In addition to a catalogue of
finds, and an extensive bibliography (with some of the titles being in German),
the work also contains a periodized prehistory of the region and a history of the
archaeological investigations which have been carried out. A sister volume
(Archeologické Studijní Materiály, 13/2) contains seventeen large-scale maps of
the region. Many finds and one of the maps relate to the mediaeval period, the
majority stretching between the palaeolithic and the first evidence of the new
Slavonic inhabitants.

History

General

122 **The Slavs: a cultural and historical survey of the Slavonic peoples.**
Roger Portal, translated from French by Patrick Evans. New
York; Evanston, Illinois: Harper & Row; London: Weidenfeld &
Nicolson, 1969. 508p. maps. bibliog.

The chapters in books 1 and 3-5 represent a good overall history of the Czechs
and Slovaks over the last thousand years, despite occupying only about one tenth
of the whole volume. Yet the coverage is attractively broad, thanks to the cultural
element, which includes arts and crafts, mining, religion, education and literature,
as well as Czech-German and Slovak-Hungarian cultural contact and conflict.
Much of this is hinted at in the meagrest detail, and the book cannot, therefore,
be taken as any more than introductory. Its raison d'être is to bring together the
highly diverse Slavonic family of nations within a single volume as, despite their
past fragmentation, they are now brought together within a single political
ideology – the author must be forgiven this overstatement!

123 **The Slavs in European history and civilisation.**
Francis Dvornik. New Brunswick, New Jersey: Rutgers
University Press, 1962. 2nd paperback printing. 688p. maps.
bibliog.

Czech history, especially in the mediaeval period, is covered here in far greater
detail than in the Portal volume (q.v.), in acknowledgement of the key role
played by early Bohemia, before and after its kings became Holy Roman
Emperors. Like Portal, however, the author stresses the unity of the Slavs, based
on 'common traits in their political history, their civilization, their national
character, and language'; and it is perhaps as well that he uses no stronger word
than 'traits' here. While some sections pick out the Czechs and Slovaks for

nominally separate discussion, the fact that this is often barely possible is tacitly acknowleged in the constant recognition of inter-Slav or international factors necessarily involved in the nations' history. The end-point of the account is the Slav Congress of 1848 and its later echoes.

124 **A history of the Czechs and Slovaks**
R. W. Seton-Watson. London, New York, Melbourne: Hutchinson, 1943. Reprinted, Hamden, Connecticut: Archon Books, 1965. 413p. maps. bibliog.

First published over forty years ago, this is still widely regarded as the best general history of both nations. A classic in its own right, it was written by one who came to be regarded, especially by the Slovaks, as a competent foreign spokesman for their nation.

125 **East-Central Europe in transition from the fourteenth to the seventeenth century.**
Edited by Antoni Mączak, Henryk Samsonovicz, Peter Burke. Cambridge, England: Cambridge University Press; Paris: Editions de la maison des sciences de l'homme, 1985. 207p. map. bibliog. (Studies in Modern Capitalism).

A number of individual studies in this collection by various leading Polish and Hungarian scholars have a direct bearing on the area that is now Czechoslovakia. These include: Eric Fügedis' 'The demographic landscape in East-Central Europe' (p. 47-58); Leonid Zytkowicz on trends in the agrarian economy, (p. 59-83); Maria Bogucka on the rise (and fall in some cases) of towns (p. 97-108); Marion Malowist on the circulation of capital, with important reference to the copper, silver and gold mines of Slovakia (p. 109-127); Jerzy Topolski's economic model of East-Central European commerce from the mid-16th to the mid-17th century (p. 128-139); and Jan Bialostocki on 'Borrowing and originality in the East-Central European Renaissance' (p. 153-166).

126 **A history of East Central Europe.**
Edited by Peter F. Sugar, Donald W. Treadgold. Seattle, Washington: University of Washington Press, 1974- . 11 vols. bibliog.

This monumental enterprise is yet to be completed, but some of its volumes already offer a good introduction to different aspects of Czechoslovak history as inseparable from that of the area generally and the Habsburg monarchy in particular. Volume 9, by Joseph Rothschild (1974. 438p. maps.), deals with the inter-war period; and volume 6, by Robert A. Kann and Zdeněk V. David (1984. 560p. maps.), reviews the political, economic and cultural development of the nations of the Habsburg lands, including separate treatment for the Czechs, Slovaks and Ruthenians, over the period 1526-1918. Other volumes, still to be published, with a direct bearing on Czechoslovakia will be: volume 1, *The Prehistory of East Central Europe*, by Marija Gimbutas (announced for 1986); volume 10, *East Central Europe since 1939*, by Ivo Banac and Jan Gross; and volume 11, *Historical atlas, general index and bibliography*.

127 **Eastern Europe 1740-1980, feudalism to communism.**
Robin Okey. London: Hutchinson, 1980. 264p. maps. bibliog.

Just over half the book covers the period from the Enlightenment to the break-up of the Habsburg Empire in 1918, and the author discusses: the prevailing trends of liberalism and nationalism; the revolutionary period of the mid-19th century; the collapse of revolutionary politics after 1860; and social and economic developments with reference to both industry and agriculture. The second half of the book covers the 20th-century history of the area since the Great War. It considers the new states formed after World War I, the effects of Hitler and Stalin on political developments and the changes which have taken place since the communist parties of the area gained control. A good wide-ranging work, which manages to pinpoint the salient local specifics for each country.

128 **The spirit of Bohemia: a survey of Czechoslovak history, music and literature.**
Vladimir Nosek. London: George Allen & Unwin, 1926. 379p. bibliog.

Although this volume is dated, it has been included here for its size and scope and for the contemporary view it gives of Czech literature and music as well as for its early, though slight, history of Slovak literature. However, it should be noted that, despite its title, Slovak music is ignored beyond a brief discussion of folksongs. Half of the book is heavily weighted towards religious history, or history as carried forward largely by the great religious, or at least religion-based, controversies of the 14th-17th centuries.

Mediaeval and Early Modern Period

General

129 **The entry of the Slavs into Christendom: an introduction to the medieval history of the Slavs.**
A. P. Vlasto. Cambridge, England: Cambridge University Press, 1970. 435p. map. bibliog.

The approximate period covered here is 500-1200 and the first third of the work is of direct, or indirect, relevance to early Czech and Slovak history. The book starts with the shadowy possible import of Christianity by Irish missionary monks operating from Bavaria and the early consecration of a church at Nitra by the Bishop of Salzburg, and then takes the reader through the better known missionary activities of Saints Constantine and Methodius from Salonika, to the demise of the Church Slavonic liturgy, which actually hung on until the mid-14th century. The text provides a detailed history of princes and bishops, and through them, of the growing strength of Christianity, especially as reflected in the history of church building and the mediaeval religious texts, many of which are listed. Equally important is the influence of especially Bohemian centres (Prague,

Sázava) on the spread of Christianity elsewhere among the Slavs, particularly in Poland.

130   **The first contacts of Czechs with Western civilization: the mission of St. Amand in the 7th century.**
       Milič Čapek.   In: *The Czechoslovak contribution to world culture.*
       Edited by Miloslav Rechcígl, Jr. The Hague, London, Paris:
       Mouton, 1964, p. 183-210.

While there is some evidence that it was Irish monks who brought Christianity to the Czechs, Čapek's thesis, based on very reasonable conjecture and a reinterpretation of the relevant Latin documents, is that priority really belongs to the Belgian St. Amand around 630 AD.

131   **Eastern and western Europe in the Middle Ages.**
       F. Graus, K. Bosl, F. Seibt, M. M. Postan, A. Gieysztor, edited
       with an introduction by Geoffrey Barraclough.   London: Thames
       & Hudson, 1970. 216p. maps. bibliog.

An illustrated history of mediaeval Europe which is informed by the belief that the traditional view of Europe as a permanent scene of recurrent Slav-German hostilities, with the Germans as the standard-bearers of the only real European civilization, is long overdue for revision. Five separate essays tackle the issue from different angles (racial, political, religious, economic and cultural), to demonstrate that the 'unity in diversity' embraces East as well as West, and that a great deal of that is to do with the shared Christian heritage. The study is of supreme relevance to the Czechs in particular as major power-holders in mediaeval Europe and as a nation which, though Slav, have sometimes been dismissed as Slav-speaking Germans.

132   **Bohemia: from the earliest times to the fall of national independence in 1620; with a short summary of later events.**
       C. Edmund Maurice.   London: T. Fisher Unwin, 1896. 533p.
       map. (The story of the nations).

This work is included here for its fascination value as a Victorian history of the Czechs, a 'lost nation' suffering from a lack of understanding by the English through the 'mischievous blunder of some fifteenth century Frenchman, who confused the gipsies who had just arrived in France with the nation which was just then startling Europe by its resistance to the forces of the [Holy Roman] Empire'. It traces Bohemian history in some detail up to the Battle of the White Mountain in 1620, with a liberal admixture of prehistoric legend in the early chapters. The summary of later events is very slender, concentrating mostly on John Amos Comenius, the National Revival and the state and status of the Czech language. The book contains a small number of illustrations and a detailed index.

133 **Böhmen im mittelalterlichen Europa: Frühzeit, Hochmittelalter, Kolonisationsepoche.** (Bohemia in mediaeval Europe: early times, the high Middle Ages, the age of colonization.)
Friedrich Prinz. Munich: Verlag C.H. Beck, 1984. 238p. map. bibliog.

The author pays detailed attention in the first half of the book to the early period of Czech history, down to the end of the reign of the Přemyslide dynasty (1306). The second half is a social, cultural, religious, literary and art history of the period. At all points the German dimension is brought in, and there is some discussion of the sources of the age-old Czech-German controversy although Prinz is more conciliatory in tone than many German writers. As is the German custom places are all given their German names, with just a few of the smaller ones identified by their Czech name in brackets. The appendix includes a list of the early Bohemian kings and their dates, and the names and dates of the bishops and archbishops of the period, whose role was often as important as that of the king.

134 **Essays in Czech history.**
Reginald Robert Betts. London: Athlone Press, 1969. 315p. bibliog.

Described by G. R. Potter, in a brief memoir (p. xii-xv) as 'an exponent of the history of Bohemia in the Middle Ages' who 'has a permanent place among those who have made enduring contributions to the history of Europe', Betts nevertheless failed to produce a single major book. This volume is a posthumous collection of scattered essays which, taken together, offer a partial history of mediaeval Bohemia including its scholarship (two essays on the University of Prague, founded 1348) and philosophy (political ideas and religious reform; the Hussite movement). There are also short monographs on Jan Hus, Jerome of Prague and Peter Payne (the English 'heretic' better known in Czech than English history; other aspects of English influence are discussed in another essay). Two further papers look at mediaeval society, and the last one is an analysis of Masaryk's philosophy of history.

Hussitism, Anabaptists and the Czech Brethren

135 **A history of the Hussite revolution.**
Howard Kaminsky. Berkeley, California; Los Angeles: University of California Press, 1967. 580p. bibliog.

This is a very detailed history of Hussitism, from the seminal stage and the contribution of John Wyclif to the solid establishment of its Taborite offshoot in the 1420s. It describes not only the conflicting theologies which developed but also the specific role of countless major and minor participants in the debates and battles that unfolded. Kaminsky is cautious in his interpretation, admitting that it may be far from the only one, and he is anxious to avoid anachronistic approaches to mediaeval 'ideology'. However, his main attitude is that 'the Hussite movement was both a reformation and a revolution, in fact *the* revolution of the late Middle Ages, the history of which period cannot be properly understood if the Hussites are left out', though, unlike some of his predecessors, he does not see this as necessarily an anti-Hussite view. Another value of the work is that it goes part of the way towards opening up some of the earlier Czech scholarship that was linguistically inaccessible.

136 **John Hus' concept of the church.**
Matthew Spinka.   Princeton, New Jersey: Princeton University
Press, 1966. 432p. bibliog.

The substance of the book is apparent from the title but what it conceals is that it also contains the ecclesiologies of some of Hus's major opponents, namely Jan z Holešova, Stanislav ze Znojma and Štěpán Páleč. A glance at the otherwise useful bibliography shows that these other reformers, representatives of other wings of the new theology, are extremely poorly served in English. Spinka has also written *John Hus: a biography* (q.v.).

137 **John Hus at the Council of Constance.**
Translated from Latin and Czech with notes and an introduction by
Matthew Spinka.   New York, London: Columbia University
Press, 1965. 327p. bibliog.

Spinka's energies have been widely devoted to the study of Hus, the results appearing either in the form of scholarly monographs such as his *John Hus and the Czech Reform* (Chicago: University of Chicago Press, 1941. Reprinted, Hamden, Connecticut: Archon Books, 1966) and others named below, or, as in the present case, by the translation of relevant documents. This work consists of Petr z Mladoňovic's eye-witness account of the trial of Hus for heresy at Constance in 1415, along with Hus's defence, and of letters by Hus himself. The translations are preceded by a biography of Petr z Mladoňovic, a history of the Constance Council and the nature of Hus's heresy, and, in the foreword, an outline of earlier attitudes, positive and negative, in Hus scholarship.

138 **John Hus: a biography.**
Matthew Spinka.   Princeton, New Jersey: Princeton University
Press, 1968. 344p. maps. bibliog.

Any meaningful analysis of the life and work of Jan Hus (often John Huss in English), the 15th-century Czech Protestant reformer, must be set in its historical and theological context, which Spinka does. He starts with an account of the reigns of Charles IV and Wenceslas IV and of the precursors of Hus, and includes, at the appropriate point, a description of the opposition to Hus's reforming efforts before summarizing the events that followed Hus's burning at the stake in 1415 and recounting details of the lives of the preachers known as Hus's successors. The volume includes an analysis of Hus's major works and many useful snippets such as the translation, in the epilogue, of the best-known Hussite battle-hymn *Ktož sú boží bojovníci*.

139 **The religion of Hussite Tábor.**
Howard Kaminsky. In: *The Czechoslovak contribution to world culture*. (Edited by Miloslav Rechcígl, Jr. The Hague, London, Paris: Mouton, 1964, p. 210-23.

The 1420s were a major period in Czech religious history. Kaminsky provides a useful account, not only of the puritanical evangelist Tábor Hussite theology, but also of the nature of the debates between Tábor and Prague, the less revolutionary centre of Hussitism, with quotations from the protagonists on both sides.

140 **John Žižka and the Hussite revolution.**
Frederick G. Heymann.   Princeton, New Jersey: Princeton University Press, 1955. 521p. maps. bibliog.

John Žižka (1360?-1424), to the Czechs Jan Žižka z Trocnova, was one of the main Hussite leaders and the eventual controller of much of Bohemia, having fallen out with the Taborites. This book is a mixture of history and biography, of the first quarter of the 15th century. Žižka was one of the foremost generals of the Hussite wars and part of his renown resides in some of the military techniques which he invented which were so successful as to have been adopted by many others far away in time and space.

141 **The nobility and the making of the Hussite revolution.**
John Martin Klassen.   Boulder, Colorado: East European Quarterly. Distributed by Columbia University Press, New York, London, 1978. 186p. map. bibliog.

Klassen's collection of essays, which only partially amount to a consecutive history, seeks to fill the gap left by earlier historians who have overlooked the role of the nobility during the Hussite revolution, or have noted only that of the Catholic nobility in the king's party during the later period. The importance of the nobility is seen in theory as they were dispensers of patronage over priests' livings and parish economies, and in practice as positive defenders of the Hussite cause around the time of Hus's death and the years immediately following. The concluding essay describes the short- and long-term advantages that accrued to the nobility in the aftermath of the Hussite revolution.

142 **The Hussite king: Bohemia in European affairs 1440-1471.**
Otakar Odložilík.   New Brunswick, New Jersey: Rutgers University Press, 1965. 337p. maps. bibliog.

The 'Hussite king', George of Poděbrady (Jiří z Poděbrad) (1458-71), was probably one of the best rulers the Czechs ever had. Certainly, that is how he is widely perceived, not only for his Hussite and Protestant connections, which despite the divisions among the Hussites' descendants are considered prime virtues, but also, and more widely than just among the Czechs, for his genuine and far-felt statesmanship. This he had tested both at home in the religiously divided kingdom and abroad. The extent of his impact on contemporary affairs means that this biography is simultaneously a history of Bohemia and at least a partial history of many of the adjacent states and provinces and some more distant ones, notably France. After dealing with the wars at the end of George's reign Odložilík, a respected post-war emigré historian, traces the next half-century of political and religious developments, including the destiny of George's children, many of whom became Catholics.

143   **The universal peace organization of King George of Bohemia: a fifteenth century plan for world peace 1462-1464.**
Edited by František Kavka, Vladimír Outrata, Josef Polišenský. Prague: Publishing House of the Czechoslovak Academy of Sciences, 1964. 122p.

The volume is in two parts: a modern Czech view of George of Poděbrady's proposal for a league of Christian nations in the form of an historical essay on its genesis, conception, contemporary responses and modern research into it, by Václav Vaněček; and a transcript of the original Latin text of King George's proposal, edited by Jiří Kejř, together with modern translations into English, Russian, French and Spanish. The work is a quinquecentennial celebration of George of Poděbrady's project, supported by UNESCO.

144   **George of Bohemia: king of heretics.**
Frederick G. Heymann. Princeton, New Jersey: Princeton University Press, 1965. 671p. map. bibliog.

The history of George of Poděbrady covers essentially the same territory as the previous entry but it is informed by the view that developments under this king were parallel to what was happening elsewhere in Europe – a 'vigorous if short-lived development of "Tudorism" in Bohemia'. The book is also a sequel to the author's earlier work entitled *John Žižka and the Hussite Revolution* (q.v.), one of the best accounts of the role of this one-eyed military leader who is to this day a revered figure in the Czech firmament of religious or political militancy whenever it surfaces.

145   **George of Poděbrady's plan for an international peace league.**
Frederick G. Heymann. In: *The Czechoslovak contribution to world culture*. Edited by Miloslav Rechcígl, Jr. The Hague, London, Paris: Mouton, 1964, p. 224-44.

King George of Poděbrady (Jiří z Poděbrad) is credited with the first attempt at a league of nations based on cooperation and understanding, mediation and arbitration, and the will of princes, not that of Rome. This paper describes some of its quite detailed provisions and the likely role of certain of George's advisers. The subject is a fascinating one in view of its antiquity – the 1460's.

146   **The political and social doctrines of the Unity of Czech Brethren in the fifteenth and early sixteenth centuries.**
Peter Brock. The Hague: Mouton, 1957. 302p. bibliog.

This remains an important work for an understanding of many aspects of religious, and hence social and political developments after Hus. It includes an account, not only of the evolution of ideology and the main split in the movement, but in particular an appraisal of the life and work of Petr Chelčický.

Chelčický, the precursor of the Brethren has hitherto been largely overlooked even by historians, but he was demonstrably one of the main figures in the history of Czech religious and political history.

147   **The anabaptists and the Czech Brethren in Moravia 1526-1628: a study of origins and contacts.**
Jarold Knox Zeman, foreword by Jaroslav Pelikán.   The Hague: Mouton, 1969. 407p. bibliog.

The particular contribution of this vast work is that it sheds new light on the history of Hussitism through its detailed and well-documented study of the Czech anabaptists, with whom the Brethren had not only negotiations for a merger, but also some serious theological polemics. Incorporated in the account is a record of other religious influences at work, especially from Germany and Switzerland. An important academic contribution is the detailed historical topography showing the times and places where and when individuals of the many religious sub-groupings could have been in contact. The work is a major contribution to Moravian, and hence Czech, religious history.

148   **Tolerance and movements of religious dissent in Eastern Europe.**
Edited by Béla K. Király.   Boulder, Colorado: East European Quarterly. Distributed by Columbia University Press, New York, London, 1975. 227p. (Studies on Society in Change, no. 1; East European Monographs, no. 13).

This volume of papers contains three of relevance to Czech mediaeval history with an emphasis on theological aspects. Frederick G. Heymann discusses 'The role of the Bohemian cities during and after the Hussite revolution' (p. 27-41) which is a story of initially strong religious and political power-seats, the towns as such, losing their power to the nobility and the crown, and a history of the various branches of Hussitism. Peter Brock, 'The Hutterites and war, 1530-1800' (p. 43-51) is a brief history of one branch of anabaptism and its attendant theology, in particular their refusal to pay war taxes either during the Turkish wars or the Thirty Years' War. Finally, Marianka Sasha Fousek writes 'On secular authority and military service among the Bohemian Brethren in the 16th and 17th centuries' (p. 53-64) and deals with the narrow limits to which the Brethren's theology would allow them to go in involvement in civil or military service.

The letters of John Hus
See item no. 994.

Bohemia under the Habsburgs

149 The Habsburg monarchy: a history of the Austrian Empire and Austria-Hungary.
A. J. P. Taylor. Harmondsworth, England: Penguin Books in association with Hamish Hamilton, 1985 (reprint of 1964 Peregrine edition). 304p. maps. bibliog.

Although concentrating on the period between the end of the Holy Roman Empire in 1806 and the break-up of the monarchy in 1918, the early chapters on the dynasty and the peoples in the Empire contribute to the longer view of the history of Austria and its many nationalities, including the Czechs and Slovaks. The history of these two nations is inseparable from that of Austria and indeed they were from time to time causes of change in Austrian affairs. Taylor's book, now a classic, is one of the handiest introductory texts and is extremely readable.

150 King and estates in the Bohemian Lands 1526-1564.
Kenneth J. Dillon. Brussels: Editions de la Librairie Encyclopédique, 1976. 206p. maps. bibliog. (Studies Presented to the International Commission for the History of Representative and Parliamentary Institutions, no. 57).

The important period considered here goes from the anarchy that preceded the election of Ferdinand of Habsburg to the Bohemian throne (the first Habsburg in a line that ended in 1918 though by then the Bohemian throne had long been a semi-ignored appendage to that of Austria) to his death in 1564. It was a period of continuing religious dispute, marked by royal attempts to cut back the old privileges of the Estates and by the background threat posed by the Turks. The ambivalent relationship between Crown and Estates – mutual reliance and mutual distrust – is illustrated by four central aspects of the history of the period: the Turkish wars; finance (dealt with throughout in considerable detail); religion; and internal political control.

151 The peasantry of Eastern Europe, vol. I: Roots of rural transformation.
Edited by Ivan Volgyes. New York: Pergamon Press, 1979. 192p. (Comparative Rural Transformation Series).

Two papers here are relevant to the economic history of the Czech Lands. Linda Longfellow Blodgett's, 'The "second serfdom" in Bohemia: a case study of the Rožmberk estates in the 16th century' (p. 1-18), is a study of the many extant *urbaria* from the Rožmberk estates to assess what economic activities dominated and the amount of forced labour they entailed; the whole seeking to assess the degree to which it can be said that there was a shift from *Grundherrschaft* to *Gutsherrschaft*, i.e. from living on feudal income to being involved in economic enterprise, on the part of the Rožmberk family. A. Paul Kubricht's, 'The national-economic implication of the formation of the Czech Agrarian Party (1899)' (p. 19-34), assesses the similarities and differences between the birth of a Czech agrarian movement and that of others in the region. Both topics have been

44

widely discussed in recent Czechoslovak historical journals, as the footnotes, in the absence of formal bibliography, show.

152 **Serf, seigneur and sovereign: agrarian reform in eighteenth-century Bohemia.**
William E. Wright.   Minneapolis, Minnesota: University of Minnesota Press, 1966. 216p. bibliog.

Maria Theresa and Joseph II were both important reformers and one significant area was the release of the peasantry from their feudal masters and, for example, the statutory obligations of labour that had gone with serfdom. Between 1740 and 1790 the Bohemian peasantry progressed from an almost total lack of freedom to complete personal freedom, with the concomitant changes in patterns of land ownership. The processes by which this monumental change came about is the subject of this work.

153 **The making of the Habsburg Monarchy, 1550-1700: an interpretation.**
Robert J. W. Evans.   Oxford: Clarendon Press, Oxford University Press, 1979. 531p. 2 maps. bibliog.

The history of the Czechs and Slovaks is inseparable from that of the Austro-Hungarian Empire, therefore this volume is of unquestionable relevance to the present bibliography. The interpretation of the title is one whereby the history is given not in terms of 'wars and armies, diplomacy and foreign relations', but in terms of social and intellectual evolution and change. Religion has always been part of the background here, and a great deal hinges on the change from peaceful coexistence between Protestants and Catholics to the recatholicization of the Counter-Reformation. For Bohemia a major consequence of this was the change in land-ownership, loyal nobility being rewarded with land confiscated from the disloyal. Evans contests that the decline of Czech culture was due to the cosmopolitanism of the newly promoted nobility rather than to the dominant influence of Austria. Useful appendixes include a political and military chronology, a genealogy of the Habsburgs and a multilingual glossary of place-names. Evans has devoted a separate study to Rudolph II entitled *Rudolf II and his world: a study in intellectual history 1576-1612* (Oxford: Clarendon Press, 1973. 323p. maps.). Rudolph made Prague his capital after 1583, and the 'intellectual history' of the title is largely tied up with the many scholars with whom Rudolph surrounded himself (Tycho Brahe, Kepler and others) and the religious question.

154 **The Thirty Years War.**
Josef V. Polišenský, translated by Robert Evans.   London: Batsford, 1971. 305p. map. bibliog. Paperback edition, London: NEL books, 1974. 314p.

The era of the Thirty Years' War is one of the periods which are very much felt to be a part of Czech history, many of the major events taking place on Czech soil (the second Prague Defenestration 1618, the Battle of the White Mountain 1620, the colourful career of the Habsburg general, later traitor, Wallenstein, murdered by Scots and Irish in 1634, and the Swedish siege of Prague in 1648). This is just one recent history of one of the longest European wars, by a highly respected Czech historian who is well served by his English colleague the translator. Other recent histories include those by G. Pages *The Thirty Years War 1618–1648* (London: Adam & Charles Black, 1970. 269p.) and Geoffrey Parker *The Thirty Years War* (London: Routledge & Kegan Paul, 1984. 340p.).

155   **The Habsburg Empire 1790-1918.**
C. A. Macartney.   London: Weidenfeld & Nicolson, 1968. 886p. map. bibliog.

This is another history of the whole monarchy, in wide use as a standard text. The emphasis is on political, social, economic and national development, and in all of these areas specific measures and other changes originating at the centre had direct consequences for the Czechs and Slovaks.

156   **Intellectual and social developments in the Habsburg Empire from Maria Theresa to World War I: essays dedicated to Robert A. Kann.**
Edited by Stanley B. Winters, Joseph Held.   Boulder, Colorado: East European Quarterly. Distributed by Columbia University Press, New York, 1975. 304p. (East European Monographs, no. 11).

These essays cover social, diplomatic and many other aspects of especially Austrian history over the period stated. As such they implicitly, and in some cases explicitly, offer a wider historical framework for various facets of pre-Czechoslovak history, but with more on the Czechs than the Slovaks.

157   **The Young Czech Party 1874-1901 and the emergence of a multi-party system.**
Bruce M. Garver.   New Haven, Connecticut; London: Yale University Press, 1978. 568p. bibliog.

A complete history, not just of one of the most important parties at the end of the 19th century, but of the entire political climate out of which it sprang and through which it evolved until its effective demise after the birth of Czechoslovakia, when it largely lost its relevance. This had been preceded by twenty years of steady decline which saw it replaced by a full range of modern right- and left-wing parties serving the interests of classes, or social groups, more than some general national idea. It had been 'the dominant Czech political party during one decade and . . . a leading force in three others, with achievements for the most part constructive' and enjoys a deservedly important place in Czech and Austrian political history.

158   **The making of a new Europe: R. W. Seton-Watson and the last years of Austria-Hungary.**
Hugh Seton-Watson, Christopher Seton-Watson.   London: Methuen, 1981. 458p. bibliog.

In essence this is a biography of Scotus Viator, as Seton-Watson was known, who was well remembered as a friend of the Slovaks in particular. The volume contains a great deal of valuable material concerning the history of the Slovak national movement before the First World War and the birth of Czechoslovakia, including Seton-Watson's contribution to Tomáš Masaryk's thinking and his influence on the British government and its policies towards Central Europe generally. The book contains generous quotations from Seton-Watson himself.

Modern history (pre-independence to Second World War)

159 **Czechoslovakia.**
William V. Wallace.   Boulder, Colorado: Westview Press; London; Tonbridge, England: Benn, 1976. 374p. maps. bibliog.

This is one of the major modern histories of Czechoslovakia, which reaches back to the middle of the 19th century and ends with the reform movement of the 1960's. It is a highly readable account of demographic, economic and social change, and of the international dimension behind all the country's major turning-points, especially in 1938, 1948 and 1968 (which provides me with the excuse to mention the popular Czech assertion that if there is to be a major event in a given decade, it will happen in the eighth year). The book contains an extensive periodized bibliography, an index of names, and an interesting selection of thirty two photographs depicting people, places and events.

160 **Twentieth century Czechoslovakia: the meaning of its history.**
Joseph Korbel.   New York: Columbia University Press, 1977. 346p. bibliog.

A fairly recent history by an émigré of the 1948 generation. It contains a wealth of detailed historical information, the full import of which may not always be readily appreciated. On these grounds the reader is advised to read one of the other works in this section first. The author is solidly pro-Masaryk, whom he sees as the country's ideal statesman and proponent of his nation's freedom and social justice.

161 **Independent Bohemia: an account of the Czecho-Slovak struggle for liberty.**
Vladimir Nosek.   London, Toronto: Dent; New York: Dutton, 1918. 190p. map. bibliog.

This work is included here as a period document, expressing the Czecho-Slovak case in English from a Czech hand, the author being secretary to the Czecho-Slovak legation in London. In the framework of its account of the pre-war history of the Czechs and their political and military virtues and claims, it also contains the texts of a number of important documents of the period. Very little is said of the Slovaks. An interesting detail is the map of the 'Czecho-Slovak Republic in future Europe' which differs somewhat from that which did materialise.

162 **The Czechoslovak Declaration of Independence: a history of the document.**
George J. Kovtun. Washington, DC: Library of Congress, 1985. 59p. bibliog.

The Declaration was published in Washington in 1918, where a certain amount of archival material has also survived which enabled this history to be written. Although there were Czech drafts, it is interesting that the final official version first appeared in English, and was then translated into Czech and Slovak, for ultimate formal issuance in Paris, the seat of the government. The work is essentially that of the first president, Tomáš Masaryk, but it also bears the names of the foreign minister Edvard Beneš and the defence minister, the Slovak Milan Štefánik. The book is supported by photographic illustrations (various facsimiles) and by the relevant Czech and English texts of the Declaration.

163 **Revolutionary war for independence and the Russian question: Czechoslovak army in Russia 1914-18.**
Victor M. Fic. New Delhi: Abhinav Publications, 1977. 270p. bibliog.

Fic takes the period of the Great War as that in which the Russian Question arose seriously for the Czechs and Slovaks for the first time. During a period of growing national aspirations for independence, or at least an improvement of their constitutional position within Austria-Hungary, the war provided an opportunity for the Czechs and Slovaks in Russia, either old settlers or, later, deserters from the Austrian armies, to take up arms against Austria. This led to the formation of the Czechoslovak Legion in Russia, the country's first army, the story of whose birth, migration across Siberia and return to the home country is a main topic of modern national history, myth and legend. This volume is a detailed history of the origins of the Legion, with all the problems of a difficult birth, disunity and conflicting interests, through the Russian Revolutions of 1917, to a discussion of its actual and possible roles up to the evacuation of the Ukraine in 1918.

164 **The march of the seventy thousand.**
Henry Baerlein. London: Leonard Parsons, 1926. 287p. maps.

This is an early, slightly idiosyncratic, very chatty account of the progress of the Czech Legions across Russia and Siberia during and after the First World War. It is told in the heroic manner common to a lot of writing of the First Republic, and is preceded by an account in like vein of Czech intelligence activities in the United States, where, in this account, they had the better of Germans, Russians and practically everyone else. The link to the main Siberian saga is one Voska, a leading American Czech, active in the Czech secret service, who was sent to Russian in 1917 as President Wilson's liaison officer with the Czechoslovaks. The book is well-illustrated and the appended maps show the positions of Czechoslovaks, Bolsheviks, non-Bolshevik Russians, Japanese, Americans and others at different junctures between 1914 and 1920.

History. Modern history (pre-independence to Second World War)

165   **The Bolsheviks and the Czechoslovak Legion: the origin of their armed conflict March-May 1918.**
Victor M. Fic.   New Delhi: Abhinav Publications, 1978. 495p. map. bibliog.

This essentially continues the history of the Legion, begun in entry no. 163. It deals with the Soviet agreement to let the Czechoslovaks leave Russia, the reversal of the agreement and the fighting which ensued. It also provides an account of the Bolshevik Czechoslovaks who preferred to join the Red Guards. One of the most hailed achievements of the campaign was the capture and temporary control of the Trans-Siberian Railway by the Czechoslovak Legion. The history is set against contemporary Allied policies, the internal politics of the Czechoslovaks and developments within the immature Soviet state. It ends with Soviet interpretations of the events. The appendix contains English texts of a number of contemporary British, Russian and Czech documents and a broadly classified bibliography, including many early English-language publications.

166   **Essays on World War I: origins and prisoners of war.**
Edited by Samuel R. Williamson, Jr., Peter Pastor.   New York: Social Science Monographs, Brooklyn College Press. Distributed by Columbia University Press, New York, 1983. 264p. (Brooklyn College Studies on Society in Change, no. 14); (War and Society in East Central Europe, vol. 5); (East European Monographs, no. 126).

Two contributions in this collection are directly relevant to this bibliography. Rowan A. Williams's 'The Czech legion in Italy during World War I' (p. 199-214), describes the internment in Italy, of Czechs and Slovaks, who were at the time treated simply as Austro-Hungarians, and their subsequent involvement in the war on the Allied side. This very readable account provides the fairly detailed scenario going beyond the handful of actions that have won a place in the national military folklore. Josef Kalvoda's 'Czech and Slovak prisoners of war in Russia during the war and revolution' (p. 215-38), deals with another area which has become part of the national folklore, but one where interpretations of the chain of events are often diametrically opposed. Kalvoda seeks to portray all the various motives and groupings of the Czechs and Slovaks who reached Russia in the course of the war, whether as captives or fugitives, describing the birth of the Legion proper, the non-belligerent elements, the conflict between the pro-Bolshevik and pro-Western sections and the way each was manipulated for and against the Bolshevik régime. The one single element of the story which is the backbone of later folklore is of course the 'anabasis' across Siberia to Vladivostok, whence they returned to Europe, and this is duly described. The legions and their history are still treated with great reverence by the man in the street, but their real significance now is as a token of pre-independence nationalism and a peg for post-independence patriotism.

167 **Siberia.**

Otto Hornung. *Stamp News*, vol. 5, no. 9 (6-19 June 1985), p. 21-25.

This is in the main a piece of philatelic historical detective work, but at the same time it offers some insight into the life and postal service of the Czech Legion in Russia during and after the Great War. It is supported by reproductions of photographs dating from 1919 showing legionaries in Siberia and a portrait of General Janin, the French commander of all Allied Forces in Russia. The same issue of the periodical also carries an article on Czech postal reflections of more recent history: the annexation of Sudetenland in 1938 and the Košice Government Plan of 1945 (ie, Peter Ibbotson's 'Forty years after liberation', p. 45-46). Ibbotson also refers to the role of the artist Alfons Mucha as a major Czech stamp designer.

168 **Essays on World War I: total war and peacemaking; a case study on Trianon.**

Edited by Béla K. Király, Peter Pastor, Ivan Sanders. New York: Social Science Monographs, Brooklyn College Press. Distributed by Columbia University Press, New York, 1982. 678p. (War and Society in East Central Europe, vol. 6).

The Treaty of Trianon was a major event in the shaping of Central Europe in the aftermath of the First World War, since it formulated the redistribution of erstwhile Hungarian territories to the 'successor states'. Czechoslovakia was among the beneficiaries. Three contributions in this collection of papers have a direct bearing on Czechoslovakia. Jozef Kalvoda's 'The Czechoslovak-Hungarian dispute' (p. 275-95), describes the events of the brief war between the two countries, including the Hungarian occupation of Slovakia and the short-lived Slovak Soviet Republic, an event of some significance to the present régime in the search for its roots. Yeshayahu Jelinek's 'The Treaty of Trianon and Czechoslovakia' (p. 439-55), explains the view that Czechoslovakia acquired more of Hungary than was really warranted, describes how Sub-Carpathian Ruthenia came to change hands, and outlines the background to the spate of vicious anti-Jewish rioting which broke out in this troubled period. Finally, Edward Chaszar's 'Trianon and the problem of national minorities' (p. 479-89), includes a list of all the international treaties and special clauses aimed at safeguarding the rights of racial, religious and linguistic minorities in Central Europe, and notes that many of the problems intended to be resolved still exist.

169 **Eastern Europe between the wars, 1918-1941.**

Hugh Seton-Watson. Cambridge, England: Cambridge University Press, 1945. 3rd ed. Hamden, Connecticut: Shoe String Press, 1963. 442p.

This is one of the best surveys of inter-war Eastern Europe, including Czechoslovakia, and is still recommended as a basic textbook.

History. Modern history (pre-independence to Second World War)

170 **Independent Eastern Europe.**
C. A. Macartney, A. W. Palmer. London, Melbourne, Toronto: Macmillan; New York: St. Martin's Press, 1966. Reprint of 1st ed. 1962. 499p. maps. bibliog. (Papermac, no. 181).
Examines the 19th- and early 20th-century background to the post-First World War emergence of the states of Eastern Europe (including Turkey, but excluding the USSR), and then describes their social and economic structure and international relations between the wars. A number of sub-sections deal separately with Czechoslovakia. The valuable bibliography is divided by period and the index is comprehensive.

171 **East Central Europe between the two World Wars.**
Joseph Rothschild, foreword by Peter F. Sugar, Donald W. Treadgold. Seattle, Washington; London: University of Washington Press, 1974. 420p. maps. bibliog.
'The several states of interwar East Central Europe present a good body of historical experience for the comparative study of the political and socioeconomic problems that confront developing multiethnic societies in general' (author). The history of each of the countries involved is described separately, but a particular emphasis is chosen in every case. The social and political history of Czechoslovakia up to the loss of independence in 1939 is chapter 3 of this work (p. 73-135), and it serves as the author's paradigm for an account of political problems arising from multi-ethnicity. It includes tables for population by province and mother tongue, religion and economic sectors, urban-rural residence and illiteracy, as well as election results for 1920, 1925 and 1929.

172 **A history of the Czechoslovak Republic 1918-1948.**
Edited by Victor S. Mamatey, Radomír Luža. Princeton, New Jersey: Princeton University Press, 1973. 534p. maps. bibliog.
Widely regarded as providing the best picture in English of Czechoslovakia's history up to the communist takeover in 1948, this is not a typical linear account, but a collection of essays on separate aspects which are partly parallel chronologically. It admits to being a response to the resurgence of interest in Czechoslovakia in 1968, but its aim is to update Western historiography on the earlier period from a longer perspective and with greater detachment than was possible in its predecessor publications of the 1940s and 1950s. It is organized in three parts: the [first] Czechoslovak Republic, 1918-38; occupation, war and liberation, 1938-45; and Czechoslovakia between East and West, 1945-48. Aspects covered include: the nature and development of democracy in Czechoslovakia; the Germans and other minorities; foreign policy; the Munich crisis; the Slovak State; exile politics; and resistance movements. There are thirteen illustrations, five maps, an impressive 'selected' bibliography, and a comprehensive index. Another item by Mamatey worth noting is his 'The role of President Wilson in the foundation of Czechoslovakia' in *Czechoslovakia past and present*, vol. 1 (q.v.), p. 19-29.

History. Modern history (pre-independence to Second World War)

173   **Czechoslovakia: keystone of peace and democracy.**
      Edgar P. Young.   London: Victor Gollancz, 1938. 394p. maps.
      bibliog.

In its day, this was one of the important surveys covering the full breadth of topics
from history and geography, through population and religion, constitution and
politics, social conditions and services, public organizations (especially the cooperatives), minorities, German grievances, and foreign relations. The last two
chapters deal with recent history and current events, all profoundly relevant to
the war which followed. The work is supported by many statistical tables and a
detailed index, and the bibliography is a useful guide to many early publications
in English, on many of the subject-areas covered in the present volume. It is
perhaps worth mentioning that its period nature extends to acceptance of the
Czechoslovak-sponsored policy myth sustained during the First Republic that
there was a single Czechoslovak nation.

174   **Czechoslovakia: twenty years of independence.**
      Edited by Robert J. Kerner.   Berkeley, California; Los Angeles:
      University of California Press, 1940. 504p. maps. bibliog.

This is one of the earlier collections of scholarly papers of the type quite common
nowadays. It was published to mark the demise of Czechoslovakia on the eve of
the last war. The coverage of topics is quite broad and includes: background
history; politics (including the minorities and the 'problem' of Ruthenia);
economic, social and cultural development (including the land reform programme,
education and religion); foreign relations (including the Little Entente); and the
then most recent events leading to the break-up of the country. The volume closes
with a comprehensive chronology. Contributors to the book represent a fair cross-
section of the time and many are people whose other works will be found in many
later bibliographies.

175   **The doomed democracy: Czechoslovakia in a disrupted Europe,
      1914-38.**
      Věra Olivová, translated by George Theiner, with an introduction
      by Sir Cecil Parrott.   London: Sidgwick & Jackson, 1972. 276p.

An instant success in Czechoslovakia when the original appeared in 1968, this is a
very readable history of the First Republic by a highly regarded Marxist historian.
It traces events from before the country emerged as a successor to Austria after
the First World War up to its demise before the Second World War, brought
about by the disaster that was Munich. Much of its value lies in the native Czech
account which it provides of the Munich Agreement, and in the unusually positive
attitude which it adopts to many aspects of inter-war Czechoslovakia and its
political and social problems. Parrott's introduction contains a flattering (in the
best sense of the word) portrayal of the First Republic and makes some telling
comparisons with Britain during the same period.

176 **Comintern and peasant in East Europe 1919-1930.**
George D. Jackson, Jr. New York, London: Columbia University
Press, 1966. 339p. bibliog.

Presents insights into the rural, social and political history of the First Republic,
set against the background of the Moscow-based Comintern and its peasant
offshoot the Krestintern. The reader interested in Czechoslovakia will need to
read: part 1, *Ideology and reality* (chapters 1-2); part II, *The conflict: international*
(chapters 3-5), and chapter 11 of part III, *The conflict: national*, which deals
specifically with Czechoslovakia. The peculiarly Czechoslovak dimension of the
whole period is the emergence of the so-called Green International, the agrarian
organization based in Prague and opposed to the spread of Bolshevism. The book
also picks out some of the unique features of the Czechoslovak Communist Party
and explains the significance of certain demographic features relevant to the
Communist successes of the 1920s (the backwardness and demographic structure
of Slovakia and, especially, Sub-Carpathian Ruthenia, and the role of nationalism
among minorities). The work contains many valuable references to pre-war
sources and secondary literature and is supported by tables.

177 **The road to World War II: a documentary history.**
Edited by Keith Eubank. New York: Crowell, 1973. 284p.
bibliog.

This book of sources for the study of the Second World War is a sequel to the
author's *The origins of World War II* (New York: Crowell, 1969), and together
they provide a good insight into 'Munich', the agreement between Hitler and the
West which saw the first stage of the break-up of Czechoslovakia.

178 **Britain and the Sudeten issue 1938: evolution of a policy.**
Harindar Aulach. *Journal of Contemporary History*, vol. 18,
no. 2 (Apr. 1983), p. 233-59.

Whatever the public's sympathies, this essay argues that there was at least no love
lost for Czechoslovakia in British official circles. It discerns five stages in British
policy up to Munich, with changes motivated by the various perceptions of, and
prevarications by, France, Czechoslovakia's unsteady ally, whose observance of
her treaty obligations would inevitably have involved Britain.

179 **From Prague after Munich: diplomatic papers 1938-1940.**
George Frost Kennan. Princeton, New Jersey: Princeton
University Press, 1968. 266p.

As a diplomat Kennan regularly reported on events to the American State
Department, and these papers provide a first-hand insight into the climate of the
country immediately before the outbreak of war. They especially reveal the
Czech-Slovak antagonisms which led to Slovakia's declaration of autonomy, and
eventual 'independence'. The work is supported by documentary evidence of
various provenance.

180   **The Second Republic: the disintegration of post-Munich**
       Czechoslovakia October 1938-March 1939.
       Theodore Procházka.   Boulder, Colorado: East European
       Monographs. Distributed by Columbia University Press, New
       York, 1981. 231p. maps. bibliog. (East European Monographs,
       no. 90).

This detailed history of the very shortlived Second Republic, which was even
spelled differently – Czecho-Slovakia, is based both on a variety of primary
diplomatic and other sources, including the memoirs of many of the politicians of
the day, mostly now exiled in the United States, and the author's personal
recollections (he was Berlin correspondent of the Czechoslovak Press Agency). It
begins with the Munich Agreement (text reproduced p. 159-61) and proceeds to
the 'surgery' which followed in the shape of territory lost by that agreement to
Germany and other territories lost to Hungary and Poland. The work ends with
the declaration of independence of the Slovak State and the momentary
independence of Ruthenia, which was swallowed up by Hungary in a matter of
hours. In between there is all the diplomatic bargaining, threatening and
vacillation, which was vain in the face of Germany's determination and her allies'
opportunism.

181   **The Second Czechoslovak Republic, September 1938-March 1939: a**
       study in political change.
       Ivo K. Feierabend.   In: *Czechoslovakia past and present.* Edited
       by Miloslav Rechcígl, Jr. The Hague, Paris: Mouton, 1968. vol. 1,
       p. 65-75.

Czechoslovakia was sorely truncated and many of its economic activities were
seriously impaired after the territorial losses stemming from the Munich
Agreement. Feierabend's description of prevailing attitudes in response to the
change, confined solely to the Czech Lands, shows how there was an abrupt move
towards authoritarianism accompanied by a growth of nationalism and a complete
'repudiation of the symbols of the First Republic'. Party political divisions were
now between the nationalities rather than between ideologies.

Masaryk, Tomáš Garrigue (1850-1937) and the Masaryk family

182   **T. G. Masaryk revisited: a critical assessment.**
       Hanus J. Hajek.   Boulder, Colorado: East European
       Monographs. Distributed by Columbia University Press, New
       York, 1983. 195p. bibliog. (East European Monographs, no. 139).

This is a biographical portrait of Czechoslovakia's first president and an
assessment of his philosophy of humanitarian democratism (humanitism) and his
social and political theories that grew out of it. Hajek also shows how, and when,

Masaryk was out of step with the age and suggests that his popularity was based more on his personality and individual actions, than on any close acquaintanceship with his works.

183 **T. G. Masaryk in perspective: comments and criticism.**
Edited by Milič Čapek, Karel Hrubý. Flushing, New York: SVU Press, 1981. 282p. bibliog.

This collection of papers, mostly by Czechs (two in Prague, the rest in North America), is an important introduction to the thought of the first president of Czechoslovakia; rather less attention is paid to his politics. As 'president-liberator' Masaryk is often elevated by Czechs beyond the range of criticism, but not all the papers here are unreservedly uncritical. One in particular, by a non-Czech, Roman Szporluk, provides a good warts-and-all assessment of the First Republic, 'Masaryk's Czechoslovakia', as it is often called by those harbouring fond memories of those days.

184 **The political thought of Thomas G. Masaryk.**
Roman Szporluk.   Boulder, Colorado: East European Monographs. Distributed by Columbia University Press, New York, 1981. 244p. bibliog. (East European Monographs, no. 85).

Czechoslovak democratic traditions are frequently seen as President Masaryk's own philosophy in action, but as is here pointed out, there was an element of chance in that it was he who, despite his moral and intellectual authority, also gained the political ascendancy. The book deals exclusively, or nearly so, with Masaryk's ideas, and not with his actual political career. However, his political belief that politics should be a domain of experts is indissolubly linked to his general moral philosophy, often, though not here, called 'humanitism', and to his conception of history, religion, education and culture, all coloured by his nationalism. Szporluk's book places Masaryk in the general Czech and European philosophical context and relates his ideas to contemporary conditions and problems, to which they of course sought to provide solutions. Another recent analysis of Masaryk's thought is *Humanity: the political and social philosophy of Thomas G. Masaryk* by Antonie van den Beld (The Hague, Paris: Mouton, 1975. 162p. bibliog.), which specifically relates 'humanity' to such concepts as nationalism, socialism, democracy and revolution and tests Masaryk for consistency.

185 **Suicide and the meaning of civilization.**
Thomas G. Masaryk.   Translated by William B. Weist, Robert G. Batson, with an introduction by Anthony Giddens.   Chicago, London: University of Chicago Press, 1970. 242p. bibliog.

This was Masaryk's first major study (Vienna, 1881) and set the tone for much of his later social and political thought. Masaryk 'diagnosed the increased incidence of suicide as due to the decay of religion' [Wellek]. The introduction to this work, by contrast to some other writings which concentrate on his thought or his political career, includes an account of Masaryk's early academic career.

55

186 **The meaning of Czech history.**
Tomáš G. Masaryk, edited and with an introduction by René Wellek, and translated by Peter Kussi. Chapel Hill, North Carolina: University of North Carolina Press, 1974. 169p.

This is a major publication for an understanding of Masaryk's views on many subjects, though as history it is distinctly idiosyncratic. The volume consists of a set of essays of various lengths and from various sources, placed in the context of Masaryk's political philosophy by Wellek's biobibliographical introduction which both describes Masaryk's attitude to history and explains the dilemmas that helped to shape it.

187 **The lectures of Professor T. G. Masaryk at the University of Chicago, summer 1902.**
Draga B. Shillinglaw. Lewisburg, Pennsylvania: Bucknell University Press; London: Associated University Presses, 1978. 172p. bibliog.

There is a considerable body of literature in English about Masaryk, rather less by him. This is a collection of seventeen lectures, by no means the most scholarly, and some quite short, on a variety of topics of Czech and Slavonic historical interest which were intended to stimulate interest in 'the Czech question' and broader historical issues at a time when the Czechoslovak state was still sixteen years away. The introductory section to the volume sets the lecture series, and Masaryk's own academic reputation, in the context of the host university's programme.

188 **The Masaryks: the making of Czechoslovakia.**
Zbyněk A. B. Zeman. London: Weidenfeld & Nicolson, 1976. 230p.

This combined biography of Tomáš Masaryk, and Jan Masaryk, his son and ultimately his country's foreign minister, covers a century of Czechoslovak history. The background of the break-up of great European empires (Russian and Austrian), great military conflicts (the two world wars) and the birth of Czechoslovakia itself (due in great part to Tomáš Masaryk) makes the book an alternative history of the country as well as a political biography. It includes not only the dominant, positive attitudes to the Masaryks, but also those of their opponents, and in the case of Russia, their enemies (Tomáš was posthumously accused of involvement in the 1918 attempt on Lenin's life). Zeman looks not only at the political background to the period, much of it of President Masaryk's making, but also at the friends and family life of the Masaryks. The absence of a bibliography is compensated for in the footnotes and the references in the introduction.

189 **Jan Masaryk: a personal memoir.**
R. H. Bruce Lockhart. London: Dropmore Press, 1951. 80p.

Jan Masaryk's life and death are mostly covered in political histories of the First Republic and the wartime government. This highly personal biography, by a well-known British diplomat, who came to know Masaryk best as the country's minister in London, traces the greater part of his career up to his death in 1948 and the propaganda haze that immediately grew up around it. The memoir is perhaps strongest on the Anglo-Saxon links in Jan Masaryk's political career; the communist or Soviet connections are too steeped in bitterness.

190   **Alice Garrigue Masaryk, 1879-1966: her life as recorded in her own words and by her friends.**
Compiled by Ruth Crawford Mitchell, special editing by Linda Vlasak, with an introduction by René Wellek.   Pittsburgh, Pennsylvania: University Center for International Studies, 1980. 251p. bibliog.
The biography of Masaryk's daughter, political prisoner in 1915, president of the Czechoslovak Red Cross in the First Republic, teacher and social worker, and émigré during the war and again after 1949. As suggested in the sub-title, the biographical narrative is interlaced with letters and shows her as feminist, patriot and practical adherent of her father's social philosophy.

Second World War: exile and Protectorate

191   **President Edvard Beneš: between East and West 1938-1948.**
Edward Taborsky.   Stanford, California: Hoover Institution Press, 1981. 299p. bibliog.
This is a political biography of the most crucial years in the life of the country's second president by one of his closest advisers. The author is understandably hostile to the present régime and its main ally, the Soviet Union – for the demise of traditional Czechoslovak democracy, the loss of Ruthenia, and the treatment accorded Beneš in the closing years of his life. The account, which is of necessity a history of the wartime government-in-exile and its foreign policy, is unreservedly pro-Beneš, who is portrayed as a tragic figure crushed at the sight of the double destruction of all that he stood for: first by the German occupation; and second by the installation of a régime with which he could not sympathize. The book benefits from its first-hand knowledge of its subject, the man and the politics of the wartime period.

192   **Master of spies: the memoirs of General František Moravec.**
Preface by J. C. Masterman, with a foreword by Hanyi V. Disher.   London, Sydney, Toronto: Bodley Head, 1975. 252p.
The memoirs of General Moravec, chief of Czechoslovak Intelligence before and during the war, are not only a good read for the lover of spy fiction (spy fact being in the event no less, and sometimes more, engrossing), but are an unusual view of the period's history. The Czechoslovaks had to cope with a great deal of German espionage activity in the run-up to the war and had their own notable successes

against the Germans. For the wartime itself, one of the major tasks was the elimination of the *Reichsprotektor* Reinhard Heydrich, which Moravec was instrumental in organizing (though at tremendous cost in German reprisals). His later troubles with the communists are also described, and his account of the Slovak National Uprising and how the Košice Government Programme came into being, place him beyond the pale for the present régime. The memoirs were completed posthumously.

193 **Wings in exile: life and work of the Czechoslovak airmen in France and Great Britain.**
Edited by Bohuš Beneš, translated by Robert Auty and Arthur R. Weir. London: 'The Czechoslovak' Independent Weekly, 1942. 165p.

This volume contains reminiscences, reproduced in a journalistic style, of various Czech and Slovak airmen from their activities with the French air force and the Royal Air Force after Czechoslovakia had been dismembered and the government and armed forces reformed in exile. There is a great deal of enthusiastic eulogizing to it, but this cannot detract from the significant contribution the Czechoslovaks made to the war effort among the Western Allies. Their work has inspired some Czech fictional writing such as Filip Jánský's *Riders in the Sky* (q.v.).

194 **The Czechs under Nazi rule: the failure of national resistance, 1939-1942.**
Vojtech Mastny. New York, London: Columbia University Press, 1971. 274p. maps. bibliog. (East Central European Studies of Columbia University).

Although the war and occupation continued after 1942, the date indicated in the title, Czech resistance was, after that date, extremely limited. That date marked the assassination of Heydrich, which was followed by ruthless repression. In the period up to then, while there were elements of resistance, as carefully defined by Mastny, the general picture is one of a curious mixture of collaboration (also carefully defined to rid it of its polemical nastiness) and resistance, with less of the dramatic extremes oberved in other countries. In addition to describing the administrative and coercive measures taken by the Germans as they absorbed the Protectorate into the Reich, and the underground responses to them, Mastny includes a useful restatement of the prevailing pre-war conditions and the chain of events leading directly to the occupation in March 1939, including the role of the Slovaks.

195 **Growing up in Europe.**
Kay Sun. New York: Vantage Press, 1980. 148p.

Despite its sentimental tone, this is an unusual view of the wartime period, being the memoirs of a woman who grew up during the years of the Protectorate. It is essentially the experiences of one small town, seen through the eyes of a child and reproduced in the same manner. The effects of the occupation on education, religious life and population changes (including the removal of Jews and the arrival of Belgian prisoners of war) as well as the various acts of quiet opposition are related. Sun also considers the split in political allegiances which evolved as the war's end approached and with it liberation, largely by the Red Army.

196   The assassination of Heydrich, 27 May 1942.
Miroslav Ivanov, translated from the French by Patrick O'Brian.   London: Hart-Davis, MacGibbon, 1973. 292p.

Ivanov is something of an eccentric literary and general historian with a nose for the unsolved mysteries of history and the detective-thriller writer's approach to unravelling them. In the case of the Heydrich assassination he has considerably more evidence to work on than in some of his other works (none translated), but something of his approach is present here too. The events are chronicled, using supporting official documents, and the more personal account of pieces of the jigsaw are provided in the form of the recollections of those who participated in any degree and survived to tell the tale. In addition to the Heydrich story, essentially familiar from the film version, this book offers some very personal insights into the resistance movements of the Protectorate and how links with the London government-in-exile were maintained. For a more general work on Heydrich see Günther Deschner's *Heydrich: the pursuit of total power* (London: Orbis, 1981).

197   Lidice.
V. Žižka.   London, New York, Melbourne: Hutchinson, 1943. 84p.

A highly charged, 'hot-from-the-press' account (it uses much fresh press material from various sources) of the Germans' response to the assassination of Reinhard Heydrich, the massacre of the people of Lidice and the destruction of the village. It includes a great deal of background material concerning Heydrich himself and German rule in the Protectorate, records the similar atrocities at Ležáky and Krasňa, and details the responses in the West, including the long poem by Edna St. Vincent Millay.

198   Lidice: sacrificial village.
John F. N. Bradley.   New York: Ballantine Books, 1972. 160p. (Ballantine's History of the Violent Century, no. 2).

Following an account of the break-up of Czechoslovakia at the hands of the Germans, the organization of the government-in-exile and the planning, from London, of the assassination of Heydrich, the book provides a detailed account of the Nazis' revenge, culminating in the total destruction of the village of Lidice.

199   The government of Bohemia and Moravia and its mail.
Otto Hornung.   *Stamp collecting*, vol. 135, no. 11 (Dec. 1979), p. 1,279-85.

This article is intended primarily as a partial postal history of the Protectorate of Bohemia and Moravia, including the use of official postage stamps by units of the 'Government Troops' (Vládní vojsko), the semi-military, semi-gendarmerie corps instituted by the Protectorate Government's decree of 25 July 1939. A large part of the article is taken up by a history of this 'forgotten army', as it is described; the general facts as presented are sound enough, but the division between officers and rank-and-file as subservient and hostile respectively to the Germans suggests a too black-and-white analysis. Many members of the Government Troops were posted to Italy to guard strategic buildings, from where there were mass desertions to the Italian partisans or, further, to the Czechoslovak Brigade in Britain.

Post-war period and developments prior to the 'Prague Spring' (1945-68)

200 **East European revolution.**
Hugh Seton-Watson. New York: Praeger, 1955. 3rd ed. 435p. bibliog. (Praeger Publications in Russian History and World Communism).

This is in essence the direct sequel to Seton-Watson's *Eastern Europe between the wars 1918-1941* (q.v.), and covers the period 1941-49, long enough to take in the communist revolutions of all the states in the area, including Czechoslovakia. Like all of Seton-Watson's works, it is highly readable, with a wealth of factual information.

201 **Communist power in Europe 1944-49.**
Edited by Martin McCauley. London; Basingstoke, England: Macmillan, 1977. Reprinted, 1979. 242p. maps.

'Czechoslovakia', by Vladimir V. Kusin (p. 73-94), deliberately seeks not to be a history, of which there are others, but an investigation of the 'formation, gradual amendment and implementation of the essential features of the strategy of takeover'. Kusin also notes the respects in which the communist rise to power differed from that in neighbouring countries. Of some significance to the topic is E. A. Radice's opening paper in this volume entitled 'Economic developments in Eastern Europe under German hegemony' (p. 3-21).

202 **Czechoslovakia since World War Two.**
Tad Szulc. New York: Viking Press, 1971. 504p. bibliog.

A political history of the country between the first and second arrivals of the Red Army, in 1945 and 1968. Much of the material is repeated in many of the other publications cited in this bibliography, but there is perhaps more here on the broader, international scale, with continuous reference to events in the other socialist states. Such references increase as the advent and course of the 'Prague Spring' are described since it was perceived as a threat to security by the country's allies. The author spends over half the space available on that period, and includes some of the relevant documents, including the '2,000 words' manifesto. A considerable amount of the writing is from a personal point of view, relating some of the author's first-hand experiences.

203   **The short march: the communist take-over of power in**
       Czechoslovakia 1945-1948.
       Karel Kaplan.   London: C. Hurst, 1985. 240p.
Kaplan was previously a firmly establishment historian of the régime, but has
since been purged and is now in exile. In the interim he was able to consult
otherwise secret documents about the post-war pre-coup period with a view to
publishing an honest history of that difficult period. In the event he was prevented
from publishing the results of his research until he emigrated. This then is the
work of a disillusioned communist with no grounds for gilding the pill; it lays bare
much of the sordid detail of the take-over and is based on notes made from (now
unverifiable) contemporary documents.

204   **Passive revolution: politics and the Czechoslovak working class,**
       1945-48.
       Jan Bloomfield.   London: Allison & Busby, 1979. 290p. bibliog.
       (Motive Series).
The crucial, immediate post-war period in Czechoslovak history ended in
February 1948 with the communist take-over, which is variously seen as a
common-or-garden election victory, a putsch or the natural and inevitable
consequence of previous events, elections or no. Bloomfield considers international relations and internal change, the Marshall Plan, relations between the
Czechoslovak Communist Party and the Soviet government, the standing of the
party in Czechoslovak society and its relations to the trade unions. Against this
background he concludes that the events of 1948 were neither the 'culmination of
a masterful Communist Party strategy clearly worked out . . . and backed by the
mass of the people' nor a coup launched against the wishes of the people. Instead
it is described as 'passive revolution', or perhaps passive acquiescence. The
bibliography quotes exact archival sources, and a glossary of names identifies the
dates of offices held by various politicians and party functionaries. Some
information is carried in tables.

205   **Schicksalsjahre der Tschechoslowakei 1945-1948.** (Czechoslovakia's
       years of destiny 1945-1948.)
       Edited by Nikolaus Lobkowicz, Friedrich Prinz.   Munich, Vienna:
       Oldenbourg Verlag, 1981. 181p.
The first paper in this collection is Harry Hanak's 'The attitude of the Western
Powers towards Czechoslovakia 1945-1948' (p. 9-19), which reveals, from a close
study of Foreign Office documents, the indecisive responses of the British
government to the post-war developments in Czechoslovakia and the conflicting
information on which the responses were based. To a lesser degree United States
and French attitudes are also described. Britain's main hope seems to have been
that affairs might be influenced via the Czechoslovak Air Force through its wartime integration with the Royal Air Force. The role of the Soviet Union in
determining the future course of Czechoslovakia is present throughout the
account. The second paper in the volume, Walter Ullmann's 'The United States
and Czechoslovakia 1945-1948' (p. 21-31), picks up the theme of Geir
Lundestad's *The American non-policy towards Eastern Europe 1943-1947* (q.v.)
using the evidence of State Department documents to show just how inadequate
United States policy was. Other papers in the collection are also of relevance but
are in German.

206 **The anatomy of communist takeovers.**
Edited by Thomas T. Hammond, with a foreword by Cyril E.
Black. New Haven, Connecticut; London: Yale University Press,
1975. 664p. bibliog.

The underlying theme of the work, which looks at all communist takeovers, anywhere in the world, the successful and the unsuccessful, is that few are the product of spontaneous domestic revolutionary forces. Czechoslovakia is mentioned in a number of the general, comparative essays, but specifically in: Pavel Tigrid's 'The Prague coup: the elegant takeover' (p. 398-432), which is a critique of earlier accounts of 'February 1948', from a variety of sources but chiefly the Czech writings of the 1968 period; and William E. Griffith's 'The Prague Spring and the Soviet intervention in Czechoslovakia' (p. 606-19), which discusses Soviet perceptions of what was happening in 1968, and sees the intervention as inevitable, with Dubček not really in control of events, and any alternatives as unthinkable. His appraisal of Husák leads to restrained optimism for the future.

207 **A history of the people's democracies: Eastern Europe since Stalin.**
François Fejtö, translated from the French by Daniel
Weissbort. Harmondsworth, England: Penguin, 1974. 565p.
Reprinted, 1977. Originally published by Pall Mall Press, 1971.

A good popular history which relates all the twists and turns of domestic and foreign, diplomatic and economic relations of, and among, the countries of Eastern Europe to developments within the Soviet Union. The work opens with the 1952 Slánský trial (the most notorious of the Stalinist judicial distortions, leading to the execution of Rudolf Slánský and many other highly placed Party members, many of them Jews) and ends with the then most recent spate of troubles in Poland (1st Epilogue) and a comprehensive continuation of the area history for 1971-72 (2nd Epilogue).

208 **Stalinism in Prague: the Loebel story.**
Eugen Loebl, translated by Maurice Michael, edited and with an
introduction by Herman Starobin. New York: Grove Press, 1969.
330p.

This edition of the author's account of the Slánský trial and his own part in it as co-accused and witness for the prosecution was preceded by another under the title *Sentenced and tried: the Stalinist purges in Czechoslovakia* with a postscript by Dušan Pokorný (London: Elek, 1969). Both are translated from the German, rather than directly from the Slovak edition published in Bratislava. The book is divided into two main sections, on the run-up to the trial (processing of the accused and witnesses) and on the actual proceedings, with a short third section covering the author's rehabilitation in 1963, with the verbatim rendering of the Supreme Court's judgment. A retelling of the author's psychological torment, as he tried to cope with the demands the judicial system placed upon him, is in the more recent work *My mind on trial* (New York, London: Harcourt Brace Jovanovich, 1976. 235p.).

209   **Fools and heroes: the changing role of communist intellectuals in
      Czechoslovakia.**
      Peter Hruby.   Oxford: Pergamon Press, 1980. 265p. bibliog.
      This is one of the more fascinating books to emerge as a result of the events of
      1968. The 'fools' and 'heroes' of the title are the same individuals but observed at
      two periods in their lives: 1948 when they 'foolishly' favoured and supported the
      introduction in Czechoslovakia of the alien Soviet ideology, and 1968, when they
      'heroically' sought to shake off the twenty-year heritage. The work poses a series
      of questions, the answers to which seek to account for the change and are based
      on an analysis of the political, social and economic developments of the period.
      The author's own allegiance is revealed in the very choice of the loaded wording
      of his title, but he does not really explain fully the reasons for the magnitude of
      the initial 'folly', for communism in 1948 was undoubtedly attractive to large
      sectors of the population, intellectuals included. The book throws an interesting
      light on the pre-history of the 1968 reform movement and, despite the distortion
      built into the chosen approach, amounts to an intellectual history of post-war
      Czechoslovakia.

The Soviet intervention of 1968 and subsequent events (1968-.)

210   **Prague Spring: a report on Czechoslovakia 1968.**
      Zbyněk A. B. Zeman.   Harmondsworth, England: Penguin, 1969.
      169p. 2 maps. (Penguin Special, S271).
      A great deal has been written about the 'Prague Spring', especially after the
      Soviet invasion of August 1968. This particular volume differs in that, according
      to its author, it was written between April and July of that year, with only a few
      pages added at the end to take the August events into account. Zeman argues
      that the Czechs and Slovaks were not asserting merely independence from
      Moscow, as had Tito or Mao, but that 'they have put forward incisive views on
      the relationship between tight bureaucratic control and the development of
      material and spiritual values'. The book's date of publication should be borne in
      mind, since not all its prognoses have actually been met, or they have been
      overtaken with the lapse of time in a manner which Zeman does not envisage. A
      useful appendage is the tabular 'Chronology of Czechoslovak events June 1967-
      August 1968' (p. 167-69).

211   **The seventh night.**
      Ladislav Mňačko, translated by Harry Schwartz.   London: Dent,
      1969. 220p.
      The autobiography of a communist who went along with the régime, even in the
      Stalinist purges, but who matured and lost his naïvety and became a leading
      Slovak journalist during the late 1960s, the period of reform. He had been pro-
      Israeli and anti-Arab during the Arab-Israeli conflict, been banned by the Czech

authorities on that account, called back again, and finally went into exile in 1968. Events and the author's reminiscences are related to the country's past and are told in a manner befitting a journalist. Mňačko now lives in Israel.

212   **Free communism: a Czech experiment.**
      Anthony Osley.   London: Fabian Society, 1969. 38p. (Young
      Fabian pamphlet, no. 19).
Although centring on the background to, and the course and aftermath of, the 'Prague Spring', this British Labour Party booklet also provides a concise and sober history of the Czechoslovak Communist Party from its inception up to the time of publication. On the way it highlights the various factors which, almost inevitably, led to the Communist coup in 1948, the emergence of Czechoslovak Stalinism and the turn against it which culminated in the Dubček experiment. All the relevant aspects of economic difficulties, intellectual unrest and the Slovak dimension are duly brought in, as is the Soviet case for the 1968 invasion as presented in *Pravda* and elsewhere.

213   **Dubček.**
      William Shawcross.   London: Weidenfeld & Nicolson, 1970. 317p.
      map. bibliog.
This is a detailed personal and political biography of the man who nominally headed the reform movement known as the 'Prague Spring' (after the eponymous Spring music festivals held in the city), the Slovak communist Alexander Dubček. It is by no means the only biography, but it has the merit of not coming from either a direct opponent or supporter of the movement. Dubček is shown to have impeccable credentials as the son of a returning migrant who early joined the communist party, a participant in the Slovak National Uprising, and an honest, thinking and studious member of his party and its apparatus. The biography is simultaneously a political history of the country and a history of the whole family of its party's shortest-ruling leader. In addition, it contains useful chronologies of Czechoslovak history 1918-70, thumbnail sketches of numerous actors in the story, diagrams of the country's power structure, translations of two of Dubček's speeches after the Soviet intervention in August 1968 and a selected bibliography of works on communism in Czechoslovakia, including some on the events of 1968. A selection of the major documents associated with the Dubček era are reproduced, with an analysis of their specific relevance, in *Czechoslovakia's blueprint for 'freedom': Dubček's statements – the original and official documents leading to the conflict of August, 1968*, with an introduction and analysis by Paul Ello (Washington, DC: Acropolis Books, 1968. Republished under a slightly different title *Dubček's blueprint for freedom . . .* and with an added profile by Hugh Lunghi, London: William Kimber, 1969).

214   **Czechoslovakia: the plan that failed.**
      Radoslav Selucký, introduction by Kamil Winter.   London:
      Nelson, 1970. 150p.
It is difficult for the non-historian to forage his way through the mass of literature generated by the events of 1967-69, but this volume is one of the early ones which continue to enjoy a reputation and are widely re-quoted. Its primary concern is with the economic reforms which lay behind the 'Prague Spring', and the political

History. The Soviet intervention of 1968 and subsequent events (1968-.)

and economic crises which preceded them in the aftermath of the Stalinist 1950s and de-Stalinization. The author had a first-hand involvement in the reform of economic thinking and is portrayed in the introduction as having made, through his lucid writings, a significant contribution to public understanding of the impending changes.

215 **The human face of socialism: the political economy of change in Czechoslovakia.**
George Shaw Wheeler. New York; Westport, Connecticut: Lawrence Hill, 1973. 174p.

The causes for the events of 1968 have been covered from every conceivable angle and many of the works they spawned have been included in this bibliography. This particular version, almost solely concerned with the economic forces at work, but also with some of the resultant social problems, differs from the others in being written by one who, though an American, had for political reasons chosen to live in Czechoslovakia since 1947. Like many, Czechoslovak or non-Czechoslovak, he had not welcomed the turn of events and returned home.

216 **The Czechoslovak reform movement: proceedings of the seminar held at the University of Reading 12-17 July 1971**
Edited by Vladimir V. Kusin. London?: International Research Documents; Santa Barbara, California: ABC-Clio, 1973. 358p. (Twentieth Century Series, no. 6).

Reproduces the proceedings of a 'Prague Spring' Seminar held at the University of Reading in July 1971 which involved professional observers and political scientists from various countries, as well as émigrés, who recounted their first-hand experiences of the events. The 1968 crisis is presented from various domestic and international points of view.

217 **Reform rule in Czechoslovakia: the Dubček era 1968-1969.**
Galia Golan. Cambridge, England: Cambridge University Press, 1973. 327p. bibliog.

This is yet another history of the 'years of crisis', from the economic and political preamble to the final clampdown in 1969. Its particular contribution is the account of worker opposition to the reforms, and the effect of the reforms on certain religious communities, notably in the short sections on the Uniate Church and the Jewish community. Despite heavy reliance on the press of the day the work provides a good account of the contemporary arguments for particular proposals, and analyses their causes and consequences. Another contribution is the detailed consideration of the rise and demise of the periodical press which typified the era. Golan has also published an account of the period which led up to the Dubček era, i.e., *The Czechoslovak reform movement: communism in crisis 1962-1968* (Cambridge, England: Cambridge University Press, 1971. 349p.).

218 **Czechoslovakia's interrupted revolution.**
H. Gordon Skilling. Princeton, New Jersey: Princeton University Press, 1976. 924p. bibliog.

For sheer bulk this must be one of the most detailed analyses of the 1968 crisis, or 'Prague Spring'. It starts with the historical background, pinpointing all the issues that were to arise when the time came, from party allegiance, nationalities and Stalinism to the role of students, writers and scholars. Then follows an almost blow-by-blow record of events and responses to them by different sectors at home, and by interested parties abroad. The major issues of the rehabilitation of the victims of Stalinism, the new economic proposals, and federalization are each given a reasoned appraisal. After dealing with the Soviet intervention Skilling discusses whether the events that led to it had been reform, revolution or counterrevolution, and explores some of the views expressed then and since.

219 **Soviet intervention in Czechoslovakia, 1968: anatomy of a decision.**
Jiří Valenta. Baltimore, Maryland; London: Johns Hopkins University Press, 1979. 208p. bibliog.

This work is an exercise in intellectual analysis, reconstructing the thought processes behind the final Soviet decision to intervene, and is based in part on documents published at the time and partly on interviews with first-hand participants. The reasoning holds up well in the light of the materials employed, but future releases of more documents may lead to some minor revisions. As one anonymous reviewer pointed out the entire KGB dimension is inaccessible to perusal and so its possible contribution to the decisions taken is here ignored.

220 **The logic of 'normalization': the Soviet intervention in Czechoslovakia of 21 August 1968 and the Czechoslovak response.**
Fred H. Eidlin. Boulder, Colorado: East European Monographs. Distributed by Columbia University Press, New York, 1980. 278p. bibliog. (East European Monographs, no. 74).

This is an American's first-hand account of the events during the month prior to the Soviet intervention and those that took place during the two days after it, followed by his observations and conjectures made from the vantage point of Radio Free Europe in Munich. It gives not only the background to that year's events in Czechoslovakia itself, but seeks to penetrate the Soviet thinking, or lack of it, which led Czechoslovakia's allies to march in. The curious nature of both the 'occupation' and the 'resistance and capitulation' that eventually ensued are major topics for analysis. 'Normalization' as in the title, and as currently understood in Czechoslovakia, did not actually come about within the time-scale of this book, which ends with the end of August 1968 and the Central Committee plenum at which the reformers, still nominally in power, had to walk the tightrope between appeasing the Russians and not disappointing their own people. For a Czech émigré view of 'normalisation' see Otto Ulč's 'The "normalisation" of post-invasion Czechoslovakia', *Survey*, vol 24, no. 3 (summer 1979), p. 201-13.

221 **Night frost in Prague: the end of humane socialism.**
Zdeněk Mlynář, translated by Paul Wilson. London: C. Hurst,
1980. 300p.

Though a one-time Stalinist, Mlynář was one of the active participants in the
'Prague Spring' of 1968. This then is an ex-Stalinist's view of, and apologia for, his
career, and as such it is highly personal in its selection of materials quoted and
even the photographs reproduced. One useful aspect of the book is its glossary of
names with a fairly detailed account of their owners' functions, and another is its
account of the Czechoslovak leadership's perceptions of the Soviet Union.

222 **The Czech black book.**
Prepared by the Institute of History of the Czechoslovak Academy
of Sciences, edited by Robert Littell. London: Pall Mall Press,
1969. 303p.

A documentary account of the events of late August 1968 prepared by
eyewitnesses, reputable historians on the spot. The sources consist of all manner
of official, semi-official and unofficial reports and articles about every major and
minor event in those critical days, when a huge amount of rapidly produced
printed matter was in circulation in addition to the regular press, which continued
to appear despite the difficulties of printing and circulation. It deals not only with
the realm of official politics and the international pressures on the Czechoslovak
government and party, but also with the effects of the situation on day-to-day life.

223 **From Dubček to Charter 77: a study of 'normalization' in
Czechoslovakia, 1968-1978.**
Vladimir V. Kusin. Edinburgh: Q Press, 1978. 353p. bibliog.

This is a periodized account of events since the Soviet intervention of 1968, from
its immediate aftermath, through Dubček's 'resignation' and the rise of Gustav
Husák as First Secretary and now president, to the contemporary issues of human
rights, brought to the fore by the emergence of the Charter 77 group as a revived
opposition. Kusin makes use of official party statements, emphasizing some of the
ambiguities they conceal.

Regional history

The Czechs and Bohemia from the National Revival

224 **A history of the Czechs.**
A. H. Hermann. London: Alan Lane, 1975. 324p. 4 maps.

A concise summary of Czech history, explicitly excluding the Slovaks, and giving
most attention to the 20th century. It underlines the Western framework of the
Czechs' cultural and political traditions, and relates the major turning points in

Czech history to international events. The Czechs are seen as a major factor in the history of Austria, and Austria is presented as having been a safe haven for the Czechs between the giants of Russia and Prussia to East and West. Very importantly, attention is drawn to the significance of cultural and literary activity, especially in the 20th century, although art, literature and politics have always been more inseparable among the Czechs than in many other nations.

225 **Social preconditions of national revival in Europe: a comparative analysis of the social composition of patriotic groups among the smaller European nations.**
Miroslav Hroch, translated by Ben Fowkes.   Cambridge, England: Cambridge University Press, 1985. 220p. maps. bibliog.

Two chapters are relevant to the present bibliography: chapter 9 'Integration heightened by revolution: the Czech national movement in Bohemia' (p. 44-61), which underlines the significance of the revolutionary stirrings of 1848; and chapter 13 'Belatedness under the influence of external oppression: the Slovak national movement' (p. 98-106), which concentrates on differences of generation and class and the role of the clergy, in addition to the 'oppression' from Hungary, which went harder with the Slovaks than Austrian attitudes to the Czechs.

226 **Die Anfänge der tschechischen Erneuerung und das deutsche Geistesleben (1740-1800).** (The beginnings of the Czech Revival and German intellectual life, 1740-1800.)
Walter Schamschula.   Munich: Wilhelm Fink Verlag, 1973. 338p. bibliog.

This is an invaluable complement to more general works on the National Revival. Written in the belief that most of the old Czech-German prejudices and animosities are dead, the work shows how far German contacts and the existence of German models was influential in shaping Czech historiography, care for the Czech language, and the renascent Czech literature in the period immediately preceding the Revival proper. Where appropriate the mediating role of learned Slovaks, who, at the time, shared with the Germans their Protestantism, is given a sober reappraisal. The German intellectual life of the title refers, of course, to both Germany and Austria.

227 **The Czech renascence of the nineteenth century: essays in honour of Otakar Odložilík.**
Peter Brock, H. Gordon Skilling.   Toronto: University of Toronto Press, 1970. 345p. bibliog.

The Czech renascence or National Revival marks the beginning of modern Czech history and its importance to the state of the modern language, the shaping of the modern literary classics, and the nation's political identity, culminating in the birth a century later of the Czechoslovak Republic, is only one aspect of a rich and varied set of processes. Brock and Skilling's book is well established as *the* authority in English on this period of Czech, as opposed to Czechoslovak or Austrian history.

228 **Czech nationalism in the nineteenth century.**
John F. N. Bradley. Boulder, Colorado: East European
Monographs. Distributed by Columbia University Press, New
York, 1984. 153p. bibliog. (East European Monographs, no. 157).
Bradley's main concern is with the evolution, as he sees it, of Czech political
nationalism out of cultural nationalism and its manifestations, negative and
positive, in social and religious life, including responses to pan-German trends
and attitudes to the Catholic Church. Unlike much of the earlier work on the
subject, this book relies heavily on archival material from Vienna, the details of
which are incorporated as a set of appendixes.

229 **The Prague Slav Congress of 1848.**
Lawrence D. Orton. Boulder, Colorado: East European
Quarterly. Distributed by Columbia University Press, New York,
1978. 187p. bibliog. (East European Monographs, no. 46).
The year 1848 is one of considerable importance in Czech history, both for the
Czechs as Slavs and for the Czechs and others as major constituents of the
Habsburg Empire. The Slav Congress, almost equally glorified and reviled as
'pan-Slavist', sought to resolve many of the issues which united and divided the
many disparate nations. This study 'traces the genesis, organization, deliberations
and results of the congress' and 'focuses attention especially on those issues which
. . . dominated contemporary evaluations and which have influenced subsequent
historical judgments of the congress'.

230 **The Czech revolution of 1848.**
Stanley Z. Pech. Chapel Hill, North Carolina: University of
North Carolina Press, 1969. 386p. bibliog.
The author uses an impressive range of archival sources including the press of the
day and other contemporary publications to illustrate the thesis that from almost
any point of view the 'revolution' in Bohemia cannot be compared with the
simultaneous stirrings in Moravia, Silesia or Slovakia.

231 **Czech nationalism: a study of the national theatre movement 1845-
1883**
Stanley Buchholz Kimball. Urbana, Illinois: Illinois University
Press, 1964. 186p. bibliog. (Illinois Studies in the Social Sciences,
no. 54).
In a period of national revival, the language and its propagation plays one of the
most vital roles, and the theatre is a major vehicle for this purpose. Equally, it
can transcend reality and recreate persons and events from the nation's past
history at a time when that history is being rediscovered. The thesis of this book is
that the movement which set out to build the Czech National Theatre is one of
the best examples of the origin, growth and development of the national
awakening. Tables record the important people involved, Czech and foreign, the
collections made and the sums realised. Due prominence is given to the 1881
tragedy when the new theatre was burnt down, to be rebuilt and finally opened to
huge and lasting acclaim in 1883. The volume is based on extensive archival
sources.

232 **Neo-Slavism and the Czechs 1898-1914.**
Paul Vyšný. Cambridge, England; London, New York,
Melbourne: Cambridge University Press, 1977. 287p. map. bibliog.
(Soviet and East European Studies).

Describes, using a wealth of primary sources, a major period in Czech politics and
brings in all relevant social, cultural and economic considerations. It is a study in
Czech intellectual history and a history of Czech-Russian relations which also
makes a significant contribution to the study of international relations before the
First World War. The bibliography is a valuable source-work in its own right.

233 **Nation and ideology: essays in honor of Wayne S. Vucinich.**
Edited by Ivo Banac, John G. Ackerman, Roman
Szporluk. Boulder, Colorado: East European Quarterly.
Distributed by Columbia University Press, New York, 1981. 479p.
(East European Monographs, no. 95).

Within this collection is one essay by Hugh LeCaine Agnew, 'Enlightenment and
national consciousness: three Czech "popular awakeners"' (p. 201-26), which,
within the context of the Josephine reforms, looks at the development, through
publishing activities, of Czech patriotism, national consciousness and learning.
The three Revivalists concerned are V. M. Kramerius (1753-1808), F. J. Tomsa
(1751-1814), and J. Rulík (1744-1812), important figures in the history of Czech
journalism, philology and literature, who are little written about in English.

234 **The development of Czech historical writing.**
Joseph S. Rouček, George Waskowich. In: *The Czechoslovak
contribution to world culture.* Edited by Miloslav Rechcígl, Jr. The
Hague, London, Paris: Mouton, 1964, p. 245-57.

Potted biographies of a number of Czech historians from the past: František
Palacký (1798-1876), the author of *the* history of the Czechs; Václav Vladivoj
Tomek (1818-1905), author of, *inter alia*, a history of Prague and of the University
of Prague; Antonín Gindely (1829-92), whose main interests were the Reformation
and Counter-Reformation and who wrote mostly in German; Josef Kalousek
(1838-1916), chiefly interested in the legal aspects of Czech history; Antonín
Rezek (1853-1909), a historian of religion and culture and founder of the first
Czech historical review; and Tomáš Garrigue Masaryk (1850-1937), moralist and
'critical realist', professor and first president of Czechoslovakia. Elements of
continuity in Czech historiography are pointed out, as are the conflicting views of
some of these men on certain key issues.

235 **Palacký: the historian as scholar and nationalist.**
Joseph Frederick Zacek. The Hague: Mouton, 1970. 137p.
bibliog. (Studies in European History, no. 5).

František Palacký is to many the uncontested leader of the Czech 19th-century
national movement and the father of modern Czech historiography. This
biography brings together both these threads in his work and draws on the
existing literature and his own analyses of primary sources.

236 **Karel Havlíček (1821-1856): a national liberation leader of the Czech renascence.**
Barbara K. Reinfeld. Boulder, Colorado: East European Quarterly. Distributed by Columbia University Press, New York, 1982. 135p. bibliog. (East European Monographs, no. 98).

Karel Havlíček, usually known with the agname Borovský, was a major almost purely political writer of the National Revival, a satirist, independent journalist and editor of his own newspapers who eventually was sent to trial over the contents of one of them before being despatched to internal exile at Brixen. This, only the second major study on Havlíček-Borovský (the first was Michael Heim's *The Russian journey of Karel Havlíček Brovoský*. Munich: O. Sagner, 1979. 194p.), includes a history of Revival politics and publications, books and serials, as the background to Havlíček's life and work. There is more on his journalistic work than his later satirical literature.

The Slovaks and Slovakia

237 **Slovakia then and now: a political survey.**
By many Slovak authors, arranged by R. W. Seton-Watson. London: George Allen & Unwin; Prague: Orbis, 1931. 356p.

This volume consists of twenty-five chapters by an assortment of leading Slovak scholars and politicians of the day and provides an excellent introduction to inter-war Slovakia, with relevant contrasts to conditions under Hungary before the First World War. The topics covered include politics, education, literature, art, music, religion, administration, justice, the economy, public works, banking and finance, the working class and social legislation, land, towns, minorities, relations with the Czechs, and Slovakia in Europe. The long introduction by Seton-Watson provides an outline history of Czechoslovakia with special reference to the Slovak 'problem' from one who is deeply sympathetic to the Slovak cause, but by no means blind to its shortcomings. In the course of the essay Seton-Watson touches on most of the topics mentioned. The volume, though old, is a valuable classic.

238 **The Slovaks, their history and traditions.**
Peter P. Yurchak. Whiting, Indiana: Rev. John J. Lach, 1947. 2nd rev. ed. 298p. bibliog.

While very patriotic in tone, this history of the Slovaks is rather less belligerently anti-Czech than many, although it does point out the shortcomings of the Czechoslovak government's policy which contributed to Slovak separatism and the destruction of the state during the last war. The place of many Slovak politicians, writers and historical figures in other areas, including Jánošík, are discussed in some detail, but a particular strength of the book is the American dimension, for at the time of writing, there were in North America about one third of all the Slovaks in the world. The final chapter deals solely with Slovakia and America, and is preceded by one on the Slovaks and Russia, which itself picks up the thread from the liberation of Slovakia by the Red Army. The author has no doubts as to the merits of the Catholic priest Andrej Hlinka, who headed the autonomy movement in the First Republic, but he does not even mention Josef Tiso (1887-1947), who was made head of the puppet Slovak State by Hitler in October 1939.

239 **The fathers of the Slovak nation: from Juraj Tranovský to Karol Salva or from the Reformation to the rise of the Populists (1500s to 1890s).**
Anthony X. Sutherland. *Slovak Studies*, vol. 21 (1981), p. 5-187. bibliog.
Essentially an outline intellectual history of the Slovaks, consisting of brief introductions to the several chapters followed by a set of bio-bibliographies of an impressive number of individual writers, teachers and preachers. The substance is mostly second-hand, but it at least makes available in English what is otherwise often only to be found in Slovak sources. The work's mission is to supply the gap left by the majority of works in English which concentrate on a very small number of leading lights.

240 **The Slovak national awakening: an essay in the intellectual history of East Central Europe.**
Peter Brock. Toronto; Buffalo, New York: University of Toronto Press, 1976. 104p. bibliog.
The best and most straightforward account in English of the evolution of Slovak linguistic and political consciousness, unhampered by any nationalist fervour or anti-Czech chauvinism. It begins with Anton Bernolák, who first set out to standardize the language in the late 18th century and takes the story through the different groupings which followed until the present standard language was given its shape by Ľudovít Štúr and his followers in the 1840s (there have been changes since, but it is to Štúr that the Slovaks look back in this context).

241 **Jean Palárik: Son œcuménisme et son panslavisme.** (Ján Palárik: his ecumenism and pan-Slavism.)
Joseph Vavrovič. *Slovak Studies*, vol. 14 (1974). 279p. bibliog.
Ján Palárik (1822-70) was a major figure in the Slovak national awakening. A Catholic priest who fell foul of both the church authorities for his ecclesiastical liberalism, democratism and ecumenism and with the Hungarian authorities who accused him of separatism, he really only aspired to Slovak unity through unity in Christianity as a defence against the threat of Magyarization. In this interpretation, based on Palárik's own writings and on contemporary documentation, he was not anti-Magyar as such, but merely sought national and religious tolerance for the Slovaks. In addition to covering the life, work and thoughts of Palárik, Vavrovič also offers some insight into the religious and political history of Hungary in the middle of the 19th century. Palárik himself was active from about 1850.

242 **Racial problems in Hungary.**
'Scotus Viator' (R. W. Seton-Watson).   London: Constable, 1908.
540p. map. bibliog.

Although the times, and frontiers, have changed, this will remain the classic study of the Slovaks in Hungary, from the period when practically all Slovaks were citizens of that state and before they became joined to the Czechs within Czechoslovakia leaving a much smaller minority behind in more recent Hungarian history. Accordingly, while the volume purports to be on a minority and ought therefore to be in the section on 'extraterritorial populations', it is much more a history of Upper Hungary (more or less Slovakia) and the Slovaks themselves, as a whole nation, not just a fragment across a frontier. In addition to being a full political, social and cultural history of the Slovaks from the Moravian Empire onwards, with special emphasis on Hungarian misdeeds in the 19th century, the volume also includes papers on: Slovak popular art by Dušan Jurkovič, a major Slovak architect some of whose best work is to be found in Bohemia; Slovak folk-poetry by Svetozar Hurban Vajanský, himself an important poet; and Slovak popular music by Milan Richard, a pupil of Dvořák, and Alois Kolísek, a musical historiographer. All three papers, in common with the rest of the book, are suitably illustrated.

243 **The lust for power: nationalism, Slovakia and the communists, 1918-1948.**
Yeshayahu A. Jelinek.   Boulder, Colorado: East European Quarterly. Distributed by Columbia University Press, New York, 1983. 185p. bibliog. (East European Monographs, no. 130).

Slovakia has a Communist Party separate from the Communist Party of Czechoslovakia, and this history of the changing policies of the Slovak communists and the Czechoslovak Communist Party, together with the different history of the two main parts of the country, helps to explain the discrepancy. This volume also represents an important history of the Slovak State, and Slovak communist attitudes to minorities (Ukrainians, Poles and Hungarians), anti-semitism (relatively mild, though no less abhorrent for all that), and, amongst many other factors associated with Slovak nationalism, the recurrent idea of a Soviet Slovakia as an answer to the need for separate national identity. Another work by the same author, but on the wartime ruling Slovak People's Party, should also be noted, ie., *The parish republic: Hlinka's Slovak People's Party 1939-1945* (New York: Columbia University Press, 1976).

244 **Slovakia. A political history: 1918-1950.**
Joseph A. Mikus, forewords by Roman Smal-Stocki, Paul Lesourd, translated from French by Kathryn Day Wyatt, Joseph A. Mikus.   Milwaukee, Wisconsin: Marquette University Press, 1963. 392p. bibliog.

Written by an American Slovak, this history seeks to give the country's history in its own right, without treating it as a part of some other nation's problems. In fact, since the theme is that Slovakia is an underdog oppressed first by Czechs and then by anti-Catholic communists, it cannot dispense with the other dimension. The work is strongly in favour of more visible Slovak nationhood or statehood, underpinned by a strong Catholic church and without the subservience of a nominal coalition with anybody. The appendixes provide the English texts of a chain of Slovak documents dating from 1861 to 1954 underlining Slovak national aspirations or confirming acts of oppression committed against (Catholic) Slovakia.

245 **History of modern Slovakia.**
Josef Lettrich, introduction by Martin Kvetko. Toronto: Slovak Research and Studies Centre, 1985. 329p. map. bibliog. First published New York: Praeger, 1955.

This is the most comprehensive modern history of the Slovaks and it differs from all others by its lack of radical nationalism or chauvinism. Its attitude to the Czechs, and the First Republic in particular, is more sober. Moreover, it does not see the Slovak State as having been an ideal solution to the Slovaks aspirations to control their own affairs, and it quotes and interprets certain sources and facts in a more liberal spirit than many. As regards the most modern period, it is an anti-communist work. The book contains the English texts of many important documents and some photographic material.

246 **Slovakia and the Slovaks.**
Joseph A. Mikus, with a preface by Michael Novak. Washington, DC: Three Continents Press, 1977. 224p. 4 maps. bibliog.

Sponsored by the Slovak World Congress, one of the main Slovak émigré organizations, this book is written in the spirit of an oppressed people who will one day be masters of their own destiny. At home the oppression has come from Hungarians, Czechs or 'communist colonialists', while abroad, in fact in North America, it has come in the form of cultural domination whereby the Slovaks cannot be educated in their own language, but are forced to learn English, or another more recognized foreign language. The volume has been written to fill the gap which is perceived to exist in literature on 'Czecho-Slovakia' (sic!) in English, what there is being heavily biassed towards the Czechs. The basic facts of the political, literary or demographic history are sound enough, but the interpretations are strongly nationalist, as reflected in other respects as well. For example: the spelling Czecho-Slovakia; the explanation of the failure of the Dubček experiment as being due to the Czechs who surrounded him; the consistent translation of *slavicus* or *slavonicus* as Slovak instead of Slav; and the fervent embrace of the idea of the universality of Slovak in that it is (perhaps) best understood by all the other Slav nations. The section on the history of the literature provides a brief introduction to all the major writers and in addition describes some of the émigré literary traditions not often covered, for example, 'Christian universalism'.

247 **The Slovak autonomy movement, 1935-1939: a study in unrelenting nationalism.**
Dorothea H. El Mallakh. Boulder, Colorado: East European Quarterly. Distributed by Columbia University Press, New York, 1979. 260p. bibliog. (East European Monographs, no. 55).

In essence this is an account of the rise to dominance in Slovakia of the Slovak People's Party which eventually took the country to independence, having first declared regional autonomy at a time when the Prague government was vainly trying to hold the country together against growing pressure from Germany. The author makes use of police reports on the party's activities, which helps to support her main contention that the nationalist movement, which the People's Party headed, was both well-defined and influential far beyond its own ranks.

248 **Aufstand in der Tatra: Der Kampf um die Slowakei 1939-44.**
(Uprising in the Tatras: the battle for Slovakia 1939-44.)
Wolfgang Venohr. Königstein i. Taunus, GFR: Verlag Athenäum, 1979. 434p. maps.

After an appraisal of the position of Slovakia in the war years and a critical assessment of the attitudes of the Beneš government in London and of the communist leadership in Slovakia and Moscow, the author, a Hamburg television editor, describes the course of the Slovak National Uprising and what became of the main participants. He makes use of documentary evidence, of which twenty-five items are reproduced in the appendix, and the work is supported by illustrations. The author clearly has considerable sympathy for the country and its people, but not for its wartime government, popular though it may have been initially, as he concedes.

249 **The Slovak dilemma.**
Eugen Steiner. Cambridge, England: Cambridge University Press, 1973. 229p. maps. bibliog. (International Studies).

The author introduces himself as a sorely disillusioned Slovak Jewish communist, in exile for the second time, having almost been reconverted to the Party faith by the events of 1968. His concern is to place a uniquely Slovak perspective on the modern history of Slovakia, with special reference to the events of 1968, about which, the majority of works published in England either centred on the country in general, or were by Czechs or Pragocentric foreigners. The opening sections are more historical, and free of some of the hysteria that besets much other émigré Slovak historiography, and the later sections are more by way of an eyewitness account and personal reminiscences of the people and events that have stood out in post-war Slovak or Czechoslovak history.

Urbanization and the formation of a Slovak intelligentsia.
See item no. 579.

Moravia

250 **Moravia's history reconsidered: a reinterpretation of medieval sources.**
Imre Boba. The Hague: Martinus Nijhoff, 1971. 167p. bibliog.

In this daring reinterpretation of history, Moravia, or 'Great Moravia' as it is traditionally called, is relocated south of the Danube and well away from its normally accepted position in what is now western Slovakia, north of the Danube. Should the theses contained in this work gain currency, and the arguments are not without some force, it will provide some essential background to early Czechoslovak history in its descriptions of what modern Moravia might have been were it not indeed the early Slavonic state hitherto assumed.

251 **The industrialization of a Central European city: Brno and the fine woollen industry in the 18th century.**
Herman Freudenberger. Edlington, Wiltshire, England: Pasold Research Fund, 1977. 220p. maps. bibliog.

A highly detailed study of an extremely specialized subject. It provides an account of the eventual proliferation of the fine woollen industry from the setting up of the first factory in 1764 (including details of the enterpreneurs involved, bank support, many statistics on looms, output and markets), and also cannot avoid including, especially in the early period, a history of the city itself and its place within the Habsburg scheme of things. Due prominence is given to other woollen centres and to the side effects of the industry in the shape of increasing machine manufacture. The whole story gives ample justification to Brno's nickname of the 'Manchester of Austria'.

Ruthenia

252 **The Ruthenian decision to unite with Czechoslovakia.**
Paul R. Magocsi. *Slavic Review*, vol. 34, no. 2 (summer 1975), p. 360-81.

The shaping of Czechoslovakia, when it was being formulated before the country actually came into being, was strongly influenced by populations abroad, in this case the Ruthenians of the United States. The outcome of the Paris Peace Conference, and the ultimate decision of the Ruthenians in Ruthenia itself, was the province's unification with Czechoslovakia in 1919. The article lacks a bibliography but the footnotes represent a useful substitute. The paper was reprinted by the Harvard Ukrainian Research Institute as their Offprint Series, no. 3 (Cambridge, Massachusetts, 1975).

253 **Republic for a day: an eyewitness account of the Carpatho-Ukraine incident.**
Michael Winch.   London: R. Hale, 1939. 286p.

This rare British account, from a correspondent with an observant eye and a lively style, tells the story of the birth and death of Carpatho-Ukraine, which declared its independence from Czechoslovakia only to be occupied almost instaneously by Hungary. The events were quick in succession and the time-span very short. Accordingly, much of this fascinating book is taken up with an external description of the country and its inhabitants—a nice piece of amateur ethnography.

254 **Diplomacy of double morality: Europe's crossroads in Carpatho-Ukraine 1919-1939.**
Peter George Stercho.   New York: Carpathian Research Center, 1971. 495p. maps. bibliog.

Carpatho-Ukraine was the name adopted by Ruthenia when it became briefly independent in 1939, before being occupied and annexed by Hungary. Stercho describes the province's history from the late 19th century, through its unification with Czechoslovakia up to the Second World War. The book is much concerned with what the author perceives as abuses by the predominantly Czechocentric government and the province's aspirations to autonomy. The work is supported by documentary evidence and a chronology of events.

255 **The Soviet seizure of Subcarpathian Ruthenia.**
František Němec, Vladimír Moudrý.   Toronto: Anderson, 1955. 375p.

This is the first full account of the events in 1944 whereby Subcarpathian Ruthenia, pre-war Czechoslovakia's easternmost province, was annexed by the Soviet Union. Němec was a government official of the day and, as the very title implies, does not favour a territorial adjustment that, yet again, like the preamble to the war, reduced the country's area by a considerable margin. Although his opinion is supported by contemporary documents, many of which are reproduced, it is not the only view; in other quarters there is rather less regret at the annexation of the most backward province which was an economic burden, and with it the loss of most of the pre-war state's largest minority, the Rusyns or Ruthenians.

Nationalities and Minorities

256 **The multinational empire: nationalism and national reform in the Habsburg Monarchy 1848-1918.**
Robert A. Kann.   New York: Octagon Books, 1950. Third reprinting 1977. 2 vols. bibliog.
This entire work needs to be known by anyone wishing to consider the early history of the minorities problem of Czechoslovakia, which has its roots in the multinational nature of Austria-Hungary and the quirks of traditional frontiers. Within Volume 1 are separate sections giving the cultural and political history of the Czechs (*inter alia*) as a national group with independent national political history (p. 150-220) and of the Slovaks (*inter alia*) as one without it (p. 271-83). The views of such leading figures as Palacký and Masaryk are outlined at relevant points in both volumes. Of particular value is the wide range of references in both the bibliography and the footnotes to each chapter. Kann has written widely on Habsburg history, cf. in this bibliography item no. 126.

257 **The shaping of the Czechoslovak state: diplomatic history of the boundaries of Czechoslovakia, 1914-1920.**
Dagmar Perman.   Leiden, The Netherlands: E. J. Brill, 1962. 339p. maps. bibliog.
Czechoslovakia's frontiers have from the outset been a bone of contention, since they were largely the product of history and could not always take account of actual boundaries between national groups (where there is inevitably a great deal of overlap or merger). This particular work considers how the national minorities were incorporated into the new republic.

258   **Bevölkerung und Nationalitäten in der Tschechoslowakei.**
(Population and nationalities in Czechoslovakia.)
Alfred Bohmann.   Cologne, GFR: Verlag Wissenschaft und
Politik, 1975. 512p. (Menschen und Grenzen, vol. 4).

The size of the German minority in pre-war Czechoslovakia produced serious
political difficulties at the time, especially after the rise of Nazism in Germany.
The problem was partially 'solved' for Czechoslovakia by the transfer of large
border areas to Germany after the Munich Conference, and by Czechoslovakia,
after the restoration of these areas when the war was over, by the expulsion of
most of the Czechoslovak citizens of German nationality. Similar issues involved
the Hungarians of Slovakia and, to a lesser degree, the Poles of Silesia. This
volume seeks to provide a complete history of demographic evolution and
population distribution up to the Second World War, during the war – the period
of the Protectorate of Bohemia and Moravia and of the puppet Slovak State – and
since 1945. The author also takes into account all the other national minorities of
any size, especially the Ukrainians (Ruthenians), Jews, gypsies, Greeks and
Croats. While seeking to be objective, it nevertheless contains some disturbing
contrasts, such as the uncertainty over the numbers of Jews who fled, or were
killed, during the wartime period as opposed to the pinpoint accuracy in the
numbers of Germans expelled by Czechoslovakia after the war. It is worth noting
at which points Czechoslovak statistics are quoted and where the source is
German.

259   **The ethnographic map of the Czech Lands, 1880-1970.**
Vlastislav Häufler.   Prague: Academia, 1973. 100p. maps. bibliog.
(Rozpravy ČSAV, Řada matematických a přírodních věd,
vol. 83, no. 6).

Statistical data and maps are used here to trace the gradual development of the
pattern of population up to the interwar period, and the huge changes in
population brought about by the war and its aftermath. Demographic changes are
then considered down to 1970, with some indication of likely further
developments. The wartime and immediate post-war changes are very much
associated with solutions to the problem of minorities, especially the Germans.

260   **The politics of ethnicity in Eastern Europe.**
Edited by George Klein, Milan J. Reban.   Boulder, Colorado:
East European Quarterly. Distributed by Columbia University
Press, New York, 1981. 279p. (East European Monographs,
no. 93).

This volume contains Reban's 'Czechoslovakia: the new federation' in which he
sees, justifiably, Czechoslovakia as second only to Yugoslavia in terms of the
mixed ethnicity in Eastern Europe thanks to the existence of the substantial
Slovak nation and some not insignificant minorities, especially Germans, within
its original frontiers. The watershed as regards the Slovaks came in 1968-69 with
the country's federalization, which solved at least partially the Slovaks' aspirations
during the 1960s, when their nationhood was the primary concern, while the
Czechs were looking more for economic reform. The article looks at the history of
official attitudes to the Slovaks and Slovakia and at some of the workings of the

new federal state. An account is also given of the state and standing of the national minorities within the federation, pinpointing the problematic nature of the relevant statistics (including some general discrepancies, no separate figures for Jews, and uncertain evaluation of gypsies). The work carries no formal bibliography, but a mass of useful bibliographical information is contained in the footnotes.

261 **Ethnic National minorities in Eastern Europe 1848-1945.**
Raymond Pearson. London; Basingstoke, England: Macmillan, 1983. 249p. maps. bibliog. (Themes in Comparative History).

Of all the recent literature on minorities this is essential reading. It constitutes an introduction to the demographic background of the whole area, showing where the minorities originated and how they evolved into nations – in the 'luckier' cases. By its general nature, including its history of emergent states and shifting frontiers, the work covers both non-Czech/Slovak minorities within Czechoslovakia and Czech and Slovak minorities outside the country. A subject which the author pays particular attention to is the effect of war on minorities. The thematic section of the bibliography is excellent.

262 **Eastern European national minorities, 1919-1980: a handbook.**
Stephan M. Horak (et al.). Littleton, Colorado: Libraries Unlimited, 1985. 375p. bibliog.

This volume contains Stephan Horak's 'Eastern European national minorities 1919-1980' (p. 1-34) and Josef Kalvoda's (with the assistance of David Crowe) 'National minorities in Czechoslovakia, 1919-1980' (p. 108-59). These are chapters 1 and 3, and further chapters are quoted in the next section of the present bibliography. The format is essentially the same in all chapters, with a historical summary first, supported by statistical tables. The summary traces the main demographic changes, in most cases associated with the approach of war and war itself, and any relevant changes of frontier. This is followed by a sectional annotated bibliography. The two chapters together constitute the most comprehensive account to date of the contemporary and recent state of minorities in Czechoslovakia. Those minorities mainly concerned are the Ukrainians, Russians, Poles, Hungarians, Germans, gypsies and Jews, though the Greeks, who are mentioned in the Polish section, and are in Czechoslovakia from the same time and for the same reasons, are not mentioned.

263 **Slovakia and its minorities 1939-1945: people with and without national protection.**
Yeshayahu A. Jelinek. *Nationalities Papers*, vol. 4, no. 1 (spring 1976), p. 1-15.

Jelinek divides the minorities in the Slovak State of the Second World War into the privileged (Germans and Magyars), underprivileged (Ukrainians, Poles and Czechs), and oppressed (Jews and gypsies). He then goes on to compare their nominal constitutional status with the reality as well as describing the tensions that existed between some of the groups. The paper is a study in nationalism, and not just of the Slovaks, and it also describes the role of external forces (including Germany, Hungary, the Vatican, international Jewry) in shaping, inhibiting or alleviating the plight of the minorities, especially the Jews.

264 **Nationalism in Eastern Europe.**
Edited by Peter F. Sugar, Ivo J. Lederer. Seattle, Washington;
London: University of Washington Press, 1969. 467p. (Far Eastern
and Russian Institute Publications on Russia and Eastern Europe,
no. 1).

The editors feel that nationalism in Eastern Europe has hitherto not been given
adequate treatment and understanding, having been too often interpreted in
terms of West European symptoms of a similar kind. This volume seeks to
remedy the shortcoming and provides background information concerning
impulses behind East European nationalism and short monographs on each
country. In 'Nationalism in Czechoslovakia' (p. 166-206) Joseph F. Zacek rapidly
dispenses with the pre-war notion of 'Czechoslovak nationalism' before dealing,
separately, with the two nations, each quite distinct in their nationalist
aspirations, which are also of quite different longevity. For the most recent period
he notes the continuing nationalist debate among the Czech and Slovak exile
communities, and believes that it is not dead in Czechoslovakia itself.

265 **The Sudeten question: brief exposition and documentation.**
Fritz Peter Habel, translated by Harry Hochfelder. Munich:
Sudeten German Council, 1984. 35p. maps. bibliog.

This new statement of the Sudeten German case, with the history of the reasons
for the anti-Czech feeling which still runs high, lays the emphasis on: the
measures perceived as 'Czechization' during the First Republic; the Allied
connivance with the Czechoslovak government-in-exile over the future expulsion
of all Germans from restored Czechoslovakia; and on the communists' seizure
and distribution to Czechs of all previously German-owned property. Separate
sections indicate the current location (and whatever staging posts there were
in between) of most of the Sudeten Germans, and describes the lot of those few
Germans who were not expelled. The Prague Treaty of 1973 and the present
attitudes of the exiled Germans and their Bavarian sponsors are described at the
end of the volume. The documents referred to in the title are texts in English of
various manifestos dating from 1950-79, all in defense of the Sudeten German
case. The bibliography contains a number of reference works and histories, all in
German.

266 **Czechoslovakia before Munich: the German minority problem and
British appeasement policy.**
Johann Wolfgang Brügel. Cambridge, England: Cambridge
University Press, 1973. 334p. bibliog.

The author concentrates on Czechoslovak domestic and foreign policy and pays
particular attention to the German minority from the birth of the Republic to the
break-up of Czechoslovakia just before the war. Responsibility for the collapse of
Czechoslovakia is laid on the Sudeten Germans and the weakness of British
foreign policy in seeking to appease Hitler at all costs, while errors of judgement
of the Czechoslovak government are also related.

Nationalities and Minorities

267 **German minorities and the Third Reich: ethnic Germans of East Central Europe between the wars.**
Anthony T. Komjathy, Rebecca S. Stockwell. New York, London: Holmes & Meier, 1980. 217p. bibliog.

The role of the many German minorities, including the Sudeten Germans, is discussed here in the light of the common assertion that they were automatically placed to become fifth columns for Germany. The period before 1933 is treated fairly scantly, and little is said of the degree to which some of the minorities were assimilated, which would make them less automatic fifth columns. Nevertheless, the book contains much background information on the many personalities and political groupings involved. Particularly relevant are 'The Sudeten German dilemma' (p. 17-41), and the Czechoslovak section in the bibliography (p. 209).

268 **The politics of ethnic survival: the Germans in Prague, 1861-1914.**
Gary B. Cohen. Princeton, New Jersey: Princeton University Press, 1981. 344p. maps. bibliog.

An impressive account of a fascinating period in Czech history, when Prague had ceased to be an almost solidly German city with a Czech lower-class minority and had become a Czech city, with a majority Czech council, Czech finance houses and a dwindling, but by no means insignificant, German minority. It is the period which saw the split of the university into two linguistically separate institutions, and the culmination of the Czech National Revival. The author realises that much has been written about the rise of the Czechs, but little work has emerged about the decline of the Germans, a study of which should contribute to an understanding of the fate of the Austrian monarchy. Involved in the story are the various socio-political manifestations of Czechdom, such as: the rise of the Sokol movement; the status of the Jews; political parties and other groupings; and religious affiliation. The work uses much archival material and statistical analyses. For a related paper see the same author's 'Ethnicity and urban population growth: the decline of the Prague Germans, 1880-1920' in *Studies in East European Social History* (q.v.).

269 **The Rusyn-Ukrainians of Czechoslovakia: an historical survey.**
Paul Robert Magocsi. Vienna: Wilhelm Braumüller–Universitäts-Verlagsbuchhandlung, 1983. 93p. maps. bibliog.

The latest of Magocsi's highly readable works on the Ukrainians of Czechoslovakia, this one concentrates on the residual Ruthenian minority in the country as presently constituted. It provides an introduction to the political, socio-economic and cultural history of the group, neatly periodized and always related to the larger area history of Slovakia, Hungary or Czechoslovakia, according to period. The work ends with a description of recent social changes brought about by the electrification and industrialization of the areas where the Ruthenians live. Magocsi has written widely on the Rusyns, whether in Ruthenia proper, or as immigrants in America. His works include 'An historiographical guide to Subcarpathian Rus', *Austrian History Yearbook*, vols. 9-10, (1973-74), p. 201-65, which was reprinted in the Harvard Ukrainian Research Institute Offprint Series, no. 1 (Cambridge, Massachusetts, 1975), and *Carpatho-Ruthenians in North America: a bibliography* (Philadelphia: Balch Institute Reading Lists, no. 31, 1976).

270 **The shaping of a national identity: Subcarpathian Rus', 1848-1948.**
Paul Robert Magocsi. Cambridge, Massachusetts; London:
Harvard University Press, 1978. 640p. 6 maps. bibliog. (Harvard
Ukrainian Series).

The first in a sequence of Harvard monographs on national movements among
ethnic groups, this volume is primarily a well-researched history of what, between
the wars, was the easternmost province of Czechoslovakia and had previously
been part of Hungary. It is a detailed and highly informative account which covers
social, cultural and ecclesiastical history, as well as political developments. The
text proper covers just under one third of the whole volume. Of the remainder a
large part (p. 359-463) is taken up by footnotes, the space between being taken up
by appendixes (p. 277-358). The latter, together with the 2,279-entry bibliography,
give the book its second function – that of general reference work. The
appendixes cover in encyclopaedic manner: the 'problem of nomenclature' (ie.,
what is Rus'?, who are its people?, what are the names they know themselves by
or are known by?); potted biographies of eighty-one post-1918 leaders; well-
chosen samples of the various versions of a literary language; and statistics for the
population as a whole as well as education and occupations, for example. From
the point of view of post-war Czechoslovakia, to which Subcarpathian
Rus'/Ruthenia no longer belongs of course, the book remains invaluable both as a
source of information about the background to the changed frontiers and for its
handling of the Ruthenian/Ukrainian areas still within Czechoslovakia.

271 **National assimilation: the case of the Rusyn-Ukrainian
Czechoslovaks.**
Pavel Mačů. *East-Central Europe*, vol. 2, no. 2 (1975), p. 101-31.

A detailed study of the different tendencies of the Ruthenians to assimilate with
the Ukrainians, Slovaks and marginally Hungarians from the birth of Czechoslovakia to the present. Involved are the various transformations of their church,
the relation of their folklore to those of their neighbours, the relation of the local
dialect to literary Ukrainian and the use of both in the local press, as well as the
Slovaks' attitudes to the Ruthenians. Treatment of Ruthenia proper and the
Prešov region of East Slovakia is partially separated.

272 **Hungarians in Czechoslovakia.**
New York: Research Institute for Minority Studies on Hungarians
Attached to Czechoslovakia and Carpatho-Ruthenia, 1959. 167p.
maps.

Now largely outdated in terms of the attitudes expressed, which are coloured by
the events of the last war and the frontier-shifting that went on before, during and
after it, this collection of essays (by F. S. Wagner, J. Holota K. (sic.), C. J.
Hokky, S. Révay and C. Brogyányi) nevertheless, despite its often virulent anti-
Czechoslovak, anti-Slovak and anti-Soviet tenor, reveals the sources and size of
the problem faced by Czechoslovakia in having enclosed within its frontiers so
many Hungarians. For its conclusions on Hungarian minority public opinion in
both post-war Czechoslovakia and the Soviet Union (as current holder of
Ruthenia – Carpatho-Ukraine) it relies heavily on the testimony of a small
handful of escapees, and for the exact extent of Hungarian-dominated territory in
South Slovakia it relies on various atlases of linguistic geography.

83

273 **From Trianon to the First Vienna Arbitral Award: the Hungarian minority in the First Czechoslovak Republic 1918-1938.**
Charles Wojatsek.   Montreal: Institute of Comparative Civilisations, 1981. Distributed by M. Kolbe Editions. 231p. 8 maps. bibliog.

The emphasis in this book is on the utter artificiality of Czechoslovakia as a state formation with somewhat arbitrary frontiers which held various minorities trapped. Contrary to the prevailing view of the First Republic as democratic and whatever else positive, Wojatsek sees President Beneš as a single-minded schemer and the Czechs as a whole as imperialists in the worst mould. Despite the unconcealed bitterness over the treatment (mistreatment) of the Hungarians and the other minorities, on which there is also considerable detail, the book manages to illustrate the difficulties faced by the young Republic and the general problem of states with minorities. The exaggerated tone goes so far as to suggest that Beneš received his just deserts by being mercilessly punished and removed by the Russians in 1948 for his misdemeanours. Appendixes provide the texts in English of various relevant documents from the Minorities Treaty of 1919 to the First Vienna Award of 1938. Edward Cháaszár's *Decision in Vienna: the Czechoslovak-Hungarian border dispute of 1938* (Astor, Florida: Danubian Press, 1978. 165p. maps.) is another work on the same vexed topic.

274 **The Hungarian minorities in the succession states.**
Sir Robert Gower.   London: Grant Richards, 1937. 123p. maps.

Sir Robert Gower acted as an unofficial spokesman for the Hungarian minorities and their grievances to the British parliament. In this volume he brings together the substance of those complaints, and in the case of 'Czecho-Slovakia' weighs the Hungarians' views against the misleading assertions of some Czechoslovak government statements and documents. The main areas of disaffection pertained to censorship, education at all levels, and finance. The Slovaks and Ruthenians are described as being affected just as badly as the Hungarians in some respects. The work may be old, but it is a valuable source for an understanding of many of the ugly developments later. The appendix contains the text of the 1919 treaty between Czecho-Slovakia and the Principal Allies on the regulation of citizenship and minority rights.

275 **Political differentiation in the Hungarian population of Czechoslovakia in the post-World War I years.**
Endre Arató.   Budapest: Akadémiai Kiadó, 1975. 31p. (Studia Historica, no. 122).

The Hungarians constituted quite a large minority in Slovakia and were therefore of considerable political significance. This Hungarian historian stresses primarily the role of the Marxist groups within the minority, especially the part played by Hungarian communists in founding the Czechoslovak Communist Party (1921).

276 **Czechoslovak policy and the Hungarian minority, 1945-1948.**
Kálmán Janics, introduction by Gyula Illyés, an English version
adapted from the Hungarian by Stephen Borsody. New York:
Social Science Monographs. Distributed by Columbia University
Press, New York, 1982. 241p. (East European Monographs, no.
122; Brooklyn College Studies on Society in Change, no. 18; War
and Society in East Central Europe: the Effects of World War II,
vol. 9).

The aim of this book is to provide in an accessible language the Hungarian (a
Hungarian?) view of what are described as the 'homeless years' between the end
of the war and the early months of 1948. That view is that the misfortunes of war,
great-power politics and small-power ambitions can all too readily be paid for by
the innocent and powerless, in this case the Hungarian minority in the south of
Slovakia, the area which during the war had been occupied by Hungary. In short,
when the boot was on the Czechoslovak, or more especially the Slovak, foot, the
Hungarian minority was made to suffer, perhaps not just for the misdemeanours
of some of them in the war years, but for the centuries past before Slovakia broke
free from Hungary in 1918. Janics is a member of the Slovak Hungarian minority,
currently prevented from publishing at home, Illyés is a major Hungarian poet
who has also fallen foul of the authorities, in Hungary, and Borsody is a
Hungarian émigré journalist and former diplomat now living in the United States.

277 **The Jews in the Soviet satellites.**
Peter Meyer, Bernard D. Weinryb, Eugene Duschinsky, Nicolas
Sylvain, preface by Morris Fine. Syracuse, New York: Syracuse
University Press, sponsored by the American Jewish Committee,
1953. 637p.

This set of country studies constitutes analyses of the effects of the war on the
Jewish populations of the states of Eastern Europe, and a contemporary (Jewish)
response to the outbreak of official anti-Semitism in those countries in the 1950s,
culminating in the infamous trials. The introduction refers to the near total
extermination of Czechoslovak Jewry, but a mass of detail is nevertheless found
which describes the situation that prevailed in the first years after the war,
especially the violence in Slovakia, and after the communist take-over in 1948.
Peter Meyer's account 'Czechoslovakia' (p. 47-204) traces the evidence of
antisemitism in newspaper reporting, from both Czech and Slovak sources, and
also uses the evidence of émigrés. The conclusion of the day is that the formerly
relatively happy Jewish community has been destroyed for good, their relations
with non-Jews in the country poisoned beyond cure.

278 **The shadow of the swastika: the rise of fascism and anti-Semitism in
the Danube Basin, 1936-39.**
Bela Vago. Westmead, Farnborough, England: Saxon House,
D. C. Heath, 1975. 431p. (Published for the Institute of Jewish
Affairs, London).

A highly specialized study, based on British Foreign Office documents,
concerning the unhappy predicament of the Jews in Romania, Czechoslovakia

85

and Hungary in the years just before the last war. During this period Germany's influence was becoming irresistible and certain domestic developments also gave cause for concern; the latter are the main theme here. Many of the relevant documents are reproduced in full, or in part.

279 **Anti-Semitism in Eastern Europe.**
Paul Lendvai. London: Macdonald, 1972. 393p.

The subject of this book is rather narrower than its title suggests, since it is mainly concerned with the period since the Second World War. It is included here for its section on Czechoslovakia (p. 243-97). The author's main concern is to show just how significant communist-party sanctioned anti-Semitism has been in Czechoslovakia's recent history, specifically during the Stalinist purges (the Slánský trial) of the early 1950s and in the methods employed in the overthrow of the Dubček régime after the country's occupation by Warsaw Pact forces in August 1968. An interesting aspect is how the Arab-Israeli War of June 1967 contributed to the formation of attitudes during the months preceding the 'Prague Spring', both on the side of the reformers and on the side of the Soviet-backed hard-liners. The book contains little of the earlier history of anti-Semitism in Czechoslovakia, but the background to the migrations and distribution of Jews in Eastern Europe, with some reference to individual events, is to be found in Part 2 (p. 3-86). In the absence of a bibliography, footnotes give full details of sources quoted (p. 351-76 [364-69 for the section covering Czechoslovakia]).

280 **Anti-Semitism without Jews: communist Eastern Europe.**
Paul Lendvai. Garden City, New York: Doubleday, 1971. 393p. bibliog.

Explores the contemporary situation of Jews in Czechoslovakia and other countries in the region with a traditionally high Jewish population. The last war led to a huge decrease in their numbers, by emigration or extermination, but Lendvai sees many of the classic problems still remaining, of which anti-Semitism is but one. Some of the forms of anti-Semitism have changed, but there are still various aspects of life that affect the minority which are interpretable as signs of anti-Semitism.

281 **The Jews of East Central Europe between the world wars.**
Ezra Mendelsohn. Bloomington, Indiana: Indiana University Press, 1983. 300p. maps.

The Jews of Czechoslovakia are described in chapter 3 (p. 131-69). The position of the Jews in inter-war Czechoslovakia is a very complex one and amounts to three different stories on account of the differences in the very nature and history of the three main areas – the Czech Lands, Slovakia and Subcarpathia – each with their distinct population mix and state of economic and cultural advancement. The author finds that all was well for the Jews under the benign rule of the Czechs, but where this weakened, in the easterly provinces at the approach of the Second World War, conditions deteriorated. Secularization and acculturation also went much further in the Czech Lands, so that they 'continued to be a good place for Jews, but not a very good place for Judaism in the sense of Jewish religious or cultural life'. A number of tables give numbers and/or percentages of Jews at different times and places.

282 **The Jews of Czechoslovakia: historical studies and surveys.**
Compiled by the Jewish Publication Society of America. New
York: Society for the History of Czechoslovak Jews, 1968, 1971.
2 vols. bibliog.

This major work, with a total of almost 1,300 pages, emphasizes the democracy of
the First Republic and asserts that the Jews have never been able to flourish in the
same way before, or since. The various studies in Volume 1 concern the early
history of, and differences between, the Jews in the different provinces of pre-war
Czechoslovakia, their legal position, social organization, religious life, welfare,
education, art and emigration. Volume 2 deals with major Jewish leaders,
Czechoslovak Zionism, economics, literature, press and publishing and Jewish
music. The detail in some sections is quite striking and the essays taken together
constitute an encyclopaedic range of information on Czechoslovak Jewry between
the wars. Each chapter has its own bibliography.

283 **Linguistic conditions among Czechoslovak Jewry: a legal-historical
guide.**
Guido Kisch. In: *Czechoslovakia past and present.* Edited by
Miloslav Rechcígl, Jr. The Hague, Paris: Mouton, 1968, vol. 2,
p. 1451-62.

A useful history on the changing social and legal pressures which have found the
Jews of Czechoslovakia, and the territories that preceded its emergence, speaking
Czech or German, and on the changing forms of Jewish names. It also includes an
historical account of the provisions for Jews in education.

284 **Mystical theology and social dissent: the life and works of Judah
Loew of Prague.**
Byron L. Sherwin. Rutherford, Madison, Teaneck: Fairleigh
Dickinson University Press; London, Toronto: Associated
University Presses, 1982. 253p. bibliog.

Rabbi Jehúdá Löw (ca. 1520-1609) is perhaps the best known of Prague rabbis,
thanks chiefly to the legends surrounding the Golem figure, his alleged robot-like
creation. He was, however, a prolific writer on theological and social matters of
some considerable influence, if not always in his own time. The relevance of this
book to the present work is that it provides an introduction to mediaeval Prague
Jewry, an account of later applications of the Golem legend in literature, theatre
and film (but little on the legend itself), and a valuable bibliography.

285 **The State Jewish Museum in Prague.**
Text prepared by a team of employees of the State Jewish Museum
in Prague, translated by Joy Turner-Kadečková. Prague:
Olympia, 1978. 40p.

This brief introductory guide to the museum also serves as an historical
background to Prague's one-time quite large Jewish community. It describes not
only the six synagogues and the famous old cemetery, but also the various
collections – textiles, metal artefacts, paintings, and exhibits connected with
World War II, during which many thousands of Czechoslovak Jews perished –

and the library, which contains many valuable prints dating from the 16th to the 18th century.

286 **Jewish cemeteries in Bohemia and Moravia.**
Jan Heřman. Prague: Ústřední církevní nakladatelství for the Council of Jewish Communities in the Czech Socialist Republic, s.d. 32p. 164 plates. map.

The brief introductory text describes the characteristics and history of Czech Jewish cemeteries (and of the community they served), and presents an idea of their regional chronology. A great number survive, even where 19th-century legislation caused the Jews themselves to move away, and many have been protected as cultural monuments. Attention is paid to the artistic merit and variety of many headstones and the location of the graves of a number of great scholar-rabbis, especially of the 17th century, is given. Then follows a catalogue of cemeteries, each entry accompanied by a brief history, and photographic illustrations of types of gravestones, ornamental motifs, the tombs of a dozen notable individuals (including Franz Kafka), and some individual cemeteries.

287 **Czechoslovak Jewry in 1979.**
Aaron Zwengbaum. *Soviet Jewish Affairs*, vol. 10, no. 3 (Nov. 1980), p. 29-46.

A good short summary of the contemporary civil and religious organization of the Czechoslovak Jewish community, with notes on, for example, its literature and arts, drawn from a judicious reading of the community's *Bulletin*, the coverage and general angle of which are characterized. There is some contrast with the community's characteristics in the past.

288 **Die Juden im Slowakischen Staat 1939-1945.** (The Jews in the Slovak State, 1939-45.)
Ladislav Lipscher. Munich, Vienna: R. Oldenbourg Verlag, 1980. 210p. bibliog.

A detailed account of a subject treated in more summary form in works by Y. A. Jelinek (cf. items nos. 243 and 263). The author covers: the pre-war attitude of the Slovak People's Party to the Jews; the removal of Jews from any position in public or business life; their eventual deportation in large numbers; the Slovak National Uprising, in which some Jews were involved; and the end of the war and the Slovak State as a separate entity. The bibliography, of mostly German and Slovak, with some English and Hebrew sources, is vast and the amount of archival material used (full references given) is impressive.

289 **Pole and Czech in Silesia.**
James Alexander Roy. London: John Lane, 1921. 212p.

Amazingly little has been written in English on the Polish minority in Czechoslovakia apart from the relevant sections in more general historical works. Czechoslovakia claimed the Teschen (Těšín) district on historical grounds, the Poles on ethnic grounds, and both nations have written extensively on the subject, each from a strong nationalist standpoint. This book offers a British view set out as a history of an area of genuinely mixed nationalities. The most comprehensive work to appear since is *Těšínsko v polsko-československých vztazích 1918-1939* (Teschen District in Polish-Czechoslovak relations 1918-1939), by Otakar Káňa and Ryszard Pavelka (Ostrava: Profil, 1970, 366p.) which contains a mass of statistical data, election results, and a good bibliography; it is in Czech but does have summaries in Russian, German and French.

290 **Notes sur le destin des Tsiganes tchèques.** (Notes on the fate of the Czech gypsies).
    Ctibor Nečas. *Études Tsiganes*, vol. 26, no. 3 (1980), p. 8-11.

This is a response to a French edition (Paris: Calmann-Levy, 1974) of Donald Kenrick and Grattan Puxton's *The destiny of Europe's gypsies* (London: Chatto-Heinemann Educational for Sussex University Press, 1972. 256p. bibliog. [Columbus Centre Series: studies in the dynamics of persecution and extermination]). It adds to the book a great deal of statistical and geographical data, specific to the Czech gypsies, on: the numbers involved in the 'final solution'; the whereabouts and nature of different camps; the dates when gypsies were transported; and their forced employment in industry. The new data comes from newly accessible archival material.

German-Czech relations in Bohemian frontier towns: the industrialization/urbanization process.
See item no. 579.

Ethnicity and urban population growth: the decline of the Prague Germans, 1880-1920.
See item no. 579.

Extraterritorial Populations

291 **The Czechs and Slovaks in Canada.**
John Gellner, John Smerek. Toronto: University of Toronto
Press, published in association with the Masaryk Memorial
Institute, 1968. 172p. bibliog.
Stressing the historical and modern bonds that unite the Czechs and Slovaks,
while acknowledging the strength of Slovak separatism during the last war, and
among the North American Slovak community, the authors, a Czech and a
Slovak, outline: the shared ancestry of the two nations (chapter 1); the early
waves of settlement by Moravian Brethren and later migrations of landless
Slovaks (chapter 2); their present-day religious, cultural and social organizations
(chapter 3); and the role they play in the life of Canada (chapter 4). Each chapter
has its own bibliography and there are a number of photographic illustrations,
especially portraits of leading figures.

292 **Czechs and Slovaks in Latin America.**
Milič Kybal. In: *The Czechoslovak contribution to world culture.*
Edited by Miloslav Rechcígl, Jr. The Hague, London, Paris:
Mouton, 1964, p. 516-22.
While North America attracted waves of Czech Protestants, South America
received its first Czechs and Slovaks as Catholic missionaries, from the time when
both Bohemia and Spain, and hence the Spanish South American colonies, were
ruled by the Habsburgs. These were Jesuits, who made a great impact on the
Christianizing of the Indians and on the general administration of the new cities oᶠ
Latin America, and their activity lasted right through the 17th and 18th centuries.
Visitors in the 19th century were mostly scientists and immigration proper only
began in the 1880s. This essay provides an account of all this, and more, and
refers to many major figures, not necessarily migrants, who have had Latin-
American connections, not least of all the doctor-writer Martin Kukučín (Matej
Bencúr), who worked for a time among the Croat settlers in southernmost Chile

90

It should be pointed out that, unusually, the footnotes offer a number of titles on the young Czechoslovak Republic in Spanish.

293 **Studies in ethnicity: the East European experience in America.**
Edited by Charles A. Ward, Philip Shashko, Donald E.
Pienkos. Boulder, Colorado: East European Quarterly.
Distributed by Columbia University Press, New York, 1980. 254p.
bibliog. (East European Monographs, no. 73).

Four papers in this collection have a direct bearing on the Czech community in North America: Henry Kučera's 'Czech linguistics in the United States' (p. 27-37); Karel D. Bicha's 'Community of cooperation? The case of the Czech-Americans' (p. 93-102); Josef Škvorecký's 'The East European émigré as writer: some personal observations' (p. 225-31); and Barbara Borowiecki's 'Geographic patterns of ethnic and linguistic groups in Wisconsin' (p. 39-67). The first concerns the state of Czech teaching and research in Czech topics, and on some areas of English-Czech contrastive study; the second is on the well-known tendency for Czechs not to band together in cohesive communities (unlike, say, the Slovaks), but it also pinpoints two striking, if tiny, exceptions (the hamlet of Snook in Texas and the village of Prague in Oklahoma); while the third is an argument against the theory of artistic decline in exile, quoting not only the author's own publishing successes (he is, largely, his own publisher, but, to be fair, his works have inspired some translations), but also those of other generations of exiles, writers and artists in other spheres. The fourth paper includes tables of statistics and maps to show the size and distribution of, amongst others, the Czech or Czechoslovak element in Wisconsin.

294 **Trends in Czech and Slovak economic enterprise in the New World.**
Vojtěch Erven Andic. In: *The Czechoslovak contribution to world culture.* Edited by Miloslav Rechcígl, Jr. The Hague, London, Paris: Mouton, 1964, p. 523-27. bibliog.

A summary account of, for example, the major Czech and Slovak industrialists, agriculturalists, bankers and publishers, who have made a mark on the immigrant community in the United States, or indeed on American life and industry generally. A detailed account of early Czech journalism in the United States, by Vlasta Vráz, follows the above in the same volume (p. 546-51).

295 **The Czechs and Slovaks in America.**
Joseph S. Roucek. Minneapolis, Minnesota: Lerner Publications, 1967. 71p. (In America Series).

One of a series concerning minority immigrant communities in the United States, this slim volume seeks to inform the average young American citizen about his fellows of Czech and Slovak origin. It provides a potted history, essentially only of the Czechs (the Slovaks only being brought into the sections from the First World War onwards, although there are historical references to the Slovaks in the introduction to the separate Slovak section). The rest of the text, supported by photographs, details: the waves of immigration into the United States; the causes of this immigration; the areas where Czechs and Slovaks are concentrated; their cultural and spiritual life; and the contribution of individual Czech and Slovak

Americans to politics and the arts and sciences, including the foundation in 1960 of the Czechoslovak Society of Arts and Sciences in America.

296 **Panorama: a historical review of Czechs and Slovaks in the United States of America.**
Cicero, Illinois: Czechoslovak National Council of America, [1970]. 328p.

The history of Czech and Slovak immigration is to be found in a variety of other sources but this review has an additional feature for it includes biographies of many of the more renowned members of the immigrant population and their descendants.

297 **The Čechs (Bohemians) in America: a study of the national, cultural, political, social, economic and religious life.**
Thomas Čapek. Westport, Connecticut: Greenwood, 1970. 293p. Reprint of the original 1920 edition.

This essential work, despite its age, offers many insights into Czech immigration into America. Its author, Thomas Čapek (1861-1950), a practising lawyer and ultimately president of a New York bank, acquired the soubriquet of 'historian of American Czechs'. He was a prolific writer, and many of the items he collected for his various publications on the American Czechs are now housed in the Library of Congress. This work also contains a distribution map of Czechs in America.

298 **The Czechs of Cleveland.**
Eleanor E. Ledbetter, foreword by Raymond Moley. Cleveland, Ohio: Americanization Committee, 1919. 40p.

This slim volume, together with *The Slovaks of Cleveland*, by Eleanor E. Ledbetter, with a foreword by Helen Bacon (Cleveland, Ohio: Americanization Committee, 1918. 32p. bibliog.), provides much detailed information on, for example: the early background of the two quite large immigrant communities; their contemporary social, religious, local and all-US societies; their participation in industry; and their role during World War I. Inevitably dated, both volumes are nevertheless valuable for the historical detail and statistics which they contain. Cleveland remains a major centre of Czechs and Slovaks in the United States.

299 **The Czechs in Texas.**
John M. Skřivánek. In: *The Czechoslovak contribution to world culture*. Edited by Miloslav Rechcígl, Jr. The Hague, London, Paris: Mouton, 1964, p. 510-15.

Texas is still an area with a large number of inhabitants of Czech descent – about 40,000 in Houston alone. Settlement began in the 1840s and 1850s, the settlers engaging chiefly in farming and the cotton industry. This paper describes the difficulties faced by the early settlers, examines some of the (Czech) names of the first settlements, and considers the Texan Czechs' modern lifestyle, religion and publishing activities. The names and achievements of many prominent Texan Czechs are also given. The essay has nothing to say on the Czech musical contribution to Texas, although there is a special brand of south-western music known as 'Czech-Tex' and some Czech Texan bands have also introduced the use of the central European hammer dulcimer (more associated with the Slovaks or Hungarians). On this and other aspects of Czech life in Texas see *The Czech Texans* (San Antonio, Texas: Institute of Texan Cultures, 1972).

300 **Augustine Heřman of Bohemia Manor.**
M. Norma Svejda. In: *The Czechoslovak contribution to world culture.* Edited by Miloslav Rechcígl, Jr. The Hague, London, Paris: Mouton, 1964, p. 500-04.

Although his involvement in America came through membership of the Dutch West India Company, Heřman is worth mentioning here as one of the early extraterritorial Czechs about whom quite a lot is known. He was instrumental in establishing New Amsterdam and Maryland, claimed to be founder of the Virginia tobacco trade and was a political opponent of Peter Stuyvesant. He received 5,000 acres of land from Lord Baltimore in return for his important cartographic work, calling it Bohemia Manor in recognition of his origins. Heřman had left Bohemia after life became difficult for non-Catholics in the aftermath of the Battle of the White Mountain (1620), and is considered co-founder of the North American branch of the Czech and Slovak nations. He died in 1686; his date of birth is uncertain.

301 **Slováci v zahraničí.** (The Slovaks abroad.)
Martin, Czechoslovakia: Matica Slovenská.

An occasional series of collected papers on the émigré communities of which the latest issue is no. 8 (1982) [1983], 188p., compiled by František Bielik and Claude Baláž.

302 **Vysťahovalectvo a život krajanov vo svete: k storočnici masového vysťahovalectva slovenského ľudu do zamoria – zborník príspevkov z vedeckej konferencie.** (Emigration and the life of expatriates in the world: to mark the centenary of mass emigration of the Slovak people – papers from a scientific conference).
Edited by František Bielik, Ján Siracký, Claude Baláž. Martin, Czechoslovakia: Matica Slovenská, 1982. 376p.

Although all of the contributions are in Czech or Slovak, interested readers will find some guidance on the subjects concerned from the foreword and contents pages, which are reproduced in English. The various papers deal, *inter alia*, with Slovak immigrant or local minority communities in the United States, Canada, Hungary, Romania, France, Poland, Austria, Argentina and Australia, and Czechs in the United States, Yugoslavia and Poland.

303 **Slovaks.**
M. Mark Stolarik. *Furdek*, vol. 23 (Jan. 1984) [1983], p. 7-26. bibliog.

From a brief history of Slovaks in Slovakia, Stolarik moves to an account of the waves of Slovak immigration into America, where they are outnumbered only by

93

Extraterritorial Populations

the Poles among Slav immigrants. Their employment (in mining and heavy industry) and their social and religious organizations as well as their family life, adherence to folk-traditions education and politics are all described, but without the chauvinism that affects so much émigré Slovak, especially Catholic, writing. (This article first appeared in the *Harvard Encyclopedia of American Ethnic Groups*. Edited by Stephan Thernstrom, Cambridge, Massachusetts, London: Belknap Press, 1980.) The same issue of *Furdek* carries a detailed social history on 'The status of Slovak American Women in Pennsylvania 1875-1914' by Janine M. Bolchazy (which refers to the domestic economy, maternity and infant mortality as well as literacy). This latter article is based in part on the memories of the older generation and in part on an analysis of the 1900 census for two towns with a high Slovak population. It is supported by a good mixed bibliography.

304 **Pittsburg-Wien-Budapest.**
Monika Glettler. Vienna: Österreichische Akademie der Wissenschaften, 1980. 504p. 4 maps.

At the end of the last century and early this century there were massive waves of emigration from Austria-Hungary to America, which included hundreds of thousands of Slovaks. This book, by a German professor with no particular axe to grind, looks at Austro-Hungarian national policy with particular regard to the Slovaks, many of whom settled in Pittsburgh. The work is richly supported by archival evidence (from some ninety collections of records in Austria, Hungary and Czechoslovakia). Amongst its other findings are the exact proportions and distribution of the various Slovak religious communities, especially Roman Catholic, Greek Catholic and Russian Orthodox; previous publications have tended to absorb the Slovaks in Ruthenian or Ukrainian statistics where the Orthodox and Greek Catholic populations were concerned.

305 **Sixty years of the Slovak League of America.**
Edited by Joseph Paučo, with an introduction by Stephen J. Tkach. Middletown, Pennsylvania: Slovak League of America, 1967. 148p.

The Slovak League is the most vociferous Slovak émigré body. Founded in 1907, it is passionately nationalist, strongly supports an independent Slovakia and is vehemently anti-communist. Members of the League also vigorously reiterate their loyalty to the United States. This anniversary volume, containing five essays, describes the history of the organization's various social, cultural and political activities, and includes some details about the life of Slovaks in the United States. Most important on the political side is Karol Sidor's paper 'The Slovak League of America and the Slovak nation's struggle for autonomy' (p. 37-70), which not only outlines the history of the League's involvement in Slovak politics, but also details the anti-Czech or anti-Czechoslovak case pursued by the nationalists since 1914 and the (mainly) Czech political activity which stirred it. Perhaps the largest single publication to emanate from the Slovak League is the illustrated history *Slovaks in America: a Bicentennial study*, compiled by the editorial board, chairman Joseph C. Krajsa (Middletown, Pennsylvania: Slovak League of America, 1978. 494p.).

Extraterritorial Populations

306 **Our people: Carpatho-Rusyns and their descendants in North America.**
Paul Robert Magocsi, with a preface by Oscar Handlin. Toronto: Multicultural History Society of Ontario, 1984. 160p. maps. bibliog.

A new, lavishly illustrated history of the Ruthenian immigrant population of North America, supported by maps and tables, by the leading writer on Ruthenian history and culture. It deals with all aspects of the people's economic, religious, organizational, cultural and political life, but its main mission is to foster an awareness of the Ruthenians' cultural heritage and to aid individuals to find their roots – a topical endeavour among North American immigrant groups. To this end it includes a village by village directory for the whole Ruthenian area, with alternative names, location (in pre-World War I Hungary or Galicia, ignoring interwar Czechoslovakia) and the country in which each parish currently lies, with many in Eastern Slovakia.

307 **Poland.**
Kenneth C. Farmer. In: *East European national minorities 1919-1980: a handbook.* Stephan M. Horak (et al.). Littleton, Colorado: Libraries Unlimited, 1985, 35-65.

In addition to Farmer's contribution on Poland this volume also contains other accounts of extraterritorial populations of Czechs and Slovaks including: 'Hungary' by Martin L. Kovacs (p. 160-74); 'Yugoslavia' by Toussaint Hočevar (p. 216-41); and 'Bulgaria' by Peter John Georgeoff (p. 274-85) (see also the important bibliographies). Surprisingly, there is no reference to the Slovaks of Romania, for which there is a body of literature (see Z. Salzmann's article 'A bibliography of sources concerning the Czechs and Slovaks in Romania' (q.v.)), nor to the Czech and Slovak communities (if not minorities) of Austria and Italy. Chapter 10 by Theodor Veiter (p. 314-26) concerns the nationality research centres in the various countries, but also includes references (an incomplete account) to the range of facilities available to the minorities (including broadcasting, the press, schools and publishing).

308 **Hungary and her successors: the treaty of Trianon and its consequences 1919-1937.**
C. A. Macartney. London, New York, Toronto: Oxford University Press, 1937. 505p. map. bibliog.

Another volume which has become a classic, and an effective sequel to R. W. Seton-Watson's (see item no. 242) at least as far as minorities are concerned. It deals not only with the surviving residual Slovak minority within Hungary (its reason for inclusion in this section), but also with the Hungarian minorities in Slovakia and Ruthenia. The account of relevant legislation, statistics, and the political behaviour of all the relevant minorities applies to the period of the Czechoslovak First Republic. Otherwise, this volume constitutes a general introduction to many aspects of interwar Slovakia and Ruthenia, especially geography, history, economics and politics. Another account of minorities, either side of various frontiers, by the same author is *Problems of the Danube Basin* (Cambridge, England: Cambridge University Press, 1942. 160p.).

309 **Wien und seine Tschechen: Integration und Assimilation einer Minderheit im 20. Jahrhundert.** (Vienna and its Czechs: integration and assimilation of a minority in the 20th century.) Karl M. Brousek. Vienna: Verlag für Geschichte und Politik, 1980. 148p. bibliog. (Schriftenreihe des österreichischen Ost- und Südosteuropa-Instituts, vol. 7).

A detailed history of the large Czech community in Vienna which demonstrates that they have been a major element in the shaping of the cultural, political and economic life of the Austrian capital, indeed of Austria generally. Of central importance is internal Austro-Czech politics, with much emphasis also on education and legal matters. Of great importance is the language issue and the author provides numerous statistics to show how far Czech survived as the first language of the minority and how far, and when, it was displaced by German. The many useful appendixes contain details of Czech cultural and other associations and the many Czech periodicals that have appeared, or still do, in Vienna. The book opens with Chancellor Kreisky's remark that nowhere has there ever been such a successful process of integration of a minority as the case of the Viennese Czechs. Some idea of the magnitude of this historic process comes out of Monika Glettler's background work on the social and political structure of this community as it stood at the turn of the century, *Die Wiener Tschechen um 1900* (Vienna: Oldenbourg Verlag, 1972. 628p. bibliog. Veröffentlichungen des Collegium Carolinum, no. 28), about one third of which consists of relevant documents, tables, a bibliography and other useful material.

310 **A bibliography of sources concerning the Czechs and Slovaks in Romania.**
Z. Salzmann. *East European Quarterly*, vol. 13, no. 4 (winter 1979), p. 465-88.

The relatively tiny and scattered Czech and Slovak communities in Romania have given rise to quite a corpus of work on their origins, their place in politics and economics, and their language and folklore, drawn together in this list of over 175 entries, dating from 1857 to the present. It is unfortunate that the listing is solely alphabetically by author, with no sub-division by subject.

311 **National minorities in Romania: change in Transylvania.**
Elemér Illyés. Boulder, Colorado: East European Quarterly. Distributed by Columbia University Press, New York, 1982. 355p. maps. bibliog. (East European Monographs, no. 112).

Very little indeed has been written on the Czechs and Slovaks in Romania in English. However, this work at least provides an idea of the number of Czechs and Slovaks in Romania (from the tables), the dates when these pockets were established, and where they are located.

312   **Ethnic minorities in Romania under socialism.**
       Trond Gilberg.   *East European Quarterly*, vol. 7, no. 4 (Jan.
       1974), p. 435-58.

Discusses Romania's general nationality problem and some aspects of internal
policy. The work contains a modicum of information, especially statistical, on the
country's Czechs and Slovaks, together with wider coverage of the Hungarians,
Germans, Jews and gypsies. This article is reproduced as chapter 9 of Bernard
Lewis Faber's (ed.) *The Social Structure of Eastern Europe: transition and process
in Czechoslovakia, Hungary, Poland, Romania and Yugoslavia (q.v.)*

313   **Kovačica: Slovak city in Yugoslavia.**
       Andrew V. Pier.   *Furdek*, vol. 22 (Jan. 1983), p. 179-80.

Although only a very brief piece, this is included here because of the general
shortage of works in English on the Slovak community in Yugoslavia. The history
of the people from 1784 onwards and their present cultural and industrial
activities are described.

Folklore, Folk-art
and Customs

314 **Fundamental problems encountered by Czechoslovak ethnographers and folklorists.**
Karel Fojtík. *International Journal of Sociology*, vol. 1, no. 1 (spring 1971), p. 67-87.

The problems referred to in the title are those of both theory and practice arising out of current research. The research programme the author refers to is connected with the preparation of a major history of Czech and Slovak folk-culture in all its breadth.

315 **Die slawische Mythologie in der tschechischen und slowakischen Literatur.** (Slav mythology in Czech and Slovak literature.)
Anton Hönig. Augsburg, GFR: Blasaditsch, 1976. 210p. bibliog.

I have found no comparable publication in English on this rich topic, which the author handles chronologically, by genre of the literature in which mythological elements appear (the range of which is closely defined in the introduction), and by dominant themes. The German dimension is, understandably, brought out wherever relevant. The book contains a detailed index of the mythological and pseudomythological concepts discussed (p. xxvi-xxxi) in the appendix, and a copious bibliography (p. i-xviii *ib.*).

316 **Look comrades: the people are laughing; underground wit, satire and humour from behind the Iron Curtain.**
Edited and compiled by John Kolasky, with an introduction by Josef Škvorecký. Toronto: Peter Martin Associates, 1972. 136p.

The political joke and anecdote is an indispensible part of life in Eastern Europe and has been for much longer than is perhaps assumed, ie., it is not just a by-product of the contemporary régimes. This collection, included here as representing one type of what may be called folk-oral literature, has a ten-page selection from Czechoslovakia, although all are contemporary.

Folklore, Folk-art and Customs

317 **An egg at Easter: a folklore study.**
Venetia Newall.   London: Routledge & Kegan Paul, 1971.
Reprinted, 1973. 423p. bibliog.

The tourist in Czechoslovakia, whatever the time of year, will be able to include among his souvenirs some of the very finely decorated Easter eggs produced in a variety of styles all over the country. Their production is now more a minor money-spinning industry than a folk-craft, though its latter function is by no means dead. This book, though its coverage is world-wide, contains some superb illustrations of many of the Czech and Slovak types. The text gives a complete account of the calendar-related background, associated legends and beliefs, methods of production and general Easter frolicking connected more or less directly with eggs, as well as other spring-time folk-customs, such as 'carrying death out of the village'. The book is comparative, but the Czechoslovak items can be located via the index (entries Bohemia, Czechs, Moravia, Slovakia and Ruthenia), which will lead to coverage also of the country's German minority.

318 **Myths and folk-tales of the Russians, western Slavs and Magyars.**
Jeremiah Curtin.   London: Sampson Low, Marston, Searle & Rivington, 1891. 555p.

This work is an example of one of the early collections of folk-tales made at a time when interest in them burgeoned. The book includes six Chekh (*sic*!) myths and folk-tales (themselves taken from early Czech collections) by no means the best known and so perhaps at least as interesting as some recent, more classical collections. Curtin is particularly interested in comparing East European (Aryan) folklore with that of the North American Indians.

319 **Folk and fairy tales from Bohemia.**
Jiří Horák, Jane Carruth, translated from the Czech by Alice Denesova and illustrated by Jiří Trnka.   London, New York: Hamlyn, 1973. 186p.

This book is one of the products of the years of collaboration between the publisher and Czechoslovakia's printing and publishing industries. It is included here not merely as another representative collection of folk-tales, but because of the illustrator, Jiří Trnka, one of the best-known and best-loved of Czechoslovakia's artists specializing in pictures for children, especially book illustrations and animated films.

320 **The palace of the moon and other tales.**
Ruzena Wood, illustrated by Krystyna Turska.   London: André Deutsch, 1981. 128p.

The Czechs share much of the European folk-tale heritage, and this selection offers twelve representatives of the Czech version of the genre. There have been other collections translated in the past, but this one contains a number of less well-known items, some not particularly familiar to the Czechs themselves. For a more classical selection see Marie Burg's *Salt and gold: tales from Czechoslovakia* (Glasgow: Blackie, 1976, 95p.).

321 Moravian tales, legends, myths.
Karel Absolon. Rockville, Maryland: Kabel, 1984, 1985. 2 vols.

The first volume of tales relates to the Macocha abyss and the underground river Punkva, rich in legend as mentioned elsewhere herein, and volume two has tales connected with other actual localities, including the haunted Pernštejn Castle. Absolon has collected here stories handed down through his family, émigrés in North America.

322 The enchanted castle, and other tales and legends.
Pavol Dobšinský, adapted by Ann Macleod. London: Hamlyn, 1967. 248p.

Dobšinský (1828-85) was the most important Slovak collector of folk-tales and other folklore which he published to constitute the national, classic corpus of folk and fairy-tales. This is a fairly representative collection of tales of various kinds, and the edition benefits from the use of illustrations by one of the best-known Slovak illustrators, Ľudovít Fulla.

323 Janosik: a Carpathian saga.
[Edited by John Okal]. [Whiting, Indiana: J. J. Lach, 1954]. 62p.

Jánošík was the Slovaks' Robin Hood and is still very much a Slovak folk hero, 'a brigand idealised by the Slovak people' (Slovník slovenského jazyka). His exploits have been retold numerous times and in many versions. Indeed, the Jánošík idea has passed into linguistic idiom and underlies many a literary metaphor and allusion. It is to be regretted that so little Slovak folklore is available in English but it is inevitable that, of all that is available, the Jánošík legend is the one that has become best known. Another Jánošík story is included in Marion M. Coleman's *A brigand, two queens and a prankster* (Cheshire, Connecticut: Cherry Hill Books, [1972]. 77p.), and three Slovak tales are included in Oldřich Syrovátka and Rudolf Lužík's *Slav Tales*, English version by Neil Jones, based on translations by Jean Layton ([London]: Dent, 1974, 197p.).

324 Ethnologia Slovaca: an international review of Slavic ethnology.
Bratislava: Slovenské pedagogické nakladateľstvo, 1968-.
annual.

This is one of Eastern Europe's main English-language serials dealing with Slavonic ethnology but because it emanates from Bratislava the emphasis in individual volumes is often on Slovak questions. There are occasionally pieces concerning Czech ethnology, and on the mixed-population areas on the fringes of Czechoslovakia.

325 Peasant art in Austria and Hungary.
Edited by Charles Holme. London, Paris, New York: The Studio, 1911. 54p.

If the illustrated plates were paginated this volume would be four or five times the size implied by the number of pages stated. In fact it constitutes an encyclopaedia of folk architecture, domestic art (in, for example, furniture, pottery, embroidery and lace) and costume for all the provinces of Austria-Hungary. Separate sections

100

relevant to the present bibliography cover Egerland, Bohemia proper and Moravia; such representations as there are of Slovak work are intermingled with those of Hungary proper, Slovakia having at the time of publication no separate identity. Many of the illustrations are in colour. Moreover, the population of Bohemia and Moravia is called Czecho-Slav, which here also includes the Czechs of Silesia, but not the Slovaks. The textual part of the volume picks out the salient features of folk-art in each region, and is a partial introduction to some of the native terminologies.

326   **Folk art of Czechoslovakia.**
       Věra Hasalová, Jaroslav Vajdiš, translated by Ivo
       Dvořák.   London, New York, Sydney, Toronto: Hamlyn, 1974.
       296p. map. bibliog.

The text, which starts with an historical survey of the country and evolves into a geographical guide with commentary on prevailing art forms and their typical features, is interlaced with 235 illustrations, many in colour, showing samples of the unique art and architecture of both Czechs and Slovaks. The art coverage includes all manner of farm and household items and their decoration, folk costumes, toys, devotional objects in a variety too vast to give an adequate impression. Each illustration carries a brief caption, but more details of, for example, source and location are given at the back of the book. The bibliography is divided into Czech and English titles, the latter mostly emanating, like this title, from Prague via one or other of the British publishers with strong commercial links with Czechoslovakia (Hamlyn Books were for years printed in Czecho-slovakia even if the titles involved did not originate there).

327   **Folk painting on glass.**
       Josef Vydra, translated by Helen Watney.   London: Spring
       Books, [n.d.]. 57p. bibliog.

Considers the history of the techniques employed by this art form as it developed in Czech culture (having originated in Bavaria), and as it evolved from a professional occupation to a folk-art form originally cultivated for supplementary income. Preferred themes, changing in time, are also described. The second part of the text deals with the regional spread of 'schools' of glass painting (which includes ten general areas, covering Bohemia, Moravia, Silesia and Slovakia), and attempts a periodization. The illustrative plates are gathered at the end of the book, but their brief iconographic descriptions precede the text (p. 7-16).

328   **Folk and traditional music of the Western continents.**
       Bruno Nettl, foreword by H. Wiley Hitchcock.   Englewood Cliffs,
       New Jersey: Prentice Hall, 1973. 2nd ed. 258p. bibliog. (Prentice
       Hall History of Music Series).

The chapter on Eastern Europe (p. 83-108) includes references to Czech and Slovak folk-music traditions, their typical features and differences, and it also compares Slovak music to the Hungarian. The meagre bibliography indicates how poorly covered this topic is in English. The book was written as a study of all the sources that play a dominant role in the music of the Americas. A little more on the American products from these sources is in Nettl's *Folk music in the United*

Folklore, Folk-art and Customs

States: an introduction (Detroit, Michigan: Wayne State University Press, 1976.
3rd ed. rev. by Helen Myers, 187p. bibliog.). Both works repeatedly refer to an
earlier article, 'Czech and Slovak songs collected in Detroit' (*Midwest Folklore*,
vol. 5 (1955), p. 37-49), which reproduces a number of songs but foresees their
demise as barely relevant to the city environment. (This latter article was co-
authored with Ivo Moravčík).

329　**Dances of Czechoslovakia.**
　　　Mila Lubínová, translated by G. B. Smith.　London: Max Parrish,
　　　1949. 40p. map. bibliog.
A brief outline of the characteristics of types of Czech and Slovak folk-dances and
the music that accompanies them, with a description of the occasions when
dancing was traditional, and of some of the costumes (partially illustrated). This is
followed by a technical guide to performing a selection of the best-known dances
(this section edited by Kathleen P. Tuck).

Religion and Theology

330 **The philanthropic motive in Christianity: an analysis of the relations between theology and social service.**
Frank Martin Hník, translated from the Czech by M. Weatherall, R. Weatherall.   Oxford: Basil Blackwell, 1938. 328p. bibliog.

This long theological treatise is a history of Christian attitudes to charity, but its inclusion here is due to the account it provides (part 5, p. 287-328) of the 'socially theological basis of charity in the Czechoslovak Church'. This is arrived at from a critique of the Roman Catholic (especially Thomist), Lutheran, Calvinist and Humanitarian (especially Unitarian) interpretations of the role of Christian charity. Hník comes down firmly on the side of the Humanitarian view and stresses the need for social services based on equality and fraternity and on the careful investigation of social needs and ills – their mere observation and 'relief' through almsgiving is no solution to them. The work is a description of a social theology, not of any integrated philanthropic practice in the Czechoslovakia of its day, but it is an important insight into the social and theological thinking of a major institution in pre-war Czechoslovakia.

331 **The soul of Czechoslovakia: the Czechoslovak nation's contribution to Christian civilization.**
Arthur Stuart Duncan-Jones.   London: Herbert Barker, 1941. 63p.

This is essentially a history of Czech theology and liberal democratic thought, the Slovaks being brought in only for the earliest period and the National Revival, then obliquely as part of the 'Czechoslovak' nation since independence (this interpretation is an acceptance of the inter-war Czechoslovak view of a unitary nation). The book offers quite a good summary of early Hussitism and its debt to Wycliffism, the latter perhaps a little exaggerated, and is a useful introduction in English to Hus's precursors. The other period to which more attention is paid is the 19th century and the spiritual and intellectual renaissance which gave rise to the Sokol movement, and the career of the important political journalist Karel Havlíček-Borovský. For the period since independence the author emphasizes the strength of Czechoslovak democracy and, importantly for the time of writing, the exemplary treatment of minorities by the Czechoslovak state. The argument is that German-minority disquiet would have been resolved to the satisfaction of all had it not been for the strategic worries of Hitler.

332 **Bohemia sacra: das Christentum in Böhmen 973-1973.** (Holy
Bohemia: Christianity in Bohemia, 973-1973.)
Edited by Ferdinand Seibt.   Düsseldorf, GFR: Schwann, 1974.
645p. map. bibliog.

Produced to mark the millennium of the foundation of the Prague bishopric, this comprehensive history of religious life in Bohemia cannot be matched by anything in English; all the papers are in German. Every period is discussed, but the emphasis is really on the 19th and 20th centuries, with the attendant relevance of politics and nationalism. The state of the church, or churches, is described for various periods, with separate sections on relevant linguistic, literary, artistic or architectural topics. Some fine black-and-white and coloured plates illustrate selected buildings, manuscripts, statuary and plate.

333 **Thoreau's influence in Bohemia.**
Otakar Vočadlo.   In: *Thoreau abroad: twelve bibliographical
essays.* Edited by Eugene F. Timpe. Hamden, Connecticut:
Archon Books, 1971, p. 119-30.

There is much in Henry Thoreau's naturalist philosophy that could not fail to attract the Czechs, or their free-thinking, increasingly anti-dogmatic intellectual leadership. This paper draws together a number of threads which underline the affinity, starting with the interests and character of Thoreau's first Czech publisher, Jan Laichter, who was also the publisher of Masaryk's works. It not only gives a history of Thoreau translations, especially of *Walden*, but *passim* refers to many of the naturalist and similar Czech writers up to the Second World War, as well as the translators and publishers active in this realm. In addition, it also contains many details of American-Czech literary and philosophical kinship, and mentions the early years of the Czech Scout and Woodcraft movements, and echoes of Sylvester Graham's dietetic system (*Grahamův chléb* – 'Graham bread' is well-known at the Czech baker's today). Three Czech moralists are picked out as genuine Thoreauists: Gustav Jaroš; Miloš Seifert; and František Kovařík. Although equally a literary topic, the moral philosophy involved here is so akin to religious philosophy that the work has been included in this section. (Many of the topics referred to here crop up elsewhere in Vočadlo's works, often quite short journalistic pieces in the Czech and English press; see *Otakar Vočadlo [1895-1974], Professor of English, Charles University, Prague: biography and bibliography of his works.* Compiled and edited by B. R. Bradbrook, [London?]: the compiler, 1980. 24p.).

334   **The Czechoslovak Church.**
Frank M. Hník, Frank Kovář, Alois Spisar.   Prague: Central
Council of the Czechoslovak Church, 1937. 101p.

The political break with Austria-Hungary which saw the birth of the Czechoslovak
Republic in 1918 was accompanied by a strong turning away from the Catholic
Church both as a dogmatic organization out of tune with modern thought and as a
pillar of the Austrian establishment. Out of this was born the new Czechoslovak
Church, national, democratic and liberal. In its national aspect it saw some
affinity with the Anglican Church and the Serbian Orthodox Church, but longer-
lived and further-reaching were its contacts with the other liberal churches,
notably the Unitarian Churches of Britain and America. The three articles in this
volume describe: the Church's origins, the social structure of its membership and
its relationship to the ecumenical movement of the day; the foundations on which
its theology and confession of faith are based; and a biography of Karel Farský,
co-founder and first patriarch of the Church. Before the war the Czechoslovak
Church shared many of the ideals of Masarykian humanitarianism, while now it
is, along with the other churches, at variance with the régime, which is actively
atheistic.

335   **The Czechoslovak heresy and schism: the emergence of a national
Czechoslovak Church.**
Ludvík Němec.   Philadelphia: American Philosophical Society,
1975. 78p. (Transactions Series, volume 65, part 1).

Undoubtedly the most comprehensive recent history of the Czechoslovak Church,
it is largely concerned with theological discussion of schism and heresy, showing
the Czechs to be the schismatics and indicating the low acceptance of the new
national church among the non-schismatic Slovaks. The historical detail covers all
the theologians and politicians of the day, before the birth of the Republic and
during its early years, who had any contribution to make. The important aspects
covered include the role of the Catholic Church, German bishops, constitutional
provisions applying at different times, the important question of relations with the
Orthodox Church (relevant to Ruthenia, the then easternmost province of the
country), statistics of denominational adherence, and, in the absence of a formal
bibliography, much of the relevant literature.

336   **The re-establishment of the Greek Catholic Church in
Czechoslovakia.**
Michael Lacko.   *Slovak Studies*, vol. 11, Historica 8 (1971),
p. 159-89.

The Greek Catholic Church is of great religious and political significance to a
section of the community in Eastern Slovakia. In the 1950s it had been forcibly
merged with the Orthodox Church, which is also described here, and only during
1968 was it allowed to be reconstituted by government decree. The article
describes the machinery of re-establishment and the problems involved, and it
includes (semi-conjectural) statistics for the nationality composition of the
adherents (Slovaks, Ruthenians and Hungarians). Continuing poor relations with
the Czechoslovak Orthodox Church are a blight on the religious interests of the
area. Another article on the same topic, 'Restoration of the Greek Catholic
Church in Czechoslovakia', by Athanasius B. Pekar (*Ukrainian Quarterly*, vol.

29, no. 3 (autumn 1973), p. 282-96), takes a more strongly political view of the event and accuses the Slovaks of a chauvinistic attempt to seize the Church from the Ruthenians.

337 **Byzantine rite Rusins in Carpatho-Ruthenia and America.**
   Walter C. Warzeski. Pittsburgh, Pennsylvania: Byzantine
   Seminary Press, 1971. 332p. map.

A history of the Uniate Church in Ruthenia and America which refers to the history of the Ruthenians themselves as a nation in revival, and to the chequered history of the province itself which was only briefly independent and was otherwise a part of Czechoslovakia, Hungary or the Soviet Union. The work includes some valuable statistics and a number of important documents. It is relevant both to the pre-war history of Czechoslovakia, the religious history of the country (there is still a small Uniate Church among the Ruthenians of the Prešov district, with some Slovak adherents as well), and to the extraterritorial populations whose homeland is/was Czechoslovakia.

338 **The Infant of Prague: the story of the Holy Image and the history of the devotion.**
   Ludvík Němec. New York: Benziger, 1958. 304p. bibliog.

The title here is basically self-explanatory, but for the uninitiated, the Infant of Prague is one of the most celebrated Czech religious effigies, the *pražské Jezulátko*, an object of pilgrimage, a reported worker of miracles and the possessor of a huge assortment of clothes which are frequently changed by the sisters in charge.

339 **Our Lady of Hostýn: queen of the Marian Garden of the Czech, Moravian, Silesian and Slovak Madonnas.**
   Ludvík Němec. New York: RCH Press, 1981. 171p. bibliog.

Hostýn is where the Tatar invasion of Europe was stopped and became associated with Marian visions. It is just one of the many places of pilgrimage important to Czech and Slovak Catholics. Němec takes a rigidly Catholic view of the country's religious history, stressing the political motivation for the switch away from Catholicism in 1918 and understating the equally important political drive against Protestantism during the three previous centuries. The book is generously illustrated by photographs of some of the many shrines and churches in all four provinces and seeks to describe their relevance to the country's contemporary religious life; there are over 1,200 Marian churches and chapels in the country. The reader's attention should also be drawn to the Czech and Slovak element in *The Penguin Dictionary of Saints* by Donald Attwater (Harmondsworth, England, 1965 and many reprintings, 364p.) which contains references in varying detail to the following saints: Adalbert of Prague, Clement Hofbauer, Elizabeth of Hungary, John of Nepomuk, Ludmila and Wenceslas (he of the fictitious story in the popular Christmas carol), and of course Cyril and Methodius, the great Slav apostles, whose major missionary endeavours began in Great Moravia.

340 **Church and state in Czechoslovakia, historically, juridically and theologically documented.**
Ludvík Němec, preface by Ambrose Ondrák. New York: Vantage Press, 1955. 577p.

Slightly misnamed, in the sense that it is concerned with the Roman Catholic church only, this is a documented account of the state of affairs prevailing up to the time of publication. The author covers the difficult time after the war and the communist take-over when church-state relations sank to their lowest. It has the authenticity of first-hand knowledge but the author discusses his subject from the church's point of view.

341 **Discretion and valour: religious conditions in Russia and Eastern Europe.**
Trevor Beeson, with a foreword by Sir John Lawrence.
[London]: Collins, 1974. 348p. map. bibliog. (Fontana Original).

The book is the product of a working party study which was promoted by the British Council of Churches because of a 'growing concern about religious conditions throughout Eastern Europe'. It aspires to be a fair account, but admits that there are obvious difficulties over statistics and the general reliability of such information as is accessible. The chapter on Czechoslovakia (p. 190-226), opens with a brief historical view of the Protestant heritage of the Czechs and a passing reference to the Slovak Lutheran tradition. However, very little information is provided about the strength of Catholicism after the Counter-Reformation, although the Catholic Church is cited as being the strongest denomination in contemporary Czechoslovakia. Each denomination is given a brief historical and statistical description before a detailed account of post-1948 church-state frictions and accommodations, especially the role of Josef Hromádka and the Prague-based Peace Movement. Religious education and publishing activities, and the nature of restrictions on them, are also included. For a book responding to the early legal limitations placed on church life after the communist take-over see the section on Czechoslovakia in *Church and State behind the Iron Curtain*, edited by Vladimir Gsovski (New York: Praeger, 1955).

342 **Thoughts of a Czech pastor.**
Josef L. Hromádka, translated by Monika Page, Benjamin Page. London: SCM Press, 1970. 117p. bibliog.

This autobiography of a leading Lutheran theologian is set against the events in Czechoslovakia during the 20th century. Indeed the force of history and the need for Czechoslovak theologians, especially Protestants, to come to terms with prevailing currents is strongly reiterated, especially for the more recent period. The early pages contain an outline theological history of the Czechs and the author then proceeds to provide an account of the position of Czech (actually Moravian – Hromádka is from Eastern Moravia) Lutheranism within the context of Czech Protestant reform generally, and vis-à-vis Catholicism. Two major trips abroad, to Scotland for study and to America at the outbreak of the last war, offer useful accounts of the Czech view of Scottish Protestantism and its role in Central Europe and of a Czech view of America's failure to understand Europe. The author's views on many currents of religion and philosophy receive an airing.

343   **Church in a Marxist society: a Czechoslovak view.**
      Jan Milič Lochman.   London: SCM Press, 1970. 198p.
The author is a professional theologian of the Czech Brethren Church and a
committed member of Czechoslovak socialist society. He is also an obviously
keen supporter of the Prague-centred Christian Peace Movement, which he seeks
to defend in the face of hostile criticism. In addition to providing an account of
the background to Czech Protestantism and an apologia for the nature of the
symbiosis between the churches and the state under socialism, he also: draws
some comparisons with the position of the church in areas where it remains part
of the establishment; summarizes the distribution of Christian denominations
throughout Eastern Europe; and in particular explores the substance of the
continuing debate between Christianity and Marxism in Czechoslovakia. His often
reiterated concern is that the Christian witness of the churches of Czechoslovakia
should be seen as a small but telling contribution to the ecumenical spirit.

344   **Religious ferment in Eastern Europe.**
      Pedro Ramet.   *Survey*, vol. 28, no. 4 (winter 1984), p. 87-116.
Includes a brief account of the state of religion in Czechoslovakia during the
1980s. The author relies on Western news reports for the accounts of repression,
and on Czechoslovak reports for arguments underlying certain anti-church (anti-
Catholic) actions. The situation is related to the fact that the Pope is from
neighbouring Poland and that the Slovaks in particular are actively church-going
Catholics, presently resorting to underground religious observance in fairly high
numbers. The underground church is of course seen as an anti-state body.

345   **Religion and atheism in the USSR and Eastern Europe.**
      Edited by Bohdan Bociurkiw, John W. Strong.   London:
      Macmillan, 1975. 412p.
Considers the conflicts between Eastern Europe's Christian traditions and the
officially atheist doctrine of the contemporary governments, and the strange
modus vivendi which many of the churches find themselves having to sustain. In
their 'Church-State schism in Czechoslovakia', p. 273-291, Peter A. Toma and
Milan J. Reban describe two periods, post-1948 and post-1968, when the state
took active steps to 'resolve the problem of religious–political interaction', by
various 'instruments of coercion and "persuasion"'. The article is rich in statistics,
from pre-war religious affiliation to the number of new churches built in Eastern
Slovakia in 1968. Different events pertaining to individual denominations, as well
as the general provisions relating to religious life, are described chronologically
against the background of recent history. A minor asset is footnote 2, which lists
the eighteen religious organizations currently recognized in Czechoslovakia.

Society, Population, Health and Welfare

346 **The people's republics of Eastern Europe.**
Jürgen Tampke.   London, Canberra: Croom Helm, 1983. 178p.

This work is different from many with similar titles in that it seeks to overcome the black-and-white view of East-West relations as reflected in writing about 'the other side'. The general, historical, sections all include Czechoslovakia in the discussion, as do the sociological sections on incipient consumerism and, *passim*, recreation. One chapter is a reappraisal of the events of 1968 and the political confusion and other negative features of the period, suggesting that there was more interest in the dimension of scandal than in the heart of the reform. Tampke also accepts the Soviet intervention as inevitable, as the only salvation of long-term Soviet interests and to avert the peril of the consequences of Czechoslovakia's potential departure from the Soviet sphere. The work includes details on contemporary opinion polls, and there are some interesting comparative tables in the section on consumerism.

347 **Socialism, politics and equality: hierarchy and change in Eastern Europe and the USSR.**
Walter Connor.   New York: Columbia University Press, 1979. 389p.

Despite the general title, Czechoslovakia is quite well covered in this work from a variety of angles, both in its own right and comparatively (see tables). It offers a picture of everyday life, at home and at work, in the context of traditional values and contemporary ideology. The author also provides for example, documentation concerning the survival of the greater status accorded to non-manual over manual work, or urban over rural, or such factors that Czech women tend to marry down slightly more than up. Social mobility, employment patterns and family structure are just some of the topics discussed, with explicit comparisons among the countries involved and some tacit comparison with modern Western society.

109

348 **The social structure of Eastern Europe; transition and process in Czechoslovakia, Hungary, Poland, Romania and Yugoslavia.**
Edited by Bernard Lewis Faber. New York, London: Praeger, 1976. 423p. (Praeger Special Studies in International Politics and Government).

The volume includes 'Classes and elites in socialist Czechoslovakia' (p. 143-65) by Jaroslav Krejčí, a sensitive, but quite widely discussed topic which needs to be faced by a society that claims to be classless. The managerial class and the working class are here called classes, the political leadership the power élite. The old middle class has become proletarianized, while paradoxically 'a larger part of the nation acquired a middle-class character', this on the grounds of the components of social status. Each element of modern society is discussed, in terms of attitudes, income and observed standard of living, and official statistics are quoted in support.

349 **Social change and stratification in post-war Czechoslovakia.**
Jaroslav Krejčí. London: Macmillan, 1972. 207p.

Krejčí considers the institutions and political processes at work in the country, the roles of planning and marketing, intellectuals and the party, Czechs and Slovaks, and peasants and the rest of the population. The main interest is in the interplay between the government-managed economy and political culture in the widest sense. Some of the questions raised concern the position and structure of the new power élite, and the author enquires whether the end product of shifts in the socio-economic groups has produced social classes.

350 **Bureaucracy and interest groups in communist societies: the case of Czechoslovakia.**
Andrzej Korbonski. *Studies in Comparative Communism*, vol. 4, no. 1 (Jan. 1971), p. 57-79.

This is based on the thesis that after totalitarianism was lifted, group pressures became operative in the 1960s, the three groups of managers, journalists and trade unions each being somehow involved in the discussion of reform, but opposed by the bureaucrats. For the period, the 'group model' of socialism is then more applicable than the totalitarian or the bureaucratic.

351 **Blue collar workers in Eastern Europe.**
Edited by Jan F. Triska, Charles Gati. London: George Allen & Unwin, 1981. 320p.

This volume of papers, of which more than one is relevant to Czechoslovakia, includes Jiri Valenta's 'Czechoslovakia: a prolétariat embourgeoisé?' (p. 209-23). It is based on a classification of workers as: 'nostalgic', ie., party bureaucrats and civil servants; 'penitent', ie., former non-workers, now disgraced; and 'authentic'. Concentrating on the latter, Valenta describes their motivation, organization (unionization), involvement in revolt (with special reference to the revolt of the Škoda workers in Pilsen in 1953 which was caused by currency reform which wiped out their savings), revolutionary potential (latent), ability to form coalitions with the intellectuals, and their capacity for opposition. The question of the title is tacitly answered in the affirmative, with perhaps some overstatement of the alleged socio-economic disadvantages inhibiting complete *embourgeoisement*.

352 Membership of the Communist Party in the 1970s: continuing divergence from the Soviet model.
Gordon Wightman. *Soviet Studies*, vol. 35, no. 2 (April 1983), p. 208-22.
Wightman explains the reasons behind the rapid increase in Party membership since the purges of 1969-70, when the Party lost over one quarter of its members. Besides giving absolute statistics, from various sources, he analyses the situation in terms of age structure, social composition, the percentage of women, and the special situation of the Prague City branch. The statistical position is compared throughout with Soviet practice.

353 Social services for women in Eastern Europe.
Bogdan Mieczkowski. Charleston, Illinois: Association for the Study of the Nationalities (USSR and East Europe), 1982. 130p. bibliog. (ASN Series in Issues Studies (USSR and East Europe), no. 3).
In addition to describing the social services including pre- and post-natal care, clinics, nurseries and kindergartens, the author also looks into: the death-rate for women, including suicide rates; employment and the economics of work and child-care; and the problems faced by women in striking a balance between the duties of housewife and mother and the frequent necessity for women to go to work to supplement the family income, not to mention the natural desire of many women for their own career. Although the book concerns the whole of Eastern Europe, there is some specific attention to Czechoslovakia, accessible via the index, and many of the generalizations also apply to the country.

354 Women under Communism.
Barbara Wolfe Jancar. Baltimore, Maryland; London: Johns Hopkins University Press, 1978. 291p. bibliog.
Jancar seeks to describe the everyday life and social role of women in all the socialist countries. One weakness is in the treatment by topic rather than by country, though the clear index makes the Czechoslovak sections readily accessible. The work is based on sources from the countries in question, with wisely cautious conclusions by the author, and on the author's first-hand experience from formal and informal contacts. Another weakness is the tendency to treat Czechoslovakia as *east* European *because* it has its particular political complexion, so that some of the generalizations appear to apply where they are not strictly applicable. The subjects covered include: employment patterns; home life and child-care; divorce and abortions; the ideological views of women's roles; legislation relevant to women; and women's own attitudes to their position at work, in the home and in society at large. For a more recent study by the same author see 'Women in communist countries: comparative public policy' in *Women and world change: equity issues in development*, edited by Naomi Black and Ann Cottrell (Stanford, California: Stanford University Press, 1981).

355 **Women and state socialism: sex inequality in the Soviet Union and Czechoslovakia.**
Alena Heitlinger. London; Basingstoke, England: Macmillan, 1979. 241p. bibliog.

This is a detailed study of official policy as regards women in society and of actual practice. It covers the development of sexual equality, contemporary life in the home, employment, women in positions of authority and pays special attention to the role of women and their social surrogates in child-care, and the effect of prevailing population policies. While women have progressed far in terms of employment, they are still hampered by traditional expectations in the home, inadequate crèche and kindergarten facilities to enable them to return to work quickly, and a Union of Women which follows the wishes of the party with regard to policy matters. The book contains a great deal of relevant statistical data, and is one of the few sources to quote substantially from Czech and Slovak women's magazines. Inevitably there is a discussion of abortion and contraception in their relation to the population policy. Another item on the same general topic is B. Korda's 'The status of women in a socialist country', *Osteuropa Wirtschaft*, vol. 3 (1976), p. 205-14.

356 **Does socialism liberate women?: experiences from Eastern Europe.**
Hilda Scott. Boston, Massachusetts: Beacon Press, 1974. 240p.

Although the title of this work is non-specific as to the countries involved, and although parts of it are general, especially the discussion of socialist theories as far as they affect women, the core of the study concerns the situation in contemporary Czechoslovakia as it has evolved since the war. The socialist would say that socialism does liberate women, and this view is weighed against those of the women's liberation movement as understood in the West. Having confronted the two views and given her interpretation of the Czechoslovak situation, the author concludes with a negative answer to the question in the title. Similar issues are tackled by Sharon L. Wolchik in 'Elite strategy toward women in Czechoslovakia. Liberation or mobilization?' in *Studies in Comparative Communism*, vol. 16, no. 2-3 (summer-autumn 1981), p. 123-42.

357 **Political socialization in Eastern Europe: a comparative framework.**
Edited by Ivan Volgyes. New York, Washington DC, London: Praeger, 1975. 201p. (Praeger Special Studies in International Politics and Government).

A collection of papers which seeks to reveal, in the absence of any East European theory on the subject, what might underlie the practice of political socialization – the process by which political cultures are changed or maintained; new socialist man is to be created, with desirable attitudes. The authors assess what such attitudes might be and then, country by country, investigate how they are achieved. Otto Ulč's 'Czechoslovakia: from the winter of discontent to the despair of Husák's autumn' (p. 38-65) takes a clearly pro-Prague Spring line and is consequently hostile to the régime, but offers a useful analysis of how the family works (is made to work). Ulč notes the special role of grandmothers, and describes the formal structures of social (youth) organizations, the media and the education system that contribute to attempts, not an unqualified success, to shape the socialist good citizen.

358 **Reproductive behavior: Central and Eastern European experience.**
Henry P. David, Robert J. McIntyre. New York: Springer, 1981.
393p. bibliog.

Beginning with an introduction to the relevant Marxist-Leninist ideology on women, population policy, abortion and pronatalist incentives, the book then analyses the situation country by country, with one chapter devoted to Czechoslovakia. Coverage is very wide, where available statistics permit, and includes not only the broader items mentioned, but also such matters as intended family sizes, contraceptive practices, preferred methods of abortion, sex and marriage, sex education, and adolescent sexuality. Two earlier papers specific to the problem are Z. Pavlík and J. Zbořilová's 'Changes in Czechoslovak marital fertility' in *Demographic aspects of the changing status of women in Europe. Proceedings of the 2nd European population seminar (p. 65-78)*, edited by M. Niphuis-Nell (Leiden, Netherlands: Nijhoff, 1978), and Tomáš Frejka's 'Fertility trends and policies: Czechoslovakia in the 1970s', *Population and Development Review*, vol. 6, no. 1(1980), p. 65-93.

359 **Eastern Europe: pronatalist policies and private behavior.**
Henry P. David. *Population Bulletin*, vol. 36, no. 6 (Feb. 1982), p. 1-47. (A publication of the Population Reference Bureau).

A detailed study of fertility-related population trends throughout Eastern Europe which summarizes the position in the post-war period and looks in particular at the most recent relevant legislation. Special attention is paid to abortion, which obviously tends to assist a population decline, and the various incentives introduced to increase population size (birth grants, paid maternity leave, family allowances, low-interest loans for newly-weds). Czechoslovakia is usually treated separately in all the sub-sections. The paper, which takes up the full issue of the *Bulletin*, gives interesting insights into the types of people seeking abortions, contraceptive practices, attitudes to sex and marriage, including aspects of what would elsewhere be called male chauvinism, and conclusions regarding the relatively limited impact of legislation of any kind. There are copious graphs and statistical tables, some of which involve comparison with selected non-East European countries (see also item no. 420).

360 **Social deviance in Eastern Europe.**
Edited by Ivan Volgyes. Boulder, Colorado: Westview Press, 1978. 198p. (A Westview Replica Edition).

Setting out from the doctrinal aspiration of ruling communist parties to eliminate social ills for good, by whatever means, the papers in this volume demonstrate that this goal is fundamentally impossible. The various authors are able to offer some evidence from each country demonstrating that there continue to be patterns of behaviour which violate the set code. Otto Ulč deals with Czechoslovakia (p. 23-33) relying largely on first-hand experience and discriminating between the main forms of political and social misdemeanours, and providing some indication of the penalties.

Society, Population, Health and Welfare

361 **Jugendkriminalität in Osteuropa: Deutungen, Dynamik, Daten.**
(Juvenile delinquency in East Europe: significance, dynamics,
data.)
Wolf Oschlies. Cologne, GFR; Vienna: Böhlau Verlag, 1979.
217p. (Sozialwissenschaftliches Forum, no. 7).

It is much to be regretted that this work has no index, since it contains a good
proportion of facts about Czechoslovakia (much of it culled from Czechoslovak
press reports). Crime is considered from a variety of social and ideological
viewpoints and is classified according to broad categories, such as theft, violence
and group delinquency. It is also related to similar trends in the West and the
author concludes that the East, in such areas as car theft and drug-inspired crime,
is only slightly lagging behind.

362 **Social consequences of modernization in communist countries.**
Edited by Mark G. Field. Baltimore, Maryland; London: Johns
Hopkins University Press, 1976. 277p.

A collection of conference papers which include passing comments on Czechoslovakia, most substantially in Walter D. Connor's paper with its references to
social deviance, notably crimes of violence, juvenile delinquency and theft.
Connor quotes official Czechoslovak statistics.

363 **Some criminological and socio-political aspects of Czechoslovak pre-
communist and communist legislation on abortion.**
Jaroslav Jíra. In: *The Czechoslovak contribution to world culture.*
Edited by Miloslav Rechcígl, Jr. The Hague, London, Paris;
Mouton, 1964, p. 425-45.

The chief criminological aspect dealt with here is the removal, by the more recent
legislation, of any incriminability from the mother in cases of otherwise illegal
abortions. The socio-political aspects on the other hand concern, in the main, the
perceived dangers that the more recent legislation could aggravate the very
situation it seeks to overcome (the illegal abortion rate) and its affect on the total
birth-rate and the declining population. The author provides an overview of all
the abortion legislation up to 1963, and, with it, an account of some of the social
and moral dilemmas specific to Czechoslovakia. The issues are all still alive, and
there have been other developments since, notably the increased financial
provisions for larger families, which have led to the abortion rate being brought
down somewhat. Of some interest is the description of the workings of the
abortion committees, which still operate more or less as described.

364 **The cultural limits of revolutionary politics: change and continuity
in socialist Czechoslovakia.**
David W. Paul. Boulder, Colorado: East European Quarterly.
Distributed by Columbia University Press, New York, 1979. 361p.
(East European Monographs, no. 48).

This behavioural study seeks to account for (long-term) revolutionary change and
underlying continuity by trying to analyse the political and non-political constants

114

and variables by which Czechoslovak society evolves. It makes no pretences that this is a simple matter because of the impossibility of verifying such things as personal motivation. The three central issues are: the values and attitudes that have come to affect contemporary political reality; the forces of inertia in a society in which the élite is dedicated to implementing the ideals of communism; and the question of the conflict between indigenous political culture and that of an imported ideology, Soviet communism. It is in these terms that all the standard issues revolving around nationalities, minorities and opposition politics, for example, are discussed.

365 Social medicine in Eastern Europe: the organization of health services and the education of medical personnel in Czechoslovakia, Hungary and Poland.

E. Richard Weinerman, with the assistance of Shirley B. Weinerman. Cambridge, Massachusetts: Harvard University Press, 1969. 201p. bibliog. (A Commonwealth Fund Book).

This valuable work is based on a field trip during which the author spent some of his time establishing the theoretical structure of the health services and the nature of professional training before proceeding to a period of direct observation supplemented by interviews with relevant personnel from a wide spectrum of health service and academic fields. A comparative chapter deals with the common ground and tabulates basic statistical data on expenditure, birth, death and related rates, main causes of death and the incidence of communicable diseases. The separate chapter on Czechoslovakia (p. 42-71) builds on the generalities and adds the country-specific data, which are broad enough to take in not just the management of the health service proper, but the more specialist areas of spas, the Red Cross, social insurance and the education of personnel. The overall appraisal of the system is guardedly positive. On a narrower topic see Z. Stembera's 'Development of maternal and child health care in Czechoslovakia', *World Health Forum*, vol. 2, no. 4(1981), p. 516-20.

366 Health care in the Soviet Union and Eastern Europe.

Michael Kaser. Boulder, Colorado: Westview Press, 1976. 278p.

This is a set of country-by-country studies, preceded by a general paper on the revolution, ie., post-war changes, in health care throughout the area, but even this also contains some facts specific to Czechoslovakia. The separate chapter on the country (p. 114-46) relates current health-care practice and legislation to the earlier social (industrial) history and pre-war provisions for the health service and to the overall demographic pattern. The core account then discusses: the general administration, facilities and financing of the health service; the legal background; the licencing of doctors; spas; the incidence of self-medication; and the existence of non-qualified naturopathic practitioners. There is a wealth of statistical data both in the text and in the tables.

Society, Population, Health and Welfare

367 **Public participation and social planning in Britain and Czechoslovakia.**
Barry Hill. In: *Planning in Europe.* Edited by Jack Hayward, Olga A. Narkiewicz. London: Croom Helm, 1978. p. 131-46.

Hill tends to stress the similarities rather than the differences between the two countries, especially the unhappy lot of planners themselves in the crossfire of criticism wherever they may be. Also noted are such factors as public ignorance of their elected representatives except, in Czechoslovakia, at the most local level, and such items of social policy as loans for young married couples and the writing off of a given percentage as each child is born. Within the book there are other passing comparisons between East and West at a more general level, and the work includes a bibliography.

368 **Public opinion in European socialist systems.**
Walter D. Connor, Zvi Y. Gitelman, with Adaline Huszczo, Robert Blumstock. New York, London: Praeger, 1977, 197p. (Praeger Special Studies in International Politics and Government).

'Public opinion in Czechoslovakia' (p. 83-103) is the part of this volume which is central to the present bibliography. For obvious historical reasons the opinion polls which it describes and analyses can only have come from the 1960's, although it also describes the brief flowering of poll-taking in the period immediately following the Second World War. These had been concerned more with social policy (such as the direction of labour, attitudes to child-rearing and the death penalty) than the more overtly political (including religious) surveys of the later period. The re-shaped Public Opinion Research Institute continued in existence after 1970, but no longer conducted political surveys. While this chapter of the book contains break-downs of the major surveys conducted, the first and last chapters also contain many references to Czechoslovakia set against the background of general discussion of the book's title subject.

369 **Public opinion polling in Czechoslovakia 1968-69: results and analysis of surveys conducted during the Dubček era.**
Jaroslav A. Piekalkiewicz, foreword by Barry Bede. New York, Washington DC, London: Praeger, 1972. 359p. (Praeger Special Studies in International Politics and Government).

Opinion polling has generally been an unknown practice in Czechoslovakia in the sense in which it is understood in the West, but between March 1968 and March 1969 some 20 polls were conducted – one of the many symptoms by which that period stands apart from the rest of recent Czechoslovak history. It was an eventful period by any reckoning, as is recalled by the chronology appended to the work, and polling, as these analyses show, was a meaningful exercise.

Society, Population, Health and Welfare

370 **Survey research and public attitudes in Eastern Europe and the Soviet Union.**
Edited by William A. Walsh.   New York: Pergamon Press 1981.
365p. (Pergamon Policy Studies on International Politics).

In addition to Walsh's introductory overview of survey research in Eastern Europe, which he finds somewhat limited, the volume contains George Klein and Jaroslav Krejčí's 'Czechoslovakia' (p. 204-41). The authors found, contrary to expectations, that quite a lot of surveying still goes on, even if it is little reported and confined to less sensitive topics. The range is quite broad but nonetheless, as the actual survey results reproduced show, the conclusions reached are always in line with contemporary party policy. The authors also note the range of specific topics on which no surveys have been conducted.

371 **The restoration of order: the normalization of Czechoslovakia, 1969-76.**
Milan Šimečka, preface by Zdenek Mlynar.   London: Verso
Editions, 1984. 167p.

This is an account, from the inside, of how Czechoslovakia has (been) returned to 'normality', ie., the state existing before the ill-fated experiment of 1968. Šimečka describes, largely from personal experience, many of the methods by which society is controlled. His conclusions represent not only an indictment of the régime, but also of the Czech and Slovak man in the street, who is found too able to adapt to circumstances, being ready to be bought off by consumer goods and an undisturbed private life; undisturbed if he makes the right motions in the course of his public life. Much is made of the equality of contemporary society; no power-group is graced by birth or inherited fortune, almost everyone is involved in everyday bribery and corruption, there is no major wage differential between intellectuals and manual workers, all aspire to the same (best possible) education for their children, whatever their own education. However, it still remains the case that, for example, envy plays a considerable role in life (Šimečka's own references to envy are not entirely consistent). In its separate chapters the work looks individually at the contemporary media, law and order, attitudes to education, and *passim* at attitudes to the West, the environment and the family.

372 **The state of sociology in Eastern Europe today.**
Edited by Jerzy J. Wiatr, foreword by Herman R.
Lantz.   Carbondale, Edwardsville, Illinois: Southern Illinois
University Press; London; Amsterdam, The Netherlands: Ferrer &
Simons, 1971. 273p. (Perspectives in Sociology).

'Czechoslovakia', by Jan Macku (p. 59-77) amounts to an historical overview, beginning with the early modern academic tradition in sociology at the end of last century and the pre-First World War division into various discernible trends, especially the 'critical realism' of Arnošt Bláha, described as a synthesis of Émile Durkheim and Tomáš Masaryk. The sparse outline continues through all the main representatives and their major works, including separate developments among the Slovaks. The main burden for the modern period is that the Marxist emphasis on social conflict was largely absent from Czech and Slovak thinking, except among Marxists, and that contemporary Marxist sociological theory is

117

Society, Population, Health and Welfare

dominated by the 'structural-functional conception of social phenomena'. Most progress is seen to have occurred in the sociology of youth, education and the family.

373 **Social guarantees in Czechoslovakia.**
Compiled by staff of the Federal Ministry of Labour and Social Affairs and the corresponding ministries of the Czech and Slovak Republics. Prague: Práce, 1977. 151p.

The government sponsors a steady trickle of publications aimed at the foreign consumer in order to explain official policy and practice. This one relates to all aspects of employment and the welfare state from the legal and executive point of view, but understandably avoids the question of abuses.

Education

374 **J. A. Comenius and the concept of universal education.**
John Edward Sadler. London: George Allen & Unwin, 1966.
318p. bibliog.
Modern education was given the essence of both theory and practice by Jan Ámos
Komenský (John Amos Comenius), the leading 17th-century Moravian Protestant
thinker. Sadler's book offers one of the most accessible descriptions and
interpretations of Comenius's basic theories and the concepts central to them,
including: the Good Man, encyclopaedic knowledge of the world about us and of
ourselves, the Good Society and the didactic process. His philosophy of language
and his ideas on the practical side of education (the nature and needs of schools,
teachers and textbooks) are all described. The bibliography contains many good
references to earlier English works on Comenius, and the notes on important
contemporaries include such interesting figures as the Polish Scot John Jonston
(1603-75) and the Rosicrucian Robert Fludd (1574-1637).

375 **John Amos Comenius, that incomparable Moravian.**
Matthew Spinka. Chicago, Illinois: University of Chicago Press,
1943. 177p. bibliog.
Written to mark the 350th anniversary of Comenius's birth in 1592, this biography
of 'the father of modern pedagogical theory and practice' and 'apostle of
reconciliation and peace' covers his entire private and professional life, giving the
full scope of his interests and activities in education and theology. The work
inevitably contains a great deal of the contemporary history of war-torn Europe in
general and the countries in which Comenius was active, in particular: Poland;
England; Sweden; Hungary; and the Low Countries. Spinka is also the author of
a translation (not the first) of Comenius's *The labyrinth of the world and the
paradise of the heart* (q.v.), a marvellous allegory on the state of the world which
has some claim for comparison with Bunyan's *Pilgrim's Progress*.

Education

376 **Comenius and the Low Countries: some aspects of life and work of a Czech exile in the seventeenth century.**
Wilhelmus Rood. Amsterdam, The Netherlands: Van Gendt; Prague: Academia; New York: Abner Schram, 1970. 276p. bibliog. (Respublica Literaria Neerlandia Series).

An important background work to the life and times of Comenius, written to mark the tercentenary of his death. The 'life' element is concerned with his movements, his contacts, especially with the important De Geer family of financiers and arms producers, and his polemics with Dutch theologians, and the 'times' element provides much information about the Thirty Years' War. The coverage is broader than the title would suggest, since it includes a section on 'Comenius and Descartes' and ample references to Comenius's connections in Sweden and England.

377 **Comenius.**
Edited by Vratislav Bušek, translations by Káča Poláčková. New York: Czechoslovak Society of Arts and Sciences in America, 1972. 184p.

A collection of sixteen very mixed papers from a symposium held to mark the tercentenary of Comenius's death in 1670. Some are theoretical, and some descriptive and historical, including one on the troubled times in England during his stay there.

378 **Slovakia 1918-1938: education and the making of a nation.**
Owen V. Johnson. Boulder, Colorado: East European Quarterly. Distributed by Columbia University Press, New York, 1985. 516p. bibliog. (East European Monographs, no. 180).

This is undoubtedly one of the most reliable recent works on Slovakia; it deliberately sets out to overcome the one-sidedness or distortions present in so many publications owing to their Slovak émigré, hyper-patriotic Tendenz. It is based on a close study of a vast corpus of archival materials covering not only its stated subject – secondary and tertiary education provision for Slovaks, civil and religious, inside Slovakia and elsewhere in the First Republic – but also the general geographic, demographic, economic and historical background and the Czechoslovak-Czech/Slovak political issues of the day. Ancillary to the central themes is a concluding chapter on related topics: the development of publishing; libraries; music and theatre; the work of the Matica slovenská national cultural foundation; and the various interest groups directly or indirectly involved in the education process.

120

379 **Die Entwicklung des tschechoslowakischen Schulwesens 1959-1970: ein dokumentarischer Bericht.** (The development of Czechoslovak education 1959-70: a documentary report.)
Rudolf Urban, foreword by Oskar Anweiler. Heidelberg, GFR: Quelle & Meyer Verlag for the Osteuropa-Institut an der Freien Universität Berlin, 1972. 259p. (Osteuropa-Institut an der Freien Universität Berlin, Erziehungswissenschaftliche Veröffentlichungen, vol. 7).

This is one of the few detailed studies in a Western language on Czechoslovak education and it covers an important period, from the major reform of 1959-60, whereby education became linked physically to production (i.e. as part of the curriculum children were taken out of the classroom and put in fields, building sites or factories for practical experience) to the period of consolidation after the Dubček era, when various issues pertaining to the gymnasia and vocational schools in particular were dealt with. The work looks separately at each layer of the system, including teacher training, and considers educational problems and how they were solved, contemporary criticisms and press commentary. Any factors specific to Slovakia are duly mentioned. The appendix contains German translations of certain key documents.

380 **Society, schools and progress in Eastern Europe.**
Nigel Grant. Oxford: Pergamon Press, 1969. 363p. map. (Commonwealth International Library of Science, Technology, Engineering and Liberal Studies).

In its day this was a major study intended as a contribution to comparative education. Reforms have rendered it out of date in some respects, but much remains of value including the background information it provides about the demography, politics, history and education of the past. Also useful is the section entitled 'general features' which covers modern East European education and ideology, discipline and moral education, science and technology, youth organizations, the education of girls and women, and administration. The common elements of the structure of education are contained in part 1, and part 2 consists of country studies, with Czechoslovakia being covered on p. 232-58. This chapter is partly historical but it also describes the contemporary position and is sufficiently detailed to include, for example, tables of entire curricula, though it must be treated as, at best, an introductory study. All basic levels are described, plus adult education, special schools, apprentice schools and training colleges.

381 **Communist education.**
Wasyl Shimoniak. Chicago, New York, San Francisco: Rand McNally, 1970. 506p. map. bibliog.

The section on Czechoslovak education (p. 291-301) is regrettably brief and inevitably dated, but it does contain an outline of the educational heritage, especially in the work of John Comenius (1592-1670), and a contrast between the pre- and post-war structural and ideological bases of education. The unsympathetic tone of the work becomes even more strident on the subject of the fate of church schools after 1949 and the hostility of the régime to religion generally. The bibliography is of little use.

121

Education

382 **Thirty years of socialist school in the Czechoslovak Socialist Republic. Vol. 1, Elementary schools; Vol. 2, Secondary schools; Vol. 3, Universities.**
Ministry of Education of the Czech Socialist Republic, translated by Till Gottheinerová. Prague: State Educational Publishing House, 1975.

Although something of a self-congratulatory collection on the achievements claimed for Czechoslovak education under a centralized, socialist system based on 'progressive Marxist principles', these volumes deal less with the history of the thirty years since the war and contain more on the conditions in the mid-1970's with reference to orgnization; curricula; types and numbers of schools – and other facilities such as children's homes; adult education; and teacher training. Some of the basic facts remain valid, though others have been overtaken by the great educational reforms of the last five or six years. The image presented is entirely rosy, as befits an official document and as is underpinned by the appended photographic record.

383 **The Czechoslovak education system.**
Pavel Jeník, translated from the Czech by Jan Nemejovský.
Prague: Orbis Press Agency, 1980. 77p.

A brief conspectus of information on education at all levels, made available specifically for foreign consumption. It includes a brief history of education in the country, from the earliest times, and of course makes much of the Comenius heritage. Since 1978 the whole education system has undergone some major changes and the consequences of these for the change-over period to 1984 are discussed. There are some tables of curricula and a list of the country's institutions of university status.

384 **Prague essays presented by a group of British historians to the Caroline University of Prague on the occasion of its six-hundredth anniversary.**
Edited by R. W. Seton-Watson. Oxford: Clarendon Press, 1949. 145p.

The seven essays in this volume vary in their relevance to the present bibliography, though most are concerned with aspects of 14th- and 15th-century Bohemian history. The first essay is the most pertinent. Written by the editor of the whole volume, and entitled 'What the Caroline University has meant to the Czechs', it is a history of Prague's university from its foundation in 1348 to its closure by the Germans in 1939. Important in modern times is the 1882 split into separate Czech and German universities and the eventual (1918) dominance of the Czech as the decreed descendant of the original institution. This whole issue is an element in the wider Czech-German antagonism referred to elsewhere.

385 **Higher education in the Czechoslovak Socialist Republic.**
Pavel Malý, Jiří Měřička, translated by Joy
Moss-Kohoutová. Prague: Státní pedagogické nakladatelství,
1982. 80p. map.

Intended as an information brochure and so not on sale, this book is likely to be obtainable only through specialist libraries and Czechoslovak embassies. However, though brief, it provides a comprehensive introduction to tertiary education in the country and its place within the overall educational structure, for which a structural diagram is given. It also summarizes the history of education in the country after 1348 when Charles University was founded. Syllabus and course structures are described and there are tables to show the kinds of tertiary institutions teaching particular disciplines. A useful asset is that the nomenclature of degrees and titles is provided in Czech as well as English, with explanations of the study or qualification they imply. A five-part list of all the country's colleges and universities, with their faculty divisions, is also included.

386 **Act No. 39 of April 10, 1980 concerning institutions of higher learning.**
[Prague]: Published with the permission of the editorial board of the Bulletin of Czechoslovak Law, [n.d.] 66p.

A verbatim translation of the relevant law as enacted by the Federal Assembly of the Czechoslovak Socialist Republic, doubtless intended for circulation through embassies and international educational conferences. It sets out in detail: all the provisions for the organization and management of colleges and universities of various categories; the nature of registration thereat, including such things as the awarding of degrees; the functions of, for example, officers of universities; research obligations; cooperation with other institutions; staffing; the provision of textbooks; the special colleges of the Communist Party and the armed forces; and the provisions enabling foreigners to study at Czechoslovak universities and allowing Czechoslovaks to study abroad. There is an appendix providing a full list of all places of tertiary education and their separate faculties.

387 **Selected bibliography of materials on education in Czechoslovakia.**
Compiled by Nellie Apanasewicz. Washington, DC: US
Department of Health, Education and Welfare, 1960. 37p.

Although of no help to students of contemporary Czechoslovak education, this partially annotated bibliography does contain a fair corpus of materials on education in the inter-war period and the early years under socialism. Many titles are in English and the presence of an English résumé is indicated for publications emanating from Czechoslovakia. Some of the titles quoted are other bibliographies.

Statistics

388 **The East European and Soviet data handbook: political, social and developmental indicators, 1945-1975.**
Paul S. Shoup. New York: Columbia University Press; Stanford, California: Hoover Institution Press, Stanford University, 1981. 482p. bibliog.

This massive assemblage of facts and figures, largely from the countries in question but supplemented from other sources such as the United Nations, is specifically intended as a research tool. The tables in many sections are directly comparable, others are subject to local differences of approach or definition. Usefully, much of the relevant terminology is cited in the original language, which is a vital asset to those conversant with the language since in some areas translations, however apparently accurate, necessarily carry with them collocations from the language of the translation. In each section Czechoslovakia is accorded separate treatment on: population, its growth and change, age-groups and sex and fertility rates; party membership, its social composition, occupations, age and nationalities; ethnic and religious affiliation; levels of education (Czechoslovakia and East Germany alone shown as having no illiterates); class structure by occupation, level of education and age, with separate treatment for the agricultural population; background and education of party leaders; major occupations and relationship to education; developmental indicators for persons in agriculture and urban population; housing, food consumption, transport, health and culture; and dates of censuses. The last named is the first of a number of appendixes.

389 **Comecon foreign trade data, 1980.**
Edited by the Vienna Institute for Comparative Economic Studies. London; Basingstoke, England: Macmillan, 1981. 509p.

Contains fairly complete original Comecon data on the volume of trade in selected years between 1960 and 1979. It also provides data for Comecon trading

Statistics

partners, drawn from the Organization of Economic Co-operation and Development (OECD) and the International Monetary Fund (IMF), which go a long way towards supplementing data on such subjects as the balance of payments, which are among those which the Comecon countries do not publish. The next volume in the series is for 1982 (published 1983, 518p.), and for the intervening, and subsequent, odd years the same editors and publishers produce *Comecon Data* (for 1981, published 1982, 464p.), which contains the widest possible range of statistics, including population, employment, investment, industrial and agricultural population, employment, investment, industrial and agricultural production, standard of living, incomes and prices, health, education, foreign trade, finance and energy. All tables give separate treatment to Czechoslovakia, which is also incorporated in summary tables. As above, some data are supplemented from other sources, for example Gross National Product from World Bank estimates.

390 **Statistical survey of Czechoslovakia.**
Federal Office of Statistics. Prague: Orbis. annual.
A concise statistical handbook covering practically every aspect of the life of the country that can be expressed statistically. This includes: population; language; health; schools; industrial, agricultural and mineral output; and international trade. Much more detailed statistical handbooks are of course published in the national languages. The 'export' versions of the statistical survey contain many tables showing how Czechoslovakia compares with the top six or so countries in a given sphere. Like all publications of this nature, it should be used with caution, since reasons of state may decree that certain statistics are distorted in some way.

391 **Československá statistika.** (Czechoslovak statistics.)
Prague: Statistický úřad, 1922-. irregular.
The title of this serial has changed over the years and it has been broken up into various sub-series, the present one running since the 1950s. In addition to providing the range of statistical data normally associated with such publications, it also includes census returns in years when a census has been conducted.

392 **Manuel statistique de la République Tchécoslovaque 1920-1932.**
Prague: L'Office Statistique d'Etat, 1920-1932. Cambridge, England; Teaneck, New Jersey: Chadwyck-Healey, 1977.
The above title and the following two statistical yearbooks, both published in 1977, are also available in this series of microfiche: *Annuaire statistique de la République Tchécoslovaque 1934-1938.* (Prague: L'Office de Statistique de la République Tchécoslovaque, 1934-1938); and *Statistická ročenka Československé socialistické republiky 1957-1970.* [Statistical yearbook of the Czechoslovak Socialist Republic 1957-1970.] (Prague: Český statistický úřad; Bratislava: Slovenský statistický úřad, 1957-1970).

393 **1000 československých nej.** (One thousand Czechoslovak superlatives.)
Ladislav Kochánek. Prague: Albatros, 1983. 2nd ed. 205p.
First published as *1000 československých rekordů: rekordy, superlativy, kuriozity* [One thousand Czechoslovak records: records, superlatives, curiosities] (Prague:

125

Statistics

Olympia, 1976), this is the country's local answer to the *Guinness Book of Records*. This later version is aimed at the junior market (Albatros is the publisher of most children's literature in Czechoslovakia), but the variety of information, while not exactly matching the original version, is of factual interest. It is impossible, if not pointless to hint at all the areas covered, but it does range from historical and geographical constants, through to the present state of affairs in areas where there will (for example, population), or may (for example, sport), be changes in future. There is even a measure of the more bizarre records, such as those for pram-pushing, barrel-rolling or plum-dumpling consumption. Although the book is in Czech, there are some useful aspects, illustrations apart, for the outsider in, for example: the lists of nature reservations and natural parks (p. 45-46); the 118 most important protected monuments (p. 176-86); a complete list of protected plants, invertebrates and vertebrates (p. 186-94); and the list of Czechoslovak Olympic gold-medal holders (p. 143-46).

Politics, Opposition and Dissent

394 Background of Czechoslovak democracy.
Václav Beneš. In: *The Czechoslovak contribution to world culture*. Edited by Miloslav Rechcígl, Jr. The Hague, London, Paris: Mouton, 1964, p. 267-76.

The Czechs have often thought of themselves as a nation democratic by nature and peace-loving by tradition. This has not always gone unquestioned, but they became the major assets, as well as a handicap, for the young Czechoslovak Republic. The background proper, as regards the Czechs in particular, comes from the ideology of some of the main historians (František Palacký and Thomas Masaryk), and from the first-hand experience of politics which the Czechs had gained inside Austria-Hungary. The Slovaks are not ignored in the paper, but, curiously consistently, all detail on developments among them is left to footnotes.

395 Communist political systems: an introduction.
Stephen White, John Gardner, George Schöpflin. London; Basingstoke, England: Macmillan, 1982. bibliog.

This work opens with a comparative study of communist states generally, and proceeds, in separate chapters, to deal with political cultures; structures of government; the communist parties; the policy process; and democracy and human rights. It ends by comparing communist states with other states with similar and dissimilar political systems. Each chapter has its own bibliography of fairly recent publications, and some are supported by tables. Czechoslovakia is well represented in the coverage, as the detailed index indicates.

127

Politics, Opposition and Dissent

396   **The Communist Parties of Eastern Europe.**
Edited by Stephen Fischer-Galati. New York: Columbia
University Press, 1979. 393p.
Of the eight separate studies here, that on 'The Communist Party of
Czechoslovakia' (p. 87-165) by Peter A. Toma, is by far the longest. This is
perhaps because its scope goes beyond that of the Party itself to include a
discussion of other, admittedly relevant, aspects, such as the industrialization of
Slovakia, economics and religion (especially the quite distinct ¨ractices of
religious observance between the Czechs and Slovaks). An important element in
the account is the changing nature of the relation between the ('semi-elitist')
working class and the Party. Of passing interest is the early reference to the
existence of other parties within the National Front, seen as 'supportive' and
'auxiliary' 'vestiges of traditional values'. There are some tables listing officials in
the Party.

397   **Communism in Eastern Europe.**
Edited by Teresa Rakowska-Harmstone, Andrew Gyorgy.
Bloomington, Indiana; London: Indiana University Press, 1979.
338p. map. bibliog.
Vernon V. Aspaturian's opening essay, 'Eastern Europe in world perspective'
(p. 1-36) is a useful background piece indicating such things as Czechoslovakia's
(and the other countries') membership of international organizations, socialist or
otherwise, and its level of diplomatic representation. This essay also includes
tables showing the country's trade, foreign aid, arms exports, its place in military
training for other states, seconded personnel, foreign student intake, population
growth, Gross National Product and hard currency deficits. Much of Otto Ulč's
paper, 'Czechoslovakia' (p. 100-20) consists of information given elsewhere, from
the tactics of takeover, through political structure, leadership, foreign policy and
foreign economic relations, to current problems. It is accompanied by a
bibliography. Paul Marer's 'East European economies: achievements, problems,
prospects' (p. 244-89) emphasizes the differences between the countries of the
area and has a great deal of information on the workings of Comecon, trade with
the West, and patterns of agricultural development; this paper is also supported
by statistical tables. Jiri Valenta's 'Eurocommunism in Eastern Europe: promise
or threat?' (p. 290-307) relates the Eurocommunist idea to the events of 1968 in
Czechoslovakia, while Teresa Rakowska-Harmstone's 'Nationalism and integration in Eastern Europe: the dynamics of change' (p. 308-27) analyses the conflict
between the pressure from an unloved Soviet presence and the various national
wills, including due references to the purges and trials of the 1950s and the events
of 1968, viewed as much from a social as a political point of view.

398   **Zealots and rebels: a history of the ruling Communist Party of
Czechoslovakia.**
Zdeněk Suda.   Stanford, California: Hoover Institution Press,
Stanford University, 1980. 412p. bibliog. (Histories of Ruling
Communist Parties; Hoover Institute Publication, no. 234).
Like Jacques Rupnik, Suda also notices the conflict between the Party's twin
experience of Stalinism and the traditions of Western liberalism. Various other

aspects are duly noted and expounded including the fact that the Czechoslovak Communist Party was never outlawed in peacetime; the role of the minorities; and the Party's sense of being the legitimate heir to the workers' movement and later the representative of the largest victor in the Second World War. The author also explores the problems facing the Party: a 'hopelessly outdated political system'; the inconsistencies in the relations between the Czechs and Slovaks; and the failure to make a clean break with the Stalinist past. Suda believes that recent experiences have been so telling that reformism, though dormant, must return, and some hope for this is seen in the sheer size and variety of the Party membership. An outline of the formation, organization and role of all the country's parties, by David W. Paul, can be found in *Political parties of Europe*, edited by Vincent McHale (London: Aldwych Press, 1983).

399 **Histoire du Parti Communiste Tchécoslovaque: des origines à la prise de pouvoir.** (History of the Czechoslovak Communist Party: from the beginnings to the seizure of power.)
Jacques Rupnik. Paris: Presses de la Fondation nationale des sciences politiques, 1981. 288p. bibliog.

Starting from the apparent contradiction that one and the same party has been profoundly Stalinist and capable of a major attempt at liberalization, Rupnik treats its whole history in terms of dichotomies: the Czech dimension and the Slovak dimension; and double background of Moscow-oriented internationalism and the experience of pre-War Czechoslovak parliamentary democracy; unwavering pro-Sovietism and deep-seated nationalism; the rough split between worker-leaders and intellectual leaders and their respective leaning to Moscow or Prague or, among the Slovaks, to Prague or Bratislava, respectively. An interesting discussion concerns the question of whether it should be accepted that the take-over was, as is customarily accepted, in 1948 with the visible change of government, or whether it should be put back to 1945. The bibliography contains a number of sections and is sub-divided into communist and non-communist sources. It has recently been announced that an account of Czechoslovakia's Marxist régime by the same author is to appear in English in 1985 (London: Frances Pinter).

400 **The Party statutes of the communist world.**
Edited by W. B. Simons, S. White. Leiden, The Netherlands: Sijthoff, 1984. 554p. (Law in Eastern Europe, no. 27).

Gordon Wightman's contribution to this volume provides the full English text of the statutes of the Communist Party of Czechoslovakia with an introduction containing basic information about the Party and its statute. Some additional reference to the statute is made in S. White's concluding essay which compares all sixteen statutes featured in the volume.

401 **Communist strategy and tactics in Czechoslovakia, 1918-1948.**
Paul E. Zinner. New York, London: Praeger, 1963. 264p.

Zinner is chiefly concerned with the manoeuvring which preceded the Communist take-over in 1948, but his outline of the main stages in the Party's development, even before the war, contributes to an understanding of the events in the years immediately after it. The work is currently available again in a recent reprint (London: Greenwood Press, 1976).

402 **Socialism and democracy in Czechoslovakia, 1945-1948.**
Martin R. Myant. Cambridge, England; London; New Rochelle, New York; Melbourne; Sydney: Cambridge University Press, 1981. 302p. bibliog. (Soviet and East European Studies Series).

Relying heavily on orthodox Czechoslovak communist sources, and ignoring practically all others, this book presents a one-sided view of the events between the end of the last war and the communist take-over in February 1948. It is superficial on the pre-war background and tends to underestimate the Stalinist line of Klement Gottwald and the inevitability of the take-over, given the firmness with which Czechoslovakia fell within the post-war Soviet sphere of influence, and the relative ineffectuality of the other parties at the time.

403 **Politics in Czechoslovakia 1945-1971.**
J. F. N. Bradley. Washington, DC: University Press of America, 1981. 231p. bibliog.

This work, partly periodized, partly thematic, is one of a number of political histories of the country since the war. It opens with an account of the essentially confused period immediately after the war which led up to the Communist take-over in February 1948, and ends with a discussion of federalism, ascribed *ad hominem* to Husák, having first discussed the Dubček era in which Husák had also figured. In between there is an account of such things as the purges of the 1950s, constitutional arrangements and parliament, and security. Tables are included containing election results and lists of the main government officers.

404 **Stalinism. Essays in historical interpretation.**
Edited by Robert C. Tucker. New York: Norton, 1977. 332p.

H. Gordon Skilling has contributed a paper to this volume on the subject of 'Stalinism and Czechoslovak political culture' (p. 257-80) in which he seeks to explain how Stalinism, introduced by Gottwald almost immediately after the communists gained power, could have come about in a country with such a distinct tradition in political culture. The answer is a complex one, based on a number of hypotheses, and includes the perceived weakness of the traditional political culture in its post-war permutation. The 1968 period is seen as a possible return to the more classical tradition, and the Husák régime as a return to a kind of neo-Stalinism.

405 **The Czechoslovak political trials, 1950-1954: the suppressed report of the Dubček government's Commission of Enquiry, 1968.**
Edited with a preface and postscript by Jiří Pelikán. London: Macdonald, 1971. 360p.

One of the larger retrospective issues raised during the Dubček period was the rehabilitation of victims o the trials of the 1950s, to investigate which a commission of enquiry was set up. In the event the commission's findings were feared to be too dangerous to publish, and most members of the commission

130

themselves have paid the price of involvement in an action which could not be sanctioned by those who replaced the Dubček régime. Part of the problem was that the events were too recent and some of the participants on the state's side were still in positions of high office. While actual publication of the report by the exiled former Director of Czechoslovak Television is an overtly political act from an opponent, which the present régime will doubtless never forgive, the trials of the 1950s were an undisputed historical fact. This report, therefore, based on previously closed archival material, offers the historian more than memoirs or hearsay. Some memoirs of the period have also been published and include: *Report on my husband* (ie., Rudolf Slánský – the Slánský trial was perhaps the most notorious of all) by Josefa Slánská (London: Hutchinson, 1969); *Truth will prevail* by Marian Šlingová, the English communist wife of Otto Šling, who was executed with Slánský (London: Merlin Press, 1968); and *On Trial* by Arthur London (London: Macdonald, 1968).

406 **The communist states in disarray 1965-1971**
Edited by Adam Bromke, Teresa Rakowska-Harmstone.
Minneapolis, Minnesota: University of Minnesota Press, 1972.
363p.

H. Gordon Skilling's 'Czechoslovakia' (p. 43-75) assesses the nature and extent of conflict within the ruling Communist Party under Antonín Novotný and Alexander Dubček. Skilling seeks to evaluate the latter's performance as a tightrope-walker balancing between the contrary pulls of domestic reform and external pressure, chiefly from the Soviet Union, the changing attitudes of which before, during, and after, the critical 1967-69 period are also described.

407 **East Central Europe: yesterday – today – tomorrow.**
Edited by Milorad M. Drachkovitch.   Stanford, California:
Hoover Institution Press, Stanford University, 1982. 417p.

The book is in two parts, part 1 deals with: general aspects; past trends and future prospects (conjectural); the region and Eurocommunism; the area as an active element in the 'Soviet Empire'; aspects of international economics; the role of the area in Soviet foreign policy; and the workings of the Warsaw Pact. Czechoslovakia is involved *passim* throughout the account. Part 2 looks at the separate countries and chapter 12 by Zdenek Suda is on Czechoslovakia, 'an aborted reform' (p. 243-65). In the context of specifically Czechoslovak social and political culture it seeks to solve the enigma of the 1968 reform movement as a manifestation of 'civilised politics' after twenty years of 'oppressive dictatorship and ruthless abuse of power'. For the period since, it looks at changes in the views of the opposition and explains the features (uncoordinated leadership, uncertain popular pressure, and the unpredictable future of the Soviet Union) which the author sees as underlying the uncertainty of future developments in Czechoslovakia itself.

408   **Political grouping in the Czechoslovak reform movement.**
Vladimír V. Kusin.   London; Basingstoke, England: Macmillan,
1972. 224p.

This might better have been called 'Political grouping in the time of the
Czechoslovak reform movement', since it shows not only the extent of groups
essentially at one with the idea of reform, but also deals with opposition to it. The
importance of the work is its broad coverage of non-Communist Party and non-
government bodies, beginning with a characterization of 'the Czech worker' and
then discussing such groups as farmers, the intelligentsia, young people and
students, national minorities, other political parties and non-party pressure
groups, and the churches. Included in the work is an almost complete list showing
the vast variety of organizations.

409   **Reform and change in the Czechoslovak political system: January-
August 1968.**
Alex Pravda.   Beverly Hills, California; London: Sage, 1975.
bibliog. (Sage Research Papers in the Social Sciences;
Contemporary European Studies, vol. 3).

Pravda avoids detailed rehearsal of the events of 1968, since these are well-
covered elsewhere. His main concern is with the actual developments of reform
and change – proposals, their synthesis and the degree to which they were put
into practice – with the notion in the background that they are of significance to
the comparative politics of communism. Comparison is, after all, worthwhile
since, despite many similarities, no two communist régimes are as alike as the
simplest traditional view would suggest. Another account of the system by the
same author is to be found in *Marxist governments: a world survey*, edited by
Bogdan Szajkowski (London: Macmillan, 1981).

410   **The secret Vysočany congress: proceedings and documents of the
Extraordinary Fourteenth Congress of the Communist Party of
Czechoslovakia, 22 August 1968.**
Edited and with an introduction by Jiří Pelikán, translated by
George Theiner, Deryck Viney.   London: Allen Lane, Penguin
Press, 1971. 304p.

The editor of this volume is a well-known émigré hostile to the Husák régime.
The Vysočany congress was extraordinary in more senses than one; first in having
been successfully convened at all in the wake of the Soviet intervention of the day
before, and secondly in having been declared retrospectively null and void, as if it
simply had not occurred. The proceedings and the various relevant other
documents will only be of interest to the historian, but the introduction and
scattered commentary provides the background to this extraordinary event. The
record in English of the Party congress which the régime does call the fourteenth,
*The speeches and resolutions of the 14th congress of the Communist Party of
Czechoslovakia (May 24th-29th, 1971)*, was published in Prague by Orbis (1971),
as other records of subsequent congresses have been.

411 **Eastern Europe and European security: a Foreign Policy Research Institute book.**
William R. Kintner, Wolfgang Klaiber, foreword by William E. Griffith. New York: Dunellen, 1971. 393p. bibliog.

Since it is the security aspect which is paramount here, the countries of Eastern Europe are discussed only in the context of periods and events which somehow jeopardized, or were perceived as jeopardizing, security. In Czechoslovakia's case this means an analysis of those elements in the 'quiet revolution of 1968' which, from the point of view of its allies, constituted such a threat. The authors therefore discuss the elimination of that threat by the Warsaw Pact intervention, and the consequences, including the return to normal and the apparent permanent stationing of Soviet troops in the country (see chapter 14, p. 271-94).

412 **The East European predicament: changing patterns in Poland, Czechoslovakia and Romania**
Peter Summerscale. Aldershot, England: Gower; New York: St. Martin's Press, 1982. 174p.

The author explicitly compares the political and economic development of the three countries. It is the external dimensions that are paramount, most notably Soviet policy, but also the European security conferences (Helsinki, for example). Internal political and economic pressures are also discussed, with the conclusion that some weaknesses are so deep-seated that change and reform are inevitable.

413 **Political culture and communist studies.**
Edited by Archie Brown. London: Macmillan, in association with St. Antony's College, Oxford, 1984. 211p.

Two papers in this volume deal with the political culture of Czechoslovakia: H. Gordon Skilling's 'Czechoslovakia political culture: pluralism in an international context' (p. 115-33); and David W. Paul's 'Czechoslovakia's political culture reconsidered' (p. 134-48). Together they constitute a debate on the topic with Skilling making reference to Paul's earlier work, and Paul responding in part to the Skilling paper. Both consider the continuity, or otherwise, of pluralism in Czech and Slovak political culture, with relation to interior and exterior forces. In the background discussion, Paul has slightly more to say on the Slovak tradition.

414 **Political culture and political change in communist states.**
Edited by Archie Brown, Jack Gray. London; Basingstoke, England: Macmillan, 1979. 2nd ed. 286p.

The volume includes Archie Brown and Gordon Wightman's 'Czechoslovakia: revival and retreat' (p. 159-96) which is an original attempt to account, at least partially, for the recent history of the country, especially the events of 1968, in terms of the political culture of the Czechs and Slovaks. In particular, it locates those points in early Czech and Slovak history which have been perceived at different times as the most and least glorious and the personages, past and present (1968), who enjoyed the greatest esteem among the respective nations. The survey results are set out in tabular form.

415 **The world economy and elite political strategies in Czechoslovakia, Hungary and Poland.**

Zvi Gitelman. In: *East-West relations and the future of Eastern Europe: politics and economics.* Edited by Morris Bornstein, Zvi Gitelman, William Zimmerman. London: George Allen & Unwin, 1981, p. 127-61.

This paper is concerned with the distinctive political strategies being pursued in the three countries. The three main factors behind the varied approaches are the different political constellations in charge after the respective countries' upheavals of recent years, the different effects of Western economic developments, and different patterns of consumer aspirations.

416 **The communist states in the era of détente, 1971-1977.**

Edited by Adam Bromke, Derry Novak. Oakville, Ontario: Mosaic Press, [1978]. 306p.

Chapter 5, 'Czechoslovakia' (p. 89-110) by H. Gordon Skilling, sees the country as 'a critical index' of Eastern European attitudes to détente, or the provisions of the Helsinki and later agreements, since its politics are furthest away from the Helsinki principles and show least sign of being affected by détente. The negative features of the Husák régime are interpreted as returns to the past of, variously, Novotný and Gottwald. The attitude to Helsinki was one of welcome, but chiefly because it recognized, if so interpreted, the territorial and political status quo, and placed sovereignty and non-interference above foreign concern for human rights. Czechoslovakia's initiatives at follow-up conferences are picked out, and the epilogue introduces the activities of the Charter 77 human rights group.

417 **Eastern Europe: political crisis and legitimation.**

Edited by Paul G. Lewis. London, Sydney: Croom Helm: 1984. 202p.

The volume includes Mark Wright's 'Ideology and power in the Czechoslovak political system' (p. 111-53) which makes out an interesting case for the essential consistency of Czechoslovak politics, to which the concept of 'workerism' is central. Workerism is described as a narrow creed, 'severely limiting the vitality and responsiveness of the elite', and certainly not to be interpreted as worker control. Unlike most modern histories of the post-war period, Wright makes light of the events of 1968, as a temporary aberration from a generally straight line brought about by a collapse of the regular system of Czechoslovak power politics. The concept of 'legitimacy', a central topic in the book as a whole, is seen to be of doubtful value in the context of Czechoslovak politics.

418 **Communist armies in politics.**

Edited by Jonathan R. Adelman. Boulder, Colorado: Westview Press, 1982. 225p. (Westview Special Studies).

'This book analyzes the historical and contemporary political roles of armies in the majority of the world's Communist countries, stressing the problems faced and overcome by Communist parties in the creation and development of legitimate and effective armies.' The particularly distinctive relation between the

Czechoslovak People's Army and the political power in the land (the two are seen to be largely isolated from each other) is described by Jiri Valenta and Condoleezza Rice (p. 129-48). The special factors are too numerous to mention, but the obvious ones include: the absence of Soviet troops from the country between 1945 and 1968; the continuity of the Czech fighting force through the war, in exile, but with many fighting in the USSR; and the complication of Slovakia's wartime 'independence' with an army of its own, initially fighting on the German side. Subsequent developments are broken down into five discernible periods, ending with the contemporary recruitment difficulties.

419 **Politics in Czechoslovakia.**
Otto Ulč, foreword by Jan F. Triska.   San Francisco: W. H.
Freeman, 1974. 181p. bibliog.
Despite its title, this work more or less solely concerns the politics of the period around 1968, though there is some historical perspective and some comparison with other socialist states in Europe. The minor parties and other party-like groups of the period are also discussed, as are many factors which are really only indirectly political: welfare; the role of women in society; incomes; car ownership; circulation of the periodical press; the media; and censorship. An unusual view which is presented is that Czechoslovakia poses a threat to the Soviet Union because of its tradition of limited sovereignty and because of the Czechs' latent capacity for violence, last seen in the post-war expulsion of the Germans. Another less common contribution is the inclusion of many of the best-known cartoons and jokes of the period.

420 **Foreign and domestic policy in Eastern Europe in the 1980s: trends and prospects.**
Edited by Michael J. Sodaro, Sharon L. Wolchik.   London;
Basingstoke, England: Macmillan, 1983. 265p.
The only contribution confined solely to Czechoslovakia is Wolchik's 'The scientific-technological revolution and the role of specialist elites in policy-making in Czechoslovakia' (p. 111-32). The author discusses the function of expertise and experts in policy-making and evaluates their changing role in Czechoslovakia, with particular emphasis on the shaping of demographic policy through due processes of research, consultation and recommendation. This is the most recent account of current pronatalist policy, including attitudes to abortion and maternity grants. One general conclusion of the work is that the ruling party élite does benefit from the work of the country's experts, while the latter, whatever their private attitude to the régime, accept the situation out of an appreciation of being appreciated.

421 **Legislative politics in Czechoslovakia.**
Otto Ulč.   In: *Communist legislatures in comparative perspective.*
Edited by Daniel Nelson, Stephen White. London; Basingstoke,
England: Macmillan, 1982, p. 111-24. bibliog.
The author's principal objective is to demonstrate the non-separation of the legislative and executive branches of the state, the former being subordinate to the latter. The legislative bodies are described as passing rather than creating

Politics, Opposition and Dissent

laws, and the executive itself is seen as subordinate to the will of the Communist Party. Much of the discussion revolves around what might have been, and the situation which temporarily existed in 1968, as opposed to the present *de facto* conditions relating, for example, to the legislature, the electoral system and the performance of elected representatives. The article contains a list of parliamentary committees (although Ulč is scathing about their work), and provides some idea of the nature of the Federal Assembly, the national assemblies and the National Front, the umbrella body under which politics are conducted.

422 The politics of culture.
   Antonín J. Liehm, translated by Peter Kussi, with an introduction by Jean-Paul Sartre, translated by Helen R. Land. New York: Grove Press, 1968. 412p.
Based on interviews, this is a collection of intellectual biographies of fifteen writers and other Czech and Slovak intellectuals involved directly in the Prague Spring.

423 Opposition in Eastern Europe.
   Edited by Rudolf L. Tőkés. London; Basingstoke, England: Macmillan, 1979. 306p. (St. Antony's/Macmillan Series).
A set of mixed papers on opposition and dissent in Czechoslovakia and three other Central European socialist states, one of which, by Vladimir V. Kusin, is devoted solely to Czechoslovakia in the decade after the 1968 Soviet intervention. The book also includes four other essays by the editor himself, Iván Szelényi, Alex Pravda and Paul G. Lewis, respectively, which deal with broader topics (such as human rights, socialist opposition, dissent in industry and opposition among the peasantry); Czechoslovakia is referred to in these contributions, often comparatively. Most of the text is factual, with some conjecture as to the cases of individual manifestations of dissent and possible future sources. Several writers are at pains to explain some of the key terms (human rights, socialist opposition) as perceived in the area. In Kusin's paper, the topic is periodized, with a special section outlining the short history of Charter 77, but perhaps overestimating public response to it.

424 Socialist opposition in Eastern Europe: the Czechoslovak example.
   Jiří Pelikán, translated by Marian Sling, V. Tosek, R. Tosek. London: Allison & Busby, 1976. 221p. (Motive Series).
The 'socialist opposition' of the title is not an abstract noun, but a label for that brand of dissidents which has avowed to pursue further the aims of the reform-minded leadership of 1968. In the main they are journalists and intellectuals currently banned from their previous positions, if not actually in prison, who have mapped out a programme which, though undoubtedly socialist, could never be tolerated by the present régime. Czechoslovak opposition, and the government's responses to it, are related variously to other opposition trends elsewhere in Eastern Europe, and to détente and the political thinking of West Europeans, especially West-European socialists. Half of the book consists of documents (including manifestos and open letters) from the opposition movement.

136

425 **White Paper on Czechoslovakia.**
International Committee for the Support of Charter 77 in
Czechoslovakia. Paris: The Committee, 1977. 269p. map.

Opening with a thumb-nail sketch of Czechoslovakia's history, population, trade
and foreign policy, the book proper carries an introduction on its purpose and a
massive corpus of authentic documents in English translation (a parallel version
exists in French). The objective is to give a hearing to those who are 'at the wrong
end of the stick' in the human rights debate and to provide, through those people,
their statements, testimonies, letters and appeals, evidence of the non-
implementation of human rights in Czechoslovakia since the Helsinki Conference
of 1975. Official attitudes are also included in the form of excerpts from the
Czechoslovak constitution, press reports and replies to the various petitioners.
The international dimension is explored through documents on, for example,
access to the foreign press, expulsions from the country and travel restrictions
placed on certain individuals. It is the compilers' stated policy to let the
documents speak for themselves, with as little editorial comment as possible. The
Charter 77, which the International Committee which published this work
supports, is now thought of as a movement of dissidents, but properly it is the title
of a single document, which is duly reproduced here in unabridged form.

426 **Since the Prague Spring: Charter 77 and the struggle for human
rights in Czechoslovakia.**
Edited by Hans-Peter Riese, foreword by Arthur Miller, translated
from the Czech by Eugen Loebl. New York: Vintage Books;
Toronto: Random House, 1979. 208p.

Just as the events of 1968 caught the imagination of many outsiders and made it
one of the most written-about periods of Czechoslovak history, so too its
aftermath, in the shape of the movement that has become known by the name of
one of its documents, Charter 77, attracts a great deal of curiosity and sympathy
from outside. Indeed the movement possibly draws more attention outside than
inside the country where there is a common belief that 'least said soonest
mended', however 'typically Czech' that may seem to some. While there already
exists a body of interpretive literature on Charter 77 and the socialist opposition,
the best idea of what any particular brand of opposition stands for comes from its
own writing, hence this volume, which reproduces a number of relevant
documents, letters and appeals, including the Charter itself. A larger, partly
overlapping collection of documents, classified by general thematic area, was
published in 1977 by the International Committee for the Support of Charter 77 in
Czechoslovakia as the *White Paper on Czechoslovakia* (q.v.) and was intended to
make a contribution to the post-Helsinki discussion of human rights.

427 **Charter 77 and human rights in Czechoslovakia.**
H. Gordon Skilling. London: George Allen & Unwin, 1981.
380p. bibliog.

With the possible exception of some of the Polish dissident groups, Charter 77 is
perhaps the best known opposition group (though some would doubtless
disapprove of such a label) in Eastern Europe. It has been active on many fronts
and its members have had to suffer domiciliary searches, expulsion from work and
imprisonment. They are the major thorn in the side of the régime and have had

considerable success in getting their activities publicized. They have to face not only the hostility of the régime, but also some hostility from fellow citizens who, while they may share the group's views, feel that change can be brought about, just as successfully in the long term, by more discreet action. In the face of the general public's adaptability (cf. item no. 371) any optimism on either side is probably misplaced. Skilling's book is a revealing account of all the Chartists' wide-ranging activities.

428   **Writers against rulers.**
Dušan Hamšík, translated by D. Orpington, introduction by W. L. Webb.   London: Hutchinson, 1971. 208p.

The Fourth Congress of the Union of Writers is widely remembered as one of the harbingers of the 1968 reform movement. A great deal of literary and political debate went on, of course, outside the narrow time-span of the congress, and these general developments, during which politics and literature became even more entwined than is habitual in the Czech context, are the topic of this book of memoirs. Being a personal recollection of events at, around and after the congress, the tone is sometimes almost gossipy. The book, however, presents a personal insight into the proceedings of the congress, without seeking to be either a history or a set of minutes, and also provides, *inter alia*, the background to the demise of the main literary journal *Literární noviny* and the rise and demise of its successor *Literární listy*, including the role of censorship. The appendix contains translations of some of the speeches by those who gained notoriety on the reform side between 1967 and 1969 and the notes provide a key to some of the main literary and political personalities and concepts relevant to the period.

429   **The power and the powerless: citizens against the state in central eastern Europe.**
Václav Havel (et al.), edited by John Keane, with an introduction by Steven Lukes.   London: Hutchinson, 1985. 228p.

The title of this collection of eleven essays is the same as that given by Havel to his own paper. The other contributions, all of them essays on ideology, democracy, civil liberty and the law, represent answers to the various questions he raises and discuss the prospects for change. The introduction places the contents of all the contributions in their historical context, between Charter 77 (the text of which is given) and the birth of Solidarity in Poland. The contributors are all Czechs and the book includes background notes on each of them.

Foreign Relations
and Contacts

430 Britain and Czechoslovakia: a study in contacts.
Josef V. Polišenský.   Prague: Orbis, 1968. 2nd rev. ed. 98p.
bibliog.

The 'contacts' of the title have a long and respectable history, though the first of
many fascinating facts in this slim volume does not count as a contact proper; this
is Alfred the Great's *Anglo-Saxon Chronicle*, where he writes about the Slavs. As
Polišenský says in the introduction, there are many manifestations of contact, but
he concentrates, in the space available, on 'a mixed company of medieval princes
and princesses, bishops and revolutionaries, industrial pioneers, diplomats,
scholars and politicians'. He also includes an outline of indirect contacts, ie., the
picture of each country in the other's literature. The book ends (p. 86-92) with a
useful comparative chronology of the two countries, and the work contains some
relevant illustrations. The volume is, of course, not widely available, perhaps no
more than one of its predecessors, 'The Czechs and the English', chapter 2 in the
wartime *Czechoslovakia* by Cecily Mackworth and Jan Stranský (London:
Macdonald, [n.d.], p. 48-60), but the British origins of the latter may mean it can
still be found.

431 Britain and the origins of the new Europe, 1914-1918.
Kenneth J. Calder.   Cambridge, England: Cambridge University
Press, 1976. 268p. (International Studies Series).

The Czechs and Slovaks were only two of the nations with émigré organizations
claiming to represent them during the First World War with which the British
government had dealings. Britain was primarily concerned with winning the war
and therefore sought the collaboration of the non-independent nations. After the
ending of hostilities the reconstruction of Europe out of the ruins of the two great
empires of Austria and Russia became the main objective and Britain again had
contacts with the non-independent nations. The book draws largely on archival
material including British government papers and the private papers of leading

civil servants. A book on American diplomacy in the same period, also dealing generously with the Czechs and Slovaks is Victor S. Mamatey's *The United States and East Central Europe, 1914-1918: a study in Wilsonian diplomacy and propaganda* (Princeton, New Jersey: Princeton University Press, 1957. 431p.).

432 Canada and Czechoslovakia.
Josef Vincent Polišenský, translated from the Czech by Jessie Kocmannová. Prague: Orbis, 1967. 60p. bibliog.

Examines Canadian-Czechoslovak relations from prehistory to the mid-19th century – relations of a frequently but understandably tenuous nature – then the involvement of North American Czechs and Slovaks in the movement for Czechoslovak independence, and finally relations, political, cultural and commercial, between the two states. Illustrations and a comparative chronology of the histories of the two countries are included.

433 Czechs and Germans: a study of the struggle in the historic provinces of Bohemia and Moravia.
Elizabeth Wiskemann. London, Melbourne, Toronto: Macmillan; New York: St. Martin's Press, 1967. 2nd ed. 299p. maps. bibliog.

Although written in the heat of the events leading up to the war (the 1st edition was published in 1938), this work is still regarded by many as a classic. It traces the full history of the rivalries, animosities and perfidies between the two nations and the conflicting claims and counter-claims to dominance in the Lands of the Czech Crown, from the prehistoric movements of Germanic tribes down to the 20th century. It is factually sound and, for the modern age, is based on the author's broad range of contacts among both communities. The author presents a wide-ranging picture, portraying economic and cultural, as well as political aspects. Wiskemann is also frank in admitting doubt as to the correctness of some of the information she was given – doubts not misplaced in the event.

434 Confrontation in Central Europe: Weimar Germany and Czechoslovakia.
F. Gregory Campbell. Chicago, London: University of Chicago Press, 1975. (Midway Reprint 1978.) 383p. bibliog.

The Sudeten crisis was a direct product of the existence of a large German minority within Czechoslovakia. An account of how that had come about through the incorporation of large numbers of Germans within the new post-1918 republic, the frontiers of which were based on history, not demography, is given in this work, which goes one better and describes first the respective national revivals in the 18th and 19th centuries and the roles of Czechs, Slovaks and Germans during the Great War. The actual political history of the Czechoslovak Germans within the Republic is traced from the shortlived government of a German-Bohemian province, autonomous within Austria, which declared its capital to be Reichenberg (Liberec), to the emergence of Konrad Henlein at the head of a Germany-orientated 'Sudeten-German Homeland Front' in October 1933.

435   The Sudeten problem 1933-1938: 'Volkstumpolitik' and the formulation of Nazi foreign policy.
Ronald M. Smelser.   Folkestone, England: Dawson, 1975. 324p. bibliog.

Before the post-war expulsion of Germans from Czechoslovakia there had been so many of them in the country that it is almost impossible to talk of a minority in any other than a purely mathematical sense. At times there were those who sought to (re-)institute a separate German Bohemia. At all events, they were so numerous as to create a major problem for the Czechoslovak government when Nazism took hold in Germany and met a sympathetic echo in many a Czechoslovak (Sudeten) German. This work relates the evolution of the Sudeten crisis (which ultimately led to the cession of Czechoslovak territory to the German Reich) to the formulation of Nazi Germany's foreign policy, and effectively contains the political biography of Konrad Henlein, the Sudeten German leader in Czechoslovakia, whose party won the largest number of votes of any party in the 1935 elections; this alone gives some idea of the magnitude of the problem for inter-war Czechoslovakia.

436   The transfer of the Sudeten Germans: a study of Czech-German relations, 1933-1962.
Radomír Luža.   London: Routledge & Kegan Paul, 1964. 365p. maps. bibliog.

The pre-history to this root-and-branch upheaval of a vast number of Sudeten Germans after the last war is given in the two preceding entries, but Luža also rehearses them as a vital element in his technically narrower subject. Luža sees the transfer as the 'last act of the long German-Czech dispute' and as 'a response to circumstances created by the Sudeten Germans themselves and implicit in the Nazi war regime'. There were, and still are, some doubts as to the morality of the enterprise, but it was a genuinely popular solution to their problems among the Czechs and the alternatives did not bear contemplation. By the end of 1946 the number of Germans in the Czech Lands was less than one tenth of the numbers in 1930 (Luža advises caution over many of his statistics because of the impossibility of verifying so many of them, but these at least seem to be correct). In gradually changing circumstances, many more Germans have left since. Other topics relevant to the study are also dealt with, if briefly, namely the fate of the Jews and how they figure in various statistics, and the post-expulsion activities of those Sudeten Germans, particularly in West Germany, who will not come to terms with the situation.

437   Czechs, Magyars, Slovaks.
Paul Ignotus.   Political Quarterly, vol. 40, no. 2 (April-June 1969), p. 187-204.

A whimsical memoir of Czechoslovak and Hungarian history by a Hungarian émigré which sets out from a comic contrast of Czechs and Hungarians as bourgeois and gentry, tax-collectors and tax-dodgers, pedagogues and playboys, respectively, and a host of other contrasting epithets, in many of which there is more than a grain of truth. The author is concerned with: Czechoslovak-Hungarian relations during the First Republic, especially the issue of Southern Slovakia with its Hungarian population; the Hungarian uprising of 1956 and the

141

'Prague Spring' of 1968; and presents a condescending view of the Slovaks as a history-making nation.

438 **Relationships between Romanians, Czechs and Slovaks (1848-1914).**
Lucian Boia. Bucharest: Editura Academiei Republicii Socialiste
România, 1977, 157p. (Biblioteca Historica Romanie, no. 54).
This work concentrates on the political relations between the Romanians and the Czechs and even more so the Slovaks, showing how the generations of contact before the Great War represented the precursor to the interwar Little Entente (with Yugoslavia) and, ultimately, of the thirty years of cooperation and friendship that have followed the Second World War. United by their respective campaigns for autonomy within Austro-Hungary, the nations continue to be united economically and politically (this overstatement of the present state of affairs reflects the tone of the whole work and is entirely suited to this kind of anniversary publication).

439 **The Little Entente: sixty years later.**
Piotr Wandycz. *Slavonic and East European Review*, vol. 59,
no. 4 (Oct. 1981), p. 548-64.
The Little Entente, born in 1920, consolidated in 1921, was a system of diplomatic and economic agreements between Czechoslovakia, Yugoslavia and Romania. This article considers such issues as how far the Entente was a barrier against Hungary or a tool in French foreign policy and assesses the many domestic and foreign policy aspects which contributed to its weakness, as well as noting such strengths and successes as it had. The introductory paragraphs contain a useful survey of the disparate literature dealing with the Entente.

440 **Czechoslovak-Polish relations, 1918-1939: a selected and annotated
bibliography.**
Chester Michael Nowak. Stanford, California: Hoover Institution
Press, 1976. 219p. (Hoover Institution Bibliographical Series,
no. 55).
An annotated bibliography of 869 publications up to 1972. It is a good source for works relating not just to the ups and downs of the two countries' political and economic relations, but also to individual border areas (Teschen, Spiš, Orava) that have mixed populations on both sides of the frontier.

441 **Czechoslovak-Polish confederation: a Czech view.**
Josef Kalvoda. *Kosmas*, vol. 1, no. 2 (winter 1982), p. 1-14.
As the author points out, a confederation of the kind named in the title has often been mooted (most recently in 1968), but has never materialized. This article summarizes the events and personalities which stood in the way of such a confederation between the wars, and deals in detail with the serious consideration of the idea which went on during the Second World War, leading up to a joint declaration in fourteen points published in 1942. It then describes the demise of the idea through Soviet opposition and renewed Polish-Czechoslovak distrust, arising chiefly out of Beneš's willingness to reach an accommodation with the

Foreign Relations and Contacts

Soviet Union (the alliance of 1944). The sorry history of Polish-Czechoslovak
relations does not prevent the author from wishfully thinking that some version of
the old idea may yet come to pass. The footnotes contain useful references to
earlier works on the subject.

442   **The United States in Prague, 1945-1948.**
      Walter Ullmann.   Boulder, Colorado: East European Quarterly.
      Distributed by Columbia University Press, New York, 1978. 205p.
      bibliog. (East European Monographs, no. 36).
The introduction provides a potted account of Czechoslovak-American bilateral
contacts up to the Second World War, but the body of the book, with its narrow
time-scale, is specifically unilateral, given the inaccessibility to the author of
relevant archival material. However, it goes beyond just the rather inadequate
American diplomatic role, with an underfinanced and under-staffed Embassy, and
considers all internal political and cultural trends and events from both the point
of view of the then American response, if any, and from a retrospective view of
what might have been in other circumstances. The work includes accounts of two
major events in which the United States was directly involved, either as one of the
Allies (the expulsion of the Germans) or as an initiator of post-war aid
programmes (the Marshall Plan, which Czechoslovakia rejected). The first, brief,
chapter deals with the messy background to America's failure to be involved more
deeply, as it easily could have been, in Czechoslovakia's liberation.

443   **The American non-policy towards Eastern Europe 1943-1947.**
      Geir Lundestad.   Tromsö, Bergen, Norway; Oslo:
      Universitetsforlaget. Distributed by Global Book Resources,
      London, and Columbia University Press, New York, 1978. 634p.
      bibliog.
Presents an unusual angle from which to look at Eastern European history as war
ended and peace began but offers a more useful explanation of later attitudes for
the author has no axe to grind on behalf of either side. In fact, he offers a critical
appraisal of both main trends in cold-war historiography (traditionalists who
apportion most blame to the Russians and revisionists who tend to blame the
Americans), before making his own analysis, which seeks to avoid blame of one
and defense of the other. The separate chapter on Czechoslovakia in American
policy (p. 149-82) reveals a history of ambiguous responses to the main events and
excessive optimism on the part of the Americans, at least up to late 1945. The
outcome of the period covered in the book is the stopping of all American aid,
owing largely to economic considerations, especially Czechoslovakia's programme
of nationalization, though the whole story is of much greater complexity. Neither
side comes off with credit.

444   **Communist powers and sub-Saharan Africa.**
      Edited by Thomas H. Henrikson.   Stanford, California: Hoover
      Institution Press, Stanford University, 1981. 137p.
The role of the states of Eastern Europe is studied en bloc by Roger E. Kanet
(p. 23-56) who perceives the greater significance of political and ideological
involvement than economic relations. The latter are, however, given most

143

attention, even though the total trade involvement is relatively minor. Other topics covered are diplomatic relations and military aid; most of the information is restated in tables. A more recent article, considering the growing involvement of Eastern Europe in Third World trade, for example, also by Kanet, is included in Michael J. Sodaro and Sharon L. Wolchik's (eds.) *Foreign and domestic policy in Eastern Europe in the 1980s: trends and prospects* (London: Macmillan, 1983. p. 234-59) (q.v.) and here Czechoslovak participation is chiefly to do with arms deliveries.

445 **The foreign policies of Eastern Europe: domestic and international determinants.**
Edited by James A. Kuhlman. Leiden, The Netherlands: Sijthoff, 1978. 302p. (East-West Perspectives, no. 4).

One of the foreign policy papers contained in this volume is Dennis C. Pirages' 'Resources, technology and foreign policy behaviour: the Czechoslovak experience' (p. 57-78) which separates the country from the others discussed, on the grounds that it has a much more transparent and more easily explained foreign policy. The historic attitude to the Russians, socialism (with a small *s*) and the liberation of 1945, the strong Soviet influence on the economy in the 1960s which led to decline and then reform, the Soviet decision to intervene militarily in 1968 and the Czech decision not to resist, are all elements that underpin the consistency of Czechoslovakia's foreign policy towards the Soviet Union. The title's reference to resources and technology reflects the country's difficulties in acquisition and renewal, both blamed on the increased Soviet domination of Czechoslovakia's foreign trade. For another general work, see Charles Gati's *The international politics of Eastern Europe* (New York: Praeger, 1976. 313p.).

446 **East-West relations and the future of Eastern Europe: politics and economics.**
Edited by Morris Bornstein, Zvi Gitelman, William Zimmerman. London: George Allen & Unwin, 1981. 301p.

Only the first three parts (out of four) are directly relevant to Czechoslovakia, and of these the first two are the most general, with discussions of the issues involved in East-West relations and prospects for the future. The third section is principally concerned with East-West interdependence, the world economy and 'elite political strategies'; in both these sections Czechoslovakia is given special attention as one of the countries specifically involved with the West. There are several tables of data on trade and the economies of the region, in which Czechoslovakia receives separate attention.

447 **The Czechoslovak Socialist Republic.**
Zdenek Suda. Baltimore, Maryland: Johns Hopkins University Press, 1969. 180p. map. bibliog. (Integration and Community Building in Eastern Europe).

Suda, in line with the aims of the series of which this is a volume, seeks to explain the genesis and development of Czechoslovakia's foreign relations since it became a communist party-state. The account is periodized into seven segments, from the time before the communists took over, through the first years after 1948, the period of rapid socialization, post-Stalinism, the period of proposed economic reform, the 'Prague Spring' experiment, down to the Soviet intervention and its aftermath (these are not all the terms in which Suda expresses the division). Czechoslovakia is viewed as a special case in terms of economic and political integration, since its pre-war traditions had been quite different from those in the other party-states. The bibliography contains a number of useful titles of a date generally earlier than most included in the present bibliography, though some are reproduced here too.

448 **Czechoslovakia 1968: reform, repression and resistance.**
Philip Windsor, Adam Roberts, foreword by Alastair
Buchan. London: Chatto & Windus for the Institute for Strategic
Studies; Toronto: Clarke, Irwin, 1969. 200p. map.

This is essentially a combined study of Czechoslovak-Soviet relations as they evolved in the course of 1968 (Windsor) and of the popular response to the Soviet intervention – large-scale national unity expressing itself in passive resistance (Roberts). Underlying the study is the belief in the value of détente and a desire to assess how far it is impaired by such events and how much the events themselves provide an object lesson on the implications for the West of crises in the East. The appendixes consist of translations of some of the major documents of the period from both the Czechoslovak side and that of its allies.

449 **Red star over Prague.**
Frantisek August, David Rees, introduction by David Rees.
London: Sherwood Press 1984. 176p.

Another 'inside view' of post-war Czechoslovak history, the first-named author having been a senior officer in the *StB* (Státní bezpečnost, State Security, ie., the secret police). It portrays the Soviet Union as almost the sole engineer of events in Czechoslovakia, from the 'coup d'état' of February 1948 (elsewhere referred to as a 'victory' or 'take-over'), through the Stalinist 1950s, to the events of August 1968 and after, with the exception of the experiment that preceded the August invasion. It goes into particular detail over the Stalin era and the trials, and devotes a whole chapter to the secret police. Part four contains an account of alleged Soviet plans for annexation of Czechoslovakia, a possibility which, in the present writer's experience, is not usually accorded any great credence. The source of the account of such plans is a new émigré body, as the authors repeatedly point out, while conceding that there could be something in the notion. Appendixes give a structural breakdown and diagram of the Interior Ministry (which oversees the *StB*) and a diagram of the organization of the Czechoslovak foreign intelligence service.

450 **The Soviet bloc: unity and conflict.**
Zbigniew K. Brzezinski. Cambridge, Massachusetts: Harvard
University Press, 1974. 5th printing of 1967 rev. enlarged ed. 599p.
bibliog.

A now standard work by a leading American politician, which offers the thesis, or wishful thinking, that the Soviet bloc is not the monolith it is sometimes portrayed as, for which there are some grounds. Czechoslovakia receives good coverage *passim*, both in its own right (various aspects of post-war history and society), and in its relations within the bloc (see index).

451 **The Soviet Union and the Czechoslovak Army, 1948-1983: uncertain alliance.**
Condoleezza Rice.   Princeton, New Jersey: Princeton University Press, 1984. 303p.

The Czechoslovak People's Army (ČSLA) is fully integrated into the forces of the Warsaw Pact and its structure is modelled fairly closely on that of the Soviet Union. This work is concerned with the ambiguities that arise out of the Czechoslovak Army's dual role of defence of the nation and service to the 'socialist alliance', with the interaction between the civil and military power in the land, and with the relations of the military élite to the society which it serves. The author begins with the Communist take-over in 1948 and traces developments to the 'years of crisis' of 1968-69 before considering the subsequent period right down to the present.

452 **Czechoslovakia's role in Soviet strategy.**
Josef Kalvoda.   Washington, DC: University Press of America, 1978. 381p.

This is a somewhat idiosyncratic history of Soviet interest in Czechoslovakia, which arose out of the country's geographical position, its arms and other industries, and, latterly, its ability to become involved in Soviet-backed aid plans to third-world revolutionary forces. Kalvoda blames Beneš for the passage of Czechoslovakia into the Soviet sphere. He also claims that Novotný was ousted for being too liberal for Moscow's liking, and sees Dubček as a Soviet tool. The author certainly exaggerates Czechoslovakia's role as an inspiration for third-world revolutions. The book is included here for its expression of viewpoints which differ conspicuously from the majority.

453 **Soviet foreign policy.**
Robin Edmonds.   Oxford, New York: Oxford University Press, 1983. 285p. maps. bibliog.

Inevitably, many aspects of Czechoslovakia's foreign relations are discussed in the literature in terms of the foreign relations of the entire Soviet bloc, and Czechoslovakia's relations with its main political and economic partner, the USSR, tend to be discussed from the Soviet point of view. This is also the case in a number of similarly titled publications, though in this one Czechoslovakia does earn a section to itself (p. 65-73) in addition to passing references elsewhere. The main concern is with relations as affected by the stationing of Soviet troops in Czechoslovakia, one of the main visible consequences of post-1968 Soviet and Czechoslovak policy.

454 **The Soviet Union and Central Europe in the post-war era: a study in precarious security.**
Kristian Gerner.   Aldershot, England: Gower, 1985. 228p. bibliog.

This study by a Swede takes the political and economic subordination of the states of Eastern Europe to the Soviet Union for granted and proceeds to discuss the various manifestations of instability that there have been within the bloc as the basis of its 'precarious security'. As such it is about Czechoslovakia's, and others', relations with the Soviet bloc-leader, but it stresses the fundamental differences in the political culture of the Soviet Union and some of its allies, including Czechoslovakia. The work, in being a discussion of sources of instability, includes references to the minorities problem, especially the Czechoslovak Hungarians. The comparison between Czechoslovakia, Hungary and Poland notes that 'viewing the whole period 1953-1981 one sees that Czechoslovakia was the last of the three countries trying to walk a national path and the first to fail'. Among the interesting elements of Czechoslovakia's distinctive political culture responsible for this are the traditionally benign view of Russia and traditional obedience to the government. Another work relating Czechoslovakia to Soviet security is Karen Dawisha's 'Soviet security and the role of the military: the 1968 Czechoslovak crisis', *British Journal of Political Science*, vol. 10, no. 3 (July 1980), p. 341-63.

455 **Soviet influence in Eastern Europe: political autonomy and the Warsaw Pact.**
Christopher D. Jones.   New York: Praeger, 1981. 322p. (Studies of Influence in International Relations).

Within the framework of this broadly based volume Czechoslovakia has its part to play as one of the examples of how, according to the author's thesis, Soviet influence boils down to: militarization, the threat and use of military intervention to cement waverings in the alliances among the states of Eastern Europe; the common schooling of Soviet and East European military leaders; and large-scale joint military exercises. The military domination is seen to have replaced the political and economic, although all three are undoubtedly closely interwoven.

456 **The deception game: Czechoslovak intelligence in Soviet political warfare.**
Ladislav Bittman.   Syracuse, New York: Syracuse University Research Corporation, 1972. 246p.

Bittman, who used to be very much on the inside, describes the aims and methods of the Czechoslovak intelligence service and the areas in which it was subordinate to that of the Soviet ally. The Czechs in particular have quite a reputation in this field, a reputation going back at least to the days of Austria, and among other things this work seeks to account for their particular aptitude for the job.

457 **Soviet policy in Eastern Europe.**
Edited by Sarah Meiklejohn Terry. New Haven, Connecticut;
London: Yale University Press, 1984. 375p. (A Council on Foreign
Relations Book).

A number of articles here involve Czechoslovakia from the point of view of
foreign relations, including the country's participation in Soviet energy and
military policies. However, one paper, Jiri Valenta's 'Soviet policy towards
Hungary and Czechoslovakia' (p. 93-124) takes a narrower view of the subject; it
is based on the comparison of the run-up and aftermath of the Soviet armed
interventions in the two countries. On the Czechoslovak side it notes the
country's changed role in relations with the Third World and the sources of
possible future instability, mostly economic in origin.

458 **Soviet-East European dilemmas: coercion, competition and consent.**
Edited by Karen Dawisha, Philip Hanson. London: Heinemann,
for the Royal Institute of International Affairs, 1981. 226p.

This collection of papers contains only one essay dealing with Czechoslovakia by
name; this is the contribution by Karen Dawisha (p. 9-25) which considers the
lessons to be learned from the events of 1968. Notwithstanding this, the country is
included in the discussions concerning the relations between the Soviet Union and
its allies in Europe in a number of separate areas: trade and economics; politics;
military cooperation; and foreign policy. In addition to problems between the
individual countries and the USSR, some of each country's internal problems,
relating, for example, to the economy and minorities, are also discussed. Major
topics recurring throughout the volume are of course Comecon (CMEA) and the
Warsaw Pact.

459 **The eagle and the small birds. Crisis in the Soviet Empire: from
Yalta to Solidarity.**
Michael Charlton. London: British Broadcasting Corporation,
1984. 192p.

Described as 'oral history', this represents a series of discussions/interviews
involving participants in, or direct observers of, the ups and downs of post-Yalta
East European history. A number of the speakers are Czechs, and several
sections deal with Czechoslovakia, especially the treaty of alliance with Russia,
the Communist Party, the 1968 events and the trials of the Stalinist era. It thereby
offers a picture of the country's foreign relations, vis-à-vis the Soviet Union.

Law and Constitution

460   The origins and development of the study of the history of law in the territory of Czechoslovakia (1775-1939).
Jaroslav Němec.   In: *The Czechoslovak contribution to world culture.* Edited by Miloslav Rechcígl, Jr. The Hague, London, Paris: Mouton, 1964, p. 381-95.

A somewhat telegraphic account of the major publishing activities of legal historians, Czech, German and, since 1918, Slovak, which also includes a good synopsis of the Czech mediaeval legal writings, including the first real land register in Europe, the 13th-century *Zemské desky.*

461   History of juridical institutions in Slovakia.
Joseph M. Kirschbaum.   *Furdek*, vol. 22 (Jan. 1983), p. 181-91.

Traces Slovakia's legal institutions from conjectures about the prehistoric period, through the religious influences of the mission of Saints Cyril and Methodius, the general evolution of the law in mediaeval Hungary, of which Slovakia was a part, down to the 20th century. The Catholic aspect is emphasized throughout. The final section makes much of the non-equality of the Slovaks with the Czechs in the modern state, but the final assertion that the two nations are still not equal is not fully supported. Nor does it consider why many Czechs are beginning to feel that the boot is on the other foot, the Slovaks having become, in their eyes, 'more' rather than 'less' equal.

462   Election laws and democratic government.
John G. Lexa.   In: *The Czechoslovak contribution to world culture.* Edited by Miloslav Rechcígl, Jr. The Hague, London, Paris: Mouton, 1964, p. 414-24.

In addition to discussing the merits of various types of election law, contemplating the possible future return of Czechoslovakia to a Western style of democracy,

Law and Constitution

Lexa provides a good summary of how Czechoslovakia's own election law operated under the First Republic. It was one variety of proportional representation with all the disadvantages thereof, and there was also a system whereby members of parliament could lose their mandate if found to be in breach of party discipline, based on the existence of undated resignation pledges given prior to nomination. This system meant the total domination of party members by the respective executive.

463 **Government, law and courts in the Soviet Union and Eastern Europe.**
Vladimír Gsovski, Kazimierz Grzybowski. London: Stevens; The Hague: Mouton (jointly as Atlantic Books), 1959; New York: Praeger, 1960. 2 vols. bibliog.

This massive compendium of over 2,000p. contains a country-by-country analysis of: all aspects of post-war pre-communist political and constitutional developments; transitional legislation (undoing wartime innovations); the administration of justice (its organization and Sovietization); judicial procedure; the new criminal law and civil law; and sections on 'worker and factory' and 'land and peasant' (covering such topics as directed labour, wages, contracts, collectivization and land tenure). Although out of date in some respects, the substance of the work, in particular the historical dimension, continues to apply. All the contributors are essentially hostile to the legal systems they are portraying.

464 **The legal systems of Eastern Europe.**
William E. Butler. Columbus, Ohio: American Association for the Advancement of Slavic Studies, 1978. 111p. bibliog. (Eastern Europe: an Interdisciplinary Series).

This summary of East European legal systems aims to present, above all, the common element which makes them a family, but there is also a preamble which picks out the salient differences in the heritages of the separate countries. The core outline describes legal education, the legal profession, the administration of 'socialist legality' (a key phrase of loose meaning which is adequately described for the uninitiated), constitutional order, the law as it relates to the planned economy, and concepts of property. Over half the work is a 'sourcebook' containing the texts of some of the constitutions of Eastern Europe and other documents, including the 'Economic Code of the Czechoslovak Socialist Republic' of 1964, with revisions up to 1970 (p. 87-98). The bibliography is solely of books in English.

465 **The judge in a communist state: a view from within.**
Otto Ulč. Ohio: Ohio University Press, 1972. 307p.

The author defected, though he objects to the use of the word, in 1959. Here he intends neither to whitewash nor to denigrate the system, but to give, in his own (perhaps inevitably negative) terms, an explanation of the processes by which one becomes a judge, the role of lay assessors, and the processes of adjudication in numerous different types of cases: anti-state crimes; murder; paternity suits; property law; divorce; and sexual crimes. Much of the book is highly personal, hence on the one hand its tendency to be anecdotal, and on the other hand its

emphasis on the people involved in court proceedings such as the secret police
and the defendant.

466 **East European rules on the validity of international commercial
arbitration agreements.**
Ludwik Kos-Rabcewicz-Zubkowski, foreword by B. A. Wortley.
Manchester, England: Manchester University Press; Dobbs Ferry,
New York: Oceana Publications, 1970. 332p. bibliog.

A full account of the stated topic, with separate treatment accorded to each
country, including Czechoslovakia. Consideration is given to the capacity to
conclude such agreements, their form, the conventions pertaining to arbitrability,
and the relevant judicial bodies. Much of the legal framework is provided, with
some examples of arbitral decisions, and the full English text is given of the
Czechoslovak Chamber of Commerce Arbitration Court's Rules, and of the
country's Act no. 98 on arbitration in international trade and the enforcement of
awards.

467 **The Czechoslovak constitutions of 1920, 1948 and 1960.**
Vratislav Bušek. In: *The Czechoslovak contribution to world
culture.* Edited by Miloslav Rechcígl, Jr. The Hague, London,
Paris: Mouton, 1964, p. 396-404.

This paper is chiefly concerned with the difference in the status of the 1920 and
1960 constitutions, as well as their particular provisions, and the difference
between a widely accepted statement of liberal democratic principles and an
imposed assertion of the will of the Communist Party in every walk of life. The
1948 constitution is seen as a kind of bridge to the 1960 one, the ultimate nature
of which, at that stage, was still concealed behind various smokescreens. Bušek is
most concerned about provisions for private ownership, and his argument would
doubtless be more compelling if it could be rid of bitterness, sarcasm and, at
times, frivolity.

468 **The constitutions of the communist world.**
Edited by William B. Simons. Alphen aan den Rijn, The
Netherlands; Germantown, Maryland: Sijthoff & Noordhoff, 1980.
644p. (Published for the Documentation Office for East European
Law, University of Leiden).

Czechoslovakia's constitutional history is outlined by Th. J. Vondracek (p. 136-
38) and this is followed by the full English text of the 1960 constitution as
amended (p. 139-58). The new federal constitution of 1968, as amended, which is
quite a different document, is included in the appendix (p. 581-624). The index to
subjects expressly provided for by the constitutions is given in tabular form to
facilitate comparative study.

Law and Constitution

469 **Constitutions of the Communist party-states.**
Edited by Jan F. Triska. Stanford, California: The Hoover
Institution, 1968. 541p.
Includes the complete translated texts of the 1948 and 1960 constitutions of
Czechoslovakia (p. 395-452).

470 **The constitutional foundations of the Czechoslovak Federation.**
Translated from the Czech by Ivo Dvořák. Prague: Orbis Press
Agency, 1978. 2nd ed. 123p.
The text, in English, of the *Constitution of the Czechoslovak Socialist Republic* of
11 July 1960, as amended by other constitutional Acts, the *Constitutional Act
Concerning the Czechoslovak Federation* of 27 October 1968, as amended by later
Acts, and the *Constitutional Act Concerning the Status of Ethnic Groups in the
Czechoslovak Socialist Republic* of 27 October 1968. Three major legal
documents. In the last-named it is worth noting that the ethnic groups for which
provision is made are the Hungarian, German, Polish and Ukrainian (Ruthenian)
minorities only.

471 **The Czechoslovak socialist federation.**
Jaroslav Chovanec, preface by Viliam Plevza, translated by Anton
Farkaš. Bratislava: Pravda, 1978. 303p. bibliog.
The country's own official account of the pre-history of its federalization in 1968,
and of the ideological principles underlying the federation. Separate chapters deal
with the leading role of the Communist Party, the position of the National Front
(umbrella organization) and the system of organs of state at the federal and
republic level. The final chapter deals with the status of the nationalities. An
appendix lists all the legislative acts (constitutions, amendments and individual
laws) concerned with government and politics with special reference to the
federalized state, or to the new constituent republics.

472 **Review of socialist law.**
Leiden, The Netherlands: Sijthoff, 1975- . quarterly.
Published under the auspices of the Documentation Office for East European
Law of Leiden University, this quarterly journal contains articles on the law and
legal systems of all the states where the Communist Party is in power. Sijthoff
also publish the series *Law in Eastern Europe*, many of the volumes dealing
globally with aspects of the law common to the area. Some, however, do pick out
countries for separate treatment, such as, *Government tort liability in the Soviet
Union, Bulgaria, Czechoslovakia, Hungary, Poland, Romania and Yugoslavia*,
edited by Donald D. Barry, vol. 17 (1970) which contains papers from a
symposium.

473 **Bulletin of Czechoslovak law.**
Prague: Ústav státu a práva, 1962-. quarterly.
This periodical quotes and/or surveys recent legal enactments, and carries articles
relative to all branches of the law. Each issue tends to be monothematic, hence
vol. 18(1979), nos. 1-2 is on parenthood and childcare; vol. 19(1980), nos. 1-2

elates to literature (copyright law), libraries and ancient monuments, while nos.
-4 deals with the functioning of the courts and legal services; and in vol.
1(1982), no. 1 concerns the legal impact of the 16th Communist Party Congress,
o. 2 covers foreign trade, and nos. 3-4 is concerned with agriculture and fishing.

egal sources and bibliography of Czechoslovakia.
ee item no. 958.

Government

474 **Communist systems in comparative perspective.**
Leonard J. Cohen, Jane P. Shapiro. New York: Anchor
Press/Doubleday, 1974. 530p. bibliog.

The 'comparative perspective' is the important aspect of this work, which needs to
be read in its entirety in order to arrive at how Czechoslovakia compares, since
regrettably, the book lacks an index. Some of the individual chapters, however
deal directly with Czechoslovakia and can be read in isolation, although some o
the content is repeated in other works by the same authors. The chapters
specifically dealing with Czechoslovakia include: H. Gordon Skilling's 'The fall o
Novotný in Czechoslovakia' (p. 129-44); Andrzej Korbonski's 'Bureaucracy and
interest groups in Communist societies: the case of Czechoslovakia' (p. 358-78)
and Galia Golan's 'Youth and politics in Czechoslovakia' (p. 427-44). All are
historical though with some hint as to present circumstances in the last-named
The volume contains a number of relevant tables, and the bibliography includes
other earlier bibliographies as its main component.

475 **Eastern European government and politics.**
Václáv Beneš, Andrew Gyorgy, George Stambuk. New York:
Harper & Row, 1966. 247p.

Czechoslovakia is one of the countries whose contemporary government and
politics are discussed here. This discussion includes a consideration of the
structure of the ruling Communist Party as it has evolved, leadership problem
and relations with the Soviet Union.

154

476   **The Soviet regime in Czechoslovakia.**
Zdenek Krystufek.   Boulder, Colorado: East European
Quarterly. Distributed by Columbia University Press, New York,
1981. 340p. bibliog. (East European Monographs, no. 81).
The very title of this work carries an expression of the attitude to the subject,
namely that except in name Czechoslovakia might as well be deemed Soviet. It is
an indictment of Communist rule in Czechoslovakia, before and after 1968 and,
within the general attitude which it sustains, gives a description of the rule of the
Party and the general political system. The author also discusses aspects of the
legal system, censorship, the economy, and the influence of the Soviet Union.
The 24 appendixes contain a wealth of statistical data on production, crime and
social structure (with reference, for example, to the population, the village and
the workforce).

477   **La Tchécoslovaquie.** (Czechoslovakia.)
Viktor Knapp, Zdeněk Mlynář.   Paris: Librairie Générale de
Droit et de Jurisprudence, R. Pichon & R. Durand-Auzias, 1965.
262p. (Comment ils sont gouvernés, vol. 11).
A popular account, in French, of how the country is governed, from the pens of a
member of the Czechoslovak Academy of Sciences and a lecturer at Charles
University. It describes: the population; the general character of the state; its
public bodies and the National Front which unites them; the organs of
government (presidency, national committees, courts, electoral system); the
economic institutions (collective ownership, state planning); and the rights and
duties of the citizen (work, health, education). It is based heavily on the law and
constitution with which there is little serious polemic.

478   **Communist regimes in Eastern Europe.**
Richard F. Staar.   Stanford, California: Hoover Institution Press,
Stanford University, 1982. 4th ed. 375p. bibliog. (Publications
Series, no. 171).
Chapter 3 (p. 62-99) deals solely with the Czechoslovak Socialist Republic and is
a brief introduction to many of the subjects covered in the present bibliography
including: the constitution; government; legislation; the judiciary; local government; the electoral system; the Communist Party and its activities; industry;
agriculture; church-state relations; and foreign affairs, most particularly its role in
Comecon and its foreign aid programmes. Seven tables summarize some of the
main statistical data.

Economy

479 **The economic history of Eastern Europe 1919-1975.**
Edited by Michael C. Kaser.   London: Oxford University Press,
1982-85. vols. 1-3. maps.

Eventually this series will comprise five volumes, but at the time of writing only
the first three have been published. The work seeks to be a comprehensive
economic history, with Czechoslovakia well represented, hence its inclusion here.
The initial and terminal dates are given by the break-up of the great empires of
the 19th century and the Act of Helsinki which confirmed the East-West division
of Europe. Volume 1 contains a survey of the demographic and social structure of
the eight countries involved, and a description of their economic structure, with
chapters on agriculture, raw materials and energy, industry, infrastructure,
foreign trade and national income. Volume 2, entitled *Interwar policy, the war
and reconstruction*, traces the erosion of market mechanisms, as the role of the
state gradually expanded, from the response to the Depression, through the
imposition of German military needs on occupied states, to the onset of central
planning once the various communist parties won control. Topics covered include
arms production and trade, government finance, the impact of hostilities on
property and finance, agriculture and food, energy and materials, and industry.
Volume 3, *Institutional change within a planned economy*, discusses comparatively
the issues underlying economic change since 1950. Volumes 4 and 5 will deal with
external relations and domestic performance of the various countries under the
five-year plans of the period 1950-70. A major component of the work is the
numerous statistical tables. Contributors are drawn from both sides of the Iron
Curtain.

480   **Economic and social structure of Czechoslovak society between the
two wars.**
Vojtěch Ervin Andic.   In: *The Czechoslovak contribution to world
culture.* Edited by Miloslav Rechcígl, Jr. The Hague, London,
Paris: Mouton, 1964, p. 359-72.

A wide-ranging account of the subject which considers: the high degree of
industrial development of the country; its active foreign trade; the stabilization of
the currency (a fact well-remembered even today); the programmes of land
reform; and the development of the middle classes. In the last-named section
there is a summary account of the kinds of social legislation instituted. The text is
supported by a number of tables and statistics.

481   **An economic background to Munich: international business and
Czechoslovakia 1918-1938**
Alice Teichova.   London, New York: Cambridge University
Press, 1974. 422p. bibliog.

The author seeks to discover why Czechoslovakia, an independent state with
relatively advanced industry, was nevertheless dependent on the Great Powers
and on important business and financial groups operating in Central and
Southeast Europe. Because the business connections went so far afield, the
account represents a portrayal of the international business network of the whole
of Europe. The chapters deal with mining and metallurgy, engineering, the
chemical industry and banking and foreign loans, as well as the role of foreign
investment and international cartels. Competition in Czechoslovakia between
German and other West European business interests played a major part in the
events known simply as 'Munich' which signalled the dismemberment of
Czechoslovakia.

482   **The Czechoslovak economy 1945-1948.**
Edited by Karel Jech.   Prague: State Pedagogical Publishing
House, 1968. 282p. bibliog. (Acta Oeconomica Pragensia, no. 28).

This collection of papers from seven Prague economists provides the economic
backcloth to the period of change between the end of the war and 1948, the year
of the communist take-over. This period was characterized by conflict in almost
every area of the economy, conflict resolved by, in many cases, nationalization,
though this could not help resolve the manpower shortages (because of the
expulsion of the Germans) and the difficulty of boosting consumption (in the
absence of adequate resources). Particularly important were the reforms of the
currency and banking and insurance systems. Many of the papers are supported
by detailed statistics.

483 **Czechoslovak national income and product 1947-1948 and 1955-1956.**
Thad Paul Alton, Vaclav Holesovsky, Gregor Lazarcik, Paul D. Sivak, Alexej Wynnyczuk. New York, London: Columbia University Press, 1962. 255p. bibliog. (East Central European Studies of Columbia University).

Over half of this volume is given over to annotations and interpretations of the many statistical tables quoted; massively detailed and possibly digestible only by the most patient and percipient economist. However, the text proper, although also aimed more at the practising economist, is a contribution to the country's economic history of recent years, in particular for the years before and after the First Five-Year Plan, which allows for some comparison of the effects of full socialization of the economy. Comparison with other countries can be made from the more recent *National income and outlay in Czechoslovakia, Poland and Yugoslavia* by Jaroslav Krejčí (London: Macmillan, 1982. 122p.).

484 **Economic and social develoment in Czechoslovakia since 1948.**
Anon. Prague: Orbis Press Agency, 1978. 80p.

Tacitly issued to mark the thirtieth anniversary of the communist régime, this is essentially a propaganda brochure setting out the achievements of the intervening years. The picture it presents is one of steady progress in all fields, to each of which some three or four pages are devoted, with accompanying statistical tables giving relevant figures for four or more of the years 1937, 1945, 1948, 1960, 1965, 1970, 1975 and 1976. The prognoses are as optimistic as previous trends with no direct reference to any kind of economic difficulties.

485 **Central planning in Czechoslovakia: organization for growth in a mature economy.**
Jan M. Michal. Stanford, California: Stanford University Press, 1960. 274p. bibliog.

In its day this book provided a valuable interpretation of the effects of the planned economy. It deals separately with: manpower supply; industry; housing development; agriculture; transport; foreign trade; money and prices; the budget; the standard of living; Gross National Product; and other indicators. The work is in part comparative and it represented a pilot study into the workings of a planned economy. The volume was based on official Czechoslovak statistics.

486 **Plan and market under socialism.**
Ota Šik. Prague: Academia, 1967. 382p. bibliog.

Published at the time of liberalization by an academic economist subsequently reviled for his innovations, this work outlines not only the then new approach to the economy but the rigid thinking of the 1950s against which the new approach was a reaction. The essence of Šik's argument is that even socialism needs to take the market into consideration and to think of price functions and that production is bad if based solely on quantitative considerations and if efficiency is overlooked. There are oblique hints that the old approach being shed is essentially alien.

487 **Czechoslovakia: the bureaucratic economy.**
Ota Šik. White Plains, New York: International Arts & Sciences
Press, 1972. 138p.
This is, in a way, a much blunter statement of much of the substance of the
previous entry. It goes further in relating the proposed economic reforms to the
political context, and demonstrates explicitly the negative effects of the Soviet
economic model on Czechoslovakia's economy during the previous twenty years.
Interestingly, the origins of the book were the author's television broadcasts in
Czechoslovakia in 1968.

488 **Economic reforms in Eastern Europe: political background and**
economic significance.
Radoslav Selucky, translated by Zdenek Elias. New York;
Washington, DC; London: Praeger, 1972. 179p. (Praeger Special
Studies in International Economics and Development).
The author was a leading Czech economist before 1968. He devotes Chapter 4 to
the 1968 market reform in Czechoslovakia (p. 79-112), presenting an outline
history of the Five-Year Plans that preceded it and stating the fifteen principles
behind the proposals for reform from the group of economists led by Ota Šik. The
new proposals, which sought to salvage the failing economy and bring in greater
democracy, were, in the author's view, 'the chief cause of the political changes of
1968'. Consideration is also given to the effects the changes had, or would have
had, on the peasantry, and to the nationalist tendencies which reared their head
at the time; these were internal, Czech versus Slovak, Slovak versus Hungarian,
and not, at least initially, anti-Soviet. Šik's own account of the proposals, though
difficult to come by, was published in English as *Plan and Market under Socialism*
(q.v.).

489 **The new economic systems of Eastern Europe.**
Edited by Hans-Hermann Höhmann, Michael Kaser, Karl C.
Thalheim. Berkeley, California; Los Angeles: University of
California Press; London: C. Hurst, 1975. 585p.
A collection of topic- or country-centred papers, including Oldřich Kýn's
'Czechoslovakia' (p. 105-54) which from its opening sentences amounts to a
lament for the economic reform programme of the middle and late 1960s (up to
1968). The analysis of the main features of the reform is preceded by a history of
post-war developments, and each aspect – organization, planning, prices and
wages – is traced as far as it progressed up to the date at which each was
eventually reversed. The second half of the paper looks at the social, political and
economic pressures which had given rise to the reforms. The notes constitute a
bibliography. Other general or comparative papers within the same volume also
have a bearing on Czechoslovakia, notably that by Ivan Lončarević, Eberhard
Schinke and Miklós Géza Zilahi-Szabó on reforms in agriculture.

Economy

490   **New economic patterns in Czechoslovakia: impact of growth, planning and the market.**
George R. Feiwel.   New York; Washington, DC; London: Praeger, 1968. 589p. (Praeger Special Studies in International Economics and Development).

Provides the economic background to the reforms of the 1960s supported by a fairly detailed account of the trends which preceded them. In dealing with the potential for economic reform and where it might lead, the author underlines the political aspect, in particular the (temporary) reassessment of Marxism and its economic theories, and then the outburst of disquiet that brought the writers to the forefront of debate and saw wholesale changes in the personnel structure at the head of the state. The economic undercurrents and innovations are, however, present throughout, documented by statistics and reports culled from the Czechoslovak press of the day.

491   **Personal and social consumption in Eastern Europe: Poland, Czechoslovakia, Hungary and East Germany.**
Bogdan Mieczkowski.   New York: Praeger, 1975. 342p.

The first section examines the Marxist and East European theory and practice of the political economy of consumption. Part 2 studies actual consumption in each of the countries considered, while the third part is comparative, and also contains the author's conclusions. This is the kind of book which inevitably ages quickly, but much of the fascinating contents continues to apply and will be of interest not just to the economist.

492   **The planned economies of Eastern Europe.**
Alan H. Smith.   London, Canberra: Croom Helm, 1983. 249p. bibliog.

In view of the high degree of integration among the economies of Eastern Europe, it is appropriate that the present bibliography should include at least one thoroughly general work which takes an integrated view of the whole area. Smith's book divides the account under thematic heads relating, for example, to models, planning, reform, money, banking, wages and institutional background. Czechoslovakia's role, including economic reforms and any specific peculiarities, are dealt with *passim*, while its proportional involvement in the common endeavour is captured in some of the tables. An earlier work on the subject is Michael Kaser's *Comecon: integration problems of the planned economies* (London, New York, Toronto: Oxford University Press, 1967. 2nd rev. ed. 279p.), which weighs cooperation and integration against the contrasting interests of member countries.

160

493 **Crisis in socialist planning: Eastern Europe and the USSR.**
Jan Marczewski, translated from the French by Noël
Lindsay. New York; Washington, DC; London: Praeger, 1974.
249p. (Praeger Special Studies in International Economics and
Development).

This study is based on the premise that communications have improved so much
that the world has now 'shrunk' to such an extent that nations are thrown into
closer contact with each other so that it becomes more difficult for an inefficient
economy in one country to survive close to a neighbour's efficient economy. To
meet such a contrast the socialist countries have relied heavily on planning.
Czechoslovakia is one of the developed socialist economies of Europe whose
potential for competing with the Western capitalist economies is discussed, but in
many sections of the book the relevant detail has to be drawn from the overall
discussion or the tables. The topics covered are: agriculture; industry before the
reforms of the 1960s; the reforms themselves; services; foreign trade; and
monetary and financial flows. The final chapter hypothesizes on the prospects for
planning in the future, summarizing the mostly positive effects of past and present
trends, but pointing out the clearly contradictory influences affecting decisions.

494 **The politics of modernisation in Eastern Europe: testing the Soviet
model.**
Edited by Charles Gati, introductory essays by Vernon V.
Aspaturian, Cyril E. Black. New York; Washington, DC;
London: Praeger, 1974. 2nd printing 1976. 389p. (Praeger Special
Studies in International Politics and Government).

I include the whole volume of papers here, rather than just pinpointing the case
study on Czechoslovakia (Otto Ulč's 'Czechoslovakia, the great leap backward',
p. 89-116), since the whole concept of modernization is discussed in relation to an
economic system of which Czechoslovakia is an integral part. Aspects covered
include: the role of the Communist Party; the Soviet impact on political, social
and economic developments; other East European experiences as models for
Soviet practice; the role of tradition; and the periods of stagnation, reform and
dissent. Both within Ulč's paper and in the appendixes there are relevant
statistical tables covering Czechoslovakia alone or comparatively (referring, for
example, to social structure, car ownership, abortions, pregnancies and live
births, urbanization, medical facilities, transport, media, economic growth, and
GNP). The statistics are, in view of the periods covered and the age of the work
itself, more of historical than contemporary interest.

495 **Quantitative and analytical studies in East-West economic relations.**
Edited by Josef C. Brada. Bloomington, Indiana: Indiana
University, 1976. 133p. (Studies in East European and Soviet
Planning Development and Trade, no. 24).

As the title suggests, there are topics in this volume which are relevant to the
'Trade' section of this bibliography. However, the book has also been included
here on account of Paul Marer's 'Tourism in Eastern Europe' (p. 87-115) which
examines the importance of tourism to the Czech economy. As with so many
topics, the coverage is for the whole of Comecon, but data specific to

Economy

Czechoslovakia can be readily isolated. The article contains statistics and considers: the role of hard and soft currency in the financing of tourism; exchange rates; the place of revenue from tourism in the economy; projections for the development of tourism; and inhibiting factors. The author also makes comparisons between the East European countries and between East and West European conditions although the charts and tables provide the clearest data for the direct comparison of various parameters.

496 **Wage control and inflation in the Soviet bloc countries.**
Jan Adam. London; Basingstoke, England: Macmillan, 1979.
243p. bibliog.

This book includes a chapter entitled 'Wage regulation in Czechoslovakia' (p. 164-74) which records the progressive waves of reform adopted since the abandonment of the 'classical' Soviet model in 1958. It necessarily includes discussion of management and tax systems and in particular the way available funds are divided between basic wages and bonuses. The most recent (1978-80) pattern of control which is described is still, in the main, in operation. Other chapters in the book are of interest from the comparative point of view. For a more detailed account of earlier practices see the author's *Wage, price and taxation policy in Czechoslovakia 1948-1970* (Berlin, 1974).

497 **Aims and methods of economic policy in Czechoslovakia 1970-1978.**
Jiri Kosta. In: *The East European Economies in the 1970s.* Edited by Alec Nove, Hans-Hermann Höhmann, Gertraud Seidenstecher. London: Butterworths, 1982, p. 139-79. bibliog. (Butterworths Studies in International Political Economy).

Kosta uses as his starting point the country's admitted state of economic crisis and looks at the likely political as well as purely economic factors underlying the Five-Year Plans of the 1980s. He then considers: the specific problem areas in development strategy; the state of the labour market; the supply of raw materials (the oil crisis and the Soviet Union's inability to sustain supplies); and investment and foreign trade (especially trade balance problems with the West). The second part of the paper considers the various traditional and some innovative methods for managing the economy, and the third considers problems of growth and efficiency. Includes 22 statistical tables.

498 **East European economic handbook.**
Anon. London: Euromonitor, 1985. 325p. maps.

Within this volume there are three general chapters by Alan H. Smith which examine: Eastern Europe in a world economic context (with reference to economic performance, trade with the rest of the world and the region as an import market); the diversity within the region and in the separate countries' economic performances; and the economic prospects of the area. The remaining chapters, including the one specifically devoted to Czechoslovakia (p. 71-103), are anonymous ('by a team of economic journalists'). The Czechoslovakia chapter consists of thirty-one statistical tables relating to all aspects of the economy in the period 1980-82, with a running text to link them, resulting in a general portrait not just of the economy, but of the country, its people and politics, mining, manufacture and agriculture, energy, transport, tourism, banking, consumption, and trade. Further comparative tables are in 'Fact File' at the end of the volume.

499   **Czechoslovakia: 'unparalleled' economic problems.**
E. A. Rahmer.   *Petroleum Economist*, vol. 49, no. 2 (1982), p. 53-54.
The oil crisis hit the communist economies just as it hit the West, though some of the resultant problems were peculiar to the Soviet bloc. The population of Czechoslovakia were warned to face up to the magnitude of their complex 'unparalleled' socioeconomic problems, with no promise of any easy solutions.

500   **A bad time for Czechoslovakia.**
'N.B.'   *Banker*, vol. 128, no. 627(May 1978), p. 36-37.
Although Czechoslovakia enjoys a high level of consumption and ownership (including second homes), and although imports suffice to meet the demand for material goods, the country is in many areas self-sufficient and has shown recent increases in production. Notwithstanding this, there are problems: the manpower shortage; apathy; obsolescence of plant (which is compared to Britain); and resistance to investment by foreign banks, though the Japanese have had some important successes here.

501   **Economic reforms in Eastern Europe and prospects for the 1980s: colloquium 16-18 April 1980, Brussels.**
Edited by the Economics Directorate and Information Directorate, NATO.   Oxford: Pergamon Press, 1980. 328p. bibliog.
Like many similar volumes this one contains some general papers with a bearing on Czechoslovakia, but also two papers specifically devoted to that country. Franz-Lothar Altmann's 'Czechoslovakia: economic prospects for the 1980s' (p. 149-62) discusses the country's acknowledged failure to meet its Five-Year Plan, the difficulties in the labour market, the export surplus in foreign trade, the growing dependency on Soviet oil supplies, and unfavourable developments in the terms of trade. Vaclav Holesovsky's 'Czechoslovakia: economic reforms' (p. 59-71) outlines the development of the economy since the war, with reference to the different Five-Year Plans and the efforts to improve the processes of planning. Both papers are supported by tables and notes which constitute an informal bibliography, especially of Czechoslovak sources. An earlier volume dealing with economic development is *The new economic systems of Eastern Europe*, edited by Hans-Hermann Höhmann, Michael Kaser and Karl C. Thalheim (q.v.).

502   **The economics of Eastern Europe in a time of change.**
Adam Zwass.   London: Macmillan, 1984. 171p.
Czechoslovakia is taken together with East Germany in this volume (p. 23-63) since both countries shared a relatively higher degree of industrial development compared with others in the region when communist economic and political systems were established after the Second World War. Within the chapter, which is not directly comparative, Czechoslovakia receives separate treatment (p. 44 onwards). The story is one of short-lived initial success, brought down by Stalinist methods, and the general theme is that management suited to a developing

country cannot work with a developed economy. A sub-chapter deals with the 1968 reform period followed by a description of current problems. The major positive aspect, also vaunted by the Czechoslovaks themselves, is that there is little in the way of foreign debt for the economy to carry.

Czechoslovakia: Lloyds Bank Group economic report.
See item no. 6.

Banking and Finance

503 **Banking and industrialization in Austria-Hungary: the role of banks in the industrialization of the Czech Crownlands 1873-1914.**
Richard Rudolph. Cambridge, England; London; New York; Melbourne: Cambridge University Press, 1976. 291p. bibliog.

This is the first study of the role of the banks, Austrian and Czech, in the industrialization of the country and it concludes that they were not as significant as has been assumed, though they did have an obvious role to play. Separate attention is paid to the part played by the big Austrian banks and the smaller banks based in the Crown Lands (some of which were purely Czech, others being Austro-German), and to their different relations with various branches of industry. All three territories, Bohemia, Moravia and Silesia, are discussed.

504 **The finance of Czechoslovakia in the new scheme of management.**
Vladimír Háčik (et al.). Bratislava: Slovak Pedagogic Publishing House, 1968. 287p. bibliog.

Finance as such appears, for bibliographical purposes, inseparable from other questions of economics, whether in terms of Czechoslovak or foreign literature. This volume of papers, compiled at the Department of Finance of the Bratislava School of Economics and the Central Economic Library, Bratislava, has of course been rendered obsolete in most respects, since the 'new scheme of management' has much to do with the economic reforms of the 1960s, most of which have been undone or greatly revised since. The book remains worth mentioning, however, for some of the constants that still apply such as the papers on currency and credit, banks and insurance. Those essays on wages policy, state and lower-level budgets, investment policy, the financing of industry, agriculture and trade are more relevant to the reform period. The last paper contains an appeal for foreign cooperation with Czechoslovakia's economists, and offers as a lure a detailed account of the departments, services and other activities of the Central Economic Library in Bratislava.

505 **Banking business in socialist economy with special regard to East-West trade.**
Iván Meznerics, translated from Hungarian by Emil Böszörményi Nagy. Leiden, The Netherlands: A. W. Sijthoff; Budapest: Akadémiai Kiadó, 1968. 383p.

In the absence of any large corpus of literature dealing specifically with banking in Czechoslovakia, this work can only be a poor substitute. However, it does state the extent to which the banks of Eastern Europe, named where relevant, adhere to Western banking practices in their dealings with the West. The account of internal banking and finance, though much of it could be generalized, is actually specific to Hungary, while that on intra-Comecon arrangements applies equally to Czechoslovakia. This is mainly because Czechoslovakia is a signatory to the agreement concerning the multilateral settlement of accounts in transferable roubles and the organization of the International Bank of Economic Cooperation.

506 **Money, banking & credit in the Soviet Union & Eastern Europe.**
Adam Zwass, translated by Michel C. Vale. White Plains, New York: M. E. Sharpe; London; Basingstoke, England: Macmillan, 1979. 233p.

The different chapters discuss: the role of money in a planned economy; the price system; inflation (an issue formulated as a question: Are the planned economies shielded from inflation? – answered in the negative); the banking system proper; credit policies and money in foreign trade; and the perspectives for East European currencies to become integrated into international trade. Regrettably there is no index, so any references to Czechoslovak practice are somewhat difficult to trace, but useful information can be gleaned, especially in the areas where data can be tabulated.

507 **Into the IMF.**
Banker, vol. 131, no. 670 (Dec. 1981), p. 54-56.

Against a discussion of the conjectured Czechoslovak application to rejoin the International Monetary Fund (IMF), this article details the country's Eurocredit liabilities and interprets the signs, in official statements, that the need to join the IMF could be genuine.

508 **Státní banka československá bulletin 1968 (et seq.): report on the economic, credit and monetary development in the Czechoslovak Socialist Republic for 1968 (et seq.).**
Prague: Státní banka československá, 1968-. annual.

A yearly report on economic conditions and development in the country prepared by the State Bank. The emphasis is on the preceding twelve months, but where appropriate some comparative statistical data is included for the previous five years or more.

509 **Socialist economic development and reforms: from extensive to
     intensive growth under central planning in the USSR, Eastern
     Europe and Yugoslavia.**
     Jozef Wilczynski.   London; Basingstoke, England: Macmillan,
     1972. 350p.
Although the history and recent changes of strategy in planning, pricing, banking
and investment are presented en bloc, Czechoslovakia's position, and contribution
to joint endeavours, is specified where relevant. The author is particularly
concerned with the role of technology and how progress here is being accelerated,
and also with the increasing dependence of Eastern Europe on Western
technology and on improved co-operation between the two economic systems.
The many tables are set out country by country, one of them, in the section on
banking and finance, describing in brief the different Czechoslovak banks.

**Banking and nationality conflict in the modernization of the Bohemian
Crown Lands.**
See item no. 579.

Employment and Labour

510 **Employment policies in Czechoslovakia.**
Franz-Lothar Altmann. In: *Employment policies in the Soviet Union and Eastern Europe.* Edited by Jan Adam, London; Basingstoke, England: Macmillan, 1982. p. 72-95.

This is a very good account, in many ways more satisfying than the more recent one below, of current labour problems and shortages, which are expounded chiefly in terms of demographic developments and economic policies (the two are sometimes inseparable). The demographic developments concern in the main the huge fluctuations in the birth-rate, where the abortion law referred to elsewhere and the recent new child benefits play a major part, and the use of imported labour. The statistics on the latter include the huge numbers of Vietnamese, but are perhaps just a little premature to include the Cubans who are now to be found in Czechoslovakia (these could have been mentioned in the work below but seem not to have been). Another important element in the labour force are the working pensioners, while among the problems faced by the country there is the increase in the numbers of white-collar workers, low mechanization and time-wasting through poor organization. Some of the methods devised to overcome these shortcomings including incentives, bonuses, perks, and the unloved 'working Saturdays', are also described.

511 **Employment and wage policies in Poland, Czechoslovakia and Hungary since 1950.**
Jan Adam. London; Basingstoke, England: Macmillan, 1984. 251p. bibliog.

Starting from an acceptance of the fact (sometimes questioned) that there is full employment in these countries, the author proceeds to analyse how the concept is understood and sustained, and what full employment actually costs. He is interested in how the system and changes to it interact with politics. In the main the work is interpretive, since it relies for most of its data on sources from the

168

countries concerned, and uses the relevant socialist terms and classifications. The development of employment policy is the primary concern, wages policy being deliberately left in second place. Since each of the three countries concerned is quite different from the others, the study is also explicitly comparative.

512 **Employment policies in the Soviet Union and Eastern Europe.**
Edited by Jan Adam. London; Basingstoke, England: Macmillan, 1982. 216p.

This collection of nine papers contains four with a bearing on Czechoslovakia: 'Employment policies in Czechoslovakia' by Franz-Lothar Altmann (q.v.); 'Similarities and differences in the treatment of labour shortages' by Jan Adam (p. 123-44); 'Regional employment policies in East European countries' by Hans-Eric Gramotzki (p. 166-88); and 'Cooperation of the CMEA countries in the sphere of employment' by Tibor Vais (p. 189-208). Adam's paper deals with a range of problems similar to those dealt with by Altmann but comparatively, considering also the Soviet, Polish and Hungarian versions of the difficulties. Gramotzki is primarily concerned with the reasons for, and practice of, equalization between the Czech Lands and Slovakia, a product of the huge demographic contrast between the two halves of the country, while Vais describes the reasons for, and benefits accruing from, the export and import of labour among the Comecon countries, in which Czechoslovakia has been involved on quite a large scale. Although there is some inevitable repetition in the book, it nevertheless provides an insight into some of the most important aspects of employment in the country. Also included are a number of statistical tables showing, *inter alia*, birth rate, women's participation in the labour market, wage differentiation, and regional employment and demographic structure as of 1978.

513 **Problematika pracovních sil v některých pohraničních oblastech České socialistické republiky.** (Labour-force issues in some frontier areas of the Czech Socialist Republic.)
Josef Brinke. *Acta Universitatis Carolinensis: Geographica 15. Supplement,* (1980), p. 171-76.

This article, which has an English résumé, deals with an interesting aspect of international cooperation in the labour market. The problem arose initially out of the Czech labour shortage after the war, to compensate for which foreign labour, especially from Poland, was brought in, notably in Northern and Eastern Bohemia and Northern Moravia. More recently, because of labour shortages in Poland and other factors which are not discussed, such international labour agreements have been terminated and this has given rise to a renewed labour shortage on the Czech side. A partial solution, arrived at since this article appeared, has been the massive influx, in some areas at least, of Cubans, which seems to be something of a mixed blessing in social terms.

514 **Workers' councils in Czechoslovakia 1968-69: documents and essays.**
Edited, with an introduction by Vladimír C. Fišera. London: Allison & Busby, 1978; New York: St. Martins Press, 1979. 200p.

Trade unions and other labour organizations tend, if mentioned at all, to be incorporated in wide-ranging discussions of the role of the state and/or the Party of which they are perceived to be just another arm. One of the features which marked out the period of reform was the innovation of workers' councils which took, and briefly held, a position of a kind unheard of before or since. It is the place of these bodies in the running of enterprises and in the economy that this book describes, fully supported by documentary evidence and bibliographical references.

515 **Cooperative movements in Eastern Europe.**
Edited by Aloysius Balawdyer. London; Basingstoke, England: Macmillan, 1980. 211p.

Despite its title, this book limits its attentions to Poland, Slovakia and Slovenia. Jozef M. Kirschbaum deals with 'The cooperative movement in Slovakia 1845-1948' (p. 23-48) and Stanislav J. Kirschbaum with 'The cooperative movement in socialist Slovakia' (p. 49-75). The former gives a detailed account of the many types of cooperative set up in Slovakia, in a tradition that goes back almost as far as cooperativism in England (only 50 days separate the first Slovak cooperative from the Rochdale one), explaining the role of the clergy and certain political parties. However, the exposition is set in a typically Kirschbaumian chauvinist history of the country, the mildest token of which is the persistent spelling 'Czecho-Slovakia'. The second paper explains, in calmer language, the developments since the Communist take-over and contrasts the old voluntary cooperatives, many of which were broken up, with their eponymous, state-controlled modern counterparts. It includes an account of the forced collectivization of the 1950s and the birth of the modern collective farms (United Agricultural Cooperatives), but underestimates their present success and even popularity.

516 **Vývoj lesního dělnictva v Českých Zemích v letech 1918-1938.** (The development of the forestry labour force in the Czech Lands 1918-38.)
Miroslav Landa. *Lesnictví*, vol. 29, no. 2 (1983), 153-68.

Together with the author's 'Lesní dělnictvo v Českých zemích za Druhé světové války' (The forestry labour force in the Czech Lands during the Second World War; *Lesnictví*, vol. 29, no. 9[1983], p. 815-26) and 'Lesní dělnictvo v Českých zemích v letech 1945-1955' (The forestry labour force in the Czech Lands 1945-55; *Lesnictví*, vol. 30, no. 3[1984], p. 251-66), this article provides a detailed history of one major area of employment. Landa not only traces fluctuations in the size of the workforce, but also: the legal provisions governing wages and accident insurance; the operation of bonus systems and payments in kind; the outflow of labour during the depression; and the inflow of Slovak labour during, and since, the war. Many of the features described amount to a 'normal' linear development, but the three sections give a good contrastive study of the topic under three quite distinctive sets of conditions: capitalism, with largely privately owned forests; the war economy of occupied Bohemia and Moravia; and post-war socialism with the forests nationalized. The articles are included here for their brief, but comprehensive and intelligible English summaries.

Agriculture

517 **The performance of socialist agriculture: a case study of production and productivity, Czechoslovakia 1934-38 and 1946-61.**
Gregor Lazarczyk.   New York: L. W. International Financial Research, 1963. 121p. bibliog.

In this report the author discusses and quantifies patterns in agriculture for the two periods named, specifically comparing the pre-war capitalist system of Europe in general and Czechoslovakia in particular with the performance of the latter since the socialization of agriculture. The same author explores the comparative costs in more detail in a related work: *Czechoslovak agriculture and output, expenses, gross and net product and productivity 1934-38 and 1946-62* (New York: Columbia University Press, 1965, 33p. Research Project on National Income in East Central Europe, Occasional Paper, no. 7), while another study in the same series (Occasional Paper, no. 20) considers *Czechoslovak agriculture and non-agricultural incomes 1948-65* (ibid., 1968, 76p.).

518 **Soviet and East European agriculture.**
Edited by Jerzy Karcz.   Berkeley, California: California University Press, 1967. 445p. (Soviet and East European Studies).

This volume contains (p. 385-410) Gregor Lazarczyk's 'The performance of Czechoslovak agriculture since World War II', which in part rehearses some of the same author's findings in the previous entry, such as the lower output per unit under socialist, as opposed to private-ownership, agriculture. In addition it compares the Czech agricultural performance with that of neighbouring Poland, where much private ownership survives. Further comparisons can also be made by consulting other papers in the same volume.

519 **A survey of Czechoslovak agriculture.**
R. Cummings. Washington, DC: US Economic Research Center,
International Economics Division, 1982. 28p. (Foreign Agriculture
Economic Report, no. 171).
The most recent investigation of Czechoslovakia's agriculture by an outside
official body.

520 **Czechoslovak agriculture.**
Jaroslav Kutil, translated by Vladimír Kosina. Prague: Orbis
Press Agency, 1983. 126p. maps. bibliog.
An official publication for external consumption which describes the position of
agriculture within the economy, from supply and consumption, through national
income and employment, to the agricultural share in foreign trade. It also
acknowledges the problems of protection and conservation of the natural and
human environment. Much of the text is taken up with the post-war land reforms,
the consequences these had for agriculture and those employed in it, and ends
with a consideration of current trends. The text contains many tables and charts
and supplementary tables show comparative statistics for selected years between
1936 and 1980 on consumption, production, growth rates and grain imports
(nineteen tables in all in the supplement). A potentially interesting, though
somewhat opaque addition are the two maps indicating the layout of the parish of
Rodinov before and after collectivization. A selection of photographs illustrating
many of the relevant topics is included at the back of the book, black-and-white
for the earlier periods, coloured for the present.

521 **Czechoslovakia.**
D. E. F. Taylor. *Agriculture Abroad*, vol. 36, no. 2 (April 1981),
p. 1-6.
A typical example of an external observer's report, in fact from the Commercial
Counsellor at a Western embassy in Prague. It provides a breakdown of current
agricultural production based on published statistics and notes: trends in
organization; areas of growth and decline; actual results compared with targets;
targets for the future (a preview for the seventh five-year plan was published in
Agriculture Abroad for April 1980); priority areas in research; and the place of
Canada in Czechoslovakia's agricultural import trade (grain, some livestock,
etc.). The article includes two tables and many other statistical data.

522 **Men versus systems: agriculture in the USSR, Poland and
Czechoslovakia.**
Arthur E. Adams and Ian S. Adams. New York: Free Press;
London: Collier-Macmillan, 1971. 327p. bibliog.
A fairly detailed field study of the subject which aims at making sense of the
conflicting views of official outpourings, disaffected émigrés and intellectual
critics. Part three is devoted to Czechoslovakia, beginning with the pre-1948
period which is rich in statistics, and proceeding to the enforced collectivization
and subsequent trends. Constant comparison is made with the quite different
Polish situation. Much of the detail in the chapters that follow comes from
interviews with people on the spot: social scientists studying trends in peasant

lifestyles and attitudes; academics of agriculture; and the personnel of a collective farm near Kutná Hora (Bohemia), the Valtice state farm (Moravia), renowned for its wines, and the state experimental farm attached to Nitra Agricultural College (Slovakia). At the end of the volume there is slight coverage of private farming which is still fairly extensive in Slovakia.

523 **The political economy of collectivized agriculture: a comparative study of communist and non-communist systems.**
Edited by Ronald A. Francisco, Betty A. Laird, Roy D. Laird. New York: Pergamon Press, 1978. 250p. (Pergamon Policy Studies).

Contains Josef Hajda's 'The politics of agricultural collectivization and modernization in Czechoslovakia' (p. 130-54) a history of the subject in three periods: the massive land redistribution after the war; the decade of the formation of state and cooperative farms; and the more recent period from the 1960s onwards. The latter period has seen much restructuring, modernization and, since 1968, adaptation to the needs of international socialist economic integration, both in production and research. The paper discusses the theoretical political background to developments, and the failures these brought in the earlier post-war period. It also contains a great deal of statistics on, for example, yields, investment and employment. For an early Western analysis of collectivization in Czechoslovakia, see Ernest Koenig's paper in *Collectivization of agriculture in Eastern Europe*, edited by Irwin T. Sanders (University of Kentucky Press, 1958).

524 **Agricultural policies in the USSR and Eastern Europe.**
Edited by Ronald A. Francisco, Betty A. Laird, Roy D. Laird, with a conclusion by Karl-Eugen Wädekin. Boulder, Colorado: Westview Press, 1980. 332p. (Westview Studies on the Soviet Union and Eastern Europe).

Many of the papers herein have an indirect bearing on Czechoslovakia but of special interest is Vladislav Bajaja's 'Concentration and specialisation in Czechoslovak and East German farming' (p. 263-93). It analyses the recent movement towards the amalgamation of smaller farms to provide bigger units capable of employing the largest plant available. Different types of units, how they are managed and financed, types of specialization, with all the relevant (official) statistics on size and output are described in some detail, as are the latest trends in agricultural policy. There is a cool appraisal not only of areas of weakness, but also of such successes as the already almost legendary Slušovice cooperative (whose very existence, let alone performance, is a constant source of amazement to the man in the street) with its great diversity of agricultural, manufacturing and marketing activities. For a discussion of the evolution of agricultural policy see Joseph Hajda's paper in the previous entry.

525 **Farm policies in socialist countries.**
Theodor Bergmann, translated from German by Lux
Furtmüller. Farnborough, England: Saxon House; Lexington,
Massachusetts: Lexington Books, 1975. 289p. maps. bibliog.

A brief introductory section outlines the history of the socialist states, particularly
the crucial dates of their birth, and pinpoints the major differences between them,
especially in terms of geographical zone, the strength of the Communist Party and
illiteracy. Czechoslovakia is considered in detail in chapter 2, 'Countries with a
collectivised agriculture' which considers its agrarian structure before and after
the communist take-over. Czechoslovak agricultural methods in the early 1970s
are seen as merely a modification of Soviet practices. The author makes
surprisingly light of peasant resistance to collectivization. The actual stages in the
process of collectivization are spelled out, and so are the changes in the country's
social structure, but the graphs and tables, which use Czechoslovak sources in the
main are more informative overall than the slender text. The work was originally
published in 1973, thus the discussion of current problems has most bearing on
the 1968 period of reform as it affected agriculture.

Industry

526 **Pre-industrial iron-making in the Czech Lands: the labour force
and production relations circa 1350 – circa 1840.**
Milan Myška, translated by Thomas Hnik, Bo Richter and
R. E. F. Smith. *Past and Present*, vol. 82 (1979), p. 45-72.
This substantial study is an investigation of early iron metallurgy in the Czech
Lands as an industry. Like glass and paper making, iron-making did not lend itself
to organization by guilds, and yet it was, even according to Marx, a manufactory.
The gradual evolution from small-scale to large-scale production is traced through
a series of major technological innovations in the first half of the 14th century,
and the author indicates how these developments led to a considerable difference
in how labour was organized, divided and specialized. The 500-year history of this
area of production is remarkable in that manpower relations were based neither
on corvée nor forced wage labour. This is a periodized history showing each wave
of innovation in both technology and management, especially the changing role of
the feudal authority and the ironmasters, and is based on copious archival and
secondary sources. A useful example of Marxist historiography.

527 **Tomáš Baťa – pioneer of self-government in industry: the effect of
self-administration of workshops and departments upon the world-
wide growth of the Bata Organization.**
Anthony Cekota.   In: *Czechoslovak contribution to world culture.*
Edited by Miloslav Rechcígl, Jr. The Hague, London, Paris:
Mouton, 1964, p. 342-49. bibliog.
The footwear industry in Czechoslovakia is still concentrated largely in Zlín (now
Gottwaldov), the town where Bata shoes originate. Contemporary views of
Tomáš Baťa vary between seeing him as a far-sighted benevolent employer,
somewhere between a Ford and a Cadbury, to seeing him as a typically ruthless
capitalist making his money out of tied labour. In any event he and his business

176

were an interesting, Czech, phenomenon, as this historical outline, and the continuing success of the business, demonstrate. The mainspring of Baťa's success was undoubtedly the system of self-administration, including responsibility for finance, which he instituted.

528 **Č-K-D employees, Prague 1871-1920: some aspects of their geographical distribution.**
Francis W. Carter. *Journal of Historical Geography*, vol. 1, no. 1 (1975), p. 69-97. maps.

Outlines the development of the three concerns which eventually merged to form one of Prague's biggest heavy industrial enterprises. The author relates this industrial growth to successive developments in industry and technology generally. The main body of the work, however, which is based on statistical analyses of extant company registers, describes changes in the geographical origins of the workforce and changes in the journey-to-work patterns, as related to shifts in the locations of dwellings and developments in public transport. It also records changes in the structure of the workforce. The whole is supported by largely self-explanatory tables, maps and graphs. A more detailed analysis of the development of Prague's transport system can be found in F. W. Carter's article 'Public transport development in nineteenth-century Prague' (q.v.).

529 **The industrial development of Prague 1800-1850.**
Francis W. Carter. *Slavonic and East European Review*, vol. 51, no. 123 (April 1973), p. 243-75. maps.

In this paper Carter argues that the mere geographical location of Prague does not explain its growth as a major industrial centre and the author bases his whole account on a model of industrial growth taken from other sources. Tables indicate the changes in the city's industrial structure and the text records in some detail the rise and fall of individual businesses and the industries they represent. The maps show the gradual relocation of industries and the statistics are supported by graphs and tables. There is also a wealth of information on the involvement of foreigners in the growth of industry and on the export markets for some of the city's goods. A more detailed study on the rise and fall of one particular industry, cotton printing, is to be found in F. W. Carter's 'The cotton printing industry in Prague 1766-1873' (q.v.).

530 **The cotton printing industry in Prague 1766-1873.**
Francis W. Carter. *Textile History*, vol. 6 (1975), p. 132-55. bibliog.

A detailed account of cotton printing, a one-time major industry in Prague. This industry went into decline with the raw cotton crisis of 1860, the collapse of the Vienna banking system and the ensuing slump.

Industry

531 Czechoslovak textiles.

Frank Lewis.   Leigh-on-Sea, England: F. Lewis, Publishers, 1962. 20p. 110 plates.

The introduction (the only textual matter in the book) sketches the development of textiles in the Czechoslovak area since the time of the earliest records (10th century) and provides a characterization of the contemporary variety of fabrics, textiles and clothing. The book contains one of the few references I have met to Czechoslovakia's fez-making industry. The plates are preceded by a brief description and statement of the relevant manufacturer.

532 Skoda builds exports on vigorous home market.

Railway Gazette International, (March 1980), p. 201-03.

A moderately technical account of innovations in the Czechoslovak railway locomotive industry, centring on the large Škoda works at Plzeň (Pilsen), in particular its new models and their export to other railway concerns in the Soviet Union, Bulgaria and Poland. The locomotive types discussed are all electric and contribute to the modernization of Czechoslovakia's own locomotive fleet. The same issue of the periodical has other articles with a Czechoslovak dimension, including the immediately preceding snippet on the locomotive, rolling stock and track testing facility at Velim, and the one before that on, *inter alia*, Czechoslovak-East German technological cooperation in the development of prototype passenger stock bogies.

533 Czechoslovak aircraft industry: alive and well 40 years on.

Brian Wanstall.   *Interavia*, vol. 40, no. 6 (1985), p. 660-64.

A detailed, positive account of the full extent of the aeroindustry, including: the location, structure, output and inter-relations between the fifteen or so main works; the state of research and development and the relation of new models to their predecessors; the manufacture and use of pilot-training equipment; and *passim*, the countries where Czechoslovak-made aircraft are in use. The civil, recreational, agricultural and military use of Czechoslovak planes is also covered.

534 Delayed reaction.

Economist (27 Oct. 1984), p. 72, map.

This journalistic commentary on the present situation concerning the country's endeavour to switch over more to nuclear power explains: the nature of the hold-ups in the programme; the consequences for the power industry generally; and the shape of Soviet-Czechoslovak trade in nuclear energy resources and production. The map locates present and planned nuclear power stations.

535 The Danube: blue is green.

Economist (8 Dec. 1984), p. 68, 70.

Examines the state of play in the Czechoslovak-Austrian and Czechoslovak-Hungarian disputes concerning conflicting ecological and economic interests arising out of certain important hydro-electric projects. The saga has gone on for some time and is regularly reported in *The Economist*.

536 **Eastern Europe: studies in industrial geography.**
David Turnock.   Folkestone, England: William Dawson; Boulder,
Colorado: Westview Press, 1978. 273p. maps. bibliog. (Studies in
Industrial Geography).

Although eventually working round to individual industries and the major
industrial regions, Turnock approaches the subject via a general appraisal of the
political background, the available natural resources, pre-war industrial development, transport and energy, and post-war economic changes. The author has
deliberately chosen the macro approach, taking the eight countries involved as
one block, though sometimes separate treatment is given to the northerly, more
advanced sub-group, which includes Czechoslovakia. The text and especially the
tables do, however, pinpoint items specific to Czechoslovakia (or any one of the
other countries) and the volume is thus a useful source for comparative studies.

537 **Planning in Eastern Europe: industrial management by the state – a
background book.**
Michael Kaser, Janusz G. Zieliński.   London, Sydney, Toronto:
Bodley Head, 1970. 184p. bibliog.

This remains a useful 'background book' for the period up to 1969. Czechoslovak
practice is described *passim* throughout, but is unfortunately not pinpointed in the
index. The authors acknowledge the assistance of L. Rychetník, author of *The
industrial enterprise in Czechoslovakia* (q.v.). A useful appendix lists the central
governing authorities concerned with industrial planning and management
(boards, ministries and banks).

538 **Planned economy and environmental problems – Eastern Europe
from a comparative perspective.**
Ingmar Oldberg.   *Bidrag til Öststatsforskningen*, vol. 11, no. 2
(1982), p. 1-64.

Emphasizes the tendency for governments in Eastern Europe to concentrate pre-
eminently on industry and to place production norms, which are to be met at all
costs, on too high a plane. As a result the environmental consequences of
industrial expansion are not being catered for in planning. The article includes a
section on Czechoslovakia.

539 **Decision-making and industrial location in Eastern Europe.**
F. E. I. Hamilton.   *Transactions of the Institute of British
Geographers*, vol. 53 (1971), p. 52-81.

The discussion of the Marxist theory and practice of industrial location is
illustrated by a number of case studies to exemplify post-war adherence to these
principles (for example, the equal spread of industrial development across a
country). It should be noted that the adoption of such principles has, in some
cases, had negative consequences, as can be seen from some examples taken from
the Czechoslovak experience. That socialism is itself not solely to blame for some
of the unfortunate locations is exemplified by some pre-war anomalies, like the
Vítkovice steelworks.

Industry

540 **Industrial progress in Poland, Czechoslovakia and East Germany, 1937-1962.**
Alfred Zauberman. London, New York, Toronto: Oxford University Press, 1964. 338p. bibliog.

Although now dated, this book nevertheless provides a good overview of: the economic mechanism and strategy for industrial growth; the labour force; and the growth in both industrial production, and in specific areas of energy, metal mining and processing, and the chemical industries for the period before the energy crisis. Many tables are supplied on topics as varied as population, the employment of women, imports and exports and natural resources. The book also describes the early nuclear energy programme.

541 **The industrial enterprise in Czechoslovakia.**
Luděk Rychetník. In: *The industrial enterprise in Eastern Europe.* Edited by Ian Jeffries. Eastbourne, England; New York: Praeger, 1981. p. 114-28. bibliog. (Praeger Special Studies; Praeger Scientific).

In addition to its historical section, this paper is most valuable for its introduction to the modern pattern of classifying enterprises. It is particularly useful for the contemporary (Czech) terminology, which is well-translated and defined, a worthwhile exercise given the possible misconceptions which can arise where so many of the terms are loan-words with meanings which do not necessarily coincide with their foreign cognates (cf. *koncern, trust, kombinát*). Other aspects covered include efficiency, pricing, development strategies and the role of the 'socialist manager'. Detailed diagrams reveal the machinery of planning procedure and the management of income and funds.

542 **East European energy and East-West trade in energy.**
Jonathan P. Stern. London: Policy Studies Institute, 1982. 94p. (Energy Paper, no. 1).

Although couched in general terms for the whole region, some specific data contained here is directly relevant to Czechoslovakia which has also been affected by the energy shortage, the cuts in Soviet oil supplies and the rise in Soviet natural gas supplies. Where statistics are given, each country is treated separately, and figures are provided for coal, oil, gas and electricity consumption as well as for hard currency indebtedness. The main East-West trade in energy which is relevant to Czechoslovakia concerns its supplies of electricity to neighbouring Austria.

543 **Problems of measuring industrial output in Czechoslovakia.**
Jan Michal. In: *The Czechoslovak contribution to world culture.* Edited by Miloslav Rechcígl, Jr. The Hague, London, Paris: Mouton, 1964, p. 373-78.

Unlike most papers in the collection in question, this one is primarily concerned with the then contemporary state of affairs, although pre-war computations are also discussed. The chief problem is seen as interpreting the relationship between the 'gross value' statistics as reported and the 'industrial income' statistics. This economist's view is that the gross-value index suggests a faster than actual growth.

544 **Herbs.**
František Starý, Václav Jirásek, English consultant F. J. Evans.
London, New York, Sydney, Toronto: Hamlyn, 1985. 12th
impression of 1973 ed. 239p.

This is another product of the cooperation between Czechoslovakia's publishing
and printing industries and Hamlyn. Its relevance to the present bibliography is
that it indirectly offers an insight into the extent to which herbal medicine is
cultivated in Czechoslovakia. There is a steady trickle of such books on the
Czechoslovak market. Wild-herb gathering and processing are major components
of the pharmaceuticals industry and the book at least provides some indication of
which herbs are cultivated in Czechoslovakia, or for which herbs the country is a
leading international supplier. What the book does not reveal is the extent of
hedgerow and field margin amateur herb-picking that is fostered by the state,
whereby individuals, or organizations, especially schools, harvest all manner of
wild plants in massive quantities for sale to the pharmaceuticals industry. Many of
the treatments described in the book are those in use by many ordinary Czech
families, and not just those in rural areas, whose medicine chest will often contain
a number of 'universal' herbs.

The world guide to beer.
See item no. 853.

Transport

545 **Public transport development in nineteeth-century Prague.**
Francis W. Carter. *Transport History*, vol. 6, no. 3 (1973),
p. 205-26. maps.
The administrative and economic development of the city is here related to
transport of all types, from cabs and horse omnibuses, horse trams to suburban
railways, and the inter-urban rail and river networks. Statistics covering: revenue
totals; home-to-work journey lengths; numbers of passengers; and the amounts of
different kinds of goods traffic are all included. Of separate relevance is the
consideration given to the evolution of Bohemia's rail network and to the
development of one of the city's largest industrial works the Českomoravská-
Kolben-Daněk (ČKD).

546 **Die museale Darstellung der Geschichte des Holztransportes im
Gebiet von Böhmen und Mähren im 19. und 20. Jahrhundert.** (The
exhibiting in museums of the 19th- and 20th-century history of
timber transportation in Bohemia and Moravia.)
Miroslav Landa. *Neue Museums Kunde*, vol. 27, no. 4 (1984),
p. 237-39.
Describes the historical forestry transport exhibition set up at the Ohrada hunting
lodge in Hluboká nad Vltavou by the Forestry, Hunting and Fishery Department
of the Prague Agricultural Museum. It includes illustrations of the early waggons
and sledges and more recent motorized and railed vehicles used. The article is
typical of many, in being in German and in setting out some of the practical
problems of such specialist displays in museum conditions. Czechoslovakia has a
great interest in this particular kind of display, for traditionally it is a country with
vast tracts of afforested land and forest exploitation remains a major industry.

547 Material relations and transport policy in the Czechoslovak Socialist Republic.
Karel Vítek. *Transport Policy and Decision Making*, vol. 1, no. 1 (1980), p. 27-46.

Presents official policy and describes the interconnections between the various sectors of the communications network and the nature of the decisions underlying investment input. Investment and production costs are also discussed.

548 Public transport in Eastern Europe: a case study of the Prague conurbation.
Francis W. Carter. *Transport Policy and Decision Making*, vol. 1, no. 3 (1980), p. 209-30. maps. bibliog.

A history of the development of transport which treats the pre-socialist and socialist periods separately. The aspects considered include: the problems of physical geography, such as the awkward location of the main station; the patterns of migration and commuting; statistics for road, rail, river and air traffic; and such limiting factors as a labour shortage, costlier oil imports, and the inefficiencies of a centrally planned economy. The new underground system was too new at the time to receive much attention; the Czechs lay great store by it, but, according to Carter, its success or failure will depend on fuel supply. So far it seems to be a success, despite his uncertainty.

549 How OK is ČSA?
Brian Wanstall. *Interavia*, vol. 40, no. 7 (1985), p. 767-68.

A brief account of the current activities of Czechoslovakia's national airline which was based on a study trip and interviews held with top company representatives. Apart from the question of profitability, ČSA is found to be OK (OK are the country's registration prefix letters) on every account, from present and future aircraft provision, staff training, maintenance programmes, and passenger and cargo payloads. The main domestic and international routes are mentioned, with special reference to recent domestic limitations brought about by the oil crisis. The question of profitability is left unanswered, but some grounds for doubt, especially in certain areas, are hinted at. The text is supported by graphs and photographs.

550 Soviet and East European transport problems.
Edited by John Ambler, Denis Shaw, Leslie Symons. London, Canberra: Croom Helm, 1985. 256p.

At the time of writing, this volume is at the 'forthcoming' stage, but it has been included for it must update parts of the two volumes by Bogdan Mieczkowski (q.v.). According to the publisher's notice the book 'looks at the different modes of transport and the problems faced by each, and examines the relationship between transport problems and problems of poor economic performance discussing the measures being taken to remedy the situation'. Moreover, transport systems are considered from the point of view of the individual countries and from that of their integration within Comecon.

Transport

551 **East European transport: regions and modes.**
Edited by Bogdan Mieczkowski. The Hague, Boston, London:
Martinus Nijhoff, 1980. 353p. maps.

Although the essays herein are conceived from the regional, East-European point
of view, they are also concerned with the increasing interaction with the transport
patterns in Western Europe. The role of Czechoslovakia within the discussion is
an important one, since she is at the meeting point. Most areas of transport are
discussed from the standpoint of integration within the public-sector systems, but
Jozef Wilczynski (p. 257-81), also considers the question of the private car, in the
context of economic planning.

552 **Transportation in Eastern Europe: empirical findings.**
Bogdan Mieczkowski. Boulder, Colorado: East European
Quarterly. Distributed by Columbia University Press, New York,
1978. 221p. maps. bibliog. (East European Monographs, no. 38).

This survey of transport in the whole area makes good sense, given the high
degree of integration between the economies of Eastern Europe. It describes the
geographic and economic factors which shape: transport patterns, planning,
growth and statistics; the costs to the exchequer and the user; and the specific
nature of international cooperation among Comecon countries and between them
and the rest of the world. All modes of transport are considered, especially rail,
road and air, including, for example, the container network, as well as related
topics such as the international movement of gas by pipeline. There are ample
references which specifically concern Czechoslovakia, which also figures indepen-
dently, or comparatively, in several of the tables. In some respects the work is
already dated, since it cannot take account of the most recent shifts away from
internal air transport to, in particular, long-distance buses and coaches.

553 **The steam locomotives of Eastern Europe.**
A. E. Durrant. Newton Abbot, England: David & Charles, 1972.
2nd ed. 160p. bibliog. (David & Charles Locomotive Studies).

Steam has now been ousted from the Czechoslovak State Railways, with the
exception of some deliberate preservations, on the Pioneer Railway in Eastern
Slovakia, near Košice, and elsewhere. However, the chapter on Czechoslovakia
(p. 90-105), provides a good outline history of all the types of steam engine ever
employed, with information on the builders, cooperation with foreign makers, the
wartime split of railway authorities with its generation of alien Hungarian and
Austrian types, and some detail on in-service use. A table offers principal
dimensions of the main classes, and the article includes photographs and some
technical diagrams. Chapter 13 deals with foreign-built wartime locomotives,
many of which operated during and after the war on Czechoslovak lines. The
important role of the Škoda works surfaces in a number of articles on other
countries in the volume.

Trade

54 International economic cooperation.
   Vladimír Wacker, translated by R. Klímová.   Prague: Orbis Press
   Agency, 1983. 85p.
This book can basically be divided into a description of trading relations between
Czechoslovakia and the other socialist countries, Czechoslovakia and the
capitalist West, and Czechoslovakia and the Third World. The emphasis is on the
latter two. What is perceived as important is the switch from straight bilateral
trade (exchange of goods), to the development of joint enterprises, related
scientific and technical contacts and the increased scale of production under
licence. All these are seen as being jeopardized by the crisis of capitalism and the
deteriorating international political situation (for which the West is blamed).
Includes official statistics.

**55 Council for Mutual Economic Assistance and the Czechoslovak
    Socialist Republic.**
   Vladimír Wacker.   Prague: Orbis Press Agency, 1979. 146p.
Describes, from a member's standpoint, the origins of Comecon and how far
economic integration among the member-states has progressed. The author also
examines the economic relations between the Council for Mutual Economic
Assistance (Comecon) and the rest of the world and the specifics of
Czechoslovakia's external economic relations. The work contains photographs
and tables for expressing the structure of foreign trade.

56 The institutions of Comecon.
   Giuseppe Schiavone.   London: Macmillan, 1981. 260p.
This recent account of all the functions, powers and institutions of the Council for
Mutual Economic Assistance, of which Czechoslovakia is an important member,
is a vital reference tool for those interested in the country's economy and foreign

trade. Financial cooperation and the machinery of payments and investment are
also described, but from the legal rather than the economic viewpoint.

557 **Oil and gas in Comecon cuntries.**
Daniel Park, introduction by Alec Nove.   London: Kogan Page;
New York: Nichols Publishing, 1979. 240p. bibliog.

The relevant specialist and general economic periodicals have sometimes singled
out Czechoslovakia for special attention during the oil crisis and the ongoing
energy crisis. However, this book, with its periodization, and detailed
presentation of the energy interrelations between Czechoslovakia and the other
Comecon partners, offers perhaps the best recent overview. It includes an implicit
explanation of the concern expressed in some of the periodical writings. The main
emphasis is on the Soviet Union's partners' dependency on the USSR for much of
their gas and oil needs, and on the consequences for the partners of changes in
the Soviet ability to supply. Czechoslovakia enjoys a handful of separate
paragraphs of coverage, and is well-represented in the many statistical tables.

558 **Coexistence and commerce: guidelines for transactions between East
and West.**
Samuel Pisar.   New York: McGraw Hill, 1970; London: Allen
Lane, Penguin, 1971. 558p.

Although now dated, there is much in this compendium that remains valid,
including the general nature of trade between East and West, with the limitations
legal and practical, exercised on both sides. It includes an analysis of the overall
legal framework and how the law operates in arbitration matters. It is also one of
the few works which deals with copyright law. Access to Czechoslovak data is
perforce via the index.

559 **Changing perspectives in East-West commerce.**
Edited by Carl H. McMillan.   Lexington, Massachusetts; Toronto
London: Lexington Books, D. C. Heath, 1974. 207p. bibliog.

The information on Czechoslovakia's foreign trade is partially submerged in the
general approach taken in this collection of papers. They are important, however
for implicitly emphasizing specific recent changes in the world – détente, the EEC
as a growing trading bloc, concern about various countries' indebtedness – and
the concomitant changing legal, commercial and financial perspectives for trade

560 **The multinationals and East-West relations: towards
transideological collaboration.**
Jozef Wilczynski.   London: Macmillan, 1976, repr. 1979. 235p.

Despite the title and the absence of any chapter devoted to Czechoslovakia, this is
a useful source on the nature and range of trade with the multinationals, all of
which are listed in the appendix. They include many Japanese-based companies
and the tables reveal that Czechoslovak-Japanese trade is no less significant than
trade within Europe. The book covers both sales of technology, end-products and
licences to the socialist countries, and the more limited range of corresponding
purchases by the multinationals. Separate sections consider: joint ventures

186

finance and the payments problem; socialist-owned multinationals (with an account of Eastern European banks operating in the West, including the Živnostenská banka); and some broader issues underlying bilateral trade.

561 **The EEC and Eastern Europe.**
Edited by Avi Shlaim, G. N. Yannopoulos. Cambridge, England: Cambridge University Press, 1978. 251p.

Much of Czechoslovakia's trading activities are tied into the overall practice of the East European trading bloc, Comecon. Accordingly, relatively little is written exclusively about Czechoslovakia, while there is quite a body of literature on area trade. This collection of essays is a case in point: within the various topics (the historical view, industrial cooperation, investment by the West in the East, financial relations between the two blocs, economic interdependence between them, and the role of international organizations) the general situation is portrayed, with a brief note *passim* on the random peculiarities of individual countries, including frequent references to Czechoslovakia (see index).

562 **Partners in East-West economic relations: the determinants of choice.**
Edited by Zbigniew M. Fallenbuchl, Carl H. McMillan. New York: Pergamon Press, 1980. 461p. (Pergamon Policy Studies on the Soviet Union and Eastern Europe).

Almost every conceivable aspect of Czechoslovak foreign trade is mentioned here, in one or other of the nineteen different papers and four blocks of 'comments' (the book is the outcome of a conference). However, only one paper is specific to the country in its own right, i.e., Jaroslav Nykryn's 'Traditional and nontraditional trade: the case of Czechoslovakia' (p. 236-52). The 'traditional' element is based on the country's highly developed industry, offering export possibilities, and its limited supply of raw materials, implying the need for imports. The 'non-traditional', which is seen as taking over from the traditional, is the area of direct cooperation, order-fulfilment for known foreign customers and more broadly formulated trading agreements, which are shown to play a part not just within Comecon, but also in trade with the West. Official statistics, and known practices show that there is considerable scope, to the benefit of both sides, for expansion in Czechoslovak trade with the West, and suggestions are made as to how this could be achieved (including recommendations concerning planning, incentives, and legal provisions). For an earlier collection of papers, reflecting one major 'determinant', though not in the sense intended above, namely the effects of the Soviet intervention in Czechoslovakia in 1968, see *East-West trade and the technology gap: a political and economic appraisal*, edited by Stanislaw Wasowski (New York, Washington, London: Praeger, 1970).

563 **East-West trade, industrial co-operation and technology transfer: the British experience.**
Malcolm R. Hill. Aldershot, England: Gower, 1983. 235p.

Many British companies have active trading relations with Comecon members, including Czechoslovakia. The channels through which this takes place, the nature of agreements, the interchange of licences and of course the specific areas

of technology in which the two sides are interested are all discussed, with many of
the substantial facts summarized in the appendixes. The book will interest both
economists and those contemplating joint ventures. A more broadly based study
of post-war trade, cooperation and economic relations is F. Levčík and J.
Stankovský's *Industrial cooperation between East and West* (White Plains, New
York: M. E. Sharpe; London: Macmillan, 1979. 286p. bibliog.).

564   **East-West trade and finance in the world economy: a new look for
the 1980s.**
Edited by Christopher T. Saunders.   London; Basingstoke,
England: Macmillan, 1985. 338p.

This valuable set of papers, which increases the reader's understanding of
Czechoslovakia's role in East-West trade and finance, is the outcome of an
international economic workshop held in Moscow in 1983 which was organized by
the Vienna Institute for Comparative Economic Studies. The topics covered
include: current trends and prospects for trade in the light of many economic
variables; hard-currency indebtedness of the Comecon states; energy, agricultural
and technical transfer; and the non-traditional nature of trade deals. Views of
both Eastern and Western economists are expressed.

565   **Facts on Czechoslovak foreign trade.**
Prague: Czechoslovak Chamber of Commerce and Industry, 1967-.
annual.

The basic facts of the year's trading are supported by statistical tables on exports
and imports in the various areas of the economy.

Science and Technology

566 Das goldene Bergbuch – Zlatá kniha baníćka. (The golden book of mining.)
Jozef Vozár. Bratislava: Veda, 1983. 675p.

Mineral resources and the scientific and technological developments involved in their extraction were a major factor in the evolution of modern Slovakia. This important historical text, in the original German of 1764 and a modern Slovak translation, offers a picture of all aspects of metal-working, from the extraction and processing of the ores to the production of metal goods and coinage in the Banská Štiavnica, Kremnica and Banská Bystrica fields. Kremnica is to this day the seat of the Czechoslovak mint. Banská Štiavnica was the first place in the world to use gunpowder in mining (1627), and it became the seat of the first college (academy) of mining (1763), which attracted students from as far away as Britain.

567 Mendel.
Vítězslav Orel, translated by Stephen Finn. Oxford, New York: Oxford University Press, 1984. 111p. map. bibliog. (Past Masters).

Gregor Mendel (1822-84) is now universally recognized as the father of modern genetics, and the laws of heredity which he discovered and explained in 1865 now bear his name. He was a monk who started experimenting with peas in his monastery garden, and although his results were published in German in 1866 it was not until 1900 that his contribution became recognized, posthumously. Orel reconstructs Mendel's experiments and explains how his remarkable achievement eventually became part of the mainstream of 20th-century science.

568 **The Purkinje Effect in the evolution of scientific thought.**
Karel Hujer. In: *The Czechoslovak contribution to world culture.*
Edited by Miloslav Rechcígl, Jr. The Hague, London, Paris:
Mouton, 1964, p. 449-57. bibliog.

Considers the part played in optics and in the philosophy of science of the
discovery, by Jan Evangelista Purkyně, that our perceptions of colour alter with
the intensity of illumination, different colours altering in different directions.
Purkyně (1787-1869) was an important figure in the National Revival and a
scholar in several fields. The optical effect here discussed is not the only discovery
to carry his name, which is more commonly associated with the study of cell
structures and the formulation of cellular theory.

569 **Jindřich Matiegka and the anthropometric approach to the study of**
body composition.
Josef Brožek. In: *The Czechoslovak contribution to world culture.*
Edited by Miloslav Rechcígl, Jr. The Hague, London, Paris:
Mouton, 1964, p. 458-61.

Matiegka was a leading anthropologist working in the 1920s at Charles University
who produced a novel approach to the calculation of tissue mass on the basis of
body measurements. This article explains the essence of the theory and why it
remained largely overlooked even though other, later theories have essentially
confirmed Matiegka's approach.

570 **Czechoslovak engineering until the Second World War.**
Joseph Z. Schneider. In: *The Czechoslovak contribution to world*
culture. Edited by Miloslav Rechcígl, Jr. The Hague, London,
Paris: Mouton, 1964, p. 477-81.

With its plethora of snippets of information, this entry could be in any one of
several sections of the present bibliography; under history, for its general
historical approach; under education, for the account of the first Czech technical
colleges (still in existence); under agriculture, for the data on malt, hops and
sugar-beet; or under extraterritorial populations for the account of engineering
endeavours by Czechs in North America. It is included in this section however,
since much of the chronological data is to do with 'firsts' in Czechoslovak industry
associated with Czech innovations in engineering and technology. It is worth
noting that this piece also refers to one and a half of the tiny handful of Czech
loan-words in English, namely *howitzer* and *br*en.

571 **The Czechoslovak contribution to the change in the concept of**
circulation of the blood.
Walter Redisch. In: *The Czechoslovak contribution to world*
culture. Edited by Miloslav Rechcígl, Jr. The Hague, London,
Paris: Mouton, 1964, p. 462-70.

This Czechoslovak contribution was the result of the work of Jan Evangelista
Purkyně and a number of later experimental physiologists who were either
Bohemian Germans, or Germans working in Prague, or, in the case of the study

of the hormonal regulation of blood flow, pure Czechs, such as Bohumil Prusík (1886-1964). The work of many Czech specialists right down to the time of writing is surveyed, with full references in the bibliography.

572 **Achievements of the Czechoslovak science and technology awarded State Prizes in 1973 and 1974.**
Central Office of Scientific, Technical and Economic Information, Department for Scientific and Technical Propaganda. Edited by František Ježek. Prague: Central Office of Scientific, Technical and Economic Information, 1974.

Issued only in very small numbers for publicity purposes, and probably matched by similar publications since, this work is representative of the approach used by the government to bring Czechoslovakia's achievements to the notice of the rest of the world. It contains more information, in condensed form, than appears to be noted by foreign publications.

573 **Czechoslovakian glass 1350-1980.**
Corning Museum of Glass and the Museum of Decorative Arts, Prague. Corning, New York: Corning Museum of Glass; New York: Dover Publications, 1981. 176p.

Glassware is one of Czechoslovakia's major exports, and glass as the raw material of countless art forms, applied and otherwise, has a long and hallowed tradition. This Corning publicaton, with the direct cooperation of the premier Czechoslovak museum concerned with glass in art, offers probably the best survey in English of the scientific, industrial and artistic development of glass in the country. It is worth noting that items relating to Czech and Slovak glass and glassmakers figure from time to time in other Corning publications, especially periodicals.

574 **Czechoslovak machine-tool developments.**
Machinery (5 Feb. 1975), p. 848-50; 9 Apr. 1975, p. 338-43; 24-31 Dec. 1975, p. 616-21.

Published at a time when Czechoslovakia was looking for ways to cope with the recent rise in imported oil prices, these articles reflect the country's attempt to sell more of its modern machine-tools as a source of hard currency. The emphasis is on technological innovation. *Machinery* is just one of the specialist trade magazines in which such innovations are publicized. Another of Czechoslovakia's traditionally strong areas in machine technology is that of textile machinery, and reports on developments in this field are included in, for example, *Textile Month*. See, for instance, W. Andrew's 'Progress in East European textile machinery shown in Czechoslovakia' in *Textile Month*, no. 12 (1976); this particular article was a by-product of one of the country's trade-fairs.

Science and Technology

575 **Management problems of Slapy Reservoir, Bohemia, Czechoslovakia.**
M. Straškraba, Vera Straškrabová. Reading, England: Water
Research Centre, 1975. 34p. (The Effects of Storage on Water
Quality, a Water Research Centre Symposium, 24-26 March 1975,
Paper 16, Session 4).

Although a technical paper based on detailed limnological studies of Slapy
Reservoir over the previous almost twenty years, it has been included here
because it presents an introduction to the Reservoir itself. Originally built as a
hydro-electric power source, it is now a major source of water for the city of
Prague and is a very popular and accessible recreation centre (boating, fishing,
weekend chalet colonies on the banks). This and another more recent paper,
'Spectral analysis of the automatically recorded data from Slapy Reservoir,
Czechoslovakia', by I. Nesměrák and M. Straškraba (*Internationale Revue
gesamter Hydrobiologie*, vol. 70, no. 1[1985], p. 27-46), illustrate not only the
specific hydrological and ecological problems of one Bohemian reservoir, but also
the state of the relevant technologies in contemporary Czechoslovakia.

576 **The place of East-West technology transfer: a study of
Czechoslovakia.**
Friedrich Levcik, Jiri Skolka. Paris: OECD, 1984. 102p.

A detailed statistical study of the range and nature of technology transfer
involving Czechoslovakia and Organization for Economic Cooperation and
Development (OECD) countries. Many aspects are considered: exports to OECD
countries; Czechoslovakia's energy requirements; research and development;
capital goods imports; and the overall problems of cooperation. A complete
account is given of specific Western corporations that have held presentations in
Czechoslovakia and individual projects and installations supplied by Western
firms. By the nature of the work, there are countless supporting tables, and the
study concludes with an assessment of the future role of Western technology in
the country's economic development. The situation appears by no means bleak.

577 **Slovak Academy of Sciences.**
Compiled by Ján Jurikovič, Ján Brechtl. Bratislava: Veda, 1980.
24p.

An information brochure detailing the history and objectives of the Slovak
Academy with: an account of current publishing and research activities; a
directory of personnel and membership; a list of institutes and facilities; the
names of learned societies associated with the Academy; and the titles of
periodicals published by it. Appended plates, unpaginated, illustrate some of the
institutes, the personnel as well as work in progress.

578   National science information systems: a guide to science information
      systems in Bulgaria, Czechoslovakia, Hungary, Rumania and
      Yugoslavia.
      David H. Kraus (et al.).   Cambridge, Massachusetts: MIT Press,
      1972. 325p.
Considers the organization of systems for the dissemination of scientific and
technical information within, first, the framework of characteristics common to all
the countries named and, second, the specific context of each country's own
system.

Urbanization

Edited by Keith Hitchins.   Leiden, The Netherlands: E. J. Brill,
1981. 2 vols. maps.

Volume 2 has as its first theme 'Urbanization in Czechoslovakia' and contains
four papers on quite disparate topics. Gary B. Cohen's 'Ethnicity and urban
population growth: the decline of the Prague Germans, 1880-1920' (p. 3-26) is
almost a mirror image of a book by the same author entitled *The politics of ethnic
survival: the Germans in Prague 1861-1914* (q.v.). Indeed it partly repeats this
latter work before approaching the pressures which led Czechs, Germans and
Jews in the city to clarify their linguistic and national allegiances once and for all,
stressing the different trends in different wards. Owen V. Johnson's 'Urbanization
and the formation of a Slovak intelligentsia' (p. 27-61) stresses the importance of
the expansion of towns to the Slovak 'intelligentsia' (which here is given a very
necessary critical definition), who wished to attain a strength capable of
combating the (Catholic) Slovak People's Party's simple village-centred political
philosophy. He includes tables to show the changing nationality and social
structure of Bratislava and other towns, and emphasizes the role of the education
services and the media during the First Republic in curtailing the Hungarian
influence. Ronald Smelser's 'German-Czech relations in Bohemian frontier
towns: the industrialization/urbanization process' (p. 62-87) is essentially a history
of the Czech gravitation from the country and small towns to the larger centres
and the friction that ensued in industry and local government, and, by the 1930s,
in central government as well. F. Gregory Campbell's 'Banking and nationality
conflict in the modernization of the Bohemian Crown Lands' (p. 88-105)
examines the growth of competitive banking among the Czechs as part of the
urbanization process, including an effective history of the important and still
extant Živnostenská banka.

580 **Urbanization in socialist countries.**
Jiří Musil. White Plains, New York: M. E. Sharpe; London:
Croom Helm, 1981. 188p. bibliog.

The book deals with urbanization in all the European socialist states except
Albania, but in varying depths according to the availability of sources.
Czechoslovakia is accorded a particularly detailed treatment, especially in the
fields of demography, economics and planning, and the sections on Czechoslovakia
can be read in isolation from the rest of the book. A more informative work
overall is R. A. French and F. E. Hamilton's *The socialist city: spatial structure
and urban policy* (Chichester, England; New York; Brisbane, Australia; Toronto:
John Wiley, 1979).

581 **Urbanization under socialism: the case of Czechoslovakia.**
Karel Joseph Kansky. New York; Washington, DC; London:
Praeger, 1976. 313p. maps. bibliog. (Praeger Special Studies in
International Economics and Development).

Kansky offers this work as a description of things as he found them and
acknowledges that statistics are not always verifiable. He certainly does not use
official Czechoslovak statistics, which he has found unreliable and prone to
deliberate political bias. This said, he seeks to provide a comprehensive account
of the urban geography, social history, landscape and life-style of modern
Czechoslovakia, and refers to such factors as: crime and delinquency; pollution;
the state of the utilities; patterns of shopping and travel; conservation; as well as
to such central topics as population growth; the development of the housing
stock; and the Party-state agencies involved in town, transport and industrial
planning. The ruling Communist Party has to take the blame for the failings,
contradictions and inadequacies observed, since it is the ultimate source of
guidelines and directives on urban development, as on most aspects of the
country's life. In this respect it is not surprising that similarities are found with
developments in neighbouring socialist states, but the overall influence of the
Soviet Union is perhaps overstated. The book is well-furnished with an apparatus
of maps, tables and graphs.

582 **Housing policy in European socialist countries: the Czechoslovak
experience.**
Jan Adam. *Jahrbuch der Wirtschaft Osteuropas*, vol. 6 (1975),
p. 231-52.

Outlines the philosophy underlying post-war housing policy in socialist Czechoslovakia, analysing the problems which the country faced, and is, in part, still
seeking to overcome through the continued building of massive satellite housing
estates, near self-contained suburban townships.

583 **Essays in world urbanization.**
Edited by R. L. Jones. London: George Philip, 1975.

Contains a short essay by O. Basovský and M. Blažek on the development of
towns in 'Czechoslovakia' (p. 236-37).

584 **Urban development in East-Central Europe: Poland,
Czechoslovakia and Hungary.**
Edited by E. A. Gutkind. New York: Free Press; London:
Collier-Macmillan, 1972. 339p. bibliog. (International History of
City Development, vol. 7).

A combined work by specialists from each of the countries named. In general
terms and by specific examples they discuss the origins and development of towns
in their own country. Although not specifically comparative, the volume does
allow some meaningful comparisons, especially in the light of the overlapping of
the countries' history and economic development at different periods.

585 **Prague: some contemporary growth problems.**
Francis W. Carter. *Bulletin of the Société Royale de Géographie
d'Anvers*, vol. 81 (1970), p. 197-218. maps.

The problems discerned relate to: the ability of the agricultural hinterland to
satisfy the food demands of the city; certain effects of the huge concentration of
industry; the great demands placed on a geographically (railways) and climatically
(rivers) constrained transport network; the city transport authority's fight to cope
with rapidly increasing numbers of users; and population growth, migration and
density. Solutions are suggested in the stabilization of the working capacity of the
city, better housing, security in the supply of building materials, specialization and
increased production in agriculture, and a major reorganization of the transport
networks. The paper contains a wealth of statistical information, a great deal of
detail on the distribution of individual industries and sections on agriculture, and
some on the historical background to the problems. A similar article, but with
more of the history and a much more detailed geography (physical and economic
and geology) is 'Prague et la Bohême centrale: quelques problèmes de croissance'
(Prague and Central Bohemia: some problems of growth), *Annales de
Géographie*, vol. 82, no. 450 (March-April 1973), p. 165-92.

586 **Concentrated Prague.**
Francis W. Carter. *Geographical Magazine*, vol. 40, no. 7 (July
1974), p. 537-44. 6 maps.

In an article as concentrated as its title, Carter provides a good introduction to the
city's evolution, in terms of its wonderful range of architectural variety, its pattern
of industrial spread and its transport network and demographic changes. As
important adjuncts to the life of this city of over a million inhabitants the
agriculture and recreational facilities of the surrounding region are also described.
Pollution and industrial planning are among the problems faced by what the well-
chosen photographs show is a truly beautiful city. Another portrait of the city,
'Prague in winter', by Peter T. White, photographs by Nathan Benn (*National
Geographic*, vol. 155, no. 4 (April 1979), p. 546-67), stresses the merging of
ancient and modern. The photographs include one of Antonín Langweil's famous
1834 cardboard model of the city and an aerial view of a mass rally held to
celebrate 30 years of communist rule.

587 **Prague and Sofia: an analysis of their changing internal city structure.**
Francis W. Carter.   In: *The Socialist city: spatial and urban policy.*
Edited by R. A. French and F. E. Ian Hamilton. Chichester,
England; New York; Brisbane; Toronto: John Wiley, 1979,
p. 425-59. maps. bibliog.
There is more in this paper than the title suggests; the author provides a potted
architectural history and examines the sale and rental of dwellings, inward
migration from the rural areas, as well as the more obvious topics such as recent
developments in architecture, the location of industry, the adaptation of a
mediaeval and capitalist city to modern socialist requirements and the elaboration
of master plans. The description of the city's contemporary specific features is
based on conditions in 1975 and includes an account of the then current problems:
shortcomings in building practice; nuisances such as vandalism and rubbish
dumping; and the restoration of historic buildings, neglected for years. Much of
what was then described as plans for the future has since come about, such as the
inner-motorway ring, the underground railway and the provision of more sectoral
amenities. The paper can be read without direct reference to the sections on
Sofia, but these do provide some interesting contrasts. The bibliography, though
beginning to be dated, contains a number of further titles in English, not all of
them included in this bibliography.

588 **Four towns in a Bohemian setting.**
A. E. J. Morris.   *Geographical Magazine*, vol. 45, no. 11 (Aug.
1973), p. 814-19. maps.
The four towns concerned are all in Southern Bohemia: Tábor; České
Budějovice; Český Krumlov; and Telč. They are each quite distinctive in
character for reasons of history, geography, and administrative status and the
discussion centres on the planning and conservation problems these different
considerations bring with them. The article is well illustrated.

Environment

589 **Conservation problems of historic cities in Eastern Europe.**
Francis W. Carter. London: University College Department of
Geography, 1981. 44p. maps. (Department of Geography,
University College London, Occasional Papers, no. 39).

Identifies the main themes in Eastern European conservationism, and the
different priorities of different countries. The study is essentially comparative and
the Czechoslovak dimension emerges throughout. There is, however, a separate
case-study on Prague. In addition, the book contains maps of the locations of
national and regional urban conservation areas and a table showing the
distribution by region of the different architectural periods represented at various
protected centres. The annotations constitute a detailed set of bibliographical
references, though a formal, ordered bibliography is absent.

590 **Pollution problems in post-war Czechoslovakia.**
Francis W. Carter. *Transactions of the Institute of British
Geographers*, vol. 10, New Series (1984), p. 17-44. maps.

An examination of the causes and consequences of long-term environmental
deterioration – air, water, soil and noise pollution – in Czechoslovakia which is
used as an example of a state with a centrally planned economy. Moreover, the
author discusses the fairly recent innovations in the law which seek to rectify some
of the damage. Most of the problems are caused by the activities of organizations
in various sectors of the 'energy industry' and by over-intensive use of artificial
fertilizers. There have already been serious consequences for the nation's health.
In addition to several references to Western secondary sources, this article also
provides a very wide-ranging introduction to the problems as aired in Czech and
Slovak primary sources. It should be noted that one of the maps shows the
location of National Parks.

591   **Pollution in Prague: environmental control in a centrally planned socialist country.**
Francis W. Carter.   *Cities*, vol. 1, no. 3 (1984), p. 258-73.
This is a more detailed case study of many of the issues raised in the previous entry. Of the many types of pollution, only that of the air is seen as having improved since peaking in 1966; before then, with no legislation, the increase had been dramatic. Noise and water pollution continue to give cause for concern.

592   **Landscape and man in socialist Czechoslovakia.**
Edited by O. Vidláková, translated from the Czech by
E. Kovanda. Prague: Orbis, 1977. 111p. maps.
A collection of five studies designed to explain what provisions Czechoslovakia has made in the direction of nature conservation and protection of the environment. It recognizes the conflicting interests of the economy and private recreation and concedes that still more needs to be achieved. The work that is actually being done is probably somewhat overstated. The maps show the administrative divisions of the country, the distribution of rivers and mountains, the network of main roads, and the location of National Parks and other protected areas. Photographic plates, some coloured, provide examples of rural and urban landscapes.

593   **The engineering of landscaping in an historical area of Central Europe.**
Vlastimil Vaniček, Antonín Hrabal.   *Landscape Planning*, vol. 1, no. 1 (June, 1974), p. 57-79. maps.
Landscape engineering is a subject of increasing importance to Czechoslovakia's environmentalists. This relatively early paper discusses some of the issues in relation to Southern Moravia.

594   **Die forsttechnischen Meliorationen und Wildbachverbauungen in Böhmen and Mähren bis 1918.** (Forest land-improvement techniques and mountain torrent regulation in Bohemia and Moravia up to 1918.)
Miroslav Landa.   *News of Forest History*, no. 1, pilot issue (Aug. 1984), p. 1-5.
This article is concerned with the 19th- and early 20th-century legal, practical and technical background to some of the geographically and ecologically important reafforestation and torrent control schemes in various areas of Bohemia, Moravia and Silesia. The localities and rivers concerned are all named, and the costs involved in the projects are given. The periodical in which the article appeared is a new Austrian venture and this pilot issue contains lists of titles of papers presented at a variety of recent forestry conferences, some of them relevant to Czechoslovakia, though all in German.

Environment

595 **Floodplain forest ecosystem.**
Miroslav Penka, Miroslav Vyskot, Emil Klimo, Ferdinand
Vašíček. Prague: Academia, 1984. 432p. maps. bibliog.
The River Dyje in Moravia has been subject to regulation because of the building
of a huge dam. This detailed ecological study of every conceivable aspect of the
ecosystem of the local floodplain forest relates to conditions before the changes to
the river, which have completely altered the humidity conditions in areas
previously prone to flooding. The Dyje Dam and reservoir is only one of a
number of major hydroengineering projects on the country's rivers.

596 **Ekológia (ČSSR).** (Ecology, CSSR.)
Bratislava: Veda, 1982-. quarterly.
This journal is published by the Institute of Experimental Biology and Ecology of
the Centre for Biological and Ecological Sciences of the Slovak Academy of
Sciences. It is described as a journal examining the ecological problems of the
biosphere, and is a respectable publication dealing with all manner of serious
theoretical and practical ecological problems. The periodical covers the whole
country, not just Slovakia, and a large proportion of the articles are in English. In
any event every contribution is preceded by a English abstract.

597 **Krkonošský národní park.** (The Krkonoše – Giant Mountains –
National Park.)
Bohuslav Sýkora (et al.). Prague: Státní zemědělské
nakladatelství, 1983. 278p. 2 maps (loose). bibliog.
Declared a National Park in 1963, the Giant Mountains are an area of striking
natural beauty on the Bohemian-Polish border with a great wealth of rare and
interesting species of flora and fauna. Published to mark the 20th anniversary of
the National Park, this compact volume offers a total description of the area's:
geology; hydrology; climate; flora and fauna; agriculture; forestry and industry;
population; folklore; architecture; conservation; and sport and recreation. The
text, which is in Czech only, but with a slender English summary, is supported by
tables, reproductions and photographs, themselves a more than adequate
introduction to the region. Where relevant, each section includes a historical
précis as, for example, for education or tourism. The *Year-book of the
Administration of the Krkonoše National Park* appears in English (Hradec
Králové: Kruh) and provides a good idea of the day-to-day research and
management activities involved in the running of the Park.

598 **TANAP: zborník prác o tatranskom národnom parku.** (TANAP:
occasional papers on the Tatra National Park.)
Bratislava; Martin, Czechoslovakia: Obzor. irregular.
Each collection of papers is internally subdivided by discipline or area, and deals
with current problems and the present state of research in, for example,
hydrology, zoology, botany, forestry, conservation and ethnography. Some
contributions are of a wide interest while others are narrowly specialist. Résumés
are given in Russian, German and English. TANAP is the main National Park in
Slovakia.

200

Chráněná území přírody ČSSR. (Nature Conservation areas of Czechoslovakia).
See item no. 50.

Sport and Recreation

599 Sokol: the Czechoslovak national gymnastic organisation.
   F. A. Toufar.   London: George Allen & Unwin, 1941. 66p.
Published during the war, this is the last major English publication concerning the
Sokol movement and idea before its jamborees (*slety*) were replaced by the
spartakiads of the new régime. The work is historical, and traces the post-1848
background out of which the movement was born in 1862 and its subsequent
evolution. It is also biographical and is particularly concerned with the founder
Miroslav Tyrš (1832-1884). In addition the author describes the organization's
insignia, slogans, the music used in its displays, celebrated members, and related
organizations among Czech communities abroad.

**600 Sport under communism: the USSR, Czechoslovakia, the GDR,
   China, Cuba.**
   Edited by James Riordan.   London: C. Hurst, 1981. 2nd ed. 181p.
This is perhaps the best account of the subject by a writer who has long studied it
especially in the Soviet context. It covers both the political and practical aspects
of the organization and performance of sport. Traditionally, at least since the
National Revival, sport has, of course, played an important part in the country's
life. Indeed, for ideological as well as health reasons sport continues to play a
significant role in Czechoslovakia.

601 Czechoslovakia and Olympic Games.
   Jan Kotrba, Zdeněk Illman, Jiří Kössl, translated by Libor
   Trejdl.   Prague: Orbis Press Agency, 1984. 143p.
The first part of this book provides an account of the Czechs' involvement with
the Olympic movement from the days well before political independence right up
to the present. It should be noted that a Czech, Jiří Guth, who also used the
pseudonym Stanislav Jarkovský, was one of the founding members of the
International Olympic Committee. Due reference is made to the strong traditions

202

of physical culture among the Czechs, starting with the 19th-century Sokol movement founded by Miroslav Tyrš, but also recalling Comenius' *Panorthosia*, in which he had recommended the re-organization of Olympic games. The second part is a photographic portrait gallery depicting Czechoslovak Olympic sportsmen and some other, non-Olympic sporting events in the country. The third section consists of short sketches on the careers and Olympic successes of nineteen Czech or Slovak, individual or team, medal-winners, and the final section is a chronological table of Czechoslovak successes from 1948 to 1980, giving all first to sixth places attained. The work is marred by the unevenness of the translation, which seeks to achieve a racy English journalistic style.

602 **Checkmate in Prague.**
Luděk Pachman, translated by Rosemary Brown. London: Faber & Faber, 1975. 216p.

Luděk Pachman, at one time Czechoslovakia's leading chess-player, gained considerable notoriety, like many other sportsmen, artists, writers and others for his opposition to the Czechoslovak régime. This book of memoirs is not only one man's view of his country's history and his own unhappy brushes with the powers that be, but also an account of the author's career in chess, with some reference to the game's organization and some of the tournaments in which he participated. Pachman is the author of numerous books on chess for players of all standards of attainment (published by Routledge & Kegan Paul).

603 **Československá Spartakiáda 1980.** (The Czechoslovak Spartakiad, 1980.)
Edited by Július Chvalný (et al.), texts by Zvonimír Šupich. Prague: Olympia; Bratislava: Šport, 1981. 176p.

Physical education has evolved into an area where sport and politics meet. This is reflected in the five-yearly mass displays of physical education known as Spartakiads which are heavily promoted by the state and in which over 150,000 people take part in the final with up to a million being involved in the regional run-ups. The 1980 event, described as a 'festival of peace and socialism' and associated with the thirty-fifth anniversary of the country's liberation by the Soviet Union, is recorded in this volume of photographs, which illustrates the sheer proportions of the undertaking and the variety and size of the individual displays. The text provides some of the historical background, but no mention of the debt to the Sokol movement, whose 'slety' were the forerunners of the modern gymnastic displays. Statistical information about the performance is, however, supplied together with details about the authors of the various compositions. For the foreign reader a summary of the 1980 events is given in Russian, English, German, French and Spanish.

604 **The Czechoslovak Spartakiad 1985.**
Zdeněk Lipský, translated by Alžběta Rejchrtová. Prague: Orbis Press Agency, 1984. 48p. map.

Published in anticipation of the 1985 Spartakiad, this somewhat dreary, ideologically laden document gives some sparse background information on the Czechoslovak physical training ethos and statistics pertaining to the previous event (1980). For those who have not seen the film of the event on British television, the photographs at least give an idea of the sheer magnitude and complexity of the undertaking.

605 **Skiing in Slovakia.**
Slovakia National Council Committee for Tourism. Bratislava: Slovak National Council Committee for Tourism [n.d.] [unpaginated] 20p. map.

This photographic introduction to the main Slovak ski resorts is in colour and is a publicity brochure designed to attract winter tourism to areas already well-patronized by natives and large numbers from neighbouring countries. More important is the twenty-eight page loose insert in English, French and German containing an introduction to the terrain and specific accounts of individual complexes, including tables giving altitudes, number of days with snow cover, daylight hours and means of access to the various sites. It is an official publication normally available through Čedok, from which similar, more general publications will also be available, such as *Winter in Czechoslovakia* (Prague: Merkur [n.d.], 8p. + 24p. insert), which extends coverage to the Czech Lands.

606 **Fishing in the Czech Socialist Republic.**
Government Committee for Tourism of the Czech Socialist Republic and the Czech Fishing Association. Prague: Merkur, 1983. [unpaginated] 22p. map.

This is essentially a publicity brochure for tourists with a mind to try their hand at angling and it is normally only available through Czechoslovak agencies (Čedok). However, it is a good introduction to the country's riverscapes and fishponds, with fairly detailed physical and distributional descriptions of twelve species of fish. A loosely inserted sixteen-page leaflet lists the best fishing grounds for individual species and provides statistical tables for sizes of catches per annum and individual record catches. The same leaflet also outlines the provisions for angling in the Czech republic with details of how to obtain permits.

607 **Náš hokej.** (Czechoslovak ice-hockey.)
Compiled by Vladimír Dobrovodský, Stanislav Halásek, text by Václav Pacina, Slovak text translated by Ferdinand Kráľovič, Russian résumé translated by I. Temnova, English résumé translated by M. Paule, and German résumé translated by Z. Bútorová. Prague: Olympia; Bratislava: Šport, 1985. 2nd updated ed. 176p.

Ice-hockey is the country's major spectator sport, alongside football. Moreover, Czechoslovakia, together with Canada, the United States, the Soviet Union, Sweden and Finland, is one of the game's main international exponents and is a frequent finalist in the international championship, which it has won on a number of memorable occasions. Czechoslovak players and trainers have also contributed to the success of foreign teams. This publication is a portrait of the contemporary game and its players, especially at the top of the league and in the national team. It also records recent Czechoslovak international successes. The text is supported by over 100 mostly coloured photographs. The same publisher produces an ice-hockey yearbook which records the year's events and statistics, with the emphasis on the home competitions.

608   **Atletika – encyklopédia.** (Athletics – an encyclopaedia.)
Andrej Kuchen, (et al.).   Bratislava: Šport, 1985. 304p.

Although world-wide in its coverage, this volume contains details about all the major national competitions and the best-known Czechoslovak athletes. It is supported by many coloured and black-and-white photographs.

609   **Chata and chalupa: recreational houses in the Czech Socialist Republic.**
Lawrence C. Herold.   *Social Science Journal*, vol. 18, no. 1 (Jan. 1981), p. 51-68.

With the vast majority of the urban population living in flats, there is a strong tendency to seek an escape to a second home. This has led to a strengthening tradition among many classes of city dwellers to acquire a *chata*, a purpose-built chalet or rudimentary shack, or a *chalupa*, which is usually a cottage or other redundant village property, of which many are available as the young rural population moves to the towns and the old generation dies out. There is some overlapping of the terminology of *chata/chalupa*, and the words may conceal some quite large second (weekend) homes.

610   **Being myself.**
Martina Navrátilová, with George Vecsey.   London: Collins, 1985. 272p.

Genuinely more about herself than her tennis, Martina Navrátilová's book nevertheless offers some insights into her pre-emigration tennis career as such, as well as providing a passing introduction to other Czech players and the running of the game in Czechoslovakia. The style will not suit everybody but somehow it fits the character who has become so familiar through her televised matches. Some photographs from childhood onwards are included.

Language

General and historical

611 **The Slavic literary languages.**
Edited by Alexander M. Schenker, Edward Stankiewicz. New
Haven, Connecticut: Yale Concilium on International and Area
Studies, 1980. 287p.

The two sections on Czech (Robert Auty, p. 163-82, bibliog.) and Slovak
(Ľubomír Ďurovič, p. 211-28, bibliog.) are the most recent general histories of the
languages. Auty presents the patterns of historicizing conservatism and waves of
purism as the main trends to have given Czech its present shape, and relates the
religious history of the nation to the history of its language. Reference is also
made to the development of the alphabet, the early grammars, and the formation
of the lexicon. Ďurovič gives religious considerations even more prominence, and
this, coupled with the disjointed geographical spread of the language has led to
different regional variations, or hybrid creations, being preferred at different
times and places. In particular he recalls the vastly different attitudes to Czech as
an alternative language for the Slovaks. There is more here than in Auty's paper
on the specific grammatical features of the language, and it is generally more
detailed on both areas of controversy and the more recent developments. The
bibliographies are separate from the main articles, on p. 271-74 and 278-80,
respectively. Auty's bibliography in particular contains a number of references to
his own earlier works dealing with specific topics in greater detail.

612   **The formation of the Slavonic literary languages: proceedings of a conference held in memory of Robert Auty and Anne Pennington at Oxford 6-11 July 1981.**
Edited by Gerald Stone, Dean Worth.   Columbus, Ohio: Slavic Publishers, 1985. 269p. bibliog. (UCLA Slavic Studies, vol. 11).

A volume of recent studies which incorporates, in both the 'General and Comparative' and 'West Slavonic' sections, papers on many topics relevant to the history or contemporary development of both Czech and Slovak. It is always invidious to mention some rather than all, but I would pick out Peter Király's paper on the role of the Buda University Press in the development of orthography and literary languages (p. 29-38) and Jozef Mistrík's on the modernization of contemporary Slovak (p. 71-76), the former since it has been little discussed in English and the Buda press was a major source of 18th- and 19th-century Slovak and Czech printings, and the latter since it summarizes a great deal of what has been appearing of late in Slovak linguistic journals.

613   **Moravian codification of the first Slavic literary language**
Ladislav Matějka.   In: *The Czechoslovak contribution to world culture.* Edited by Miloslav Rechcígl, Jr. The Hague, London, Paris: Mouton, 1964, p. 105-11.

The most widely accepted view is that Old Church Slavonic, the first written Slav language, and a major contributor to the cultural versions of many of the younger Slavonic languages that have evolved out of the early dialect divisions, was given its written form by the Slav evangelists Cyril (Constantine) and Methodius. Although they originally came from Macedonia, they carried out their task of translating the scriptures and other liturgical works into Slavonic in Moravia at the request of Prince Rastislav in 863. This paper reviews the earliest manuscripts in Slavonic, including those acknowledged to be the first representatives of Old Czech.

614   **Die historische und sprachwissenschaftliche Entwicklung der slowakischen Sprache: die Streitfragen der Vergangenheit und die neuesten Theorien.** (The historical and linguistic evolution of the Slovak language: the disputed issues of the past and the most recent theories.)
Milan St. Ďurica.   *Slowakei*, vol. 17-18 (1979-80), p. 24-51.

Some recent publications in Slovakia (notably those by Rudolf Krajčovič, and František Kopečný's work on the common core of the Slav lexicon) have led to an increasing popularity of the notion that Slovak is of respectable antiquity and no mere offshoot of Czech. There is little in the way of new evidence, the entire issue being one of interpretation. This article summarizes the latest thinking on the subject against the background of the 'offshoot-of-Czech theory' and the inter-war linguistic policy of a 'Czechoslovak' language in two local variants. It carries an anti-Czech bias and contains one or two controversial assertions, but it nevertheless highlights the various aspects of the problem of Slovak as a separate language.

Language. General and historical

615 **Czech historical grammar.**
Stuart E. Mann. London: Athlone Press, 1957. 183p. bibliog.
This is the only complete history of the language available in English. The author deals with different segments of the grammar in turn, rather than providing a consecutive history, periodized with each major shift in any part of the system, which is the presentation followed by more recent works of Czech origin (see below). However, the work does draw generously on etymologies and the prehistoric periods of evolution, in accordance with the generally accepted reconstructions. The book also contains a summary account of the modern dialects, the Old Czech textual sources, some illustrative Old Czech literary extracts and a note on the composition of the Czech vocabulary. The best recent historical grammar from Czechoslovakia itself is *Historický vývoj češtiny* [The historical evolution of Czech] (Prague: Státní pedagogické nakladatelství, 1977. 309p. maps. bibliog.) by Arnošt Lamprecht, Dušan Šlosar and Jaroslav Bauer, while on the dialects readers should consult the various works by Jaromír Bělič or Slavomír Utěšený.

616 **The role of calques in the early Czech language revival.**
G. Thomas. *Slavonic and East European Review*, vol. 74, no. 4 (Oct. 1978), p. 448-504.
A major process within the National Revival was the re-shaping of the Czech language which was perceived as inadequate to many modern needs. In some cases there were indeed no satisfactory Czech expressions, in others there were, but German in origin. This paper deals with one of the two processes by which the situation was rectified, calquing, the other being borrowing direct from other Slavonic languages, though this was more typical of the later stage in the Revival. For another paper on the re-shaping of the modern Czech literary languages see Yves Millet's 'Continuité et discontinuité: le cas du tchèque' in *Language reform, history and future, vol. II*, edited by István Fodor and Claude Hagège (Hamburg, GFR: Buske Verlag, 1983. 521p.), p. 479-504.

617 **Guide to the West Slavonic languages. (Guide to the Slavonic languages, part 2.)**
R. G. A. de Bray. Columbus, Ohio: Slavica Publishers, 1980. 3rd ed. 483p. bibliog. (Previous editions were published by Dent).
This is the standard reference work providing traditional descriptive grammars of all the West Slavonic grammars. The section on Czech was revised for the second edition, that on Slovak for this most recent version. Each section contains an historical introduction and some literary passages as examples of the language at work, as well as the grammar proper. This is likely to remain, despite its flaws, the major scholarly reference work in English for some time.

Dictionaries

618 **Slovník spisovného jazyka českého.** (Dictionary of the Czech
literary language.)
Compiled by the lexicographic collective of the Institute for the
Czech Language of the Czechoslovak Academy of Sciences, led by
Bohuslav Havránek, Jaromír Bělič, M. Helcl, Alois Jedlička,
Václav Křístek, František Trávníček. Prague: Academia, 1971.
4 vols.
In the absence of any comparable dictionary this *is* the basic modern lexicon. It is
descended from the nine-volume *Příruční slovník jazyka českého* (Reference
dictionary of the Czech language) of 1935-57, which was equally without
competition. From the dates of publication it is clear that these dictionaries
cannot be easily obtained, but most Slavonic libraries will have them. It is really
rather remarkable that the national language community should not be better
served by having ready access to a large dictionary. The situation is only partially
saved by the publication of Josef Filipec and František Daneš's *Slovník spisovné
češtiny pro školu a veřejnost* (q.v.).

619 **Slovník spisovné češtiny pro školu a veřejnost.** (Dictionary of
literary Czech for school and public.)
Edited by Josef Filipec, František Daneš. Prague: Academia,
1978. 799p.
Amazingly, the Czechs were without a single-volume dictionary of their language
for over a quarter of a century, the last having been the 1952 edition of the 1937
Slovník jazyka českého (Dictionary of the Czech language) by Pavel Váša and
František Trávníček. The present dictionary, although dated 1978, has gone into a
number of reprintings since and is fairly widely available. It differs from both the
preceding entry and the Váša-Trávníček work in concentrating on those areas of
the vocabulary that have recently begun to dominate, namely the more technical
element, deliberately omitting much that is purely 'literary'. It also contains much
of a theoretical nature, relating to lexicography in general and recent changes in
the Czech standard language.

620 **Etymologický slovník jazyka českého.** (Etymological dictionary of
the Czech language.)
Václav Machek. Prague: Academia, 1971. 3rd ed. 866p. bibliog.
This is the standard etymological dictionary of the language. Usually, prefixed
words do not appear as separate entries, so a knowledge of basic forms, even if
obsolescent is essential. The work contains a wealth of peripheral words –
regional, dialectal or even some Slovak items and various types of interjections –
in addition to the central native word-stock. The bibliography is presented only in
the form of explanations to the list of abbreviations employed. However, a
language-by-language list of all the words referred to in the etymological glosses
to the entry-words is provided (p. 732-866). Although widely accepted and
generally reliable, Machek's magnum opus is the subject of constant revisions and

reappraisal and new etymologies frequently appear on the pages of *Naše řeč* and other Czech philological journals.

621 **Stručný etymologický slovník se zvláštním zřetelem k slovům kulturním a cizím.** (Concise etymological dictionary with special reference to cultural and foreign words.)
Josef Holub, Stanislav Lyer. Prague: Státní pedagogické nakladatelství, 1967. 527p. bibliog.

This work is a complement to the foregoing and contains for the most part those words whose foreign origin has been obliterated, more recent loan-words that are becoming thoroughly domesticated, often in the absence of an adequate native synonym, and a large portion of the 'international' vocabulary essential to everyday life and certain areas of learning with which the man in the street cannot avoid at least a passing familiarity. The introduction outlines the structure of the Czech word-stock and the evolution of Indo-European. This provides the background to the systematic cross-referencing between entries to reveal inter-relations between loans across language boundaries, e.g. both *mykorrhiza* and *ředkev* are cross-referenced to *radikál*. The work has re-appeared sporadically since in unnumbered reprints. A much wider range of scientific, technical and cultural words in use in Czech is to be found in Lumír Klimeš's *Slovník cizích slov* (Prague: Státní pedagogické nakladatelství, 1981. 791p. bibliog.).

622 **Retrográdní morfematický slovník češtiny.** (Reversing morphemic dictionary of Czech.)
Eleonora Slavíčková. Prague: Academia, 1975. 645p.

Another valuable aid to the study of the language, this reversing dictionary differs from many in being compiled using morphemes, certainly a more feasible undertaking than for, say, English, rather than using letters. It contains inventories of root, prefixal and suffixal morphemes as well as the main *a tergo* list. The theoretical introduction is in English, as well as Czech, Russian and French.

623 **Frekvence slov, slovních druhů a tvarů v českém jazyce.** (Frequency of words, word-types and word-forms in Czech.)
Jaroslav Jelínek, Josef V. Bečka, Marie Těšitelová. Prague: Státní pedagogické nakladatelství, 1961. 587p. bibliog.

This is the Czech frequency dictionary, and although it is becoming dated, and is certainly hard to obtain outside libraries, it is unlikely to be replaced for some time. A complex introduction, itself a major piece of scholarship, explains the methods of collecting and processing the material, while the main body is in two lists – for frequency order with absolute frequency indexes and for alphabetical order with indexes for absolute frequency and frequencies for the eight genre types encompassed by the analysis.

624 Český slovník věcný a synonymický. (Czech dictionary of subjects and synonyms.)
Compiled by Jiří Haller. Prague: Státní pedagogické nakladatelství, 1969-1977. 3 vols.

This is the only genuine Czech thesaurus to go beyond lists of synonyms. The vocabulary is classified by semantic fields, all relevant items brought together irrespective of, for example, word class. Overall the classification evolves in a logical sequence, as follows from the contents table. There is a certain amount of exemplification under some of the entries. Work on the dictionary has been arrested by the death of the compiler and a number of the members of the editorial committee, but an alphabetical index to the existing volumes is in preparation.

625 Slovník synonym a frazeologismů. (Dictionary of synonyms and phrasal units.)
J. V. Bečka. Prague: Vydavatelství Novinář, 1979. 2nd ed. 431p. bibliog. (Knihovnička novináře, no. 16).

Unlike many lexicographical reference works, this dictionary from Prague seems fairly readily obtainable. This is probably because it is specifically intended for journalists, and journalism plays such a major role in handing on the Party line, in addition to normal news functions. The phraseological section seeks to arm the journalist with a choice of clichés, each entry being based on a core concept. Possibly most informative for the foreign user or learner is the brief section (p. 418-29) on foreign tags current in Czech, since many do not occur in any other dictionary and since some of the Latin tags in particular happen to be quite familiar in Czech while not having the same currency in English, e.g. *nomen omen*; it is also of some interest for the somewhat idiosyncratic range of English tags used in Czech, especially journalese.

626 Anglicko-český a česko-anglický slovník. (English-Czech and Czech-English dictionary.)
Ivan Poldauf, Jan Caha, Alena Kopecká, Jiří Krámský. Prague: Státní pedagogické nakladatelství, 1982 (1983). 5th ed. 1,232p.

This is the most convenient general-purpose two-way dictionary for Czech, being a somewhat condensed combination of Jan Caha and Jiří Krámský's *Anglicko-český slovník* (q.v.) and Ivan Poldauf's *Česko-anglický slovník* (q.v.). It is, however, tailored more to the native user's requirements in that it contains less grammatical information under each entry than the foreign user might well need.

627 Anglicko-český slovník. (English-Czech dictionary.)
Jan Caha, Jiří Krámský. Prague: Státní pedagogické nakladatelství, 1982. 5th ed. 880p.

The usually available general-purpose one-way dictionary intended in the first instance for native Czech learners of English from school-age upwards. It contains approximately 30,000 entries and the grammatical and semantic annotations are in Czech.

628 **Velký anglicko-český slovník** (Large English-Czech dictionary.)
Karel Hais, Břetislav Hodek. Prague: Academia, 1984-. 3 vols.

This much needed and long-awaited work is the first large English-Czech dictionary to appear since 1911. It seeks to enable the Czech user to cope with idiomatic English from the 18th century to the present, thus it has a good stock of phrasal and other idiomatic expressions. It is inevitably flawed, the more so for the apparent failure to collaborate with any English scholars in its production ('the British Road Services depot in Oxford' is not a bus station!). Each entry has the pronunciation marked, with any necessary grammatical, stylistic or other indicators (American vs. British usage, for example) given. The work has a generous proportion of lexical items from many specialist fields.

629 **Slovník amerikanismů.** (Dictionary of Americanisms.)
Jaroslav Peprník. Prague: Státní pedagogické nakladatelství, 1982. 612p.

This useful supplement to the usual English-Czech dictionaries covers all modern American English, literary and non-literary, and is almost entirely reliable. It also includes a US-British differential glossary and differences of pronunciation.

630 **Česko-anglický slovník.** (Czech-English dictionary.)
Ivan Poldauf. Prague: Státní pedagogické nakladatelství, 1968. 3rd ed. 1,237p.

In the absence of the long-awaited, entirely new and larger Czech-English dictionary, by the same author with the collaboration of R. B. Pynsent, this dictionary continues to be re-issued as the sole work of its kind – a counterpart to item no. 627, from which it differs in having more concessions to the English user, including an abstract of Czech grammar.

631 **Česko-slovenský slovník.** (Czech-Slovak dictionary.)
Edited by Gejza Horák. Bratislava: Veda, 1979. 790p.

Previous Czech-Slovak and Slovak-Czech dictionaries have tended to be of the differential type, given the vast areas of overlap between the two languages. The ten authors of this work have, presumably, decided that on the contrary it is just as important to know that a word is shared by the two languages. Accordingly, this has become a standard bilingual dictionary of some 60,000 entry words and a vital instrument to Czechs, Slovaks and foreign users of both alike. Besides the core vocabulary it contains a fair measure of the modern technical vocabulary which is so asserting itself in everyday usage. A companion Slovak-Czech dictionary is in preparation at the time of writing.

632 **Say it in Czech.**
M. Fryščak. New York: Dover Publications, 1973. 277p. (Dover Say-it Series).

A typical tourist phrase-book covering all the allegedly typical situations in which the tourist might find himself. The guidance on pronunciation is through a non-standard, unsophisticated pattern of transliteration.

633 **Say it in Czech: English-Czech phrasebook with figured pronunciation.**
Alois Krušina.   Prague: Státní pedagogické nakladatelství;
Wellingborough, England: Collet's, 1971. 2nd ed. 387p.

More substantial in every respect than the foregoing, this phrasebook is also more up-to-date linguistically and more refined in its phonetic transcription. The range of vocabulary for which it allows is quite broad.

634 **Slovník slovenského jazyka.** (Dictionary of the Slovak language.)
Edited by Štefan Peciar.   Bratislava: Vydavateľstvo Slovenskej akadémie vied, 1971. 2nd ed. 6 vols.

The Slovak counterpart of *Slovník spisovného jazyka českého* (q.v.) it contains to all intents and purposes the full modern lexicon, minus the most technical stratum and the rash of neologisms coined to keep pace with modern technology. Many of the latter are embodied in the series of bi- and multilingual technical dictionaries published by Alfa in Bratislava, which are too many and various to be included here. A Slovak counterpart to *Slovník spisovné češtiny pro školu a veřejnost* (q.v.) above is still awaited.

635 **Frekvencia slov v slovenčine.** (Word-frequency in Slovak.)
Jozef Mistrík.   Bratislava: Veda, 1969. 726p. bibliog.

This is the Slovak frequency dictionary. It includes a detailed theoretical and methodological introduction and lists the lexicon by both frequency and alphabetical order. It also covers the distribution of words and the stratification of the language in terms of style.

636 **Retrográdny slovník slovenčiny.** (Reversing dictionary of Slovak.)
Jozef Mistrík.   Bratislava: Univerzita Komenského, 1976. 735p.
bibliog.

This *a tergo* dictionary contains approximately 100 pages of background information, on reversing dictionaries generally and on specific matters regarding Slovak including its homonyms, productivity of morphological types and distribution of word-finals.

637 **Hrobak's English-Slovak dictionary.**
Philip A. Hrobak.   New York: Robert Speller, 1965. 2nd ed.
702p. bibliog.

Very North American, even idiosyncratic, this is the only English-Slovak dictionary of any size of Western provenance. Many words given as translations are distinctly archaic and some are even felt by recent émigrés to be pure invention. Accordingly, this work must be used with caution. Besides the word-corpus, it also contains a summary grammar and guidance on spelling, word-order and certain general conventions (such as forms of dates and time expressions).

Language. Dictionaries

638 **Anglicko-slovenský slovník.** (English-Slovak dictionary.)
Ján Šimko. Bratislava: Slovenské pedagogické nakladateľstvo,
1967. (Many reprintings). 1,443p.
In practice this is the counterpart to Jan Caha and Jiří Krámský's *Anglicko-český*
slovník (q.v.) but overall it is more satisfactory in volume, in the amount of
additional linguistic and lexicological information for the (Slovak) user, and in the
number of phrases incorporated in addition to the head-words.

639 **Anglicko-slovenský frazeologický slovník.** (English-Slovak
phraseological dictionary.)
Pavol Kvetko. Bratislava: Slovenské pedagogické nakladateľstvo,
1984. 599p.
Based on editions, if not works, of the period 1950s-70s, this dictionary offers a
reasonable repertoire of English, and some American, idiomatic phrases and
other lexical quirks. Where reasonable, they are translated by their Slovak
equivalent, or near-equivalent, duly marked, and in the absence of a
corresponding idiom in Slovak, a translation-explanation is given, mostly perfectly
adequate. Almost all entries, which are ordered according to key-words, are
exemplified from one or other of the works consulted, which are mostly literature,
but with some press and a range of scholarly works – grammars and other
dictionaries; these are all listed in the back and, though not intended as a
bibliography in the normal sense of the word, the section of scholarly works
(p. 594-95) can be seen in that light.

640 **Slovak-English phraseological dictionary.**
Jozef J. Konuš. Passaic, New Jersey: Slovak Catholic Sokol,
1969. 1,664p.
This is aimed at the North American Slovak user and both languages reflect this
up to a point, the Slovak less so, however, than in *Hrobak's English-Slovak*
dictionary (q.v.). It is a standard translating dictionary, 'phraseological' only in
the sense that it contains some set phrases and idioms nested under certain
headwords.

641 **Slovensko-anglický slovník.** (Slovak-English dictionary.)
J. Vilikovská, P. Vilikovský. Bratislava: Slovenské pedagogické
nakladateľstvo, 1983. 4th ed. 522p.
A medium-sized general-purpose translating dictionary of about 23,000 entries
which deliberately avoids archaic, technical or regional words. It pre-eminently
serves the Slovak user.

642 **Slovensko-anglický frazeologický slovník obchodnej korešpondencie.** (Slovak-English phraseological dictionary of commercial correspondence.)
Dušan Závada, Slovak edition prepared by Eugen Klimo.
Bratislava: Alfa, 1973. 554p.

The Czech work on which this is based, *Čech anglickým korespondentem* [The Czech as English correspondent] (Prague: SPN, 1960), has long been out of print, but this Slovak version can be used by speakers of both languages, not only on account of their similarity, but also thanks to the inclusion of a Czech-Slovak differential glossary. The phrases employed are introduced by key-words ordered alphabetically with generous cross-referencing.

643 **Anglicko-slovenský technický slovník.** (English-Slovak technical dictionary.)
Edited by Ľubomíra Csáderová. Bratislava: Alfa, 1975. 1,357p.

The work of some thirty-seven different authors, this general dictionary covers over 110,000 terms drawn from science, technology and economics. It does not shun many quite ordinary words that have a technical reference and so constitutes a valuable addition to the range of bilateral dictionaries at the disposal of the ordinary, as well as the technical, user.

644 **Slovensko-český slovník.** (Slovak-Czech dictionary.)
Želmíra Gašparíková, Adolf Kamiš. Prague: Státní pedagogické nakladatelství, 1967. xliii + 812p.

Pending the appearance of the new Slovak-Czech dictionary, this is the best available. It is compiled with the reader of Slovak literature in mind rather than seeking to portray the actual core of modern Slovak, ie., the modern literary language with a telling share of the kind of technical language which is becoming used everyday. Hence it only contains a modicum of the latter, but a fair proportion of peripheral vocabulary – colloquial, obsolescent, regional or bookish – where such elements show a high incidence in major authors. It is differential only in the area of proper names, ie., it includes only those with a purely Slovak form. The long introductory pages form a précis of Czech grammar.

645 **Malý synonymický slovník.** (Small dictionary of synonyms.)
Mária Pisárčiková, Štefan Michalus. Bratislava: Slovenské pedagogické nakladateľstvo, 1978. 2nd ed. 210p.

Another useful tool for anyone involved in actively employing Slovak, marred for the non-native by the absence of any guidelines on style or register.

Grammars

646 **Grammaire de la langue tchéque.** (Grammar of Czech.)
André Mazon. Paris: Institut d'études slaves, 1952. 3rd rev. ed.
252p.
A once highly regarded, now classical but dated reference grammar which
remains extremely useful.

647 **Česká mluvnice.** (Czech grammar.)
Bohuslav Havránek, Alois Jedlička. Prague: Státní pedagogické
nakladatelství, 1981. 4th rev. ed. 582p.
This is the standard Czech systematic reference grammar intended primarily for
university level. It is revised periodically to take account of the changing norms –
recent years have seen several waves of spelling reform and some quite
conspicuous upward shifts, from the common colloquial to the literary standard,
of a number of words and forms. The work is exhaustive, structuralist in approach
and is generous with examples. Appendixes discuss the lexicon, style and the
history of the language. A sister work for secondary schools, *Stručná mluvnice
česká* (Concise Czech grammar), from the same authors and publishers also
appears at frequent intervals.

648 **Contemporary Czech.**
Michael Heim. Columbus, Ohio: Slavica Publishers, 1982.
2nd ed. 271p. bibliog. (UCLA Slavic Studies, no. 3).
This very dense course in fourteen lessons and fourteen review lessons is intended
for university study; it does not lend itself to self-tuition. While not specifically
intended for those with a prior knowledge of Russian, it does cater for them, with
notes *passim* on specific areas of similarity or contrast. The exercises (no key) are
more generous than in many course books and there are useful appendixes
(grammar tables and geographical names, for example). The pilot edition was
published in 1976 by the Slavic Department of the University of Michigan.

649 **A modern Czech grammar.**
William E. Harkins. New York: King's Crown Press, 1960.
Reprint of 1st ed. 1953. 338p. (Columbia Slavic Studies).
One of the aging but still standard course books, which introduces the grammar in
thirty lessons through reading passages, fairly conservatively selected, from the
literature. The vocabulary which it introduces is fairly limited.

650 **Čeština pro cizince – Czech for English-speaking students.**
Milan Šára, J. Šárová, A. Bytel. Prague: Státní pedagogické
nakladatelství, 1979. 2nd ed. 564p.
In many respects this is the fullest course available since its main purpose is the
linguistic preparation of anglophone Third-World students prior to their courses
of study. It seeks initially to facilitate the user's contact with the man in the street

before passing to higher styles and more varied registers. It is worth mentioning here that many college faculties produce their own language courses for foreigners in the form of *skripta* (paper-bound cyclostyled A4-format short-life volumes), which the visitor to Prague may find it useful to seek out.

651 **Czech.**
William R. Lee, Z. Lee. London: Hodder & Stoughton, 1985. 13th impression of 2nd ed. 1964. 243p.

A useful, if skeletal, course with only minor changes from the first edition. Like William E. Harkins's *A modern Czech grammar* (q.v.) it requires updating as regards orthography and some details of grammar and vocabulary. Of the materials available, this is perhaps the best of what is a poor selection designed for the totally uninitiated beginner.

652 **Colloquial Czech: an easy course for beginners.**
J. Schwartz. London; Henley-on-Thames, England; Boston: Routledge & Kegan Paul, 1980 (reprint of 2nd ed., 1945). 252p.

The title is that of the first edition (1943) and has become a slight misnomer, since some of the utterances and forms contained would not now pass for colloquial. Intended for the linguistically unsophisticated and even shorter on exercises than W. R. and Z. Lee's *Czech* (q.v.), its limited vocabulary is nevertheless perhaps more useful overall for the intended users.

653 **Czech through Russian.**
Charles E. Townsend. Columbus, Ohio: Slavica Publishers, 1981. 263p.

For the majority with a Slavonic interest, Russian will have been the first language studied. It is perhaps unfair, but realistic, that the other Slavonic languages are often in the position of Cinderellas, but it is beyond question that a knowledge of any one is a major asset before another is tackled. Townsend's book seeks to provide a good working knowledge of Czech for those who have previously acquired Russian, and arrives at a book which is at once a serious comparative study and a workable course book. The comparisons are made at all levels of analysis that are conventionally recognized, and in the particular standard problem areas of Slavonic grammar. Examples abound and a fair number of exercises and a reasonable vocabulary are included.

654 **Čeština jazyk cizí: mluvnice češtiny pro cizince.** (Czech as a foreign language: a grammar of Czech for foreigners.)
Ivan Poldauf, Karel Šprunk. Prague: Státní pedagogické nakladatelství, 1968. 418p.

This was an interesting experiment, a kind of Basic Czech, taught through the medium of the language itself, with only a brief 'Explanation of purpose' in English and other foreign languages at the end. In its attempt to simplify the grammar it makes some radical new departures, such as the reduction of the number of members in the case system. Hard to come by except second-hand, but worthy of being known.

655 **A grammar of contemporary Slovak.**
Jozef Mistrík. Bratislava: Slovenské pedagogické nakladateľstvo, 1983. 159p. bibliog.

A fairly concise descriptive grammar of the standard language ordered in the traditional manner. It is preceded by a brief historical section and finishes with a summary of the dialects and grammatical reference tables. The English text is at times bizarre.

656 **Slovenská gramatika: opis jazykového systému.** (Slovak grammar: a description of the language system.)
Eugen Pauliny. Bratislava: Slovenské pedagogické nakladateľstvo, 1981. 322p. bibliog.

This descriptive grammar consists of a general introduction to language and linguistic analysis and sections on the lexicology, word formation, word classes (including morphology), phonology and phonetics, and syntax (unusually but justifiably in that order) of contemporary Slovak. It has replaced, in the bookshops though not entirely in fact, the previous normative grammar of Eugen Pauliny, Jozef Ružička and Jozef Štolc entitled *Slovenská gramatika* (Bratislava: SPN, 1962 and several later revised editions in the intervening years). Both works have served as the Slovak counterpart to Bohuslav Havránek and Alois Jedlička's *Česká mluvnice* (q.v.).

657 **Grammaire de la langue slovaque** (Grammar of Slovak.)
Jozef Bartoš, Joseph Gagnaire. Paris: Institut d'Études Slaves; Bratislava: Matica slovenská, 1974. 2nd ed. 267p.

A reference grammar in the classical style adopted by the Institut d'Études Slaves, hence a sister publication to André Mazon's *Grammaire de la langue tchèque* (q.v.).

658 **Slovak for slavicists.**
Peter Baláž, Miloslav Darovec, Heather Trebatická. Bratislava: Slovenské pedagogické nakladateľstvo, 1976. 302p.

As its title suggests, this work sets out to be a 'conversion' course for those with a prior knowledge of some Slavonic language. This means that a measure of grammatical explanation is omitted, the emphasis being on those features that are specific to Slovak. In twenty-seven lessons the grammar is covered quite adequately, and a reasonable vocabulary is obtained. The Slovaks' efforts to propagate their language in the world at large have meant that parallel textbooks have appeared in other languages, namely: Peter Baláž, Jozef Bartoš and Miloslav Darovec's *Manuel de slovaque à l'usage des slavisants* (Bratislava: SPN, 1980. 2nd rev. ed.); Peter Baláž and Miloslav Darovec's *Lehrbuch der slowakischen Sprache für Slawisten* (Bratislava: SPN, 1978. 2nd ed.); P. Baláž, M. Čabala and M. Darovec's *Učebnik slovatskogo jazyka dlja slavistov* (Bratislava: SPN, 1983. 3rd ed.).

659   **Slovak for beginners.**
Philip A. Hrobak.   Middletown, Pennsylvania: Jednota Press,
1963-76. 3 vols. (various reprints).

Volume 1 concentrates on the sounds of the language and volumes 2 and 3 on the grammar, which is explained in traditional terms. The work relies heavily on random sentences and hence the random acquisition of vocabulary, though there are some consecutive passages. The Slovak of North America has become slightly out of step wtih the Slovak of present-day Czechoslovakia, and this work betrays its North-American origins.

660   **Basic Slovak.**
Jozef Mistrík.   Bratislava: Slovenské pedagogické nakladateľstvo,
1981. 155p.

In the field of Slovak studies, Mistrík is perhaps best known for his work in stylistics and for his authorship of the Slovak *a tergo* dictionary entitled *Retrográdny slovník slovenčiny* (q.v.). He has also written on word frequency, and the present skeletal beginner's textbook is an offshoot of that work. It introduces in fifteen simple progressive lessons the essentials of Slovak grammar, using only 800 of the most frequent words in the language. The book may be used for self-teaching, but ideally guidance from a qualified teacher should be sought. The course is specifically aimed at speakers of English.

661   **Základný kurz slovenčiny.** (Basic course in Slovak.)
Jozef Prokop.   Bratislava: Slovenské pedagogické nakladateľstvo,
1980. 263p.

A course intended for audio-visual teaching which is based on the verb as the organizational centre of the sentence. The verbal core is then extended grammatically and semantically as the course progresses, due attention being paid to the frequency of individual verbs and morphological classes. Prokop acknowledges the priority of the spoken language and relies heavily on situational dialogue and question-and-answer drills. The work derives in part from the same author's *Lexikálne a gramatické minimum slovenského jazyka* [Lexical and grammatical minimum of the Slovak language] (Bratislava: SPN, 1978), which is a beginner's picture dictionary, an exemplar of the relevant vocabulary in use, a reference grammar and a Slovak-English-French-German-Russian glossary. It is intended as an introduction to Slovak for foreign students at summer schools, or on intensive courses, preceding their full-time studies.

Miscellaneous

662   **The Czech language in America.**
J. B. Dudek.   *American Mercury*, vol. 5 (1925), p. 202-07.

If it were not so amusing, on a number of counts, and relatively substantial for such a recondite topic, I should have been tempted to have omitted this item, at

Language. Miscellaneous

least on the grounds of age and relative inaccessibility. It does provide, however, a good overview of what was happening at the time to the language outside its native environment, particular the range of loan-words in use and how American meanings have accreted gradually to them. Its main weakness is in the unscholarly assumption that practically any modern, international, loan-word in Czech, wherever spoken, represents a debt to the American (sic!) language. At best this applies only to the genuine North-Americanisms; the pearls such as *trafiční kop, plumbařský kontraktor* or *běžeti pro ofis* will be appreciated by the reader with a knowledge of more standard versions of the language.

663 **Sound, sign and meaning: quinquagenary of the Prague Linguistic Circle.**
Edited by Ladislav Matějka. Ann Arbor, Michigan: Department of Slavic Languages and Literatures, University of Michigan, 1976. 622p. (Michigan Slavic Contributions, no. 6).

No bibliography on Czechoslovakia could be complete without some reference to the Prague Linguistic Circle, one of the prime movers of 20th-century linguistics. It is invidious to risk quoting some names and not others, but three at least must be mentioned: Vilém Mathesius; Roman Jakobson; and Jan Mukařovský. The many papers in this collection, some of them specifically on these three, must suffice as an introduction to the Prague School, though there is no shortage of other specialist works concerning it. Jakobson in particular has been well served by critical studies and reprints of his many major works.

664 **Nástin české dialektologie.** (Outline of Czech dialectology.)
Jaromír Bělič. Prague: Státní pedagogické nakladatelství, 1972. 463p. maps. bibliog.

This is the standard modern work on the Czech dialects. After the introduction, which includes a note on the extraterritorial dialects, the second section describes the many distinguishing phonetic and morphological features and their distribution, while the third section is based on the geographical areas and describes the features which specifically mark them out. Section four looks at contemporary trends, and an appendix provides an account of current work in the subject. The maps are included loose, but the commentary on them is in the body of the book. There is a comprehensive sectional bibliography and a full index of words quoted.

665 **České nářeční texty.** (Czech dialect texts.)
Under the general editorship of Arnošt Lamprecht. Prague: Státní pedagogické nakladatelství, 1976. 425p. bibliog.

Preceded by a brief outline of the emergence and evolution of the Czech dialects, this is a comprehensive collection of sample texts, duly annotated, including representative passages from the Czech enclaves and immigrant communities abroad, especially in Yugoslavia, Romania and the United States.

666 **O českých slanzích.** (Czech slang.)
Jaroslav Hubáček. Ostrava, Czechoslovakia: Profil, 1981. 2nd ed.
bibliog.

This work is included here, despite the fact that the theoretical introduction and definitions of terms, for example, are in Czech, since there is little alternative material available on social dialects. The book was immensely popular when it first appeared and this second edition was brought out, with some additions, remarkably quickly by Czechoslovak standards. The slangs are a mixture of true slang and professional jargon words and are classified by source areas – such as the railways, the army, student life and the theatre. The thirty-page list of all the words included (three columns per page) is a useful source of countless expressions that will not be found in any of the standard dictionaries of Czech, and the bibliography contains information about many publications that deal in more detail with individual slangs.

667 **Morfill and the Czechs.**
James D. Naughton. *Oxford Slavonic Papers*, vol. 17 (1984),
p. 62-76.

Richard Morfill (1834-1909) was one of the first English scholars with a strong interest in Czech and Slovak affairs (though with a greater interest in the former, for obvious chronological reasons). Naughton offers here a scholarly biobibliography of Morfill's work, especially concerning the other scholars of the day with whom he was in contact, or dispute. Not to mention the many writers and historians with whom he corresponded, or indeed met on his visits to Prague. Morfill was clearly something of a Czechophile, and was well-liked by the Czechs in turn, ultimately being honoured by corresponding membership of the Royal Scientific Society of Bohemia in 1905. This, despite their having found fault, with absolute justification, with his *Grammar of the Bohemian or Čech Language* (1899), the first major work of its kind in English. The text and footnotes to this paper together provide an interesting period bibliography of Czech studies, especially in England.

668 **Historio de la Esperanto-movado en Ĉeĥoslovakio: iom da historio
kaj iom da rememoroj.** (History of the Esperanto movement in
Czechoslovakia: some history and some reminiscences).
Stanislav Kamarýt. Prague: Český esperantský svaz (Ĉeĥa
Esperanto-Asocio), 1983. 256p. bibliog.

The history of Esperanto in Czechoslovakia goes back to before the Republic was even born, with the first textbook being produced as early as 1890 and the Prague Esperanto club being founded in 1902. This book, compiled from the author's manuscript materials (he died in 1956) by members of the Czech Esperanto Association, under the editorship of Jan Werner, traces the history of the movement from its humblest beginnings in 1887 up to 1969, when the two modern Esperanto organizations were constituted after the federalization of Czechoslovakia. The period between 1956 and 1969 has been written up by the editors. Membership of the Czech Esperanto Association is around 6,000, while the Esperanto Association of the Slovak Socialist Republic has approximately 3,000 members. Of some interest to the international Esperanto-using community is the periodical *Auroro* (1926-.), published in braille for foreign blind Esperantists.

Literature

General

669 **Comparative history of Slavic literatures.**
Dimitrij Čiževskij, translated by Richard Noel Porter, Martin P.
Rice, and edited, with a foreword, by Serge A. Zenkovsky.
Nashville, Tennessee: Vanderbilt University Press, 1971. 225p.
bibliog.

Essentially the only comparative history of Slavonic literatures in English, the
work is periodized, with, in most cases, a nation-by-nation summary of what was
happening in a given period. The Hussite period is treated separately. Slovak
literature only starts being considered in the Baroque period, for which there is
some justification, but since the time when Čiževskij was writing rather more
attention has been paid to earlier Slovak (Slovakized Czech) literature. The book
is well supported by quotations in the original and in parallel translation, and
there is some useful discussion of the development of the literary languages as
they diverged.

670 **Modern Slavic literatures. Vol. 2. Bulgarian, Czechoslovak, Polish,
Ukrainian and Yugoslav literatures.**
Edited by Vasa D. Mihajlovich, Igor Hájek, Zbigniew Folejewski,
Bogdan Czaykowski, Leo D. Rudnytzky, Thomas Butler.   New
York: Frederick Ungar, 1976. 720p. (Library of Literary
Criticism).

Czech, and to a lesser degree Slovak, prose, verse, drama and even literary
history are fairly well-represented in translation. It is distinctly less usual for
works of literary criticism to be so treated. However, this volume contains a
selection of portraits of writers by well-known critics, though with the doyen of
Czech 20-century criticism, F. X. Šalda, over-represented. There is a minimum of

biographical detail on the writers concerned. The relevant section, edited by Igor Hájek, is on p. 38-230.

671 **The realm of rime: a study of rime in the poetry of the Slavs.**
Thomas Eekman. Amsterdam, The Netherlands: A. M. Hakkert, 1974. 364p. bibliog.

Contains (p. 210-34) a separate study on rhyme in Czech and Slovak poetry, which quotes many early and modern examples as well as some theoretical works on rhyme. The types of rhyme occurring are classified.

672 **White stones and fir trees: an anthology of contemporary Slavic literature.**
Edited by Vasa D. Mihailovich. Rutherford, Teaneck, New Jersey: Fairleigh Dickinson University Press; London: Associated University Presses, 1977. 603p.

Anthologies have their good and bad points, but the main good point would appear to be that they are often the only place from which to gain at least some idea of the work of writers who are not translated 'in bulk'. Such is the case of some of the writers included here, though others are in fact more widely known. The Czechs represented are: Ivan Diviš; Vladimír Holan; Václav Havel; Miloš Macourek; Miroslav Florian; Jiří Šotola; Vladimír Vondra; Jan Skácel; Josef Škvorecký; Ivan Vyskočil; Miroslav Holub; and Bohumil Hrabal. The Slovaks included are: Ladislav Ťažký; Ján Stacho; Vincent Šikula; Dominik Tatarka; Peter Karvaš; Štefan Žáry; Rudolf Jašík; Laco Novomeský; and Miroslav Válek. The selection is roughly equally split between prose-writers and poets, with Havel and Karvaš representing drama. Many other anthologies are listed in George J. Kovtun's bibliography of *Czech and Slovak literature in English* (q.v.).

673 **Tchèques et Slovaques entre l'Est et l'Ouest.** (Czechs and Slovaks between East and West.)
Revue de Littérature Comparée, vol. 57, no. 4 (Oct.-Dec. 1983), p. 403-534.

The several papers in this all-Czech/Slovak volume of *Revue de Littérature Comparée* would, if entered separately, appear in different sections of the present bibliography, but they have been included *en bloc* in view of the volume's tacit mission to bring to the French public a general idea of Czech and Slovak literature and its international connections. Hana Jechova's 'Entre l'Est et l'Ouest' (p. 405-15) gives a superficial overview of those connections (mostly Czech, little Slovak). Mojmír Vaněk's 'L'Histoire de l'art comme histoire de la pensée' (p. 417-41) compares the different art historical theories of the Viennese Czech Max Dvořák and the Frenchman Henri Focillon, while Vladimír Peška's 'Albert Camus et la Bohême' (p. 443-63) reassesses the impact of Camus's 1936 trip to Prague on his 'Absurd Thinking' as it evolves from the personal, through the literary to the philosophical in the course of his literary career. In another article, 'Poètes tchèques et modèles français. La dénomination poétique de Baudelaire à Apollinaire et ses parallèles tchèques' (p. 465-93) Jechova discusses the influence of the French Symbolists and Surrealists on Czech verse and the purely native elements in Czech Symbolism and Surrealism. Miloš Tomčík, one of the main contemporary Slovak literary critics and historians, offers an introduction to an important, if not prolific Slovak poet in 'Ivan Krasko dans le contexte européen' (p. 495-501) and mentions in particular his knowledge of modern French poetry and how it influenced his work. The review section is devoted both to Václav Hájek z Libočan's *Czech Chronicle* (1541), of which a new critical edition has appeared, and to Czech structuralism (it provides a review on a new history of the subject and an anniversary vignette on René Wellek, one of its main exponents).

674 **Translation in Czechoslovakia.**
    Bohuslav Ilek, Dušan Slobodník, Ján Ferenčík. [Prague,
    Bratislava?]: Czech Literary Fund and Slovak Literary Fund for
    the Czechoslovak Translators' Coordination Committee, 1982. 78p.
Czechoslovakia has a vast wealth of native literature, both Czech and Slovak, stretching back to the 14th century. Less well-known or appreciated is that it has a very respectable tradition in translation, indeed its annual production of translations from other literatures far exceeds that of most countries. This odd little volume, which was distributed free and unsolicited to potentially interested parties outside the country and which will therefore not be easy to locate, nevertheless deserves a mention here since it is a mine of information on centuries of translation into Czech and Slovak, and is at the same time a potted history of the two literatures. It also contains facts on the organizational aspects of translation in Czechoslovakia, on translating, interpreting and dubbing for science, tourism, conferences and films.

Czech

History and criticism

675 **The native literature of Bohemia in the fourteenth century.**
    A. H. Wratislaw. London: George Bell & Sons, 1878. 165p.
The four popular lectures contained in this work still remain a fascinating curio. They give an outline of many of the major works of Old Czech literature with, importantly, copious sections in English translation, in verse where relevant. At all events the wealth of Old Czech literature, prose and verse chronicle, satire, disputation and theological writings, is well represented. Where an English dimension can be found it is duly pointed out.

676 **A sacred farce from medieval Bohemia. Mastičkář.**
    Jarmila F. Veltruský. Ann Arbor, Michigan: Horace H. Rackham
    School of Graduate Studies, University of Michigan, 1985.
    396p. bibliog.
The *Mastičkář* (Quacksalver) is the best known of the Czech mediaeval plays, but practically only among speakers of Czech. Veltruský surmises that had it been an

English work, it would have been much better known, and to overcome at least
the language barrier, she includes full transcriptions *and* parallel English
translations of both extant fragments of the play (p. 332-76). The rest of the book
is a history of mediaeval drama and of the detail of the Easter story underlying
this and other European plays involving apothecaries, spice merchants and the
like in particular. There is also a literary, linguistic, dramatic and semantic
analysis of the play, and an account of the role of farce and laughter in the
mediaeval religious context. Comparisons are drawn throughout with some better
known English and French plays of similar antiquity.

677 **A history of Bohemian literature.**
The Count Lützow. London: Heinemann, 1907. 2nd imp. 437p.
(Short Histories of the Literatures of the World, no. 7).

This is another curio of similar antiquity to item no. 675, but covers the literature
right up to the 18th century. Like later literary historians Lützow notes the depth
to which Czech literature, more than some others, is bound up with the nation's
general and religious history. Many quotations are given in translation. One way
in which this early work differs from later ones is the unusual emphasis on certain
of the writers quoted. The work is of sufficient significance to have merited
reprinting by Kennikat Press in 1970.

678 **Czech literature.**
Arne Novák, translated from the Czech by Peter Kussi, edited with
a supplement by William E. Harkins. Ann Arbor, Michigan:
Michigan Slavic Publications, under the auspices of the Joint
Committee on Eastern Europe, American Council of Learned
Societies, 1976. 375p. (Joint Committee on Eastern Europe
Publication Series, no. 4).

The text selected for translation here is a posthumous (1946) edition of Novák's
classic, prepared for publication by Antonín Grund, who also brought the text up
to that date. Harkins' supplement then follows Czech literature up to 1976. The
work seeks to be a complete history, within the limitations of space, from the
earliest extant texts right down to the present, and it largely succeeds. In the
absence of any other complete history of Czech literature in English one is
grateful that it exists, but it is nevertheless marred by certain omissions – a
consequence of its triple authorship at the points where the sections meet, and the
translation contains a number of malapropisms, mostly fairly transparent, and
some serious mistranslations of the Czech titles of works. However, even as it
stands it is a useful introduction and has the added benefit of a section on folk
literature and, in the supplement, it takes note of literary output both inside
Czechoslovakia and among the émigré community.

679 **Essays on Czech literature.**
René Wellek, introduced by Peter Demetz. The Hague: Mouton,
1963. 214p. bibliog. (Slavic Printings and Reprintings, no. 43).

Now a classic collection of essays, some of the survey type, others dealing with
specific narrow problems. The interpretations have not all been received without
criticism, and some are openly polemical, as the one on K. Čapek and T. G.

Literature. Czech

Masaryk's philosophy in its literary dimension. There are also highly instructive studies on, for example, Bohemia in English literature, where the coverage extends from the 9th to the 19th centuries, or Mácha and English literature, which explores the 'Byron problem' in relation to K. H. Mácha, perhaps the best Czech poet of all time. There is also a sober history of Czech-German literary contacts. Each essay is accompanied by its own bibliography.

680 **Narrative modes in Czech literature.**
Lubomír Doležel.   Toronto: University of Toronto Press, 1973. 152p. bibliog.

A set of specialist literary essays by a leading Prague scholar and recent émigré, providing detailed structuralist accounts of several major works in Czech literature by writers who all merit translation, though some are still waiting attention: J. A. Comenius, Karel V. Rais, Karel Čapek, Vladislav Vančura and Milan Kundera. Another structuralist essay, on the cycles and circles in Jaroslav Hašek's life and the structure of his novel is Doležel's 'Circular patterns: Hašek and the Good Soldier Švejk' in *Poetica Slavica: Studies in honour of Zbigniew Folejewski*, edited by J. Douglas Clayton and Gunter Schaarschmidt (Ottawa: University of Ottawa Press, 1981, p. 21-28).

681 **Two paradoxes of Czech literary evolution.**
George Pistorius.   In: *The Czechoslovak contribution to world culture*. Edited by Miloslav Rechcígl, Jr. The Hague, London, Paris: Mouton, 1964, p. 39-43.

Pistorius seeks to discover why Czech literature, unlike even Danish, Portuguese and other literatures of small nations, has failed to become a part of universal literature. In essence the argument is that: Czech literature has always been weighed down by non-literary considerations (such as the service of national emancipation); that the search for style has in part stifled the search for ideas; and that while foreign borrowings (translations) have been readily admitted, the influences they might have brought to the formation of a native system of values have been lost beneath the weight of the 'patriotic emancipative function' of literature and were irrelevant to an undemanding readership. Accordingly there is little of value to export, or re-export. This evaluation is a little harsh, as a perusal of some of the other works listed here may demonstrate.

682 **Tschechische Erzählkunst im 20. Jahrhundert.** (Czech narrative art in the 20th century.)
Heinrich Kunstmann.   Cologne, GFR; Vienna: Böhlau Verlag, 1974. 466p. bibliog.

This is the first synthetic work on the development of the Czech novel, *novella* and short story. For the period up to the war the treatment is basically by sub-genre and themes, with a general introduction to the topic and separate paragraphs on the main authors represented. The last chapter (p. 349-402) is on the period 1939-72 with most on the period since the late 1950s. So many individual authors are considered in the book that it can be taken as no more than an introduction to the subject, despite its length. The bibliography is a particularly useful one in that it follows the structure of the main text.

226

683 **Der Poetismus: das Programm und die Hauptverfahren der
tschechischen literarischen Avantgarde der zwanziger Jahre.**
(Poetism: the programme and main progressions of the Czech
literary avant-garde in the 1920s.)
Vladimír Müller.   Munich: Verlag Otto Sagner, 1978. 215p.
bibliog.

The movement known as Poetism, which is claimed by the Czechs to be uniquely
theirs, has received more attention from German rather than English scholars.
Poetism was actually broader than just literary, being represented in music,
painting and architecture, and in the performing arts. It 'was based on the
principle of pure poetry . . . poetry that did not serve the purposes of actual
existence and that scornfully rejected all tendentiousness: it was a poetry that
cultivated sheer playfulness, plunged headlong into inventive fantasy in order to
heighten the delights of hedonistic existence, reached with the magic of carefully
selected words, oxymoronic concepts and paradoxical images of an esthetic
intensity hitherto unknown' (Novák). Many of these characteristics are picked out
by Müller and are exemplified and analysed in great detail; he concentrates on
four central figures: Karel Teige, Vítězslav Nezval, Konstantin Biebl and Jaroslav
Seifert.

684 **Czech writers and politics, 1945-1969.**
Alfred French.   Boulder, Colorado: East European Quarterly.
Distributed by Columbia University Press, New York, 1982. 435p.
bibliog. (East European Monographs, no. 94).

'The social importance of the intelligentsia in Czechoslovakia was not only due to
the traditionally high role conceded by public opinion to the artist and writer. At
a time when no opposition politics were permitted – when no official opposition
was deemed to exist – then its place was taken, in the eyes of the pubic, by the
officially tolerated opposition of artists and intellectuals'. Against the background
of the periodized post-war history of the country, from the communist take-over,
through Stalinization to the reformist experiment of 1968, thence to the renewed
stiffening of orthodoxy, Czech literary output is followed in readable essay form.
The work of many writers is traced, and various works, especially those open to
allegorical interpretation are described in detail, with generous quotations.

685 **Slovník českých spisovatelů: pokus o rekonstrukci dějin české
literatury 1948-1979.** (A dictionary of Czech writers: an attempt to
reconstruct the history of Czech literature 1948-79.)
Compiled by Jiří Brabec (editor), Jiří Gruša, Igor Hájek, Petr
Kabeš, Jan Lopatka.   Toronto: Sixty-Eight Publishers, 1982.
537p.

The word 'reconstruction' in the title refers to the reinstatement in a reference
work of those many authors, some in Czechoslovakia, many abroad, who have
fallen foul of the régime at some time or another. In other words it seeks to
provide a complete biography and bibliography of all émigré and dissident writers
and those who, while denying dissidence are, or have been, denied the
opportunity to publish. Manuscripts and other inedita are included with

appropriate annotations, coverage being broad enough to include, for example, literature proper, criticism, travel writing and theological writings. The work is based on the 2nd edition of the Prague underground version. In addition to the writers' careers, details of professional and political affiliation are included (such as signatory of Charter 77). Given the specific range of authors included the 'reconstruction' cannot be complete, since it excludes those writers who have never been involved in controversy, which of itself does not disqualify them from a place in the literature. Three dictionaries of writers produced inside Czechoslovakia need also to be mentioned: The *Slovník českých spisovatelů* [Dictionary of Czech writers], compiled by the Czechoslovak Academy of Sciences' Institute for Czech Literature (Prague: Československý spisovatel, 1964. 625p.), which in addition to describing, after its fashion, the work of most writers, includes an index of pseudonyms and a summary account, in the Foreword, of all predecessor works; a sequel to this is *Slovník české literatury 1970-1981: básníci, prozaici, dramatici, literární vědci a kritici publikující v tomto období* [A dictionary of Czech literature 1970-81: poets, prose writers, dramatists, literary scholars and critics publishing in the period] edited by Vladimír Forst (Prague: Československý spisovatel, 1985. 502p. bibliogs.) which contains approximately 600 entries and includes an index of works and a particularly good index of pseudonyms and ciphers; and *Čeští spisovatelé literatury pro děti a mládež* [Czech writers of literature for children and young people], by Otakar Chaloupka (who also edited it), Hana Mirvaldová, Vladimír Nezkusil, Václav Stejskal and Jaroslav Voráček (Prague: Albatros, 1985. 476p.), which gives on the whole better accounts of many of the same writers, mostly of the 19th and 20th centuries; the personal bibliographies are, however, less complete, since they are confined to works for the book's stated readership.

686   **Recent Czech literary history and criticism.**

René Wellek.   In: *The Czechoslovak contribution to world culture.*
Edited by Miloslav Rechcígl, Jr. The Hague, London, Paris:
Mouton, 1964, p. 18-28.

Relatively little Czech literary criticism is available in English and it is therefore difficult for the non-Czech speaker to appraise. Wellek's paper takes a number of (then) recent major works of criticism, including the first two volumes of the Czechoslovak Academy's history of literature (the third appeared in 1961), and proceeds to show the weaknesses and contradictions inherent in the rigid one-sidedness of Marxist criticism. While perhaps killing off any desire on the reader's part to go off and read for himself any of the works mentioned (for which he would have to learn Czech first, although one of the works is in German and some contain an English synopsis), Wellek does acknowledge the latent scholarship present and, in passing, mentions some of the highlights of Czech literature, especially of the earlier periods.

687   **Czech literature since 1956: a symposium.**

Edited by William E. Harkins, Paul I. Trensky.   New York:
Bohemica, 1980. 161p. (Columbia Slavic Studies).

Described by one reviewer (R. B. Pynsent) as an *omnium gatherum* of eulogies for post-Thaw writing, this collection of ten essays by six authors contains a lot of information that is unavailable elsewhere and it is therefore a useful supplement to the other literary histories quoted here. Survey essays discuss: the Czech novel since 1956 (W. E. Harkins); the playwrights of the Krejča Circle (P. I. Trensky); Czech culture and politics in the 1960s (Antonin J. Liehm); and Czech poetics and semiotics in the 1960s (Thomas G. Winner). Individual writers whose works are discussed include: Bohumil Hrabal (George Gibian); Vladimír Páral (W. E. Harkins); Milan Kundera (Antonin J. Liehm, Peter Kussi), and Ludvík Vaculík (Antonin J. Liehm).

688 **Czech literature for children: its development and present output.**
Otakar Chaloupka. Prague: Dilia, 1980. 221p.
More detailed than the same author's policy-centred *Children's Books in Czechoslovakia* (q.v.) but confined to Czech children's literature proper, this volume was prepared as a source of information for participants at the 17th Congress of the International Board on Books for Young People. It deals separately with the various age-groups but lacks a bibliography, although the running text contains references to a plethora of authors and titles. Due reference is also made to the specialist publications in the field, notably *Zlatý máj* (1959-.), and to the literary theorists and critics currently working in this area of study. Great emphasis is placed on the moral value of children's literature and its role in shaping the identity of the future generation of socialist citizens.

689 **The contemporary Czech historical novel and its political inspiration.**
Walter Schamschula. In: *Selected Papers from the Second World Congress for Soviet and East European Studies, Garmisch-Partenkirchen, Sept. 30-Oct. 4, 1980: East European Literature.* Edited by Evelyn Bristol. Berkeley, California: Berkeley Slavic Specialities, 1982, p. 57-68.
The historical novel in Czech literature has a long, not to say hallowed, tradition, with Alois Jirásek as a pivotal author. Many 20th-century historical novelists earn a brief mention here, but the core of the paper deals with František Křelina (1903-.), Miloš V. Kratochvíl (1904-.), Václav Kaplický (1895-.) and František Kubka (1894-1969), all writers widely published since the war for whom patriotism is the leading inspiration, but who have tempered their patriotism by shifting emphases over each of the last four decades.

690 **Fiction and drama in Eastern and Southeastern Europe: evolution and experiment in the postwar period, proceedings of the 1978 UCLA conference.**
Edited by Henrik Birnbaum, Thomas Eekman. Columbus, Ohio: Slavica Publishers, 1980. 436p.
Amongst the essays included in this volume are: Walter Schamschula's 'Václav Havel: between the theater of the absurd and engaged theater' (p. 337-48) which concerns a writer who is frequently in the news and whose plays have been fairly widely translated and performed; Michael Heim's 'Hrabal's aesthetic of the powerful experience' (p. 201-06), on Bohumil Hrabal, some of whose work has been translated, but who is perhaps better known through film versions of *Closely*

watched trains and *Cutting it short*; and Thomas G. Winner's 'Mythic and modern elements in the art of Ladislav Fuks: *Natalia Mooshaber's mice*' (p. 443-61) which discusses a contemporary writer, two of whose earlier works have been translated (*The cremator* (q.v.) and *Mr. Theodore Mundstock*, London: Cape, 1969, 214p.).

691 **Assimilation, childhood and death: new Czech fiction-writers of the 1970's.**
Robert B. Pynsent. *Slavonic and East European Review*, vol. 59, no. 3 (July 1981), p. 370-84.

Czech fiction is far from dead or dormant, as is sometimes claimed, and this article goes a long way towards showing just how much of interest is being produced. The 'assimilation' of the title is primarily concerned with that of the outsider, and this is seen as a common feature of much of the writing. Childhood is the state of pre-assimilation and many writers are concerned with the processes of physical and emotional development. Death is the great universal assimilation. Literary theoretical questions apart, we are given an insight into contemporary Czech society with some incidental comparison with society in Britain.

692 **Adolescence, ideology and society: the young hero in contemporary Czech fiction.**
Robert B. Pynsent. In: *The adolescent hero.* Edited by Ian Wallace. Dundee, Scotland: GDR Monitor, 1984, p. 65-86. (GDR Monitor Special Series, no. 3).

The protagonists of many recent works of serious and popular Czech literature are young people and Pynsent sees two main reasons for this: they are the future backbone of the state which must nurture them accordingly, and part of this process involves their indoctrination through literature about and for them; and they represent one group separate from the main body of society, marked out by specific characteristics, which gives authors some scope for imaginative writing. In the space available an impressive number of writers and works of the 1970s and 1980s are discussed. The author shows that within the general type of the *Bildungsroman*, which dominates the period, there is no shortage of variety, of either themes or treatment, and a fair number of genuinely interesting works offering more than just an insight into contemporary Czech society.

693 **Julius Zeyer: the path to decadence.**
Robert B. Pynsent. The Hague: Mouton, 1973. 264p.

Zeyer (1841-1901) was a prolific poet, dramatist and novelist, some of whose works continue to be regularly re-published. Surprisingly little of his work is available in English – a few scattered poems and no prose. Pynsent provides here not just an appraisal of a major writer in his Czech and European context, but includes a detailed analysis of six individual works. One of Pynsent's main academic interests is the Decadence, and the book contains, among much else on Czech literature, an account of where and why Czech Decadence differs from that of Western Europe. Zeyer himself is discerned as standing on the path leading to the Decadence from Romanticism.

694 **Karel Matěj Čapek-Chod: proceedings of a symposium held at the School of Slavonic and East European Studies, 18-20 September, 1984.**
Edited by Robert B. Pynsent. London: School of Slavonic and East European Studies, University of London, 1985. 276p. bibliog. (SEES Occasional Papers, no. 3).

Čapek-Chod (1860-1927) is an example of a major writer from a 'minor' literature, yet one who has been unjustly overlooked by translators. Nor has he received, hitherto, full critical or editorial treatment on his home ground. The symposium from which these papers come was unusual in that it was held outside its subject's home territory, and benefited from balanced treatment by both Western and Eastern European scholars. The papers place the writer in both his Czech and European context and consider him in his own right, from both the literary and linguistic angle. The contributors are, in addition to the editor: D. Rayfield, J. Naughton, K. Brušák and D. Short (all from Britain); A. Stich, V. Křivánek, D. Moldanová, J. Pavelka and J. Hrabák (all from Czechoslovakia); W. Schamschula and W. Annuss (West Germany); L. Dobossy (Hungary); C. Barborică (Romania); H. Jechova (France); L. Doležel (Canada); and T. Z. Orłoś (Poland). The bibliography is the first accurate record of Čapek-Chod's works in book form.

695 **The First World War in fiction: a collection of critical essays.**
Edited by Holger Klein. London: Macmillan, 1976; New York: Barnes & Noble, 1977. 246p.

Robert Pynsent's 'The last days of Austria: Hašek and Kraus' (p. 136-48) draws some interesting parallels between Karl Kraus's *Die letzten Tage der Menschheit* and Jaroslav Hašek's *Švejk* and decides that of the two Kraus has the more general literary satire. The argument is well exemplified.

696 **Jaroslav Hašek and the good soldier Schweik.**
Radko Pytlík, translated from the Czech by David Short. Prague: Panorama, 1983. 90p.

Published simultaneously in Czech, Russian, German and French as well as English, this volume is one of countless writings published to mark the centenary of the birth of Jaroslav Hašek. It contains a new biography of Hašek, describes the genesis of the Schweik character and the history of his appearances in print, and looks in some detail at all the derived versions of the character, in film and on the stage, within Czechoslovakia and abroad. Not the least interesting are the illustrations – period photographs, portraits of Hašek and many other individuals mentioned in the book, and, inevitably, some of Josef Lada's by now classic Schweik illustrations.

697 **The bad Bohemian: a life of Jaroslav Hašek.**
Cecil Parrott. London, Sydney, Toronto: Bodley Head, 1978. 296p. 3 maps. bibliog.

As the preface indicates this is the first attempt outside Czechoslovakia to produce a full-scale biography of Hašek. The author utilizes the maximum of

231

accessible data consisting of established fact and a modicum of the legend. While there are plenty of references to works which the English reader cannot know, and to which the book represents a useful if patchy introduction, much more attention is paid to those aspects of the writer's confusing and tortuous life, as a down-and-out, a soldier in the Austrian army and eventually a Red Army commissar and bigamist, which have some bearing on *The Good Soldier Švejk* and its eponymous 'hero'. The book is marred by some transparent translations from secondary Czech sources and an occasional tendency to moralise. Parrott returned to his favourite author with *Jaroslav Hašek: a study of Švejk and the short stories* (Cambridge, England; New York: Cambridge University Press, 1982. 219p.) which provides the English reader with, *inter alia*, an insight into less well-known Hašek stories in which Švejk also figured in anticipation of the main Švejk novel.

698 **The real legacy of Karel Čapek.**
William E. Harkins. In: *The Czechoslovak contribution to world culture.* Edited by Miloslav Rechcígl, Jr. The Hague, London, Paris: Mouton, 1964, p. 60-67.

Čapek and the reputation which he acquired abroad constitutes an exception to the generally unfavourable picture painted in George Pistorius's essay 'Two paradoxes of Czech literary evolution' (q.v.). Harkins' argument is that Čapek's legacy is not primarily literary, however enduring the popularity of his plays in particular, but political, which he shows by an analysis of the novel trilogy, *Hordubal, Meteor* and *An ordinary life.* The same volume contains another essay on Čapek ie., 'Čapek and communism', by Jaroslav Dresler (p. 68-75) which analyses both Čapek's attitudes to communism and the communists' (largely negative) attitudes to him.

699 **Miroslav Holub and William Carlos Williams.**
Herbert J. Eagle. *Germano-Slavica*, vol. 1, no. 6 (fall 1975), p. 43-52.

This article is included here for the 'Western' dimension. The two poets, Czech and American, both experimental, exhibit, despite their disparate backgrounds, many similarities of rhythm, structure and theme. Holub is one of the Czech poets who has been translated into English, see, for example, *On the contrary and other poems* (q.v.).

700 **Jaroslav Seifert:** *All the beauty of the world – or what's left of it.*
Igor Hájek. *Scottish Slavonic Review*, no. 3 (autumn 1984), p. 115-18.

In this brief paper, Hájek is not only reviewing Seifert's first major prose work *All the beauties of the world* (*Všecky krásy světa*), but also pinpointing some of the political background to literature in Seifert's lifetime, for Seifert is here writing a personalized history of literature and society. The essay is followed by a translation (by Ruth Leadbetter) of chapter 12 of *Všecky krásy světa*, which gives an idea of Seifert's prose style, a sample of personalized literary historiography, and, in the translator's notes, thumbnail sketches of the sixteen Czech writers mentioned. The chapter in question is chiefly an attack on the cult of the Proletarian poet Jiří Wolker.

701 **Milan Kundera: a voice from Central Europe.**
Robert C. Porter. Aarhus, Denmark: Arkona Publishers, 1981.
82p. bibliog.

This is the first monograph on a writer who has long been well-known in the West, where he now lives. His works have been among the most explicitly political, which added to his popularity at a time when political criticism of the system was a relative novelty. Kundera's main novels up to the time of writing, from *The joke* through *Life is elsewhere* to *The book of laughter and forgetting*, are all discussed. They are all currently banned in Czechoslovakia, but have been translated; *The joke*, translated by Michael H. Heim (New York: Harper & Row, 1982. 267p.) – an earlier and different translation is abridged and has the chapters re-ordered; *Life is elsewhere*, translated by Peter Kussi (New York: Knopf, distributed by Random House, 1974. 289p.); *The book of laughter and forgetting*, translated by Michael H. Heim (Harmondsworth, England; New York: Penguin Books, 1981. 237p.). It is worth pointing out that recently Kundera's works have tended to appear in other languages before Czech, and also that some readers in Czechoslovakia who have managed to see the foreign editions of his works since he emigrated find him now so un-Czech as to be a literary irrelevance to them, whatever his writings may have meant in the early period.

702 **Czech opinion of America in the mid-nineteenth century.**
Rudolf Sturm. In: *The Czechoslovak contribution to world culture*. Edited by Miloslav Rechcígl, Jr. The Hague, London, Paris: Mouton, 1964, p. 51-59.

Translations have always played a major part in Czech literature, both as a source of information and as an extension of the general book market (though for different reasons at different times). This essay provides, amongst other more or less interesting snippets about Czech-American contacts of the period, a consideration of: early translations from American literature; news reporting about America and American democracy; the Czechs' antipathy to slavery; aspects of the life of Czechs in America; and the coverage of American themes in the first Czech encyclopaedia – *Slovník naučný* of 1860 onwards.

Translations

703 **The labyrinth of the world and the paradise of the heart.**
John Amos Comenius (Jan Ámos Komenský), translated by Matthew Spinka. Ann Arbor, Michigan: University of Michigan, 1972. 203p.

Comenius, the Czech (Moravian) 17th-century polymath, is undoubtedly best known for his educational theories and teaching aids. One of his best known literary works, 'the culmination of native literary traditions' (Novák), is the Bunyanesque allegory of the world of his day which Comenius satirizes mercilessly before contrasting it with the inner world of profound Christian spirituality. Its moralizing didacticism does not detract from its readability, and it is still read in Czechoslovakia. The present edition in translation is accompanied by a facsimile of the 1663 edition of the Czech original.

704 **May.**
Karel Hynek Mácha, translated by Hugh Hamilton McGoverne. London: Phoenix Press, 1949. 177p.

It is widely agreed that Mácha's *Maj* (1836) is *the* verse classic of Czech literature, with a place in European Romanticism generally. Neither this, nor the translation which preceded it in English, is entirely satisfactory, but it is a notoriously difficult task anyway, chiefly on account of Mácha's exploitation of the acoustic side of Czech. The volume also includes translations of some Mácha occasional works, prose, letters and a biographical sketch. *Máj* is overdue for re-translation, but until that happens, the reader with a knowlege of German may at least turn to the twin translations in *Máj: zweisprachige Ausgabe*, translations by Otto F. Babler and Walther Schamschula (Cologne, GFR; Vienna: Böhlau, 1983. 132p. bibliog. Schriften des Komitees der Bundesrepublik Deutschland zur Förderung der Slawischen Studien, no. 6). Though differently conceived, the translations are generally excellent.

705 **Granny: scenes from country life.**
Božena Němcová, translated by Edith Pargeter. Westport, Connecticut: Greenwood Press, 1976. 349p.

This work is the Czech prose classic of the 19th century, widely revered despite its sentimentality, and compulsory reading in all Czech schools. The work is semi-autobiographical, and if the main story is too much of a moralizing idyll, much of the background of northeast Bohemian folklore (customs, proverbs) is of general interest. The authoress's somewhat idealized grandmother has become, in the popular imagination, the measure of what a good grandmother should be like, though that same popular imagination is also, and quite properly, selective.

706 **Tales of Little Quarter.**
Jan Neruda. Westport, Connecticut: Greenwood Press, 1976. 296p.

Neruda was more prolific as a poet, but only a few of his poems have been translated. As a prose-writer he was no less important and these *Tales* are his best-known work – and another volume of compulsory reading for schools. The tales are a set of observations, indulgent, ironic, humorous, on life among the little people of the Little Quarter, Malá Strana, that part of old Prague caught between the Castle and the river. Neruda's style and method greatly influenced many Czech writers who followed him, and he has been an inspiration to some non-Czechs as well (the Chilean writer Neftalí Ricardo Reyes is said to have chosen his pen-name, Pablo Neruda, out of admiration for his Czech predecessor).

707 The fireflies.
Max Bolliger, translated and adapted by Roseanna Hoover, with
illustrations by Jiří Trnka. London: Evans, 1977. 43p.

This is based on Jan Karafiát's *Broučci*, a children's classic that the present
generation still recalls, although its heavy-handed Victorian morality is quite out
of tune with the rest of children's literature. First published in 1876, the book had
reached its seventy-sixth edition by 1948 and its eighty-third by 1971, so its
popularity can be said to endure. Karafiát's original text has also been translated,
as *Fireflies* (translated by Rose Fyleman, London: George Allen & Unwin, 1942.
116p.). Karafiát was a minister of the Czech Brethren.

708 Legends of Old Bohemia.
Alois Jirásek, translated by Edith Pargeter, with illustrations by Jiří
Trnka. London: Hamlyn, 1963. 337p.

Jirásek is widely seen as a father-figure of modern Czech literature, author of
countless long historical novels based in Bohemia's past, and the kind of writer
whose 'collected works' are apt to grace the shelves of many a patriotic
household. By the nature of things, he has not been widely translated, but this
collection has been included here since Jirásek's absence would be indeed a
glaring omission. The legends are part of almost every Czech child's literary
experience, and many of them are best known in Jirásek's version.

709 The good soldier Švejk and his fortunes in the World War.
Jaroslav Hašek, translated by Cecil Parrott. London:
Heinemann, 1973; Harmondsworth, England: Penguin Books,
1974. 752p.

Švejk is almost too well-known to comment on, having appeared in many
editions, under the other spelling *Schweik*, of the first translation by Paul Selver.
This new translation is complete and unabridged, if not free of certain infelicities.
Critical opinion on Hašek and Švejk varies immensely, but whatever their
shortcomings as person and literary figure they remain immensely popular among
large sections of the Czech reading public. Others, however, express a sense of
national disgrace that this particular breed of political rebel (Hašek) and
ingenuous-ingenious anti-hero (Švejk) should have come to be held in such high
esteem by so many. Švejk himself has given birth to his own literary myth, in
having attributed to him the catch-phrase 'To chce klid' (ie., 'take it easy' or 'no
sweat') which he actually never says, and in the common Czech word *švejkovina*,
used to express any bit of underhand, petty, anti-authoritarian guile, often quite
different from the actions of the original character. The Švejk character was
obviously resilient enough as a literary character for him to be borrowed by
Brecht for the latter's *Schweik in the Second World War*, which makes him into a
more overtly political creation. There have also been dramatizations and film
versions of the original *Švejk*, but perhaps best known of all Švejkiana are Josef
Lada's illustrations.

710   **R.U.R. and The insect play.**
Karel Čapek, Josef Čapek, translated by Paul Selver.   London:
Oxford University Press, 1961. 179p. (Oxford Paperbacks, no. 34)

R.U.R. (Rossum's Universal Robots) is the work which gave the world the word
robot. It is also possibly the most frequently published Czech work in English, in
a variety of versions and adaptations. Like the novels referred to in Karel Čapek'
Apocryphal stories (q.v.) it is a warning against tinkering with a technology which
may go out of control. *R.U.R.* is nominally by Karel Čapek alone but both
brothers were involved in *The Insect Play*, which has also been widely translated
and published in English, indeed under no less than four different titles. It is a
critical portrait of society, expressed as a dramatic allegory with a mixture of
human and insect characters. Both plays are products of the period following the
Great War. Despite its apparent age, this edition was still in print at the time of
writing. For an appraisal of the symbolism and ideology of the robot play see
James D. Naughton's 'Futurology and robots: Karel Čapek's *R.U.R.*', *Renaissance
and Modern Studies* (Nottingham University Press) (1984), p. 72-86, and on the
science fiction element in Čapek generally see Darko Suvin's 'Karel Čapek, or the
aliens among us' in his *Metamorphoses of science fiction . . .* (New Haven,
Connecticut: Yale University Press, 1979, p. 270-83).

711   **Apocryphal stories.**
Karel Čapek, translated by Dora Round.   Harmondsworth,
England: Penguin Books, 1975. 160p. (Modern Classics).

Čapek was once the most translated Czech author, see George F. Kovtun'
bibliography of *Czech and Slovak literature in English* (q.v.). Recently, however
he has not been nearly so popular. The jolly, quite readable *Apocryphal Stories*
are among the few Čapek works which have been republished recently. Other
Čapek works to have reappeared in recent years, in the form of re-prints, are *The
absolute at large* (New York: Garland, 1975.) and *War with the newts* (New York:
AMS Press, 1978.), two of Čapek's science-fiction-esque novels in which he warns
against the dangers inherent in technological experimentation.

712   **Elegie – Elegies.**
Jiří Orten, translated by Lyn Coffin, introduction by George
Gibian.   New York: SVU, 1980. 111p.

Orten (1919-41) was one of the generation of lyric poets affected directly by the
war – in his case death came in the shape of a German ambulance. This edition
contains the Czech text and English translation in parallel.

713 **Three Czech poets: Vítězslav Nezval, Antonín Bartušek and Josef Hanzlík.**
Vítězslav Nezval, translated by Ewald Osers; Antonín Bartušek, translated by Ewald Osers, George Theiner; Josef Hanzlík, translated by Ewald Osers, with an introduction by Graham Martin. Harmondsworth, England: Penguin Books, 1970. 158p. (Penguin Modern European Poets).

Nezval (1900-58), Bartušek (1921-.) and Hanzlík (1938-.) were deliberately chosen for this collection as members, if not entirely typical representatives, of three generations of Czech 20th-century verse. Bartušek's and Hanzlík's poems are taken from various collections, while Nezval's are all from the volume entitled *Prague with fingers of rain* (1936); Nezval is undoubtedly the best known of the three. The translations are competent, and any difficulty of reception in their non-native environment is smoothed away by the brief but useful introduction (p. 11-22). This treats each poet separately, but draws relevant comparisons, however fleeting, with other poets – Miroslav Holub, T. S. Eliot, Thomas Hardy and Philip Larkin. For an essay on the Nezval collection see Maria Němcová Banerjee's 'Nezval's *Prague with fingers of rain*: a surrealist image', *Slavonic and East European Journal*, vol. 23, no. 4 (winter 1979), p. 505-14.

714 **Curious tales.**
Miloš Macourek, translated by Marie Burg. Oxford, New York: Oxford University Press, 1980. 76p.

Macourek is perhaps best known for his whimsical animal stories, modern fairy tales which rely heavily on bizarre distortions and juxtapositions, of which these are samples from two collections.

715 **On the contrary and other poems.**
Miroslav Holub, translated by Ewald Osers, foreword by A. Alvarez. Newcastle-on-Tyne, England: Bloodaxe Books, 1984. 126p.

Holub is another modern Czech poet who has been fairly widely translated prior to this selection, and who has been found to be of sufficient merit to earn inclusion in an Open University course (see *East European poets*, Milton Keynes, England: Open University Press, 1976). In particular Holub takes the natural sciences as the material for his verse, which often assumes the form of complex allegory.

716 **The cremator.**
Ladislav Fuks, translated by E. M. Kandler. London: Marion Boyars, 1984. 176p.

This is a bizarre, not to say horrifying, tale about a man who works in the crematorium in Prague at the time of the Nazi occupation. It is a powerful story of a mind gradually distorted by the 'hero's' belief that his family's existence is in jeopardy thanks to his wife's Jewish background. At the time this was no unique state of affairs, but set in the context of the crematorium it takes on a particularly gruesome aura. This was one of Fuks's earlier works (1967) and it enjoyed considerable success, as did the film based upon it.

Literature. Czech

717 **An umbrella from Piccadilly.**
Jaroslav Seifert, translated by Ewald Osers. London: London
Magazine Editions, 1983. 80p.

This is another work which was published illictly in Prague and then abroad,
before seeing 'normal' publication in Czechoslovakia. It is highly personal poetry,
charged with melancholy. Other translations of Seifert include *The casting of
bells*, translated by Paul Jagasich and Tom O'Grady (Iowa City, Iowa: The Spirit
that Moves us Press, 1983. 61p.), which is a slightly earlier work (1967) ill-served
by the translation, and the samples included in the *Exhibition notes* (London:
British Library, 1985. 4p.) to accompany the small display mounted at the British
Library in reponse to the poet winning the Nobel Prize for Literature.

718 **The plague column.**
Jaroslav Seifert, translated by Ewald Osers, introduction by Cecil
Parrott. London, Boston: Terra Nova Editions, 1979. 106p.

Jaroslav Seifert is a very popular Czech poet, if not the most outstanding or
original. Some indication of his popularity comes in the appearance of translations
of his work in English even before his nomination for the Nobel Prize, which he
won in 1984. *The plague column* is a fairly recent work (1977), first published in
Cologne and only later in Prague (1981), a fact which indicates that he was out of
favour with the régime and is not unconnected with the Nobel Prize nomination.
Certain other works met a similar fate. *The plague column* is also a rarity among
Czech literature in that it produced not one, but two different translations, the
other being by Lyn Coffin (Silver Spring, Maryland: SVU, 1980. 57p.), which also
contains the Czech text.

719 **My merry mornings: stories from Prague.**
Ivan Klíma, translated by George Theiner. London, New York:
Readers International, 1985. 154p.

Ivan Klíma was one of the respected authors of the 1960s. He is still writing
although his work is now proscribed. These often whimsical, sometimes almost
absurdist tales are representative of his recent writing and are, for the most part
apolitical, though many of them give a realistic picture of details of contemporary
life (for example, the snapping up of deserted village houses by townies as second
homes and the undeniable pilfering from building sites), some of which inevitably
acquire a political interpretation. Somewhat wastefully, Theiner has retranslated
one story already available in English in Antonín Liehm and Peter Kussi's, eds.,
The writing on the wall: an anthology of contemporary Czech literature (q.v.).

720 **Riders in the sky.**
Filip Jánský, translated by Joy Kadečková. London: Hodder &
Stoughton, 1969. 192p.

This was a major hit when it appeared in Prague, as was the film based upon it
since it brought into literature the role of Czechs and Slovaks fighting on the
western front, with the Royal Air Force, an aspect of the hostilities which had
been largely ignored in favour of the military effort based on cooperation with the
Red Army. The dramatic story, with its realistic plot and romantic sub-plot, was
awarded a prize when it appeared in 1965 and three editions had been published
by 1967.

721 **A close watch on the trains.**
Bohumil Hrabal, translated by Edith Pargeter. London: Cape,
1968. 93p.

Known from other editions and the film, which has a different ending, under the
alternative titles of *Closely watched trains* or *Closely observed trains*, and most
recently republished under the former title (New York: Penguin Books, 1981.)
with an introduction by Josef Škvorecký, this is a humorous and touching story of
a young railway employee battling with impotence and finding himself a hero after
sabotaging a train during the Second World War (when of course the Germans
were running the railways). Hrabal is a popular writer who, like others, has been
in trouble with the régime, and some of his more recent work has been initially
published outside Czechoslovakia. Some shorter pieces by Hrabal are also
available in translation such as is *The death of Mr. Baltisberger*, translated by
Káča Poláčková (Garden City, New York: Doubleday, 1975. 193p.).

722 **A night with Hamlet.**
Vladimír Holan, translated by Jarmila Milner, Ian
Milner. London: Oasis Books, 1980. 44p.

A night with Hamlet (1964) is a long, unrhymed poem by a major modern poet
who has been fairly widely translated but in a piecemeal fashion. It is
individualistic, pessimistic verse, with religious undertones and full of allusions
which cannot all come across in translation. Holan is essentially a poet's poet but
nevertheless enjoys considerable popularity. The same translators have published
a selection of his other work as *Selected poems* (Harmondsworth, England:
Penguin Books, 1971. 127p.).

723 **The memorandum.**
Václav Havel, translated by Vera Blackwell. London: Cape,
1967. 112p.

This is the first Havel play published in English, dating from before the 'years of
crisis' of 1968-69. It is an absurdist drama which, in many ways, sets the tone for
much of his later work and undoubtedly prepared the ground for his subsequent
notoriety. Havel's work has put him at variance with the régime, which has seen
fit to keep him under surveillance both in and out of prison. He is undoubtedly
the major dissident playwright and on these, as well as on purely literary grounds,
he has had most of his works translated. These include: *The garden party*,
translated by Vera Blackwell (London: Cape, 1969. 79p.); *The increased difficulty
of concentration*, translated by Vera Blackwell (London: Cape, 1972. 78p.), and
Sorry . . .: two plays, translated by Vera Blackwell (London: Eyre Methuen for
the British Broadcasting Corporation, 1978. 64p.). The last consists of the two
one-act plays *The audience* and *The private view*. Several of the plays have seen
more than one edition and all have been performed in England.

724 **The swell season: a text on the most important things in life.**
Josef Škvorecký, translated by Paul Wilson. London: Chatto &
Windus, The Hogarth Press, 1983. 226p.

Škvorecký was one of the most popular writers of the 1960s and he first achieved
notoriety with his novel *The cowards* (1958). In this latter work he provided an

unorthodox picture of popular responses to the end of the war, with young individuals more interested in private enjoyment and foolhardy bravado than in the grander tones of national liberation and the defeat of Nazism. *The cowards* was also one of the first works to bring jazz into literature (in more than just the thematic sense). Danny, the hero of *The cowards*, which has long been available in translation, and jazz both return in this collection of war-time stories, in which sexual adventures and mishaps play a role proportionate to that of many of Škvorecký's intervening works, most of which have also been translated. Since emigrating Škvorecký has continued to write and publish in Czech, largely through his wife's publishing house (Sixty-Eight Publishers) in Canada.

725 **The abortionists.**
Valja Stýblová, translated by Edith Pargeter.   London: Secker & Warburg, 1961. 176p. 2nd. ed. London: New English Library, 1963. 143p.

This very popular novel (the first Czech edition appeared in 1957 under the title *Mne soudila noc*), deals with a subject which at the time had not been fully worked out legislatively. The problem of abortion is considered from both the individual and the social point of view. The authoress heads the Prague neurological clinic.

Anthologies

726 **Lyra Czecho-slovanská: Bohemian poems, ancient and modern, translated from the original Slavonic, with an introductory essay.**
A. H. Wratislaw.   London: John W. Parker, 1849. 120p.

Included here for its curiosity value, this somewhat bizarre early anthology of Czech verse in translation was inspired by the translator's blood-affinity with the Bohemians' 'oldest, once their royal family'. The author was also encouraged by the well-founded belief that there is much Czech literature worthy of translation (though he cannot be said, in retrospect, to have made the best selection even of what was available in his day).

727 **Czech prose: an anthology.**
Translated and edited by William E. Harkins.   Ann Arbor, Michigan: Michigan Slavic Publications, Department of Slavic Languages and Literatures, University of Michigan, 1983. 321p. (Michigan Slavic Translations, no. 6).

This volume contains some thirty-four excerpts from the 14th century to the end of the First World War, together with a brief conventional history of the literature and a cameo on each author or work. The 19th-century section is very conservative in its choice of authors, even if some of the passages selected are less so. The real value lies in the fairly well represented Old Czech and Baroque periods, with meditational, hagiographic, allegorical and travel genres all included. The extracts are supported by brief straightforward annotations and reproductions of some of the manuscripts and portraits of some of the authors. Previously Harkins had edited an *Anthology of Czech literature* (New York: King's Crown Press, 1953. 226p.) with extracts, in the original, from twenty-two Czech 19th- and 20th-century authors, with English commentaries. For breadth of choice and depth of commentary, the work bears no comparison with Pynsent's *Czech prose and verse: a selection with an introductory essay* (q.v.).

728 **Czech poetry: a bilingual anthology.**
Alfred French, with an introduction by René Wellek. Ann Arbor, Michigan: Department of Slavic Languages and Literatures, University of Michigan and the Czechoslovak Society of Arts and Sciences in America, 1973. 372p. (Michigan Slavic Translations).

This volume's utility is as a parallel text, as well as offering an insight into Czech poetry. The seventy-one items selected stretch from the earliest times up to the Second World War and are accompanied by a brief introduction by René Wellek, one of the best known émigré literary critics and historians. Prior to this French had published the monograph *The poets of Prague: Czech poetry between the wars* (London, New York: Oxford University Press, 1969. 129p.).

729 **Czech prose and verse: a selection with an introductory essay.**
Robert B. Pynsent. London: Athlone Press, 1979. 204p. (London East European Series).

This is an anthology of extracts in the original, far less conservative than that referred to in William E. Harkins's entry on *Czech prose: an anthology* (q.v.), and deliberately so. The selection covers the period 1774-1939, beginning with Karel Thám and ending with Jan Zahradníček, and despite being less conventional than many collections, translated or otherwise, it nevertheless gives a fair representation of the modern literature. The work is primarily intended for students of literature with a prior knowledge of the language, though some language points and other vital annotations are given. The 'introductory essay' takes up over a third of the book and is a useful alternative history of Czech literature.

730 **The writing on the wall: an anthology of contemporary Czech literature.**
Edited by Antonín Liehm, Peter Kussi. Princeton, New Jersey; New York: Karz-Cohl Publishing, 1983. 252p.

The short-story and the *feuilleton* are two genres which have a long and respectable tradition in Czech literature. All the pieces in this collection fall within these two categories, all are translations from works published in *samizdat* by the underground *Edice petlice* and most are from very well-known writers. Moreover, they all date from the period since 1968, since when all their authors have been proscribed. Some are still living in Czechoslovakia, some have since emigrated. Czech literature has almost always been closely tied to contemporary political affairs, and this applies in most cases here too, though many of the pieces can be read even without any knowledge of the political sub-text. The translations are by various people and vary somewhat in their quality, but as a collection, it gives a fair impression of the range of styles and themes at the heart of underground literature. The Czech texts of many of the stories are available in the West, having been reprinted by two of the main exile publishing houses, Sixty-Eight Publishers of Toronto and Index of Cologne. The foreword, by Antonín Liehm, contains thumbnail sketches of the writers presented.

John Amos Comenius, that incomparable Moravian.
See item no. 375.

Slovak

History and criticism

731 Slovak language and literature.
Joseph M. Kirschbaum. Winnipeg, Canada: University of Manitoba Press, 1975. 336p. (Readings in Slavic Literatures, no. 12).

Kirschbaum is one of the most prolific of émigré Slovak historians, and this is essentially a history book, dealing in outline with the evolution, primarily, of the Slovak literary language. The émigré view has long been firmly on the side of the uniqueness and separateness (from Czech) of Slovak, a view now officially held also in Slovakia itself. The literary side of the title is incomplete, since the period 1860-1948, ie., the bulk of writing since the codification of the literary language, is omitted, which is to be regretted in the absence of any other major synoptic works. There is, however, a generous discussion of the pre-codification controversies, though conveyed in strongly nationalist terms.

732 One hundred and twenty years of Slovak literary language.
Juraj Slávik. In: *The Czechoslovak contribution to world culture.* Edited by Miloslav Rechcígl, Jr. The Hague, London, Paris: Mouton, 1964, p. 44-50.

Despite the title this is more a potted history of Slovak modern literature. It is necessarily superficial, but the major writers are all mentioned. Unlike many North American, or other émigré Slovak writings, it is not chauvinistic in tone, in particular not anti-Czech, and it specifically seeks to place Slovak literature firmly in the Western literary tradition and is against what it sees as distortions of the most modern i.e., communist, period.

733 **Slowakische Literatur: Entwicklungstrends vom Vormärz bis zur Gegenwart.** (Slovak literature: evolutionary trends from the *Vormärz* to the present.)
Ludwig Richter.   East Berlin, GDR: Akademie-Verlag, 1979.
272p. bibliog. (Literatur und Gesellschaft).

This East German history of Slovak literature is one of the most complete in a 'Western' language, incomplete though it may be in some of the trickier areas of the 1960s and 1970s (though it does acknowledge the existence of some of the otherwise banned authors). It follows contemporary Slovak histories of the literature in where it lays emphasis and which authors it tends to praise (ideologically). An asset for those who read German is the bibliography of translations (1949-79) from Slovak literature, which considerably extends the range of sources available.

734 **Contemporary Slovak literature.**
Pavol Števček, translated by Oľga Horská.   Bratislava: Obzor, 1980. 122p.

This work was produced on behalf of the Slovak National Book League (Slovenské ústredie knižnej kultúry), a quango that oversees every aspect of book production, including advice and coordination. It is a somewhat unhappily translated volume by one of the better known Slovak literary critics and historians and was intended for distribution to foreigners, rather than for normal sale (unlike ordinary Czechoslovak publications, it carries no price). Thus it should be accessible wherever contacts with the country are fairly strong. The opening essay outlines post-war Slovak literature, looking at its main themes and relating them to contemporary events in Slovakia and abroad. The two main sections, on verse and prose, take the form of brief biobibliographies of the main representatives (except for those currently black-listed) and each is accompanied by a summary essay and a photograph of the writer concerned. Three much shorter sections provide a sketch of the modern literature for children as well as drama and literary history and criticism. The whole book is a rather telegraphic but reasonably useful introduction to a little-known literature. A French permutation of the same work appeared in 1982.

735 **Encyklopédia slovenských spisovateľov.** (Encyclopaedia of Slovak writers.)
Karol Rosenbaum (et al.).   Bratislava: Obzor, 1984. 2 vols. bibliog.

A large and beautifully produced scholarly dictionary of writers which inevitably omits those currently out of favour. This will serve for many years to come as the major (only) work of its kind. Each entry contains a full biography and bibliography, with pseudonyms noted, and a selection of critical Slovak literature. The work needs to be known, even if it is of limited use to the non-speaker of the language.

736 **Byron in nineteenth century Slovak literature.**
Zuzana Hegedüsová. *Slavica Slovaca*, vol. 18, no. 2 (summer
1983), p. 144-52.

The article offers a partial study of Slovak Romanticism with the emphasis on the
changing role of Byronism as a source of direct or indirect influence, or as a set of
recurring patterns and themes that happen to parallel the Byronic model but
which are born equally out of the indigenous literary context. It offers an insight
into a number of the better known Slovak Romantic classics and their authors
and to some of the relevant writings by other Slovak literary historians.

737 **Kollár and Štúr: romantic and post-romantic visions of a Slavic
future.**
Peter R. Black. New York: Institute on East Central Europe,
Columbia University, 1975. 45p.

A monograph on two of the leading figures in the literary and cultural life of 19th-
century Slovakia, the one a Slavophile poet, antiquarian and folklorist, who did
not believe in the need for a separate literary Slovak language, and the other a
leading ideologue of Slovak linguistic and literary independence and forefather of
the modern Slovak literary language. For a separate, larger study on Štúr in
English see Fráňa Ruttkay's *Ľudovít Štúr (1815-1856)*, translated by Svetozar
Simko (Bratislava: Obzor, 1971. 115p.).

738 **A man of stars: the Slovakian national poet Hviezdoslav: an
illustrated summary.**
Alfred Lubran. London: Narbulla Agency Press, 1974. 52p.

Pavol Orságh Hviezdoslav (1849-1921) is one of the few Slovak poets to have
received attention in monographs, and this is the most recent. None of the works
which have been published have been very long, the most substantial being
Stanislav Šmatlák's *Hviezdoslav: a national and world poet* (Bratislava: Obzor-
Tatrapress, 1969. 122p.) which is not easy to obtain.

Translations

739 **Bloody sonnets.**
Pavol Országh Hviezdoslav, translated by Jaroslav
Vajda. Scranton, Pennsylvania: Obrana Press, 1950. [not
paginated].

Hviezdoslav (1849-1921) is widely seen as Slovakia's national poet. It is to be
regretted that he is not better represented in English translation (at least one of
his long narrative poems ought to be available; as it is there are just a few poems
scattered through anthologies). The *Bloody sonnets* (1914) are the poet's reaction
to the Great War and contain a synthesis of his social philosophy and ethics.

'40 **Seven Slovak stories.**
Martin Kukučín, translated and edited by Norma Leigh Rudinsky,
foreword by William E. Harkins.   Cleveland, Ohio; Rome: Slovak
Institute, 1980. 235p. bibliog.

Kukučín, real name Matej Bencúr (1860-1928), is held by many to be the best
writer to emerge from Slovakia, at least among those writing predominantly in
prose. Much of his writing was produced outside Slovakia and is thematically
remote from his country. This collection of short stories and novellas is set firmly
in Slovakia, however, and they belong really to the period of the National
Awakening, giving insights into the life and times of the rural population.
Allowing for certain infelicities of the translation, the reader will gain an
appreciation of the atmosphere of the age, with both its amusing and more
troubling dimensions. The stories contained are: *Obecné trampoty* (Village
quabbles); *Dedinský jarmok* (A village fair); *Z teplého hnízda* (From a warm
nest); *Rysavá jalovica* (The mottled heifer); *Neprebudený* (An unawakened boy,
or The village idiot); *Na obecnom salaši* (At the community sheepfold); and *Dies
irae*. Each is accompanied by a short introduction, and the book also contains a
brief literary biography of Kukučín. The bibliography incorporates a number of
English-language titles, and includes a reference to *Slovak Studies*, vol. 18 (1978)
edited by Michael Lacko which deals exclusively with Kukučín and was published
to commemorate the 50th anniversary of his death. It includes an important
Annotated bibliography of English-language sources on Martin Kukučín' (p. 169-
79).

741 **The taste of power.**
Ladislav Mňačko, translated from Slovak by Paul Stevenson, with
a preface by Max Hayward.   London: Weidenfeld & Nicolson,
1967. 235p.

This was one of the best-known works by Mňačko, see his biography, *The seventh
night* (q.v.) a best-seller in its day in the original and in Czech translation. It
describes the political career of the hero's friend, who rose to the highest position
in the state, and is a disturbing account of the use and abuse of power. In
Czechoslovakia it became quite strong medicine in the light of events and has
since been banned, along with its author, now exiled in Israel.

Anthologies

742 **An anthology of Slovak poetry: a selection of lyric and narrative
poems and folk ballads in Slovak and English.**
Edited and translated by Ivan J. Kramoris.   [Scranton,
Pennsylvania]: Obrana Press, [1947]. 146p.

Few major individual works are available in translation from Slovak literature, so
the enquirer has to depend chiefly on anthologies, although few of these have
been published. Accordingly, the reader must resort to this fairly early volume,

which contains selections from fifteen poets, some classics, some peripheral, but including one representative, Ján Silván, of the 16th century (the remainder are from the 19th and 20th centuries). In that early period most poetry claimed for Slovak literature, including Silván's, was written in Czech, though with some Slovakisms.

743 **Anthology of Slovak literature.**
   Compiled by Andrew Cincura. Riverside, California: University Hardcovers, 1976. 425p.

A quite varied and fairly representative collection of excerpts from the work of sixty-two poets and prose-writers from the early 19th century down to the present. It is unusual in that it draws not only on domestic Slovak literature, but also on the work of Slovak writers living in the United States. For size and variety there is nothing to match this among translations from Slovak.

744 **The world of a child.**
   Compiled by Bernardette Lézer, translated by Jana Ruppeldtová, Heather Trebatická. Bratislava: Lita, 1981. 94p. bibliog.

The Slovaks, like the Czechs, traditionally, and now as a matter of policy, lay great store by literature for children. This slim anthology is aimed at the foreign reader and interested foreign publishers simply as a sample of Slovak literature produced for children of different age groups. It includes fourteen stories from twelve authors, many of whom are also well-known writers of mainstream literature. The appendix contains thumbnail sketches of the writers concerned and a selected bibliography of their works. The book also serves as an introduction to the work of some of the contemporary Slovak illustrators.

Literatures of other nationalities

745 **Die Prager deutsche Literatur und die tschechische Literatur in den ersten zwei Jahrzehnten des 20. Jahrhunderts.** (Prague German literature and Czech literature in the first two decades of the 20th century.)
   Antonín Měšťan. In: *Slavistische Studien zum IX. Internationalen Slavistenkongress in Kiev 1983.* Edited by Reinhold Olesch (et al.). Cologne, GFR; Vienna: Böhlau, 1983, p. 339-46. (Slavistische Forschungen, vol. 40).

Měšťan's central thesis is that for the period in question Prague literary life was marked by a high degree of cooperation, friendship and even some joint publishing ventures between the two linguistic and literary communities. The links worked to the advantage of Czech literature in that thanks to translations by their German colleagues into the more widely-known German, many Czech writers became read outside the narrow confines of the Czech Lands.

746 **The relationship of the Prague German writers to the Czechoslovak Republic 1918-1919.**
Eve C. Bock. *Germano-Slavica*, vol. 2, no. 4 (fall 1977), p. 273-83.

Describes more the political allegiances of the major Prague German writers than their literary qualities. The two major groupings, the 'Prager Schule' which was pro-Masaryk and anti-Austrian, and the left-wing group with ties to like-minded writers among the Czechs and in Russia and Germany, produced a major contribution to German literature quite distinct from their pro-Nazi Sudeten compatriots. The two wings united in the face of Nazism, but eventually, after the occupation of the country, this led to their demise, either in exile or in concentration camps. Although these writers sought to be fully involved in the Czech cultural scene, they were, and still are, with some politically motivated exceptions, largely ignored by, and unknown to, the Czech reading public. The article does not discuss the Sudeten writers, but, usefully, does name some of them, and also points out the Prague German contribution to the translation of Czech authors into German. It should be noted that many Prague German writers were Jews.

747 **The world of Franz Kafka.**
Edited with an introduction by J. P. Stern. London: Weidenfeld & Nicolson, 1980. 263p.

A collection of twenty-four essays divided into three sections: 'Local and biographic'; 'Summonses and interpretations'; and 'Fictions and semi-fictions'. The papers consider, from many different angles, the life and times, works and ideas, and literary and social (Prague Jewish) context of the best-known non-Czech Bohemian writer.

748 **Kafka: Judaism, politics and literature.**
Ritchie Robertson. Oxford: Clarendon Press, 1985. 256p.

Although traditionally assigned to German literature plain and simple, there is undoubtedly a sense in insisting that there is a distinctive Prague or Bohemian German literature, and more narrowly still, a Prague German Jewish literature, of which Kafka is by far the best known representative. This new general study is less concerned with this kind of assignment and more with Kafka's works just as literature, relating it to his life and the historical background, and picking up the threads of the Jewish element. In addition to the literary and historical context, the social context, not merely Jewish, is also brought out.

749 **Franz Kafka of Prague.**
Jiří Gruša, translated by Eric Mosbacher. London: Secker & Warburg, 1983. 125p.

A photographic record of Kafka and his family and of the Prague of his day, using both recent and early photographs, including some of buildings that have disappeared. The pictures are accompanied by snatches of quotation from Kafka's works, with emphasis on such ideas as the 'omnipresent shadow of the Castle', and the introductory text is in a similar vein, with some rambling thoughts on Time.

750 **Conversations with Kafka.**
Gustav Janouch, translated by Goronwy Rees, with an introduction by Hugh Haughton. London, Melbourne, New York: Quartet Books, 1985. 205p. (Encounter).

An idiosyncratic introduction to Kafka's thoughts as recalled well after his death. There is a good deal of scepticism as regards authenticity, although many things 'fit' well enough. A discussion of the authenticity problem is given in the introduction, which also relates the 'conversations' to Kafka's works.

751 **Diamonds of the night.**
Arnošt Lustig, translated by Jeanne W. Němcová. Washington, DC: Inscape, 1978. 234p.

These stories, originally published in 1958, are about young people in concentration camps, an essentially Jewish theme from a Jewish author. The work was ideologically respectable and was first translated into English in Czechoslovakia itself. Since then Lustig has written, up until his emigration, solely on Jewish themes and has been widely translated and published especially in America. However, since he emigrated he has, unlike Milan Kundera, been largely forgotten, though he continues to publish through émigré publishing houses. In their day, many of his works were bestsellers, notably *Dita Saxová*, which was translated in 1966 by George Theiner as *Dita Sax* (London: Hutchinson) and again in 1979 by Jeanne W. Němcová as *Dita Saxova* (New York: Harper & Row). Although Lustig is dealt with in histories of Czech literature, I place him in this section because of the total Jewishness of his output; even his works in exile remain consistent in this respect.

752 **The development of Ukrainian literature in Czechoslovakia 1945-1975: a survey of social, cultural and historical aspects.**
Josef Sirka. Frankfurt am Main, GFR; Berne, Switzerland; Las Vegas, Nevada: Peter Lang, 1978. 198p. 3 maps. bibliog.
(European University Papers, Series XVI – Slavonic Languages and Literatures, vol. 2).

Although appallingly translated and marred in certain other respects as well, this little volume does give an overall portrait of Ukrainian literature in Czechoslovakia since the war. It is useful for the historical background and the demographic data as well as the vast bibliographical section. The main body of the text is conveniently divided by genre, the information being rather restricted to biographical data, the barest critical appraisal of the works mentioned and a heavy reliance on quotations. Some consideration is also given to the religious, educational and general cultural position of the Ukrainians of the Prešov region.

753   **The Prague group of Ukrainian nationalist writers and their
      ideological origins.**
      Roman Olynyk.   In: *Czechoslovakia past and present.* Edited by
      Miloslav Rechcígl, Jr. The Hague, Paris: Mouton, 1968. 2 vols.,
      p. 1,022-31.

The Ukrainians in Prague were a short-lived group as a cohesive unit, their
activities there being confined to the period 1920s-30s. They were numerically
strong enough to sustain more than twenty professional, educational and scholarly
institutions and included a number of writers. This is a detailed account of the
pressures which gave rise to this ethnic and literary minority with some detail on
individual writers and works.

754   **Selected poems.**
      Ondra Lysohorský, selected and introduced by Ewald Osers,
      translated from the Lachian and German by Ewald Osers, Hugh
      McKinley, Isobel Leviten, W. H. Auden, Lydia Pasternak-Slater.
      London: Jonathan Cape, 1971. 116p.

Ondra Lysohorský, or in his own language Óndra Łysohorsky, is an unusual
phenomenon in that he writes in an even less-known language than Czech or
Slovak and yet has been quite widely translated, not just into English, German,
French and Russian, but, in the case of individual poems, into as many as sixty
languages. That language is Lachian, to some merely a hybrid dialect of mixed
Czech and Polish features, spoken in Silesia. His position is comparable then to
that of Burns or Hugh MacDiarmid. He is a working-class poet, born in 1905,
with strong working-class passions and an almost fierce regional patriotism,
though free of xenophobia and accepting that Poles and Germans, the other
nations inhabiting his area, have a right to their existence. He is less happy about
the Czechs, whom he sees as oppressors, and has, like many other Czechoslovak
poets, had his political ups and downs. It is probably fair to say that he is not
widely known to many Czechs. This particular collection contains seventy-five
poems. More recently there have been two more collections: *In the eye of the
storm*, 110 poems translated by D. Gill, E. Osers, W. H. Auden, H. McKinley
and L. Pasternak-Slater (Youlgreave, Derbyshire, England: Hub Publications,
1976, 94p); and seventy-five poems, translated by D. Gill, E. Osers, K. Mason
and H. McKinley in *Poet*, vol. 21, no. 7 (July 1980).

755   **Pits and pitfalls: the fate of Ondra Lysohorsky.**
      David Gill.   *Scottish Slavonic Review*, no. 3 (autumn 1984),
      p. 27-44. bibliog.

This is a quite detailed account of the life and literary career of the poet,
expanding all the points mentioned in the previous item, especially on the status
of Lachian, and also including much more on relevant events in history and
political attitudes to the poet. It also bemoans the fact that since 1958 he has not
been published in the original. The article is illustrated by quotations, in the
original and in translation, and the bibliography contains three studies in German
or French, editions of Lysohorský's Lachian and German verse, and the main
editions of translations, into German, French, English and Russian *inter alia*.

756 **Maďarská literatúra v ČSSR.** (Hungarian literature in the
Czechoslovak Socialist Republic.)
Compiled by Karol Rosenbaum, introduction by Rudolf Chmel,
Karol Rosenbaum, translated from Hungarian by Katarína
Králová. Bratislava: Slovenský spisovateľ, 1983. 160p.

A collection of papers by several Hungarian and Slovak critics on various aspects
of the birth, evolution and present state of literature among the Hungarian
minority in South Slovakia. The subject still awaits a detailed treatment in
English.

Foreign literatures on Czechoslovak themes

757 **Mozart's journey to Prague.**
Eduard Mörike, translated from the German by Leopold von
Loewenstein-Wertheim. London: John Calder, 1957. 93p.

The Czechs in general, and Praguers in particular, are proud of their association
with Mozart, whose *Don Giovanni* was first produced there in 1787. This story by
the Swabian poet Mörike is included here solely for the picture which it gives,
albeit a literary one, of the Bohemian German aristocracy of the day.

758 **The Golem.**
Isaac Bashevis Singer. London: André Deutsch, 1983. 85p.

Retold by a Nobel-prize-winning author in an appropriately inimitable Jewish
style, this is the story of the legendary clay giant, a forerunner of Frankenstein
and others, created by Rabbi Jehúdá Löw of Prague during the time of Rudolph
II.

759 **Letters from Prague 1937.**
H. Gordon Skilling. *Kosmas*, vol. 1, no. 2 (winter 1982), p. 63-
73.

A small selection of thoughtful letters by the then young student of things Czech
(and later scholar) written from Prague to his parents and fiancée. Not the kind of
letters most of us would write, more a political diary laced with the writer's frank
Czechophilia, they nevertheless offer an unusual insight into the country at a
critical juncture in its history.

Literature. Foreign literatures on Czechoslovak themes

760   **La rose da Bratislava.** (The Bratislava rose.)
Émile Henriot.   Paris: Plon, 1959. 243p. (Le livre de poche, no. 465).

Set in Czechoslovakia after the *Anschluss* and before the Nazi occupation, this is a story of two rival antiquarians, French and Lithuanian, scouring the country for a lost manuscript by Casanova, who worked at Duchcov Château library and is buried at the local cemetery. The narrative abounds in descriptions of Czechoslovak towns, landscapes and châteaux, and references to the country's history and contemporary problems.

761   **The plotters.**
Friedrich Bruegel, translated by Anthony Dent.   London: Victor Gollancz, 1952. 256p.

This is one of the early thrillers set in post-1948 Eastern Europe, dealing with the outcome – arrest, imprisonment, search for incriminating evidence and death – of a vague failed plot hatched by a handful of people disenchanted by the new régime. In particular it catches the mood of topsy-turvey values, where justice and injustice may mean the same thing or where black is, may be, or must be seen as, white.

762   **The night of Wenceslas.**
Lionel Davidson.   Harmondsworth, England: Penguin Books, 1968. Reprint of first Penguin edition, 1960. 227p.

First published by Gollancz in 1960, so quite separate from the wave of interest in Czechoslovakia in the late 1960s, this is a very successful modern thriller about the troubles of an indigent young Londoner of Czech descent. He becomes embroiled in a sordid espionage venture, not political, but industrial, the plot hinging on the smuggling of secret formulae connected with glass-making. The atmosphere of the Prague scenes is conveyed with persuasion.

763   **The fabulous Englishman.**
Robert McCrum.   London: Hamish Hamilton, 1984. 274p.

This curious story of a formerly successful English writer and his tenuous contacts with Prague in the 1960s and 1970s is a hybrid between the epistolary novel, memoirs of the hero as ghosted by the *Ich*, a political history of the 'years of crisis' in Czechoslovakia and a social history of contemporary England, the latter two elements making for some telling contrasts between the two nations' cares and values. The 'hero' is firmly on the side of the losers in the 1968 experiment. To persuade the reader of the truth of his case and the depth of his feeling, the author incorporates a maximum of authentic detail, though with some lapses (Stará Boleslav is not a frontier town, but a small dormitory commuter-town a few miles northeast of Prague).

764   **Czechmate.**
David Brierley.   London: Pan Books, 1985. 285p.

At the time of writing this is the latest thriller to use East-West hostility in an Anglo-Czechoslovak context as its basic theme. It is a properly convoluted adventure involving an émigré employed by 'The Glasshouse' who makes an unscheduled return to Czechoslovakia and begins to unravel an old mystery concerning his father's (now suppressed) role in the resistance. Each side tries to outdo the other in nastiness, just to keep us in the dark as to who is on who's side – and why.

765 **Every good boy deserves favour and Professional foul.**
Tom Stoppard.   London, Boston: Faber & Faber, 1978. 93p.

Professional foul is a play (also a film) about an English academic making some discoveries about the social and political situation in Czechoslovakia, having gone nominally to attend a conference and a football match. Caught up in political intrigue, he manages to miss both. The play may be found in other editions combined with other Stoppard dramas. The dramatist is of Czech descent.

766 **The liberators: inside the Soviet army.**
Viktor Suvorov.   London: Hamish Hamilton, 1981. 202p.

The selected and selective memoirs of the pseudonymous Ukrainian author, an erstwhile officer in the Red Army with a flair for barrack-room story-telling. It provides a light-hearted and anecdotal view of the events of 1968, when the Soviet Union felt obliged to intervene militarily in Czechoslovakia to stop the perceived counter-revolutionary rot setting in.

Arts, Architecture, Crafts and Photography

767 **Románské umění v Čechách a na Moravě.** (Romanesque art in
Bohemia and Moravia.)
Anežka Merhautová, Dušan Třeštík, photography by Prokop Paul,
Russian summary translated by Valentina Boturová, German
summary by Dagmar Bílková.   Prague: Odeon, 1983. 365p.
3 maps. bibliog.

Amid the sheer wealth of Gothic and Baroque in the Lands of the Czech Crown
the Romanesque element is almost overlooked. There are in fact large numbers
of surviving monuments from this earlier period and a great deal of work has gone
into the restoration of some of them. The brief German résumé is the token
gesture towards making the book more accessible to the foreign reader, but its
main value is in the pictorial record it offers of the many sacred and some non-
sacred buildings and the book illustrations, coins and ornaments that the specialist
will appreciate. Captions are in Czech only, but each item is dated. The maps
cover Prague and Bohemia only.

768 **The art of the Renaissance in Eastern Europe: Hungary, Bohemia,
Poland.**
Jan Białostocki.   Ithaca, New York: Cornell University Press,
1976. 256p. bibliog.

Since the author is Professor of Modern Art at the University of Warsaw and
Curator of Foreign Art at the National Museum in Warsaw, it is not surprising
that his valuable work on a relatively little-known area has most to say about
Poland. However, it does contain a valuable introduction to the wealth of artistic
activity at the court of Rudolph II. A work of this nature requires the support of
illustrations and this requirement is admirably met, but only in black-and-white.

Arts, Architecture, Crafts and Photography

769 Česká barokní gotika: dílo Jana Santiniho-Aichla. (The Czech
     Baroque Gothic: the work of Jan Santini-Aichl.)
     Viktor Kotrba. Prague: Academia, 1976. 197p.

Jan Blažej Santini-Aichl (1677-1723) was a major figure during the transition from
Gothic to Baroque in Czech architecture. One of the main problems in
determining styles, dating works and agreeing their authorship is the widespread
tendency to historicism and, in the case of ecclesiastical architecture, the
conservative belief in the inherent suitability of the Gothic. This book not only
assesses various manifestations of historicism in Europe, and especially in
Bohemia, but also gives a full account of the life and work, creative evolution and
influences of Santini-Aichl. The book's value for the present bibliography is the
collection of eighty black-and-white photographic plates which it includes and
which are an excellent testimony to the nature of this transitional style in
Bohemia. The absence of a bibliography is made up by the copious references in
the footnotes appended after each chapter.

770 Baroque in Bohemia: an exhibition of Czech art organised by the
     National Gallery, Prague.
     Foreword by Gabriel White. London: Arts Council, 1969. [not
     paginated]. bibliog.

No less than the Gothic, the Baroque is an important period in the history of
Czech art (and architecture and literature). This book is a catalogue and guide to
an exhibition held in London and Birmingham and it cannot hope to illustrate all
the exhibits. However the sixty-nine reproductions it does contain, of which a
small number are in colour, provide a very fair representation of Czech Baroque
art in painting, sculpture and glass, with samples of some other areas (cabinet-
making, chasubles). In addition the catalogue contains essays on: the 'Baroque
period in Bohemia', 'Architecture' and 'Sculpture' (all by Oldřich J. Blažíček);
'Painting' (Pavel Preiss); and 'Applied arts' (Dagmar Hejdová); all of them refer
to the main exponents and the last-named deals in particular with furniture and
carving, glass-engraving and silverware. Blažíček is also the author of *Baroque art
in Bohemia* (Feltham, England: Hamlyn, 1968. 194p. bibliog.).

771 Baroque in Bohemia.
     Milada Součková, postscript by Roman Jakobson. Ann Arbor,
     Michigan: Michigan Slavic Publications, University of Michigan,
     1980. 216p. (Michigan Slavic Materials).

For the shortcomings of style and somewhat random lay-out of the material this is
not an entirely satisfactory book but it does at least open up whole areas which
are largely unfamiliar or inaccessible to the English reader. These include not just
painting and architecture, but literature, painting on glass, wayside crosses,
gingerbread design and much else. The author provides a jumble of copious
information.

772   **Cubism in architecture and the applied arts: Bohemia and France 1910-1914.**
Ivan Margolius.   Newton Abbot, England; London; North
Pomfret, Vermont: David & Charles, 1979. 128p. bibliog.

Inspired by Cubism in painting and born as a reaction to Art Nouveau, Cubist architecture in Bohemia was an abrupt creation without a counterpart elsewhere, except for a much smaller-scale flowering in France. This volume seeks, in its dense and cumbersome text (it suffers from countless linguistic Czechisms), to introduce the reader to the main architects who adopted the style through descriptions of their works, quotations from their philosophical and aesthetic writings, and well-chosen photographic records of actual buildings. Also reproduced are some of their plans which were not actually carried out. The movement is firmly located in its general architectural historical context by descriptions of the transitional predecessor movements, later developments (Rondocubism), and contemporary movements in the other countries of Europe, most of which are likewise represented in the illustrations. The Czech Cubist architects also turned their attention to furniture and other items of interior decor. A useful appendage to the book is its 'Chronology 1900-1920', with year-by-year entries for architectural and artistic events in Bohemia, France and elsewhere in three separate columns. The visitor to Prague with an eye for the city's great and varied architectural wealth will find this a handy introduction to a cross-section of the buildings from this short-lived but striking period.

773   **The wooden churches of Eastern Europe: an introductory survey.**
David Buxton.   Cambridge, England; London; New York; New
Rochelle, New York; Melbourne, Australia; Sydney: Cambridge
University Press, 1981. 405p. map. bibliog.

'There are timber-built churches in many parts of Eastern Europe whose building involved skills comparable to those of the stonemason, whose planning shows genius and whose impact on the spectator is an architectural experience.' This highly readable and well-illustrated book deserves to be called more than the modest 'introductory survey' of the sub-title, since a remarkable amount of historical and architectural fact is included in the text. The chapter divisions are partly typological, partly geographic, though the headings suggest more the latter. Four of the seven chapters have a direct bearing on Czechoslovakia: chapter 1, 'The Introduction'; chapter 3, 'Ukrainian Galicia and Carpathia', which includes Ruthenian northern Slovakia and Subcarpathia, until 1945 part of Czechoslovakia; chapter 6, 'Catholic churches in Poland and Czechoslovakia'; and chapter 7, 'Protestant churches of the margins'. It seems churlish to quibble with a work of such excellence, and everyone, not least an author, is entitled to his own preferences and emphases, but it does strike me that Bohemia is perhaps underrepresented. The bibliography, however, offers some pointers to where further coverage is to be found.

774   **Drevené stavby na Slovensku.** (Wooden buildings in Slovakia.)
Eugen Lazišťan, Ján Michalov.   Bratislava: Osveta, 1983. 2nd ed.
236p.

The visitor to Slovakia cannot fail to notice the number and variety of wooden buildings still standing, especially in the rural areas. This largely pictorial publication provides an excellent record of human ingenuity in the use of timber in construction, not merely as church-building, where it is perhaps most apparent, but also in many secular and thoroughly functional buildings such as barns and cottages.

775   **The contribution of the sculpture of Czechoslovakia to the world of art.**
      Jan Zach.   In: *The Czechoslovak contribution to world culture.*
      Edited by Miloslav Rechcígl, Jr. The Hague, London, Paris:
      Mouton, 1964, p. 175-79.

This is a very slender history of Czech (not Slovak) sculpture from the Gothic period up to the Second World War which recognizes that Václav Myslbek (1844-1922), perhaps the best known Czech sculptor, represented the turning-point between the old and the new. For the more modern period Zach confines his attentions to Czechs active abroad, having decided that, in the plastic arts, only the animated film and puppetry (Jiří Trnka) continue the tradition of creative experiment. On Czech sculptors active abroad, it is perhaps worth recalling the announcement in the London press on 1 December 1982 that it was a Czech sculptor, Franta Bělský, whose design had been chosen for the statue of Lord Mountbatten to be erected on Foreign Office Green. Another Czech sculptor, Marie Norma Svejda, produced a bust of A. Heřman for the State Office Building in Baltimore.

776   **Czech sculpture 1800-1938.**
      Peter Cannon-Brookes, in collaboration with Jiří Kotalík, Petr
      Hartmann and Václav Procházka.   London: Trefoil Books, for the
      National Museum of Wales, 1983. 128p.

Published to coincide with an exhibition from the Czechoslovak National Gallery's collection at Zbraslav held at the National Museum of Wales in Cardiff, this is much more than a catalogue, for it includes a quite detailed history, relating developments in sculpture to the Czech sculptural tradition, and to contemporary events, beginning with the National Revival and the foundation of the National Museum. The history is periodized, each period closing with fairly detailed vignettes of the life and work of the many sculptors whose work is represented. Although these are far too numerous to mention individually, it is worth mentioning Otakar Španiel, the creator of many Czech medals and coins over a long period.

777   **Czechoslovak painting from its beginning until the Second World War.**
      Mojmír S. Frinta.   In: *The Czechoslovak contribution to world
      culture.* Edited by Miloslav Rechcígl, Jr. The Hague, London,
      Paris: Mouton, 1964, p. 141–55.

The unfortunate solecism of the title of this paper is tacitly acknowledged by the author as he points out the impossibility of tackling the subject in a straightforward linear manner. There has been a long and respectable tradition of Czech art and/or artistic activity in Bohemia from very early times, while art in Slovakia has only been partly linked to the same set of traditions. However, the author does provide a useful summary of the art history of all of what is now Czechoslovakia, giving all the relevant background of political history. It is particularly useful to have stated where some of the most representative pieces, especially of mediaeval art are to be found. Many artists are discussed, including many not widely known outside Czechoslovakia; it would be invidious to select any one in particular for special mention here. The bibliography offers a wide selection of earlier works, including a number in English.

778 **Czech Gothic painting.**
Antonín Matějček, Jaroslav Pešina, foreword by T. S. R. Boase. Prague: Melantrich, 1950. 94p. bibliog.

This is possibly the largest work in English on the subject, though some books have been published since, many of which have been in Czech. The author covers the period from ca. 1350 to the end of the 15th century. The Oxford professor's foreword points out the international character of Prague as an artistic centre of the period, and its particular relevance to the English on account of the dynastic tie between Charles IV's daughter Anne and Richard II (they were married in 1382). The introduction then goes more deeply into the history of the period as a background to its art history before concentrating on some of the major works and artists. The main body of the book is taken up by the plates (only a few in colour), which are each preceded by brief artistic appraisals, date, external history and current location.

779 **Gothic mural painting in Bohemia and Moravia 1300-1378.**
Vlasta Dvořáková, Josef Krása, Anežka Merhautová, Karel Stejskal, translated by Roberta Finlayson-Samsour, Iris Unwin. London: Oxford University Press, 1964. 160p. maps. bibliog.

This collection of eleven essays, by individual members of the team of authors, provides the history and social background to mural painting and accounts of more specific topics such as: the development of court art under Charles IV; the castle at Karlštejn; Prague Cathedral; and paintings from outside the court circle. The 'Catalogue' lists and describes the twenty-seven main sites from which the photographic reproductions come, with an indication of sources from which the particular building's history is known, and sources for modern writings on them, cross-referenced to the 464-entry bibliography. One map is of the Bohemian Kingdom during the reign of the Luxembourgs, and the other indicates the location of the sites discussed (all but one in Bohemia). A useful asset to the work is its iconographical index.

780 **Illuminator egregius temporibus Wenceslai IV in Regno Bohemiae florens.** (An outstanding illuminator flourishing in the time of Wenceslas IV in the Kingdom of Bohemia.)
Mojmír S. Frinta. In: *The Czechoslovak contribution to world culture.* Edited by Miloslav Rechcígl, Jr. The Hague, London, Paris: Mouton, 1964, p. 156-66.

The author's aim is to re-evaluate Bohemian mediaeval painting to rebut previous claims that it was a somewhat stagnant art. He does so by describing and

257

Arts, Architecture, Crafts and Photography

analysing the work of the Master of the Gerona Martyrology – his own name for the painter – all of whose work has found its way to collections abroad. Other works and artists from the same milieu are also discussed. The Gerona Master was active ca. 1400-20. Footnotes supply additional bibliographical data.

781 **Wenceslas Hollar Bohemus.**
Otakar Vočadlo. *Czechoslovak Life*, vol. 20, no. 11 (Nov. 1965), p. 18-19, 32.

A biography of Hollar, inspired by the British General Post Office's decision to use Hollar's 1647 engraving of Parliament House, Westminster Hall and the east end of Westminster Abbey on a stamp to commemorate the 700th anniversary of Simon de Montfort's Parliament. Hollar's life is here set in its historical perspective, relating it to the restoration of the Habsburgs, the exile of Comenius, the English Civil War and the restoration of Charles II. Although short, the article manages to convey the magnitude and variety of Hollar's work.

782 **Les artistes tchèques en France à la fin du XIXe et au début du XXe siècles.** (Czech artists in France in the late 19th and early 20th centuries.)
Pascal Varejka. *Études tchèques et slovaques*, vol. 4 (1983-84), p. 7-34.

Most readers will be familiar with the work of Alfons Mucha, the best known of all the Czech artists with a French connection. However, as Varejka shows, Mucha was only one of many, and was by no means among the first to seek a way out of Bohemia into the world. The process began with Jaroslav Čermák in 1852 and continued right through to the Great War and beyond. All the artists mentioned are accorded a place within the context of both Czech and French art, and their relative long-term success or renown, or ultimate failure to make any lasting mark, is recorded. An appraisal of one Czech artist active in Paris in the period, Frank Kupka, is given by Jaroslav Šejnoha in *The Czechoslovak Contribution to World Culture* (q.v.) by Miloslav Rechcígl (ed.) (p. 167-74, bibliog.).

783 **Icons in Czechoslovakia.**
Heinz Skrobucha, photography by Ladislav Neubert, translation by Neil Morris. London, New York, Sydney, Toronto: Hamlyn, 1971. [not paginated]. map. bibliog.

The introductory text (p. v-xxii) represents a history of icons in Czechoslovakia. It deals separately with those from further afield which have found their way into national and other galleries, and those which are still *in situ* in various churches of East Slovakia where there is an Orthodox tradition, the sources of which are also described. The East Slovak icons are thought not to be uniquely indigenous, but a part of a wider Carpathian tradition. The body of the book contains reproductions of sixty icons with, on the facing page, details of date, provenance and present location and an artistic appraisal.

784 **Naive painters of Czechoslovakia.**
Arsen Pohribný, Štefan Tkáč, translated by George
Theiner. London, New York, Sydney, Toronto: Hamlyn, 1967.
159p. bibliog.
A great deal of Czech and Slovak art is quite unknown outside the country's
frontier, and the same goes even more so for the fascinating area of naive art, of
which there has been no shortage. The book contains a history of the subject in
Czechoslovakia which, among other things, relates the 'Czechoslovak school' to
the other arts; not that the 'school' is any kind of monolith, since the particular
nationality – Czech, Moravian, Slovak, Jewish – of each painter represented is
always stated. Interestingly, the work includes a number of items of commercial
art. The text is supported by 191 reproductions.

785 **Mittelalterliche Glasmalerei in der Tschechoslowakei.** (Mediaeval
glass painting in Czechoslovakia.)
František Matouš. Prague: Academia, 1975. 99p. bibliog.
Czechoslovakia has inherited a strong tradition of stained and painted glass
techniques with a vast heritage of surviving works. Over two dozen places
(castles, churches, museums) where glass paintings can be found are described
here with special reference to a selection of the more striking pieces. The items
discussed are illustrated (colour or black-and-white) either in the body of the text
or in the eighty-three plate appendix (not paginated). Bibliographic information is
included after each section, to which the entries explicitly relate.

786 **Bohemian engraved glass.**
Zuzana Pešatová, photographs by Jindrich Brok. Feltham,
England: Hamlyn, 1968. 61p. bibliog.
Like many of the works mentioned in this bibliography, this is of Czech
provenance and seeks primarily to inform by illustration. The text provides a
history of this major branch of the Czech glass-worker's craft from the earliest
times to the present and it is supported by 132 black-and-white plates.

787 **Painted dreams: Slovak folk painting on glass in the 20th century.**
Irena Pišútová, photography by Klement Šilinger, translation by
Eva Vajdová. Bratislava: Tatran, 1983. 19p. bibliog.
Considers the history of the glass painting tradition and its techniques, the
geographical spread of the art and the main themes favoured. The introductory
essay describes the work of a number of the main exponents and makes constant
reference to the West Slovak Alexander Salzmann (1870-1959). The main body of
the book consists of eighty quite large-format reproductions in full colour which
illustrate the range of variety of the glass paintings discussed in the text.

788 **Masters of Czech glass 1945-1965.**
Preface by Hubert Matějček, introduction by Dan
Klein. London: Dan Klein, 1983. 24p.
Czech glass is widely known abroad, especially for the cut-glass ashtrays, fruit-
bowls and stemware which is widely sold in the West. Less well-known are the

259

other types. The 1950s, the decade chiefly represented here, saw a burst of quite adventurous work using a wide variety of techniques, which ultimately inspired the Studio Glass Movement which started in America in the 1960s. This booklet, the catalogue to an exhibition of the work of twenty-three artists held in London, contains illustrations, some in colour, of forty-seven of the eighty-seven pieces exhibited together with a brief external description of all of them (size, artists' marks, colour and techniques). The short textual part of the work, by Alena Adlerová of the Prague Museum of Decorative Arts, outlines the general trends and techniques of the period and points out salient features in the work of some of the artists.

789   **Silver marks of the world.**
Jan Diviš, illustrated by Jaromír Knotek, translated from Czech by Joy Moss-Kohoutová.   London, New York, Sydney, Toronto: Hamlyn, 1976. 246p. bibliog.
A book of interest perhaps only to a restricted number of people. However, it is included here for it does cover Czechoslovakia and is of Czech provenance. All marks are recorded (indexation is by town-names) and a history of metal-marking is included.

790   **Porcelain marks of the world.**
Emanuel Poche, translated from Czech by Joy Moss-Kohoutová.   London, New York, Sydney, Toronto: Hamlyn, 1974. 255p. bibliog.
The same remarks apply here as in the foregoing entry, except that classification is by emblems. Bohemia is undoubtedly better-known for its glass, but there is a no less respectable tradition of porcelain and the work contains many entries for Czechoslovakia itself.

791   **Goldschmiedekunst in der Slowakei.** (The goldsmith's art in Slovakia.)
Eva Toranová.   Bratislava: Tatran, 1983. 2nd rev. ed. 262p.
Gold and silver working have in the past been a major craft in Slovakia, thanks to the occurrence of the precious metals and their early exploitation, notably by German immigrants. The book outlines the history and evolution of the craft, the methods and organization of the work (the guilds, for example), and contains 300 illustrations (some in colour) of the various goblets, monstrances and other objects produced by Slovakia's goldsmiths. The personal marks of the latter are reproduced in 191 drawings. The same work appeared simultaneously in Slovak under the title *Zlatníctvo na Slovensku*, and this edition may be more readily available in view of the much larger printing.

792   **Historické orgány na Slovensku – Historische Orgeln in der Slowakei.** (Historic organs in Slovakia.)
Otmar Gergely, Karol Wurm.   Bratislava: Opus, 1982. 367p.
Enthusiastic amateurs are perhaps not always the best people to provide serious introductions to any subject. However, the authors of this book, a doctor and a

historian, have demonstrated admirably that equally they may be. They make a major contribution to the current debate on the values of past practice in organ-building, providing on the way a six-century history of organs in Slovakia and a three-century pictorial review of over one hundred of the finest organs in the country. Each organ is illustrated by superb colour photographs with a fairly detailed parallel, Slovak and German, text on the external description, builder and related matters, and sometimes additional illustrative material – detail decorations and relevant manuscripts – is provided. The organs are ordered by period and partly by builder.

793 **Črpáky v slovenských muzeách.** (Ladles in Slovak museums.)
Marta Komorovská. Martin, Czechoslovakia: Osveta, on behalf of the Slovak National Museum, 1982. 135p. (Museum Nationale Slovacum. Institutum Historicum, Fontes, vol. 6).

A major feature of Slovak life is mountain sheep-farming, although many of the traditional aspects have become erased. During the season when they were alone in the mountains, cut off from the rest of society, the shepherds had a lot of time to themselves and one of the ways in which they filled it was in producing various artefacts relevant to their work. Accordingly, woodcarving in particular led to the production of great numbers of items, of which the present volume gives excellent examples. *Črpáky*, scoops for water, milk or specifically sheep cheese, were just one of the types of artefacts produced; others included wooden spoons, ladles and musical instruments. This volume describes the local distribution of types of scoops, is richly illustrated and contains a full catalogue of those held in the National Museum. It should be noted that their interest lies chiefly in the decoration of the handles. A brief account of the main regional types (north, east and central) is provided in the German résumé.

794 **Pilgrims.**
Markéta Luskačová, introduction by Mark Haworth-Booth.
London: Victoria and Albert Museum, 1983. 48p. bibliog.

The book was published to illustrate the work of Luskačová as a photographer, and as a sample of modern Czechoslovak photographic art. At the same time it constitutes a pictorial ethnographic study of East Slovakia, in particular its religious life, since the photographs record moments during religious pilgrimages by the local peasants to a number of important centres which have evolved around the Marian cult, or events in the general course of the people's religious life.

795 **Prague in colour.**
Text and photographs by Miroslav Kopecký, translated by Joy Turner-Kadečková. London, New York, Sydney, Toronto: Hamlyn, 1975. 230p.

It is not so much a history of the city which underlines this pictorial record but a history of representations of it. For it contains not only a splendid collection of modern colour photographs, but also reproductions of engravings, in which Prague is particularly rich, some of considerable antiquity; many represent the same subjects as the photographs. The texts amount to an artist's (photographer's) appraisal of the whole view, with a description of the architectural or topographical points of interest. Some history of individual subjects is also given.

796 **Praha.** (Prague.)
Jiří Doležal, Ivan Doležal, introduction by Miroslav Florian, text and captions by Jiří Burian, Russian translation by Margarita Rogačová, German translation by Valter Kraus, English translation by Joy Kadečková. Prague: Olympia, 1983. 272p.

A book essentially in the 'coffee-table' mould, but offering, in its 370 colour photographs, an excellent introduction to the city of Prague, its architectural variety and the natural grace of many of its buildings and backwaters. It includes a number of less commonly photographed parts of the city.

797 **Praha objektivem mistrů.** (Prague through the lens of the masters.)
Biographical notes by Ludvík Baran, résumés translated into English by Joy Kohoutová. Prague: Panorama, 1983. 2nd ed. 248p.

The 'masters' of the title are fifteen of Czechoslovakia's most successful photographers, whom this volume, with its 162 black-and-white and twelve colour photographs, serves to introduce to the outside world. Simultaneously it provides a series of photographic portraits of Prague, a truly photogenic city, dating from the period 1924-78.

798 **The Agnes Convent reborn.**
J. Vitula. *Czechoslovak Life*, vol. 35, no. 11 (Nov. 1980), p. 24-27.

The Convent of the Blessed Agnes is one of the finest historic monuments in Prague, an Early Gothic foundation with later additions and alterations. After suffering years of neglect it has recently been restored thanks to a major exercise in conservation. As this account and illustrations show it is also an example (admirable in the view of many Prague residents) of the principle of new uses for old buildings; it currently houses a major art collection and restaurant. For a more recent brief illustrated account of the history and renovation see Vladimír Tintěra's 'The Agnes Convent' *Welcome to Czechoslovakia*, vol. 19, no. 3 (autumn 1984), p. 30, 62-63.

799 **Die Sankt Wenzels-Krone und die böhmischen Insignien.** (The crown of St. Wenceslas and the Bohemian insignia.)
Karl Fürst Schwarzenberg. Vienna, Munich: Verlag Herold, 1960. 68p. bibliog.

The tourist to Prague will have no difficulty in obtaining locally produced descriptions of the Bohemian crown and crown jewels, even in English, but this little work by a member of one of the oldest Bohemian aristocratic families at least has the virtue of possibly greater accessibility in view of its places of publication. It combines an art historical description of the crown jewels and the royal arms with a history of the throne and the coronation ceremony. Many of the items are illustrated, and there are also reproductions of some royal portraits.

300   **Peter Parler at Prague (1353-1399) and the style of the Cathedral of St. Vitus.**
       J. S. Groseclose.   *Germano-Slavica*, vol. 1, no. 1 (spring 1973),
       p. 87-106.

Peter Parler, a member of a large family of architects active in various parts of Europe, was Royal Architect to Charles IV. Though the purview of this article is quite narrow, other examples of Parler's work are mentioned. The text is supported by black-and-white photographic illustrations (p. 100-06). 'The choir of the Cathedral of Prague appears as a vast experiment, and it retains even today a freshness and vitality which derive from Parler's fusion of forms.'

301   **Bratislavské rokoko.** (Bratislava Rococo.)
       Ladislav Šášky.   Bratislava: Tatran, 1982. 125p. (Pamiatky
       Bratislavy, no. 7).

Although much of Rococo Bratislava has been lost, thanks to modern redevelopment of the city, much survives, as illustrated by this work. The author does not look exclusively at the architecture, but also considers the other Rococo arts and crafts featured not only in the large mid-18th-century town houses of the city, but also in some of the quite modest dwellings in the period. This is a superbly produced book, illustrative of the series, accessible through the reproductions and, partially, through the Russian, German and Hungarian résumés and translations of the captions.

Music

802 **The music of Czechoslovakia.**
Rosa Newmarch. Oxford: Oxford University Press, 1942. 244 p.
Widely referred to as the only book covering the totality of music in
Czechoslovakia and of the Czechs and Slovaks, it is to be regretted that it has not
found a more recent successor. Ian Horsburgh has described it as 'enlightened,
but not always accurate'.

803 **Music in Czechoslovakia.**
Karel B. Jirák. In: *The Czechoslovak contribution to world
culture.* Edited by Miloslav Rechcígl, Jr. The Hague, London,
Paris: Mouton, 1964, p. 119-33. bibliog.
With such familiar names as Dvořák, Smetana, Janáček and Martinů appearing
regularly on concert programmes and in broadcasting, the foreign awareness of a
Czech musical contribution to world culture is perhaps stronger than in any other
context. In this outline history of Czech music these composers are accorded
places which match their significance, but they are of course not the only
musicians the country has produced. Their many predecessors and some
successors are described not only in terms of the periodization of Czech music,
but also in terms of contemporary developments outside the Czech Lands, with
which, especially in the early days, Czech music was not always in step. Slovak
music begins to feature only in the 20th century, thanks largely to the lateness of
the Slovak National Revival. The Slovak capital, Bratislava, is however proud of
its association with the German composer and pianist, Johann Nepomuk
Hummel, a fact perhaps deemed irrelevant to, and hence omitted from, this
survey. The bibliography contains titles of serious musicology and musical history
relating to Czech music, some of which are in Czech, as well as the titles of some
biographical works not included in the present bibliography.

804   **An outline of Czech and Slovak music. Pt. II: Slovak music.**
Ladislav Šíp, translated by Margaret Milner.   Prague: Orbis, 1960.
57p.

Part 1 by Vladimír Štěpánek and Bohumil Karásek and translated by Iva
Drápalová, entitled *Czech music* (Prague: Orbis, 1964. 145p.) is a more
substantial work. The different sizes of these two companion volumes is indicative
of the relative wealth, length and density of the two musical traditions, at least as
they are known from extant records. (The index of composers in the Czech
volume runs to over two and a half pages, while that for Slovak composers barely
covers two thirds of one page.) Only the Czech composers Smetana, Dvořák and
Fibich earn chapters to themselves, other chapters being on whole periods. The
books are a useful source of somewhat telegraphic information on the earliest
periods, on which less is known outside the country, and, in view of their dates,
they also offer an insight into the music of the Stalinist 1950s.

805   **The praise of music: five chapters on Czech music and musicians.**
Jiří Berkovec.   Prague: Orbis, 1975. 79p.

Five somewhat rambling, occasionally telegraphic chapters on various aspects of
music and its importance in the cultural history of the Czechs. Roughly speaking
the chapters can be described as discussing: the history of performers and
performances since early times; the role of music in education and the history of
musical education, including published works since the 16th century; famous
vocalists and instrumentalists, especially of the 19th and 20th centuries, the 17th-
century school of violin makers, and major ensembles, including the National
Opera; the main Czech composers, including the 18th- and 19th-century
predecessors of Smetana; and the symbolic nature of music for the Czechs, from
the martial Hussite hymn *Ktož jsú boží bojovníci* through occasional pieces to
mark sundry religious and political events, to the 'peace symphonies' at the end of
the last war.

806   **Czechoslovakia.**
Pavel Eckstein.   *Opera*, regular contributions, 1960-.

This sectional heading introduces Eckstein's regular reports and reviews of
current events in the world of Czech and Slovak opera. He is an accomplished
Czech musician and acts as the periodical's roving reporter, offering an up-to-the-
minute picture of works, composers and performances unlikely to be covered
elsewhere. For example: vol. 35 (1984) included his 'Cikker's comedy' (no. 5
(May), p. 512-13) on the first comedy by perhaps the best known Slovak opera
composer Ján Cikker (b. 1911); in 'Horký's new opera' (no. 6 (June), p. 633-34,
655) he considered Karel Horky's (b. 1909) fifth opera which although
monumental was not an unqualified masterpiece, and 'New operas' (no. 8 (Aug.),
p. 897-99) was devoted mostly to Jan F. Fischer's *Copernicus*, one of the works
entered in the competition held to mark the reopening of the National Theatre.
Most of these Eckstein cameos review both the works and the performances. In
the March issue (p. 307-09) he describes the refurbished and extended National
Theatre complex about which he has more positive to say than many of the
citizens who have to pass it daily.

Music

807 **Česká opera a její tvůrci: průvodce.** (Czech opera and its creators: a guide.)
Ladislav Šíp.   Prague: Supraphon, 1983. 400p. bibliog.

Long and intimately involved in the world of opera in various capacities including leading the National Opera, Šíp is well placed to produce a guide which is both historical and critical. Some works only appear in the chronological synopsis of first performances, but a total of 110 are discussed in greater detail within the cameos on twenty-nine major Czech opera composers. Although only in Czech, the work is an essential reference source for the many composers who have not won monographic treatment in English outside standard reference works (and not all are even included in the latter). In addition to the bibliography a 'discography' is included.

808 **Contemporary Czechoslovak composers.**
Edited by Čeněk Gardovský.   Prague, Bratislava: Panton, 1965. 564p.

The Czechs delight in their hyperbolic description of themselves as a nation of musicians ('Co Čech, to muzikant'), and it is true that they have made a not inconsiderable contribution to the world's concert repertoire. Although now seriously dated, this volume does go some way in defence of the popular description of the nation, since it contains biographies and musicographies of some 360 then living composers, Czechs and Slovaks, in the fields of serious and light, though not popular, music. Useful appendixes describe the country's various musical institutions and organizations (specialist schools, societies and publishers), and furnish a list of gramophone recordings. The former is still largely valid, the latter is inevitably out of date.

809 **Slavonic and Romantic music: essays and studies.**
Gerald Abraham.   London: Faber & Faber, 1968. 360p.

Several of the chapters herein concern Czech music: chapter 1 examines the contacts between the Slavs and Western music, and includes an account of, *inter alia*, the big Czech music dynasties and individual Czechs active abroad (Tomášek, Voříšek); chapter 3 considers the genesis of Smetana's *Bartered bride*; chapter 4 discusses the musical personality of Dvořák, which is basically comparative; chapter 5 concerns Fibich's *Moods, impressions and memories*, presented as an 'erotic diary for a piano' of the events underlying the individual pieces; and chapter 6 explores realism in Janáček's operas.

810 **Forgotten musicians.**
Paul Nettl.   New York: Philosophical Library, 1951. 352p. bibliog.

Four sections here have a direct bearing on Czech music, or the history of Bohemian music. The two important sections are chapter 6, 'Johann Stamitz "Another Shakespeare"' (p. 65-74) which starts with the English musicologist, Charles Burney's (1726-1814), comments on music in Bohemian schools and identifies him as the source of the Shakespeare label, and chapter 8, 'Schubert's Czech predecessors Johann Wenzel Tomaschek (1774-1850) and Hugo Voříšek (1791-1825)' (p. 90-109) which starts with Tomášek's encounter with Goethe, some of whose poems he had set to music. Tomášek's life is recounted through a mass of period gossip, but in his consideration of Voříšek (he was a pupil of Tomášek) the author says rather more about his musician's innovations. Stamitz (Stamic) (1717-57), whether seen as Czech or German, was the Bohemian deemed to have fathered much of modern orchestral practice through his Mannheim school. The other relevant items in the book are chapter 9, 'Musical monarchs' (p. 110-55) of interest for the number of musically active Habsburgs, and Part II, subsection 1 (p. 204-45) the 1763 autobiography of another of the Bohemian composers active outside the country, Franz (František) Benda (1709-86), the member of the Benda musical clan best known as a representative of the Berlin violin school and composer of pieces for the violin.

811   **Schubert's Bohemian contemporary: career of Jan Václav Voříšek.**
Ateş Orga.   *Music and musicians*, vol. 21, no. 6 (Feb. 1973),
p. 30-45.

Voříšek (1791-1825) is seen as one of the many Czechs of the generation that preceded their better-known countrymen, Smetana and Dvořák, and one who, had he lived longer, might have not only enjoyed the same kind of fame, but also been placed alongside Beethoven and Schubert. The author traces Voříšek's life, from the time when, at the age of ten he was a regular deputy organist in and around his native Vamberk, through his general, musical and legal education in Prague and Vienna, to his eventual appointments as second, and then first, court organist. Ample and consistent reference is made to the large numbers of more, and less, well known composers important to the period generally, or Voříšek's life in particular, as well as to the important publishers who first brought Voříšek's work out. The second half of the article provides an account of the oeuvre, first performances, a chronology, and musicological analyses, often comparative, with some examples of the scoring of different versions of the last work, a Piano Sonata in B flat minor. There is no bibliography, but the main period texts and modern critical editions are all mentioned.

812   **Smetana.**
John Clapham.   London: Dent; New York: Octagon Books, 1972.
161p. bibliog.

Perhaps the first of the now well-known Czech composers to make a mark worldwide, Smetana (1824-84) is also arguably the most 'national', although the Czech national flavour is quite strongly present in all of the country's internationally renowned composers. Clapham's book gives us not just a full, readable biography and analysis of the works, genre by genre, but also a summary history of music in Bohemia before Smetana. The author also adequately recognizes many earlier composers who ought to be better known. In addition, there is also a chronology, a full list of Smetana's works, a good set of thumbnail sketches on many of the musical and literary figures relevant to Smetana's life and works, a generous bibliography, and even the text of the report on Smetana's post-mortem. The work is supported by quotations from scores and the composer's correspondence and several photographs.

Music

813　**Smetana.**
Brian Large.　London: Duckworth, 1970. 473p. bibliog.

In addition to being a detailed biography and musicography of 'the founder of modern Czech music' and probably the one composer the Czechs most revere themselves, this work covers a great deal of other territory in passing, from mediaeval Czech history to literature, and from music contemporary with Smetana to the history of some of the theatres of Prague. The text is generously illustrated by photographs of people, places and manuscripts, and by passages from all the scores discussed. Among the many useful appendixes there is: a family tree; a detailed genesis of *The bartered bride* and another for *The two widows*; translated extracts of correspondence between Smetana and Eliška Krásnohorská; a chronology of works; a classified list of works; and synopses of the operas. Large is also the author of a similarly broad work entitled *Martinů* (London: Duckworth, 1975).

814　**Bedřich Smetana: letters and reminiscences.**
František Bartoš, translated by Daphne Rusbridge.　Prague: Artia, 1955. 295p.

A valuable collection of 263 documents in translation, many taken from Smetana's own diaries and many from the diaries, letters and papers of others, which provide an overall profile of the composer in his lifetime. Many of the extracts are accompanied by useful thumbnail sketches of the correspondents or others referred to.

815　**Dvořák.**
Hans Hubert Schönzeler.　London, New York: Marion Boyars, 1984. 239p. bibliog.

This is the latest in the run of Dvořák biographies, lavishly illustrated, and more concerned with the man than the music, though the latter is by no means overlooked. It is much concerned with context, so it opens with a history of Czech music from the earliest extant sacred song down to Dvořák's predecessor, Smetana. The author then proceeds to place Dvořák's work in the Czech, European and American framework, while stressing his nationalism and populism. The usual range of technical appendixes on the numbering, chronology, and classification of the works completes the volume.

816　**Dvořák.**
John Clapham.　Newton Abbot, England; London: David & Charles, 1979. 235p. bibliog.

Clapham's main intention is to update and correct accepted opinion on the life and work of Dvořák, the misunderstandings on, and misinterpretations of which, often go back to this author's forerunner Otakar Šourek (see next entry), whose efforts have, however, earned a generous accolade from Clapham. Besides discussion of the principal compositions this book contains: a complete biography; a 'pathologist's assessment of the sequence of events leading up to the composer's final illness'; a chronology; a list of compositions; and a select bibliography, containing many other biographies and critical works; a number of photographs; and quotations from the scores. The author has also written *Antonín Dvořák: musician and craftsman* (London: Faber, 1966).

817 **The orchestral works of Antonín Dvořák.**
Otakar Šourek, English version by Roberta Finlayson
Samsour. Prague: Artia, [1956]. 351p.
A systematic analysis of Dvořák's chief works in eight major sections, one per
genre. It is well-illustrated by extracts from the scores which reveal the
composer's method of developing his themes, their relation to Slavonic song and
folk-dance, and the idiosyncracies of his orchestration. Sixteen black-and-white
plates record some of the places and faces associated with Dvořák's performances
and there are also photographic reproductions of manuscripts, correspondence
and an 1898 concert programme. This and the following entry are just two of
Šourek's many Dvořák titles. For others see the bibliography in John Clapham's
Dvořák (q.v.) where Šourek is, incidentally, described as the founder of Dvořák
research.

818 **Antonín Dvořák: letters and reminiscences.**
Otakar Šourek, translated from the Czech by Roberta Finlayson
Samsour. Prague: Artia, 1954. 234p.
This volume with its 235 annotated extracts (which consist of letters, or parts of
letters, to and from Dvořák, other letters and fragments of memoirs by Dvořák's
friends and contemporaries) seeks to trace the composer's rise from obscurity to
fame, showing the impact he had on the cultural life of the time. The translator's
foreword draws attention to the English and American dimension in Dvořák's
career, while the introductory and closing comments by the compiler emphasize
Dvořák's Czechness and the magnitude of his contribution to music and culture.
The twenty-three illustrations show some of the people and places important in
the composer's life, but there is a regrettable absence of any index or table of
contents.

819 **Antonín Dvořák.**
Václav Holzknecht, translated from the Czech by Jan
Nemejovský. Prague: Orbis, 1977. 3rd ed. 83p.
A concise, general and somewhat sentimental appraisal of Dvořák's life and
work, with a list of main works and supporting illustrations – ie., family
photographs, pictures of Dvořák's homes and scenes from two operas. An earlier
Western biography drawing together the man and his work is Gervase Hughes's
Dvořák, his life and music (London: Cassell, 1967).

820 **Slavonic and Western music: essays for Gerald Abraham.**
Edited by Malcolm Hamrick Brown, Roland John Wiley. Ann
Arbor, Michigan: UMI Research Press; Oxford: Oxford University
Press, 1985.
John Clapham's 'Dvořák's visit to Worcester, Massachusetts' (p. 207-14) is a
gossipy piece detailing the correspondence and news reporting surrounding the
composer's successful attendance at the 1893 Worcester Festival, including his
unhappy exchange with the local paper.

Music

821 **Dvořák symphonies and concertos.**
Robert Layton. London: British Broadcasting Corporation, 1978. 68p. (BBC Music Guides).
Traces both the influences which shaped Dvořák's artistic personality and the development of his style and method through the nine symphonies and three concertos (one each for piano, violin and cello). The work balances the attention fairly in order to do justice even to the early, often overlooked symphonies and finds in them signs that already point to the maturity of the later works.

822 **Bohuslav Martinů.**
Jaroslav Mihule, translated from the Czech by J. M. Kohoutová. Prague: Orbis, 1978. 2nd rev. ed. 72p. bibliog.
A brief review of Martinů as a composer of symphonies and chamber music, with a special chapter on Martinů as a dramatist. The book also contains a chronology of important dates in the composer's life, a list of his main works, classified by genre, an index of names, a useful bibliography and a small number of illustrations – portraits, and samples of Martinů's scores and stage-sets.

823 **My life with Bohuslav Martinů.**
Charlotte Martinů, translated by Diderik C. D. De Jong. Prague: Orbis Press Agency, 1978. 176p.
An intimate biography of the Czech composer, periodized through his different stays in France, the United States and elsewhere. In addition to recording the people and places he visited, the book provides some idea of the genesis of Martinů's major works.

824 **Bohuslav Martinů: the man and his music.**
Miloš Šafránek. London: Dennis Dobson, 1946. 135p. bibliog. (Contemporary composers).
A description of Martinů's compositions prior to 1945, interwoven with his biography. This is an intimate book on account of the author's close and long-standing friendship with his subject. A total of 135 main compositions are listed (p. 123-30) with details of their first and subsequent performances – the place and, in many cases, the orchestra and conductor concerned. The book contains ten photographs as well as extracts from scores built into the text, and closes with a single name and subject index.

825 **Two losses to Czech music: Josef Suk and Otakar Ostrčil.**
Vladimír Helfert. *Slavonic and East European Review*, vol. 14 (1935), p. 639-46.
An early critical appreciation of the life and works of the then recently deceased Suk and Ostrčil, two of the main representatives of the modern Czech school of music. Suk is the grandfather of the Josef Suk who, with his Suk Trio and as a soloist, is well known for his appearances abroad.

270

826   **Leoš Janáček: a biography.**
      Jaroslav Vogel, foreword by Charles Mackerras, translated by
      Geraldine Thomsen Muchová, new edition revised by Karel
      Janovický. London: Orbis Publishing, 1981. 439p. maps. bibliog.

A biography of another major modern Czech (Moravian) composer whose works
regularly feature on English and Welsh concert and opera stages. Each period in
the composer's life is followed up by detailed musicological analyses of his works,
which are brought together in the appendix as a catalogue. This is followed by the
bibliographies, which list separately books, articles and Janáček's correspondence.

827   **Leoš Janáček: the field that prospered.**
      Ian Horsbrugh.   Newton Abbot, England; London: David
      & Charles; New York: Charles Scribner's, 1981. 327p. bibliog.

Janáček (1854-1928) was practically ignored in Britain during his life-time which
seems almost unimaginable these days from even the most cursory glance at the
concert listings or the BBC's *Radio Times*, where his works are constantly
cropping up. He had visited England in 1926 and gained the support of Sir Henry
Wood, but this had not been enough. Not until 1951, when Sadler's Wells put on
his *Káťa Kabanová* at the instigation of Charles Mackerras, did his popularity
become assured. Horsbrugh's book will doubtless remain the authoritative work
in English for many years to come. It is an illustrated biography which examines
all the works in considerable detail, bringing in relevant aspects of other
contemporary music and something of the Czech literary scene. The appendixes
(p. 241-316) contain items relevant to England (Janáček's 1926 diary and a list of
early BBC broadcasts of his works), synopses of the operas, and a classified,
annotated list of the other compositions.

828   **Leoš Janáček: leaves from his life.**
      Edited and translated by Vilem Tausky, Margaret Tausky.
      London: Kahn & Averill, 1982. 159p.

Janáček was not only a composer whose genius is now unquestioned, but also a
music critic and feuilletoniste. Over thirty of his pieces for the Brno daily
newspaper are gathered here, roughly classified by topic. Vilem Tausky was one
of his pupils and so is well placed to make a telling selection, revealing the best of
the composer's personality and his responses to people, places and events; some
of his own recollections of Janáček and others make up the opening section.
Margaret Tausky's preface stresses Janáček's qualities as a listener and recorder
of sound memories. The book includes two unpublished compositions, a penny-
polka and a fanfare for the 1926 Sokol *slet* (jamboree).

829   **The operas of Leoš Janáček.**
      Erik Chisholm, foreword by Charles Mackerras, editorial note and
      tribute to Erik Chisholm by Ken A. Wright.   Oxford: Pergamon
      Press, 1971. 393p.

That this idiosyncratic work is already dated is clear from a number of points, not
least of all the assertion (p. 375) that 'only *Jenůfa* and *Kátja* (*sic*) *Kabanová* have
really crossed the national frontiers of Czechoslovakia to any purpose' (consider

the number of recent London performances of others). However, the work is worth consulting for its detailed analyses of each opera separately, dealing in turn with the plot, the music and the relation to the textual source (in some cases only – Chisholm would not have had ready access to the originals of *The cunning little vixen, Jenůfa* or *Mr. Brouček*). For a more recent account of *Janáček's tragic operas* see Michael Ewans book of that name (London: Faber & Faber, 1977).

830   **Leoš Janáček:** *Katya Kabanová.*
       Compiled by John Tyrrell.   Cambridge, England; London; New York; New Rochelle, New York; Melbourne; Sydney: Cambridge University Press, 1982. 234p. bibliog. (Cambridge Opera Handbooks).

Janáček is one of the best-known Czech composers (with Smetana, Dvořák, Martinů and Suk), and *Katya Kabanová* is perhaps his most widely known opera and the one most frequently performed in both Britain and the United States. This volume contains letters, reviews and other documents, many translated here for the first time. There are also a number of different interpretations of the work, the history of its many performances, discussions of the authenticity of rediscovered interludes, a discussion of Ostrovskij's *The thunderstorm*, which was the source for the libretto, and illustrations from productions and of items in the score. Tyrrell has written elsewhere on Janáček, including the relevant entry in *The New Grove dictionary of music and musicians* edited by S. Sadie (London: Macmillan; Washington, DC: Groves Dictionaries of Music; Hong Kong: Peninsular, 1980. 20 vols.).

831   **Early Czech organs and composers.**
       Bryan Hesford.   *Organ*, vol. 58, no. 231 (Jan. 1980), p. 102-07.

Hesford pinpoints the salient features of an important, individual, but neglected school of organ music, describing the manuals of a selection of organs dating from between the 16th and 18th centuries which formed the basis from which the Czech school grew. Like others, such as Adrienne Simpson in 'An introduction to Czech Baroque music' (q.v.), he stresses the lateness of some aspects of Czech musical development. The work describes eight important early composers from Čzernohorský (1684-1740) to Rejcha (1770-1836), who was a teacher of Berlioz, Franck, Gounod and Liszt.

832   **An introduction to Czech Baroque music.**
       Adrienne Simpson.   *Consort*, no. 34 (1978), p. 283-92.

Czech Baroque music is certainly being studied and played more and more, with a number of dissertations devoted to individual composers appearing at American universities in particular and early Czech composers being regularly represented in the concerts of such ensembles as Sanssouci of Windsor. This article is part of the growing literature and is a useful introduction to the subject, which it places in the broad, not just musical, historical context. It discusses not only some of the main composers (Michna, Benda, Stamic, Mysliveček), but also the instruments used, the places at which they played and the role of foreign influences. The subject of Jesuit musical education is also referred to.

833 **The influence of 18th century Czech composers on the development of classical music.**
Edith Vogl Garrett. In: *The Czechoslovak contribution to world culture.* Edited by Miloslav Rechcígl, Jr. The Hague, London, Paris: Mouton, 1964, p. 134-40. bibliog.

In the 18th century Czech musicians, composers and performers, were much in evidence around Europe, especially at Mannheim, Berlin, Paris and Vienna. Mannheim is associated with the career of Jan Václav Stamic (Johann Stamitz) and František Xaver Richter; Berlin with various members of the Benda family, especially Jan Jiří and his third son Jiří Antonín; Paris with Antonín Rejcha and Jan Václav Stich (Giovanni Punto); and Vienna with a number of lesser-known but not uninteresting figures, including Leopold Koželuh, who became best known for his arrangements of Scottish folksongs for George Thomson in Edinburgh. Italy's main Czech connection is through Josef Mysliveček. The influence of many of these men was quite notable, not only in terms of changing compositional practice and style, but also in shaping the modern orchestra (Stamic), developing J. J. Rousseau's melodrama (in the technical sense, J. A. Benda), and generally providing much of the period's musical backbone throughout Europe; Beethoven, Haydn, Mozart all owe something to them.

834 **Essays on Russian and East European Music.**
Gerald Abraham. Oxford: Clarendon Press, 1985. 193p.

This collection of essays contains 'Czechoslovakia song' (p. 172-84) which consists mostly of a history of the *Lied* in Bohemia from the 18th century to the present. In each period too many musicians are mentioned for them all to be named here, but this is a valuable source on many of the early composers simply omitted from standard reference works. Coverage includes 18th-century émigrés, and the author concludes with references to modern Slovak song-composers.

Theatre and Cinema

835 **Politics, art and commitment in the East European cinema.**
Edited by David W. Paul. London; Basingstoke, England:
Macmillan, 1983. 314p.

This collection of sociological and socio-historical essays on many aspects of film
has many sections directly or generally relevant to Czechoslovakia. History has
always been an important factor in the heritage of the Czech cinema, and current
events and the changing political tide continue to influence it. The sub-sections of
the book indicate the approaches taken: the first deals in terms of 'pathos and
irony'; the second concerns 'aesthetics and ideology'; and the third 'style and
substance'. In the last there is an important discussion of the role of the Czech
puppet film. The book also includes an essay by Liehm on one of the best known
contemporary directors, Miloš Forman.

836 **The most important art: Eastern European film after 1945.**
Mira Liehm, Antonín J. Liehm. Berkeley, California; Los
Angeles; London: University of California Press, 1977. 467p. map.
bibliog.

The book consists of four main parts, subdivided in the last three on a country-by-
country basis, each country's film history being roughly periodized as a reflection
of general trends in current affairs and political development. For Czechoslovakia
the main turning points are, with some justification, 1955-56 and 1962-63. All
major and many minor films are discussed and the careers of many directors and
actors can be traced. One of the book's assets is the attention it pays to the often
overlooked Slovak output. Part I is essentially introductory, summarizing
developments up to 1945 and includes references to Czech, and a few Slovak films
for the period of the First Republic and even the first stirrings among Czech film-
makers during the last years of Austria-Hungary. The bibliography reveals that,
with few exceptions, items in French are the major source of secondary literature.

274

837   **Cinema beyond the Danube: the camera and politics.**
       Michael Jon Stoil.   Metuchen, New Jersey: Scarecrow Press, 1974.
       198p. bibliog.

Stoil takes the view that film-making is inevitably a product of the social and
political context, and contends that this aspect is overplayed by Eastern critics and
underplayed or ignored by Western critics. He seeks to combine film criticism
with 'political and social analyses to provide a more complete picture of Eastern
European cinema'. Stoil does so not only for the post-war period, where the
dichotomy of approaches tends to be assumed most readily, but also for the entire
preceding period. Several sub-sections deal with film in Czechoslovakia, but the
coverage is necessarily less complete than, for example, that provided in Mira and
Antonín Liehm's *The most important art: Eastern European film after 1945* (q.v.).

838   **Closely watched films: the Czechoslovak experience.**
       Antonín J. Liehm, translated by Káča Poláčková.   White Plains,
       New York: International Arts and Sciences Press, 1974. 485p.
       bibliog.

This useful background book to the Czechoslovak film industry consists of short
biographical sketches of, and interviews with, some thirty-two directors, Czech
and Slovak, available for interview at the time. Wisely the book takes in more
than just the new wave of the 1960s, and looks back, where relevant, to the First
Republic and the war period. The emphasis is always on the tensions between
film-making and the social and political environment. Included in the volume are
photographic portraits of each director and a complete filmography for each,
some sub-classified by leading stars. For the alphabetical index of films, and the
filmography, it is an invaluable reference work for the film scholar and layman
alike.

839   **Jiří Menzel and the history of the Closely Watched Trains.**
       Josef Škvorecký.   Boulder, Colorado: East European
       Monographs. Distributed by Columbia University Press, New
       York, 1982. 100p. filmography. (East European Monographs,
       no. 118).

Written in the same vein as the following, this highly interpretive work looks not
just at Menzel's best known film, but at all his work before and since, including
films that have been banned. It also examines in detail the genesis of the Hrabal
works on which some Menzel films are based, and the relevant section almost
counts as an essay on the life and work of Bohumil Hrabal as much as on Menzel.

840   **All the bright young men and women: a personal history of the
       Czech cinema.**
       Josef Škvorecký, translated by Michael Schonberg.   Toronto:
       Peter Martin Associates, in association with Take One magazine,
       Montreal, 1971. 280p. filmography.

The 'personal' element of this history is twofold. Firstly, in that, although tracing
the Czech film back to its earliest origins, where some interesting facts are
revealed, it concentrates most heavily on the generation with which Škvorecký is

Theatre and Cinema

most acquainted, ie., his own. Secondly, because having known many of the film-
makers personally, Škovorecký is able to fill out the relevant historical detail with
many reminiscences, not to say gossip, some bordering on the bitchy, about many
of the individuals mentioned. The personal descends to the obtrusively intimate,
the widespread use of first-names being no contribution to a serious study.
Nevertheless, a wealth of information is contained herein, including in particular
the fate of particular films and film-makers of the 1969-70 period. The
filmography lists the essential facts concerning all the major films produced since
1898. Peter Hames' illustrated *The Czechoslovak New Wave* (Berkeley, Los
Angeles, California; London: University of California Press, 1985. 322p. bibliog.)
is the latest work on post-war Czech *and* Slovak film, in the general historical
and cinematographic context. It consists largely of cameos on individual directors
and films, and contains a full index of the latter.

841   **Gentlemen of a company: English players in Central and Eastern
      Europe 1590-1660.**
      Jerzy Limon.   Cambridge, England: Cambridge University Press,
      1985. 191p.
A fascinating recent curiosity, based in part on reasonable conjecture, and in part
on hard evidence. The territory of present-day Czechoslovakia was visited by
various English companies between 1610 and 1658, some of which can be named,
though there are none recorded for the bulk of the period taken up by the Thirty
Years' War. In some instances the plays performed are known.

842   **Czech drama since World War II.**
      Paul I. Trensky, with an introduction by William E. Harkins.
      White Plains, New York: M. E. Sharpe, 1978. 250p. bibliog.
      (Columbia Slavic Studies).
The Western theatre and television audience should be well-acquainted with the
work of Václav Havel, and some may know something of Pavel Kohout, Milan
Kundera or Josef Topol. They are, however, but a tiny fraction of the sum of
Czech post-war dramatists, to which Trensky's book is a comprehensive
introduction. Relevant political background information and some comparison
with non-dramatic Czech literature and some non-Czech literature add meaning
to the chapter divisions, which are: the rise and fall of Socialist Realism; the
drama of poets; political drama; drama of the absurd; other playwrights of the
1950s and 1960s, and an epilogue on the 1970s. The bibliography includes not
only secondary literature, but also full personal bibliographies of the dramatists
discussed, complete with details of first performances and English translations
where relevant.

843   **Kommunikative Strukturen im tschechischen Drama der 60er
      Jahre.** (Communicative structures in the Czech drama of the
      1960s.)
      Karel Diviš.   Frankfurt am Main, GFR; Bern: Peter Lang, 1983.
      220p. bibliog. (Symbolae Slavicae, vol. 16).
This is a major semantic-pragmatic study of communication, backed up by a
complex theoretical apparatus, but it has been included here despite its technical

approach on account of the introduction it provides to some plays and playwrights not covered elsewhere. These include six plays by Václav Havel, certainly the best known, and one each by Ivan Klíma, Milan Kundera and Milan Uhde. The bibliography includes a list of first book, periodical and translated German editions of these and all other plays by the same writers.

844 **Sowjetrussisches und tschechisches Drama von 1964 bis in die siebziger Jahre: Materialen zur Produktion und Rezeption (Situationsanalyse und Bibliographie).** (Soviet Russian and Czech drama from 1964 to the 1970s: materials on production and reception [situational analysis and bibliography]).
Wolfgang Friedrich Schwarz, Nina Gütter. Neuried, GFR: Hieronymus Verlag, 1984. 490p. bibliog. (Typoskript-Edition Hieronymus: Slavische Sprachen und Literaturen, vol. 3).

A very complete analysis of recent developments in Czech (and Soviet) drama, which relates the subject not only to contemporary developments in politics but also to the social function which it has traditionally had, going back to the time when there were no Czech institutions of state. The main sections treat Czech and Soviet drama separately, but some sub-sections pertain to both (and examine, for example, relations between the two dramas, Soviet plays on Czech stages and Czech drama through Russian eyes). Other topics covered include the drama-critical tradition, Czech theory of drama, the relationship between Czech and Slovak drama, theatre organization and actors and the public. The (Czech half of the) bibliography (p. 359-460) is roughly divided into critical and theoretical works and actual plays, the latter with appended, cross-referenced secondary literature on the given play or dramatist.

845 **The silenced theatre: Czech playwrights without a stage.**
Marketa Goetz-Stankiewicz. Toronto: University of Toronto Press, 1979. 319p. bibliog.

The author seeks to present as full an account as is possible of many of the contemporary Czech playwrights whose works cannot for the time being be performed in Czechoslovakia, although some have been seen in the West. The situation is compared and contrasted with that which existed in the 1950s (Stalinism) and the 1960s (the thaw). Besides discussing the playwrights and their plays the volume describes some of the other outstanding features of modern Czech theatre – direction, production and stage design. She also introduces the uninitiated reader to as much of the cultural and political background as is needed for an understanding of the current situation. The playwrights discussed include Václav Havel, Pavel Kohout, Ivan Klíma, Josef Topol, Peter Karvaš (a Slovak), Milan Kundera and Vratislav Blažek. Proper recognition is given to the Czech dramatists' connections with, and/or debt to, writers outside Czechoslovakia (including Jarry, Brecht, Pirandello, Genet, Dürrenmatt, Beckett, Albee, Pinter and Stoppard).

Theatre and Cinema

846 **Who is Josef Svoboda.**
Vladimír Jindra, translated from the Czech by Marian
Wilbraham. Prague: Orbis, 1968. 30p.

A brief outline, with photographic documentation, of the scenic art of the
constructivist stage designer Josef Svoboda, relating him to his Czech predecessors
and to such earlier theorists as Craig and Stanislavsky. Even briefer, but more
readily obtainable, items on this major figure in Czech theatre are to be found in
the *Fontana biographical companion to modern thought* (q.v.) and J. W.
Freeman's 'The theatre of Josef Svoboda' *Opera*, no. 43 (Dec. 1978), p. 42-44.

847 **Theatre on a string.**
Barbara Day. *Index on Censorship*, vol. 14, no. 1 (1985), 34-36.

This is on the one hand an introduction to certain traditional responses of the
Czech public to its theatre, especially in the realm of real or imagined political
allegory, and on the other an account of the work of some of the contemporary
fringe theatres, their innovative methods and some of the obstacles which they
face. The modern work is actually a continuation of a very long tradition. The
author mentions *passim* the names of several plays, companies, directors and
actors, including some seen in Britain, and the article's title is taken from the
name of a Brno theatre which in the Autumn of 1985 participated in the Bristol
Czech festival.

848 **A censored life: the story of Vlasta Chramostová and her Living
Room Theatre in Prague.**
Karel Kyncl. *Index on Censorship*, vol. 14, no. 1 (1985), p. 37-42.

One type of fringe theatre not mentioned in the previous article, which it follows,
is the private theatre managed in living rooms by a mixture of amateur and
professional actors who for political reasons can no longer play in the mainstream
theatres. The actress named in the title is the indomitable leader of the group.
Some of the group's plays, the equally 'underground' (a word studiously avoided)
critical response to them, and the obstacles the group faces are all described by an
author whose sympathies are firmly on the side of the country's dissidents.

849 **Národní divadlo.** (The National Theatre.)
Russian summary translated by Tamara Ševčenková, German
summary by Helena Krausová, English summary by Till
Gottheinerová, and French summary by Růžena
Semrádová. Prague: Panorama, 1982. 287p.

Anticipating the year of the Czech Theatre, but showing nothing of the newly
extended and refurbished premises of the National Theatre (re-opened 1983), this
is a useful documentary record of the settings, designs, details of décor and the
internal development of the building since it opened a century earlier. It also
contains portraits and thumbnail biographies of leading actors past and present.
The English element consists of translations of the captions to the illustrations and
a résumé of the theatre's history with the emphasis on its unique role in Czech
political life in the second half of last century.

Czech nationalism: a study of the national theatre movement 1845-1883.
See item no. 231.

Food and Drink

850 **Culinary delights: specialities of eight countries.**
Vera Lévai, translated by Dick Sturgess, Mary Sturgess.
Budapest: Korvina, 1985. 174p.
Czechoslovakia is represented here (p. 130-43) by a good mixture of fifty-four
genuine Bohemian, Moravian and Slovak recipes. They are regional specialities
not necessarily widely known, even elsewhere in Czechoslovakia in some cases
and the recipes have not been adjusted to make allowances for the average, and
arguably intolerant, English palate. Cookery books seem to come and go very
quickly and tend not to reach many libraries, especially if they represent
'minority' cuisines. At the time of writing (late 1985) this one is still in London
bookshops. Others will doubtless follow in their sporadic manner. Less easy to
obtain will be those already out of print, of which two examples follow. Those
with a special interest in cheese will find a brief guide to the cheeses of
Czechoslovakia in the East European section of *The Mitchell Beazley pocket guide
to cheese* by Sandy Carr (London: Mitchell Beazley, 1985. rev. ed. p. 30-33).

851 **The Czech book: recipes and traditions.**
Compiled by Pat Martin, edited by Miriam Canter (et al.). Iowa
City, Iowa: Penfield Press, 1981. 60p.
An illustrated cookery book aimed primarily at the North American market. The
'traditions' angle adds a dimension not usually included.

852 **Czech cookbook: recipes translated from Národní domácí
kuchařka.**
Marie Rosická, translated by Lillian Stavinoha. Rosenberg,
Texas: Fort Bend County Historical Museum, 1976. 37p.
The origins of this cookery book lie at the beginning of the century when the
source work, *The national home cookery book*, was a minor classic of the genre

280

•f the kind that contemporary Czech grandmothers will still use in preference to
•ome more modern works.

53   The world guide to beer.
      Edited by Michael Jackson.   London: New Burlington Books,
      1982. 255p. maps.
'he Bohemian town of Plzeň – Pilsen in German – is the source of one of the few
'zech words to have gained currency in other languages, as the designation for a
•articular type of beer. This is only part of the 'lavish and long' history of beer in
'zechoslovakia, which goes back to the 9th century. The separate chapter on
'zechoslovakia in this work (p. 25-35) offers a general outline history and a true
•eer lover's guide to all the major, and many minor, beers and breweries in all
•hree provinces, and includes some guidance on where some of them can be
•ampled in Britain. The text is generously supported by photographs and a map.
'zechoslovakia produces much, but exports little, wine. Although there are
•umerous general guides to wine currently available, Czechoslovakia is normally
•nly dealt with in a cursory fashion and is dismissed in one or two pages.

The Media

854 **Radio and television broadcasting in Eastern Europe.**
Burton Paulu. Minneapolis, Minnesota: University of Minnesota
Press, 1974. 592p. bibliog.

The generous section on Czechoslovakia (p. 313-60) includes some outline
information and examines the legal structure of the country. The evolution of
broadcasting is traced down to the organization of the contemporary radio
network and a chronology of developments in both wireless and wired radio is
included. Other topics covered include: the role of ČTK, the national press
agency, the locations of its offices and the sources (other agencies) on which it
draws; the extent of cooperation with Eurovision; radio and television in
education including schools broadcasts; music in broadcasting; the content of
television drama and film schedules; audience research; external broadcasting
and Czechoslovak radio and television's organization of, and participation in
international festivals. The book appeared fairly soon after the 1968 period when
the media had enjoyed a higher degree of freedom from supervision than before
or since, and this distinctive period in the development of the role of radio and
television is accorded special attention.

855 **The role and evolution of press agencies in the socialist countries.**
Theodore E. Kruglak. In: *Education and the mass media in the
Soviet Union and Eastern Europe.* Edited by Bohdan Harasymiw.
New York; Washington, DC; London: Praeger, 1976, p. 80-98.

The brief references to Četeka (ČTK), the Czechoslovak national news agency, in
the outline history of all the agencies of the area can be ignored in favour of the
separate summary history (p. 92) which also includes the war-time Zpravodajská
agentúra Slovenska (for the Slovak State). The rest of the paper discusses the
take-up rate of items from the main Western agencies by those of the East, and
the latter's basic reliance on TASS. There is some comparison of practice between
Western and Eastern responses to the same news item.

282

856   **The bureaucracy of truth: how communist governments manage the news.**
Paul Lendvai.   London: Burnett; Boulder, Colorado: Westview Press, 1981. 285p. bibliog.

Czechoslovak practice is only one of many described here, but a certain amount of other information is provided, either of an international nature since Prague is home to the International Organization of Journalists, or of a local nature, such as the case of Pavel Minařík, the Czech mole at Radio Free Europe.

857   **Censorship and political communication in Eastern Europe: a collection of documents.**
Edited by George Schöpflin.   London: Frances Pinter, in association with Index on Censorship, 1983. 175p.

Czechoslovakia is dealt with, fairly slenderly and mostly at second hand (p. 7-31). The documents concerned are of varying antiquity, from the 1967 statement on the reasons for the non-registration of a well-known literary journal, *Literární noviny*, together with an extract from Dušan Hamšík's *Writers against rulers* (q.v.), to a 1981 notice in the Prague Catholic newspaper simply disclaiming any responsibility for delivery delays or unavailability of individual issues. Other items include an interpretation of current book-censorship practices (considering, for example, the fate of a translation of *Ulysses*), the text of the censors' report on why a particular book should be banned, and a list of blacklisted writers. Since the date of publication of this book, some of these names have been deleted from the list since some of the named writers have begun publishing again.

858   **Winter into Spring: the Czechoslovak press and the reform movement 1963-1968.**
Frank L. Kaplan.   Boulder, Colorado: East European Quarterly. Distributed by Columbia University Press, New York, 1977. 208p. bibliog. (East European Monographs, no. 29).

Describes and explains the undeniable role played by the daily press and the 'cultural' periodicals in the process that led to the 'Prague Spring' of 1968. The appendix contains detailed statistics on many periodical publications including newspapers.

859   **'Svoboda'. The press in Czechoslovakia 1968.**
Anon. foreword by Ernest Meyer.   Zurich, Switzerland: International Press Institute, 1969. 125p.

The press and other media continued to function under peculiar circumstances after the Soviet intervention in August 1968. Many of the journalists involved got together and produced this selection of testimonies, reproduced in anonymity, on just how the media and its voluntary helpers kept going through the early days. It is incidentally a history of some, at least, of the short-lived periodicals of the period. Appended is a list of relevant names with an indication of their significance, and a list of mass media, mostly newspapers and periodicals, with their affiliations.

The Media

860 **Abbreviations in the Czechoslovak press.**
Compiled by the Joint Publications Research Service and incorporating material from the Library of Congress publication *Czech and Slovak abbreviations* (1956). Washington, DC: US Government Printing Office, 1970. 185p.

This is a vital tool for the reader of Czech and Slovak newspapers, which can be a maze of abbreviations. An average of about twenty-two are listed here on each full page, accompanied by the full Czech or Slovak wording behind the abbreviations and their English translation. Acronyms are also included.

861 **Czech and Slovak press outside Czechoslovakia: its status in 1978.**
Vojtěch N. Duben, with a preface by Rudolf Šturm. Washington, DC: Czechoslovak Society of Arts and Sciences in America, 1978. 62p. bibliog. (SVU Publications Occasional Paper, no. 4).

Three separate lists give the title, specific areas of interest and source address for Czech, Slovak and 'other language' periodicals circulating outside Czechoslovakia. Part II contains a regional index to the corpus; dates of first publication are supplied where known. The work's own bibliography lists titles of articles on the ex-patriate press and details of certain earlier similar bibliographies, while the preface contains a useful list of North American colleges, libraries and archives with a Czech or Slovak connection. The approximately 275 titles include not only the numerous fairly recent publications associated with the post-1968 wave of emigration, but many long-standing organs of the larger émigré communities, such as *Nedělní hlasatel* (1898-. weekly), which describes itself as the oldest Czechoslovak newspaper in the world; it is published in Chicago and carries items in both languages. Individual articles by the same author will be found in Miloslav Rechcígl, Jr.'s (ed.) *The Czechoslovak contribution to world culture* (q.v.) and *Czechoslovakia past and present* (q.v.) and other North American émigré publications.

862 **Czechoslovak TV programmes abroad.**
Karel Čapek, Eva Švecová. *Czechoslovak Life*, vol. 38, no. 4 (April 1983), p. 28-29.

Many will have seen the children's cartoons which often appear on our television screens, but there have been other programmes, again often, though not solely, for children, with which the country has enjoyed success. Here the author presents some details of the variety of films marketed and the purchasing countries.

863 **Children's books in Czechoslovakia.**
Otakar Chaloupka. Prague: Orbis Press Agency, 1978. 87p.

Czechoslovakia is rightly proud of its per capita output of books generally, and children's books in particular. This slim volume outlines trends and policies in publishing for children, separately for Czech and Slovak, looking at the work of many of the best-known authors and illustrators and at the organization of publication through specialist publishing houses for children's literature. It also considers the role of the teaching of reading in schools, but emphasizes the social benefits rather than the leisure aspect.

864 **Slovak newspapers (and other publications) in the U.S.**
Andrew V. Pier. *Furdek*, vol. 22 (Jan. 1983), p. 95-106.

Traces the history of a number of Slovak periodicals that have appeared in the United States, in Slovak, English or a mixture, since the publication of the first weekly on 21 October 1886. The information is drawn from the more detailed work by Konstantin Culen entitled *Slovenské časopisy v. Amerike* (Middletown, Pennsylvania: Jednota Printers, 1970).

Newspapers, Magazines and Periodicals

Czechoslovak dailies and weeklies

865 **Rudé právo.** (Red Right.)
Prague: Rudé právo, 1920-. daily.
The country's main daily newspaper and the organ of the Central Committee of the Czechoslovak Communist Party. The paper is in Czech and has a circulation of approximately 950,000.

866 **Pravda.** (Truth.)
Bratislava: Pravda, 1920-. daily.
The main Slovak daily and organ of the Central Committee of the Slovak Communist Party. It has a circulation of about 330,000.

867 **Új szó.** (New Word.)
Bratislava: Pravda, 1948-. daily.
A Hungarian-language version of the Party daily, partly tailored to Hungarian minority interests with a circulation of about 85,000. It has a Sunday mutation entitled *Vasárnapi Új szó*.

868 **Práce.** (Labour.)
Prague: Práce, 1945-. daily.
The second major daily newspaper, published for the Central Council of Trade Unions, whose interests it reflects. It has a circulation of about 317,000. There is a sister Slovak daily called *Práca* which is the organ of the Slovak Trades Union Council (1946-. circulation ca. 230,000).

Newspapers, Magazines and Periodicals. Czechoslovak dailies & weeklies

869   **Mladá fronta.** (Young Front.)
      Prague: Mladá Fronta, 1945-. daily.

This newspaper, which has a circulation of about 239,000 is the organ of the Central Committee of the Socialist Union of Youth (SSM), but it is one of the more widely read dailies of general interest and is not solely aimed at the younger generation (the definition of which is in any case rather loose; SSM officers can be well into their thirties). Its Slovak sister publication is *Smena* [Shift] (1947-. circulation ca. 129,000).

870   **Zemědělské noviny.** (Farming News.)
      Prague: Ministry of Agriculture and Food, 1945-. daily.

This is the official organ of the Ministry and it has a circulation approaching 342,000. The paper has a wide coverage of news, but is especially relevant to the rural interest. The Slovak Ministry of Agriculture publishes its own *Roľnícke noviny* (1946-. circulation ca. 73,000).

871   **Svobodné slovo.** (Free Word.)
      Prague: Svobodné slovo, 1907-. daily.

This is the organ of the Czechoslovak Socialist Party, which continues to exist as a quasi-separate entity, though its policies echo those of the ruling Communist Party. News coverage is not necessarily the same as that of *Rudé právo*. Its circulation is about 228,000. The Slovak weekly *Sloboda* (Freedom, 1946-. circulation ca. 4,500), organ of the Slovak Freedom Party, is in a similar position.

872   **Lidová demokracie.** (Popular Democracy.)
      Prague: Lidová demokracie, 1945-. daily.

This is the organ of the Czechoslovak People's Party and it has a circulation of approximately 217,000. This party continues to exist as a separate entity and is the body that represents, within the constraints of the régime, the Catholic interest. On the question of national and international politics, it generally follows the line required by the ruling Communist Party, but news coverage includes far more items of an ecclesiastical or theological nature. Slovak Catholic interests are catered for by the weekly *Katolícke noviny* (Bratislava: St. Vojtech League, 1849-
      circulation ca. 130,000).

873   **Ľud.** (The People.)
      Bratislava: Slovak Party of Reconstruction, 1948-. daily.

The party system in Slovakia was badly upset by the Slovak People's Party's monopoly during the Second World War, as the controlling power in the Slovak State. The unhappy situation of post-war Slovak party politics was resolved by the creation, alongside the Communist Party of Slovakia, of a Party of Reconstruction (or Revival), of which this is the official organ. The paper's circulation is about 17,000.

Newspapers, Magazines and Periodicals. Czechoslovak dailies & weeklies

874 **Československý sport.** (Czechoslovak Sport.)
Prague: Central Committee of the Czech Association for Physical Training. daily.

By any reckoning this is a good daily sports paper of broad coverage, including many of the minority sports. It has a circulation of approximately 185,000 and includes football results from major foreign leagues as a regular feature. There is more political commentary than in an equivalent journal from a non-socialist country. The Slovak sister publication is *Šport* which has a circulation of about 60,000.

875 **Večerní Praha.** (Evening Prague.)
Prague: Prague City Committee of the Communist Party of Czechoslovakia, 1955-. daily.

Like evening papers the world over, this is the only Prague daily to be hawked and sold on street corners. Its circulation is about 120,000 and coverage is almost solely to do with events of direct relevance to, or occurring in, Prague, though with some major national items as well. A number of other cities rise to an evening paper, such as Bratislava (*Večerník*), Brno (*Brněnský večerník*) and Košice (*Večer*).

876 **Prager Volkszeitung.** (Prague People's Newspaper.)
Prague: Central Committee of the Czechoslovak National Front and the Cultural Union of the German Citizens of Czechoslovakia, 1951-. weekly.

This newspaper with a circulation of ca. 17,000 is more or less all that is left of a long tradition of Prague German journalism, now serving on a weekly basis a very small German minority. In essence it is an ordinary newspaper with a typical mixture of political and cultural news.

877 **Dikobraz.** (The Porcupine.)
Prague: Rudé právo, 1945-. weekly.

This paper, which has a circulation approaching 525,000, seeks to be a satirical weekly, but depending on the prevailing atmosphere is apt to be rather tame. There are several regular columns including some which are a useful source of Czech witting and unwitting linguistic humour, and it is home to the country's main cartoonists, political or otherwise. Its Slovak counterpart is *Roháč* (The Stag-beetle; 1948-. weekly, circulation ca. 120,000). The relatively high circulation figures speak for themselves.

878 **Nové knihy.** (New Books.)
Prague: Panorama, on behalf of the Czech and Slovak wholesale book trade. weekly.

A news sheet containing details of most, but by no means all, of the new books appearing in both republics. It is edited simultaneously in Prague and Bratislava and the articles in any one issue will be in a mixture of the two languages. The current week's releases are listed with the barest bibliographical identification (Czechoslovakia, unlike some of its socialist neighbours, does not use the ISBN system), while the next week's issues are more generously annotated. It is worth

288

Newspapers, Magazines and Periodicals. Czechoslovak dailies & weeklies

mentioning here that new books always appear on the market on Thursdays, often inspiring some of the country's longest queues. *Nové knihy* also carries reviews and similar articles on selected current titles.

879 **Květy.** (Flowers.)
Prague: Rudé právo, 1834-. weekly.

A general interest magazine with a circulation of about 360,000. It contains some current affairs items at the beginning, then a mixture of travelogues, innovations in industry or agriculture, news from the arts, serialized stories, fashion, philately, a children's corner, jokes and crosswords. It is emphatically not the same periodical that originally appeared under this title in 1834, but more a case of a modern, post-war socialist weekly adopting an old title of no small symbolic value, with its roots in the period of the National Revival. Its nearest Slovak equivalent is *Život* (1951-. circulation ca. 180,000).

880 **Ahoj na sobotu.** (Hallo Saturday.)
Prague: Czechoslovak Socialist Party. weekly.

An illustrated general interest family magazine for the weekend with a circulation of about 200,000.

881 **Mladý svět.** (Young World.)
Prague: Central Committee of the Socialist Union of Youth, 1959-. weekly.

This is certainly one of the most widely read popular weeklies (circulation ca. 420,000) which contains items primarily, but by no means solely, of interest to the younger generation. It includes a very wide range of topics and publishes a sort of agony aunt (Sally!) column and a lonely hearts page, though it is by no means the only periodical to do so.

882 **Vlasta.**
Prague: Union of Czech Women, 1946-. weekly.

The name of this women's weekly is suitably patriotic – an old Czech name, full of legendary association, still popular and etymologically equivalent to Patricia. It can be quite vocal on feminine, if not feminist in the Western sense, issues and on problems relating to the family and education. It has counterparts in *Slovenka* [Slovak woman] (Bratislava: Slovak Union of Women, 1949-. circulation ca. 220,000) and *Nö* [Woman] (Bratislava: Slovak Union of Women, 1952-. circulation ca. 35,000), which is for the female half of the Hungarian minority.

883 **100 + 1ZZ.**
Prague: Czechoslovak News Agency, ČTK. fortnightly.

This is a digest (circulation ca. 100,000) of the foreign press, sometimes notoriously difficult to obtain, although it is no real substitute for actual foreign newspapers which, except for those of the fraternal countries and fraternal parties, are not obtainable. Even individual issues of newspapers such as the fraternal *L'Humanité* or *Morning Star* may not be available because of some offending article.

289

Newspapers, Magazines and Periodicals. Czechoslovak periodicals in English

Newspapers of East Central and Southeastern Europe.
See item no. 956.

Czechoslovak periodicals in English

884   **Czechoslovak Foreign Trade.**
Prague: Rapid, 1961-. monthly.
Contains a record of relevant current events (including, for example, trade delegations, exhibitions and international agreements) and articles on specific products, producers or whole branches of industry, their present performance internationally and their future prospects. It also publishes papers on trade and economic news, statistics, and, for the philatelist, details of new stamp issues. The periodical is illustrated and appears simultaneously in German, French, Spanish and Russian. It has a circulation of approximately 12,000.

885   **Czechoslovak Heavy Industry.**
Prague: Rapid, 1955-. monthly.
Deals with all aspects of research, development and marketing of Czechoslovak heavy industrial goods, in which there is a long and respectable tradition. Unavoidably technical in its bias, it is illustrated and appears simultaneously also in French, German, Spanish and Russian. The periodical has a circulation of ca. 10,000.

886   **Czechoslovak Life.**
Prague: Orbis Press Agency, 1946-. monthly.
A colourful general interest magazine which covers all aspects of life in contemporary Czechoslovakia, such as food, fashion, sport, cultural festivals and youth activities, with occasional popular pieces on art and architecture, aspects of industry and agriculture, historic anniversaries and so forth. The periodical appears simultaneously in German, French, Italian and Spanish.

887   **Czechoslovak Motor Review.**
Prague: Rapid, 1955-. monthly.
A good mix of popular and technical writings on the Czechoslovak automobile industry, sport and trade, an area in which the country is more visible on the British scene than in many of its export efforts, thanks to the numbers of Škoda cars, ČZ motorbikes and Velorex sidecars to be seen on the roads. The language of the English edition carries more infelicities in the translation than many of Rapid's publications, which may be just a sporadic aberration in the issues I have seen. Illustrated, it appears simultaneously also in French, German, Russian and Serbo-Croat.

Newspapers, Magazines and Periodicals. Czechoslovak periodicals in
English

888 **Czechoslovak News Bulletin.**
London: Embassy of the Czechoslovak Socialist Republic, 1973-.
monthly.

A digest of current affairs in Czechoslovakia, especially those accorded greater
importance by the Czechoslovak authorities than by the world's press, which
consequently may not have covered them. The publication also presents the
Czechoslovak view or interpretation of wider international issues. Similar
bulletins are put out by some other Czechoslovak embassies.

889 **Democratic Journalist.**
Prague: International Organization of Journalists, 1953-. monthly.

The glossy organ of the 'largest democratic organization of journalists in the
world', the contributors to which come in the main from Eastern Europe, with
some Western communists and 'progressive' Third-World journalists. For a
characterization of this journal see Paul Lendvai's *The bureaucracy of truth: how
communist governments manage the news* (q.v.). It is also published in French,
Spanish and Russian.

890 **For You From Czechoslovakia.**
Prague: Rapid, 1960-. quarterly.

A glossy magazine for the export fashion trade, with illustrations of the latest
Czechoslovak fashion fabrics and made-up garments for formal and leisure wear,
mostly for women and children. It also appears simultaneously in German,
Russian, Spanish and French.

891 **Glass Review: Czechoslovak Glass and Ceramics Magazine.**
Prague: Rapid, 1946-. monthly.

An illustrated magazine with a mixture of popular and technical, artistic and
historical articles on all aspects of glass and ceramics manufacture, use and
exhibitions. It includes appreciations of the work of individual artists working in
glass and ceramics and also appears in French, German and Russian.

892 **Investa.**
Prague: Rapid, 1969-. quarterly.

'Devoted to the technical development of the commodities exported by Investa
Co. Ltd.', namely machinery in the fields of precision engineering, footwear, and
textiles. The periodical also records Czechoslovak involvement at international
exhibitions and fairs. It is illustrated and appears simultaneously in German,
French, Spanish and Russian.

893 **Kovoexport.**
Prague: Rapid, 1955-. bimonthly.

'Devoted to the technical development of the commodities exported by the Kovo
foreign trade corporation', such as electronic and electric apparatus, measuring
and regulating instruments, telecommunications equipment, laboratory instruments, computers and office machines and printing machines, for example. It
describes research, development and foreign trade activity in these areas, and

291

Newspapers, Magazines and Periodicals. Czechoslovak periodicals in English

Czechoslovak involvement at international exhibitions and fairs. It appears simultaneously also in German, French, Spanish and Russian.

894 **Meridians 12-23.**
Bratislava: Slovak Writer, 1977-. annual.

The function of this publication is to bring to the attention of the world at large what the Union of Slovak Writers deems to be representative and meritorious among recent literary output. It carries some translated excerpts and many mini-essays on individual works or the publications of particular writers. It also covers the output of selected non-literary publishing houses, especially those dealing with the social sciences or the arts. It includes potted biographies of authors mentioned and a directory of publishing houses and trade-union organizations involving writers and the arts (Czech, Slovak and Czechoslovak). For Czech literature a similar publication exists, *Panorama of Czech Literature* (Prague: Panorama, 1979-. annual), sponsored by the Union of Czech Writers and the Czech Literary Fund, with some involvement of DILIA, the national theatrical and literary agency. There are more translations than in *Meridians* and fewer background articles. Implicit in both annuals is the hope that eventually more translations from the literatures will be inspired and published outside the country.

895 **Welcome to Czechoslovakia: Tourist Review.**
Prague: Orbis Press Agency, in co-operation with the Czech and Slovak Government Committees for Tourism, 1966-. quarterly.

Published in English, French, German and Russian editions, this is perhaps regrettably described as only a tourist review for it contains many beautifully illustrated articles of quite a wide interest to anybody curious about the country and its history, architecture, sport, music and a host of other areas. It is tempting to see it as a kind of 'national geographical' for the non-academic reader. The political content is minimal and tends to occur coincidentally with major anniversaries and other political events of importance to the régime. Similar to this in many respects is the quarterly *Panorama of Slovakia* (Bratislava: Government Committee for Tourism of the Slovak Socialist Republic, 1970-.), which concentrates solely on Slovakia. It appears simultaneously in English, German and French, and quarterly in Russian.

Price list of Czech newspapers and journals from the Czechoslovak Socialist Republic.
See item no. 973.

Émigré periodicals

896 **Carpatho-Rusyn American.**
Edited from Pittsburgh, Pennsylvania, for the Carpatho-Rusyn
Research Center Inc. [n.p.], 1978-. quarterly.
Describes itself as a newsletter on Carpatho-Rusyn Ethnic Heritage. Although
Ruthenia (Subcarpathia, Carpathian Rus') is no longer part of Czechoslovakia,
there is still a Ruthenian (Rusyn) population in Eastern Slovakia, and many of
the Ruthene émigrés in North America look to Czechoslovakia as their ancestors'
home. This is reflected in the periodical's content, as also is the shared
background of both Ruthenes and Slovaks in North America, a product largely of
the simultaneous adoption by sections of both peoples of the Greek Catholic
Church.

897 **Czechoslovak Newsletter.**
New York: Council of Free Czechoslovakia, 1975-. monthly.
A duplicated broadsheet voicing the exile and dissident view of current events in
Czechoslovakia, especially those ignored or covered only partially by the official
Czechoslovak media. At the present time it contains wide coverage of anything
connected with the Charter 77 movement, which it supports.

898 **Furdek: Jednota Annual.**
Cleveland, Ohio: First Catholic Slovak Union of the United States
and Canada, 1961-. annual.
This is the English-language counterpart to the North American Slovaks'
almanach *Kalendár Jednota*. Although bearing the stamp of its Catholic and right-
wing political orientation (with much harking back to the time of the Slovak State
during the last war), this illustrated publication also contains a wide variety of
articles on the Slovak Catholic community in North America, parish histories,
biographies of leading Slovak Catholic émigrés and ex-patriates, as well as pieces
on Slovak art and architecture, films, the press and past and present culture.

899 **Kosmas: Journal of Czechoslovak and Central European Studies.**
New York: Czechoslovak Society of Arts and Sciences (SVU),
1982-. biannual.
Contains items in many fields from the pens of Central Europeans, especially
Czechs and Slovaks, who have taken up residence in the English-speaking world.
The content tends to represent the interests of the mid-century generation of
exiles and the political aspect is accordingly less virulent than in some of the more
recent émigré journals. The broad scope also means that politics and political
history do not have the monopoly of space which they enjoy in some journals.
The name *Kosmas* comes from that of an early Czech chronicler (1045?-1125)
who wrote in Latin.

900 **Londýnské listy: Zpravodaj Naardenského hnutí.** (London
Newsletter: Bulletin of the Naarden Movement.)
London: Naarden Movement, 1977-. monthly.

This is a small format mimeographed news-sheet serving primarily the Naarden
Movement, an exile organization which exists to promote the ideas of John Amos
Comenius (Komenský). In addition it serves as a general source of information
for Czechs and Slovaks living in Britain on local events of specific interest to
them. The émigré or exile communities in most of the countries of Western
Europe, and the long-standing extraterritorial communities such as those in
Yugoslavia, are all served by a variety of local periodicals, for full details of which
see item no. 861.

901 **Most.** (The Bridge.)
Cleveland, Ohio: Slovak Institute, 1954-. quarterly.

The Slovak Institute was founded in 1952 to promote and support the work of
Slovak (émigré) writers and scholars, for whom *Most* is an important publishing
venture. It contains original writings, some translations and critical essays. The
Institute also collaborates with the Slovak Institute of Saints Cyril and Methodius
in Rome, with which it publishes the annual *Slovak Studies* (1961-.); this carries
articles in Slovak, English and French on a variety of linguistic, literary historical
and general cultural topics.

902 **Proměny/Premeny.** (Metamorphoses.)
Flushing, New York: Czechoslovak Society of Arts and Sciences in
America, 1964-. quarterly.

The Czechoslovak Society of Arts and Sciences in America, known by the
abbreviation of its Czech name SVU, was founded in 1958 as an expatriate
academy of arts and sciences. *Proměny* carries a variety of political commentaries
and articles of wide cultural interest. It does not aspire to being over-scholarly;
contributions are in Czech or Slovak.

903 **Slowakei.** (Slovakia.)
Munich: Matúš-Černák-Institut, 1963-. annual.

Large sectors of the Slovak nationalist right-wing are now concentrated in West
Germany having emigrated after the war. The Slovak National Council and other
bodies produce, or are supported by, a number of periodicals of various levels of
seriousness, of which *Slowakei* seeks to be one of the more scholarly. It carries
articles on many aspects of culture (language, literature, religion, history and
politics), but always with a strong nationalist, Catholic and anti-communist bias, a
resilient offshoot of the wartime Slovak State. The Matúš Černák Institute,
besides its publishing activities, maintains an archive of Slovak materials. A
similar archive for Czech materials is at the Bohemia cultural and social
association in Cologne.

904 **Svědectví.** (Testimony.)
Paris, New York, Vienna: Svědectví, 1956-. quarterly.

Described as political and cultural, this widely circulated periodical expresses the
views of various shades of exile opinion in opposition to the régime in

Czechoslovakia, though not all the subjects covered are directly concerned with
that country. The cultural contributions are often as political as the explicitly
political, but this has long been the case of Czech culture, especially literature.
Book reviews are a regular feature. One particular branch of exile opinion, that
of the Socialist Opposition, represented by exiled ex-members of the Czechoslovak
Communist Party, is voiced through the bimonthly *Listy* (Rome; 1970-.), of which
versions in German, French and Italian also appear occasionally.

905   **Zprávy SVU.** (SVU News.)
      Washington, DC: SVU, 1959-. bimonthly.
Carries reports of events in the life of the branches of SVU, personalities, and
books published, or supported, by the Society. The Washington chapter of SVU
also publishes the quarterly *Bulletin: English supplement to Zprávy SVU* (1969-.),
which contains less on the Society's activities and more on personalities and book
reviews, by which means some knowledge of Czech and Slovak publications may
reach the non-Czech/Slovak-speaking public.

Slovak newspapers (and other publications) in the U.S.
See item no. 864.

Non-Czechoslovak periodicals and scholarly journals

906   **Bohemia: Zeitschrift für Geschichte und Kultur der Böhmischen
      Länder**—A journal of history and civilization in East Central
      Europe.
      Edited at the behest of Collegium Carolinum by Karl
      Bosl.   Munich: R. Oldenburg Verlag, 1960-. biannual.
A sane West German periodical, with contributions by Germans of various
origins, including the Sudetenland (though without the virulence often associated
with the latter), it covers all periods of Czech history and civilization, and
especially, but not solely, events and affairs with a Jewish or German connection.
The journal contains an extensive review section with the emphasis being on titles
in German.

907   **Canadian Slavic Studies – Revue Canadienne d'Études Slaves.**
      Montreal: Loyola College, 1967-. quarterly.
One of the main North-American Slavonic studies periodicals from a country
which like the United States has a sizeable Slav immigrant population. It
occasionally carries items with a Czech or Slovak interest, as well as being a
source for reviews and bibliographical information.

Newspapers, Magazines and Periodicals. Non-Czechoslovak periodicals and scholarly journals

908   **Cross Currents: a Yearbook of Central European Culture, 1982.**
Edited by Ladislav Matějka, Benjamin Stolz.   Ann Arbor,
Michigan: Department of Slavic Languages and Literatures,
University of Michigan, 1982. 379p. (Michigan Slavic Materials,
no. 20).

Cross Currents has continued to appear since this first volume, and this is not the place to provide a break-down of the subsequent issues. Suffice it to say that among the mixture of items included there are always some contributions of a Czech or Slovak interest, whether translations, discussions of current issues in literature and the arts, or essays on individual works or writers. The first volume gives a fair idea of the publication's intended scope, with articles on the: 'Liberated Theatre (Osvobozené divadlo) of Voskovec and Werich' (Jarka M. Burian); 'Slovak surrealism as a parable of modern uprootedness' (Peter Petro); 'Rilke's early contacts with Czech and Jewish Prague' (Daria Rothe); 'American motifs in the work of Bohumil Hrabal' (Josef Škvorecký); 'Kafka's Milena as remembered by her daughter' (on Milena Jesenská, Kafka's mistress) (Jana Černá); 'Jiří Orten's Elegies' (George Gibian; with five poems translated by Lyn Coffin); an interview with Milan Kundera (Alain Finkielkraut); and a translation of Škvorecký's *Swell season . . .* (q.v.).

909   **East European Quarterly.**
Boulder, Colorado: East European Quarterly, University of
Colorado, 1967-. quarterly.

Czechoslovak topics are included in this periodical fairly regularly, many of the contributing authors and editors appearing under book titles in the present bibliography.

910   **Études Tchèques et Slovaques.** (Czech and Slovak Studies.)
Paris: Centre de Recherches Slaves de l'Université de Paris,
Sorbonne, 1980-. annual.

This French journal is more concerned with culture (language, literature and the arts) than with politics or economics. It also contains translated excerpts from Czech literature and a review section. The journal is currently edited by Hana Jechova.

911   **Index on Censorship.**
London: Index on Censorship, 1971-. bimonthly.

This publication is concerned with explicit and implicit, or covert censorship worldwide. Accordingly, coverage of Czechoslovakia, which has explicit censorship, is fairly regular, most recently in the context of literature, translations and banned authors (see, for example, Josef Škvorecký's 'A cabaret of censorship', vol. 13, no. 5 (Oct. 1984), p. 38-41).

Newspapers, Magazines and Periodicals. Non-Czechoslovak periodicals
and scholarly journals

912 **Problems of Communism.**
Washington, DC: United States Information Agency, 1952-.
bimonthly.

The conception of 'problems' takes in both the difficulties faced by individual
communist societies (social, political, economic and international), but also the
problems faced by the United States in its negotiations with the Soviet Union on
various fronts. Czechoslovakia features herein only when it is 'in the news'.

913 **Radio Free Europe Research.**
Washington, DC; Munich: Radio Free Europe, 1976-. weekly.

Although covering current affairs throughout Eastern Europe, much space is
devoted to an analysis of events in Czechoslovakia and the provision of 'Western'
interpretations to reporting in the Czechoslovak media. In view of the function of
Radio Free Europe, the contents also include material relevant to the country's
past and present which is apt to go unnoticed in the country itself (certain political
anniversaries and the like). Reporting is inevitably hostile to the present régime.

914 **Religion in Communist Lands.**
Keston, Kent, England: Keston College, 1973-. quarterly.

Keston College is an educational charity specializing in the study of religious
communities in the Soviet Union and Eastern Europe. It pursues current research
into religious practice, church history and the politics of religion, including in
particular restrictions on religious liberty. Coverage of Czechoslovakia's religious
affairs in this journal is sporadic and reflects the general trend in current affairs in
that country. Keston College also publishes a fortnightly *Keston News Service* for
day-to-day items.

915 **Revue d'Études Comparatives Est Ouest: Économie, Planification,
Organisation.**
Paris: Centre National de la Recherche Scientifique, 1970-.
quarterly.

A major periodical in the subjects of its sub-title, which actually gives the
publication more breadth than at first sight. The articles are in French, but there
are summaries in English and the contents page is also reproduced in English.

916 **Slavic Review: American Quarterly of Soviet and East European
Studies.**
Stanford, California: American Association for the Advancement
of Slavic Studies, 1942-. quarterly.

The emphasis in this, one of the main US periodicals, is on literature, history and
politics, Czechoslovakia being just one of the countries covered quite regularly.
Of great value is the extensive review section.

Newspapers, Magazines and Periodicals. Non-Czechoslovak periodicals and scholarly journals

917　**Slavonic and East European Review.**
London: Modern Humanities Research Association, 1922-. quarterly.

A serious scholarly periodical covering all aspects of the languages, literatures and history of all of Eastern Europe although the emphasis tends to be historical. Czechoslovakia has been fairly well-represented among the contributions. The long review section provides a valuable guide to recent relevant publications.

918　**Soviet Studies: a Quarterly Journal on the USSR and Eastern Europe.**
Harlow, England: Longman, for the University of Glasgow, 1949-. quarterly.

One of the main outlets for Scottish academics working in the field of Soviet and East European studies. Coverage is predominantly within the socio-political and economic spheres.

919　**Survey: a Journal of East & West Studies.**
London: Survey, in association with the Institute for European Defence and Strategic Studies. 1955-. quarterly.

Each issue tends to concentrate on a small number of topics, each covered by a number of contributions. The emphasis is on current affairs, politics and economics with some historical items.

Encyclopaedias and Directories

20 Subject collections in European libraries.
Compiled by Richard C. Lewański.   London, New York: Bowker,
1978. 2nd rev. ed.
Within the Dewey system for ordering subjects, this directory lists, country by
country, the main libraries, noting any special collections and services. In addition
to providing a guide according to subject it also represents a piecemeal guide to at
least some of the main libraries of each country, including Czechoslovakia.

**21 Eastern Europe and Russia/Soviet Union: a handbook of West
    European archival and library resources.**
Richard C. Lewański.   New York, Munich, London, Paris: K. G.
Saur, 1980. 317p.
Each archive or library listed here, country by country, is described telegraphically
in terms of history, range of holdings, the names of its main staff members and
details of any publications issued. A valuable research tool.

**22 Resources for Soviet, East European and Slavonic studies in British
    libraries.**
Gregory Walker, with the assistance of Jenny Brine.
Birmingham, England: Centre for Russian and East European
Studies, University of Birmingham, 1981. 240p.
This is an invaluable source book which covers Czechoslovakia. Details are given
of all 104 relevant British libraries, and reference is made, for example, to the size
and nature of their collections and their published catalogues. The work also
provides a directory of useful relevant addresses (embassies, trading organizations,
airlines, broadcasting bodies, and academic institutes), and details on the relevant
journals published in Britain as well as specialist booksellers.

Encyclopaedias and Directories

923 **East Central and Southeast Europe: a handbook of library and archival resources in North America.**
Edited by Paul Louis Horecký, David H. Kraus.   Santa Barbara, California: ABC-Clio, 1976. 466p. (Joint Committee on Eastern European Publication Series, no. 3).
Covers the holdings in forty-three different institutions in the United States and Canada, with separate listings for Czechoslovakia.

924 **Slavic and East European resources in Canadian academic and research libraries.**
Bohdan Budurowycz.   Ottawa, Canada: National Library of Canada, 1976. 595p. bibliog. (Research Collections in Canadian Libraries, Special Studies, no. 4).
This is a survey in a running text, divided by province, the holdings being divided by language and country. The index enables the reader to gain easy access to the commentary on Czech and Slovak collections.

925 **Slavic ethnic libraries, museums and archives in the United States: a guide and directory.**
Lubomyr R. Wynar, assisted by Pat Kleeberger.   Chicago: Association of College and Research Libraries, American Library Association, and the Center for the Study of Ethnic Publications, School of Library Science, Kent State University, 1980. 164p.
Includes coverage of the collections, services and publishing activities of twenty-one Czech and fourteen Slovak institutions (with some overlapping).

926 **Carpatho-Ruthenica at Harvard: a catalog of holdings.**
Compiled by Paul R. Magocsi, Olga K. Mayo.   Englewood, New Jersey: Transworld, 1977. 149p.
Inevitably, many of the 1,030 items housed at Harvard and relating to Ruthenia are in Ukrainian, Russian, Polish, Czech or Slovak, and it is a pity that so few of the catalogue cards provide any indication in English of the content of the work to which they refer. However, the field is narrowed for the user by a nineteen-section subject classification, subdivided, where possible, geographically. Only a portion of the titles are really relevant to the present bibliography in that they concern inter-war Czechoslovak Ruthenia, but some relate expressly to the Prešov Region of contemporary Czechoslovakia where the Ruthenian minority still lives, and there are a number relating to the Ruthenian émigré community in the United States.

927 **Russia, the Soviet Union and Eastern Europe: a survey of holdings at the Hoover Institution of War, Revolution and Peace.**
Edited by Joseph D. Dwyer. Stanford, California: Hoover Institution Press, 1980. 233p. (Hoover Press Survey, no. 6).
The part-survey of holdings on Czechoslovakia (p. 33-54) provides, like the rest of the volume, a general categorization of the collection (periods, topics, types of publications), with a brief description of individual salient titles.

928 **Czech and Slovak.**
London: Centre for Information on Language Teaching and Research, 1983. 58p. bibliog. (Language and Culture Guide, no. 5).
This comprehensive guide on opportunities available in Britain for the study of Czech and Slovak contains a directory of all the relevant teaching institutions, libraries, travel services, ex-patriate centres and booksellers. It also includes an annotated bibliography of some of the available textbooks, dictionaries, readers, periodicals, research registers, and some background works on the language, literature and history.

929 **Jahrbuch der Wirtschaft Osteuropas – Yearbook of East-European Economics.**
Munich, Vienna: Günter Olzog Verlag, 1975-. biannual.
(Veröffentlichungen des Osteuropa-Instituts, Munich).
Each issue of this serial, which describes and comments on current economic or financial thinking in Eastern Europe, is divided into a section on planning theory and one on 'empirical studies' which examines the wider issues of economic policy. Most articles are in English, the remnant in German, and all are accompanied by an abstract. Czechoslovakian developments are covered as and when topical.

930 **Czechoslovakia.**
London: British Overseas Trade Board. (Hints to Exporters).
This guide, which is periodically up-dated, is normally available only to bona fide exporters, but it can be consulted at the BOTB. In addition to the advice uniquely useful to exporters, the booklet contains much general information on law, language, the day-to-day life of the country, useful addresses and telephone numbers, and other facts useful even to the short-term visitor.

931 **Kulturní adresář ČSR.** (Cultural directory of the Czech Socialist Republic.)
Milan Hromádka, assisted by Marie Poláková, Jarmila Valentová. Prague: Ústav pro výzkum kultury, 1973. 501p.
Like all publications of this kind which do not appear with sufficient frequency, this has become slightly outdated and it reflects the state of affairs in 1971. The work provides details on all the state organs, academic and research institutes connected with film, theatre, music, art, publishing, libraries, museums and

archives, conservation areas, tourism, education, the media and foreign cultural centres on Czech soil. Intended for foreign consumption, the index is in Czech, Russian, German, French and English. Despite its age this directory can still be used as a first recourse.

932 **Directory of Czechoslovak officials: a reference aid.**
Directorate of Intelligence. [Washington, DC]: CIA, 1985. 166p.
A complete and indexed directory in twelve sections, correct according to available data as of 19 April 1985. The sections cover: the federal and republic governments and their various ministries and commissions; the political parties; the legislature; regional and municipal Party and government officials; diplomatic and other personnel involved in foreign relations and international bodies; mass organizations; economic and commercial organizations; scientific and academic organizations; cultural, professional and religious organizations; and media organizations. The work is a good guide to the organizations themselves as much as to the officials representing them.

933 **Biographical directory of the members of the Czechoslovak Society of Arts and Sciences Inc.**
Eva Rechcígl, Miloslav Rechcígl, Jr. Washington, DC: SVU, 1978. 4th ed. 137p.
Due to be updated, this directory provides a complete account of the academic and other professional persons associated with the 'émigré academy of sciences', which consists mainly of Czechs and Slovaks now resident in various countries of the world.

934 **Ilustrovaný encyklopedický slovník.** (Illustrated encyclopaedic dictionary.)
Encyclopaedic Institute of the Czechoslovak Academy of Sciences. Prague: Academia, 1980-83. 3 vols.
This is Czechoslovakia's answer to the *Larousse* type of handy reference work, with almost 1,000 pages per volume. The coverage is extremely broad, no field of knowledge being omitted and entries vary from brief histories of states, wars or other human activities (such as voyages of discovery), to brief characterizations or some longer biographies of major political, industrial, cultural or military figures, past and present, to such details as the names of the Rolling Stones. The prevailing political attitudes inevitably pervade the work (the 1968 reformers, where mentioned at all, are 'right-wing opportunists', the Communist Party always heads the list of political parties of a particular country). Although coverage is worldwide, entries with any special relevance to Czechoslovakia provide a useful source of primary data, for example, the number of species of a particular genus actually occurring in the country. Most of the numerous illustrations are in black-and-white, colour being reserved for maps, flags and plates of, for example, small but excellent photographs of plants and animals. Volume 1 is up to date to the return of Mrs. Gandhi to the Indian premiership in 1980, volume 2 to the appointment of General Jaruzelski as head of the Council of Ministers in Poland in 1981, and volume 3 to the Argentine capitulation in the 'Malvinas' in June 1982. (These indicators are chosen more or less at random to

give an approximate idea of the time-scope). The year 1985 saw the delayed appearance of Vol. 1 of *Malá československá encyklopedie* [Small Czechoslovak encyclopaedia] (Prague: Academia, 1984-. 6 vols.), collectively compiled, under the editorship of Bohumil Kvasil and Miroslav Štěpánek, by the same Institute. It will be the most comprehensive work of its kind to have appeared for many decades (over 110,000 entries all told).

935 **Československá vlastivěda.** (Czechoslovak national history and topography.)
The Socialist Academy in collaboration with the Czechoslovak Academy of Sciences (Parts I, II/2 and 3); The Czechoslovak Association for the Dissemination of Political and Scientific Knowledge in collaboration with the Czechoslovak Academy of Sciences (Part II/1).
Prague: Orbis, Horizont, 1963-69. 5 vols. maps. bibliog.

Part I/1 describes the geology and physical geography, part I/2 the living world, part II/1 history from the first settlements up to 1781, part II/2 history from 1781 to the present, and part III the material and spiritual culture of the Czechs and Slovaks. The whole work is a compendium of information on the separate fields, although it is not organized encyclopaedically, the internal subdivisions within each volume being by thematic areas rather than an alphabetic system of entry words. Clearly much of the information will also be available in some of the English-language publications quoted elsewhere in this bibliography, but part III may be the only source for many aspects of the life of the people. Separate treatment is given here to such items as folklore, crafts, food, family life, dwellings, superstitions and art-forms, and the Czech and Slovak nations are reviewed individually.

936 **Encyklopédia Slovenska.** (Encyclopaedia of Slovakia.)
Edited by Vladimír Hajko (et al.). Bratislava: Veda 1977-82. 6 vols.

This beautifully produced and illustrated encyclopaedia is a complete compendium on the country, its economy, natural environment, social, political and cultural evolution and nationalities. Interpretations of events or the lives of individuals in recent times are firmly in line with current Party opinion, which, along with the emphasis on the Slovaks' 'revolutionary traditions', the 'revolutionary labour movement', and the progress of the building of socialism in Slovakia, makes it a politically one-sided work. Unlike the *Encyclopaedia Britannica* or the *Great Soviet Encyclopedia*, however, it is a purely national work: there are no entries which do not bear some relevance to Slovakia and the Slovaks. Thus the Czechs come into it as sharers in common statehood with the Slovaks, and the other socialist states on account of far-reaching contacts, long-term cooperation and so forth. For a long time to come this will be *the* source of much information which cannot be readily found elsewhere.

937   **Vlastivedný slovník obcí na Slovensku.** (National historical and topographical dictionary of communities in Slovakia.)
Compiled by the Encyclopaedic Institute of the Slovak Academy of Sciences under the general editorship of Miroslav Kropilák.   Bratislava: Veda, 1977-78. 3 vols. maps. bibliog.

This major publication, with over 500 pages per volume, lists all Slovakia's towns and villages in alphabetical order. Each entry carries a wealth of local information: first recorded mention; other names a particular place has had at different times; population figures at eleven dates between 1869 and 1970; the history and character of the place; dominant architecture with special reference to individual architectural treasures and curios; major trades and industries, past and present; and any important historical events in which a particular place has been involved. The latter tends, inevitably, to be very strong on strikes and other actions in the life of the local working class. The work is more of a reference book than a tourist handbook, but for the outsider with a knowledge of Slovak it can be an invaluable source concerning even the smallest places, many of them well off any of the beaten tourist tracks.

938   **Ukraine: a concise encyclopaedia.**
Prepared by the Shevchenko Scientific Society, edited by Volodymyr Kubijovyč, foreword by Ernest J. Simmons.   Toronto: University of Toronto Press, for The Ukrainian National Association, 1963. 2 vols. bibliog.

It should not be forgotten that until the last war Czechoslovakia's easternmost province was Subcarpathian Ruthenia, which is now part of the Soviet Union. This encyclopaedia deals with the whole of the Ukraine, but many of its sections deal separately with Subcarpathian Ruthenia in several sub-sections. Each section is followed by a bibliography, but most of the references will require a knowledge of Ukrainian, Russian, Polish or Czech.

939   **The Fontana biographical companion to modern thought.**
Edited by Alan Bullock and R. B. Woodings.   London: Collins, 1983. 867p. (Fontana Paperbacks).

Although only a small number of entries in this volume have a direct Czech or Slovak relevance, it has been included here because of the paucity of material available in English on certain areas of Czech/Slovak literature and learning. Each entry contains a brief biography and an outline of the salient ideas and unique contribution of the quoted individual. The Czechs and Slovaks listed are: Karel Čapek, Jaroslav Hašek, Václav Havel, Bohumil Hrabal, Vítězslav Nezval, Vladimír Páral, Ivan Klíma, Emanuel Rádl, Otakar Březina, Edvard Beneš, T. G. Masaryk, Josef Svoboda, Leoš Janáček, Ladislav Novomeský and Alfonz Bednár.

940 **Biographisches Lexikon zur Geschichte der Böhmischen Länder.**
(Biographical lexicon for the history of the Czech Lands.)
Heribert Sturm, on behalf of the Collegium Carolinum.   Munich,
GFR: Oldenbourg Verlag, 1974-. bibliog.

This very broadly based biographical master-work is appearing in fascicles to be
re-issued in bound form as each volume is completed. Volume 1 (A-H, 715p.)
appeared in this form in 1979. This work will be an invaluable reference aid to
many branches of history, with its detailed entries on cultural, political and
industrial figures from the earliest times. In addition to the biographical notes
proper each entry is accompanied by its own bibliographical data and cross-
references to the work's central bibliography, itself a major reference source.

Archives and
Libraries

941   **A report on the library scene in Czechoslovakia, with particular
reference to interlending.**
E. S. Smith.   *Interlending Review*, vol. 8, no. 2 (1980), p. 64-65.
A brief outline of the hierarchical organization and ultimate superior authority of
the libraries under the different Czech and Slovak systems. The statutory
obligations of libraries, including the interlending service and operation of the
system, are described, as is the range of union catalogues (no national one exists).
The current state of photocopying services is rightly found to be poor, but there is
news of proposals to remedy this by increased resort to microfiches, especially for
journals. Some statistics are included.

942   **Libraries and librarianship in the Czechoslovak Socialist Republic.**
Vincent Kútik, Mirko Velinský.   *IFLA Journal*, vol. 4,
no. 2 (1978), p. 90-102.
A moderately detailed account of the history and practice of library services,
librarianship training and the legal provisions connected with libraries from
qualified sources, the authors being, respectively, Director of the Bratislava
University Library and Head of the Services Division of the Czech State Library
in Prague. The article includes the dates of foundation for many of the major
institutions and statistics on, for example, the number and types of libraries, sizes
of collections, and the number of borrowers. Reference is made *passim* to such
discrepancies as there are between the Czech and Slovak republics.

943   **The regional planning of library activity in Slovakia.**
Vlasta Kalinová.   Bratislava: Central Economics Library, 1969.
10p.
The existence of this pamphlet, which has the double disadvantage of having
become partially outdated and being inaccessible outside specialist libraries, is

306

ndicative of the fact, referred to elsewhere, that Slovakia does have certain
ibrary practices distinct from those of the Czech Lands. Another pamphlet from
he same source is Ján Irmler's *Problems of country libraries* (1969, 24p.).

944 Libraries in the Czechoslovak Republic.
Publishing Committee of the Commission for Organizing the 44th
International Federation of Library Associations (IFLA)
Council. Martin, Czechoslovakia: Matica slovenská, 1978. 49p.
bibliog.

Despite the appalling translation, this booklet, a free handout at the 44th IFLA
conference, but presumably available at major libraries abroad, does provide an
overview of library services, the number of libraries, staffing rates and staff
training, acquisition rates and so forth. The historical preamble outlines the
development of printing, publishing and library services, since the time of the
missionary brothers Cyril and Methodius in the 9th century. Basic statistical data
and a thumbnail sketch are given for the twelve most important libraries, and the
bibliography covers the regular and less regular serials published in Czechoslovakia
on librarianship, bibliography and information science.

945 Státní vědecká knihovna. (The State Scientific Library.)
Edited by Olga Jiránová, Jaromír Kubíček. Brno,
Czechoslovakia: Blok, 1983. 298p. bibliog.

In the absence of much information on libraries in Czechoslovakia in English, this
anniversary publication must act as a partial substitute. With a history going back
to 1808 and much growth by merger and amalgamation with other libraries, in
recent times, this library in Brno is one of the country's most important. This
history of the institution, its premises, collections (many illustrations of important
holdings) and librarians (with biographical vignettes), has chapter summaries in
English, and translations in English of the librarians' biobibliographies.

946 Centenary of the Matica slovenská.
Paul L. Horecký. *Quarterly Journal of the Library of Congress*,
vol. 21, no. 3 (July 1964), p. 203-06.

The Matica slovenská is the Slovaks' national cultural foundation whose mission
has changed during the century of its existence. Today it is a major national
literary archive, bibliographical centre, publishing house and one of the
coordinators of contacts with the huge numbers of Slovak expatriates. This brief
account of its history is one of the few references in English to this important
institution.

947 Archivy ČSR. (Archives of the Czech Socialist Republic.)
Compiled by Gabriela Čechová, Jana Pražáková, introduction by
Gabriela Čechová. Prague: Naše vojsko on behalf of Archivní
správa MV ČSR, 1974. 211p.

A brief quadrilingual (Czech, Russian, German and French) history of archives in
Bohemia and Moravia from the 14th century to the present, including the recent
waves of reorganization. It also provides a list of standardized abbreviations for

Archives and Libraries

the various contemporary state archives and photographic reproductions o
documents of various types and antiquity (oldest 1057); this, with the Russian
German and French keys takes up three quarters of the book.

Bibliografie českého knihovnictví, bibliografie a VTI 1981.
See item no. 985.

Bibliographies

948 **ABSEES: Abstracts Soviet and East European Series** (Soviet and
East European abstracts).
Oxford: Oxford Microform Publications. 1970-. 3 times per year.
A useful reference work for recent scholarly articles on East Europe generally,
but with a steady coverage of Czechoslovakia. Prior to 1977 coverage was
particularly useful in the fields of history and politics but since 1977 only economic
articles have been covered. Between 1970 and 1977 the publication was available
in hard copy only but since 1977 it has been published in both hard copy and
microfiche.

949 **European bibliography of Soviet, East European and Slavonic
studies.**
Edited by M. Armand, M. Aymard, Cl.-L. Charbonnier.   Paris:
Institut d'Etudes Slaves, 1980-. annual.
One of the largest general bibliographies, not to be overlooked despite the
preponderance of titles in German. It has sections on religion, geography, history,
economics, law, politics, nationalities and minorities, external relations, social
conditions, culture and the arts, and linguistics. Volume 6 (1985) contained 372p.

950 **Öststatsforskning i Sverige, 1950-1983: forskningsöversikt och
bibliografi.** (Swedish research on Eastern Europe, 1950-83: a
review of research and bibliography.)
Claes Arvidsson.   Stockholm: Riksbankens Jubileumsfond, 1984.
100p.
This work is included here for its bibliography which is classified by subject and
country, since much Swedish scholarly output is published in English. There are
sections on Eastern Europe in general (p. 29-42) and on Czechoslovakia (p. 89-
92).

Bibliographies

951 **Bibliografický katalog. České knihy.** (Bibliographical catalogue:
Czech books.)
Prague: Státní knihovna, 1922-. monthly.

The classified register of supposedly all Czech books published. It has gaps,
however, owing to the number of short-run printings which should be submitted
statutorily, but which the producers are sometimes loth to part with, needing
every copy for their own purposes. The classification is that used in Soviet
practice. An annual index is also produced. The same publisher, the National
Library, has produced, since 1954, another series, *Články v českých časopisech*
(Articles in Czech periodicals), similarly classified, indexed in each issue and
containing a list of periodicals processed. These include the national newspapers,
which have no index of their own.

952 **East European and Soviet economic affairs: a bibliography (1965-
1973).**
Alexander S. Birkos, Lewis A. Tambs.   Littleton, Colorado:
Libraries Unlimited, 1975. 170p.

Czechoslovakian entries are on p. 33-40 and include references from the country
itself as well as from outside. Many items refer to the 1968 period. All titles are in
English and classification is by standard sub-division of the field.

953 **The Habsburg monarchy 1804-1918: books and pamphlets
published in the United Kingdom between 1818 and 1967, a critical
bibliography.**
Francis Roy Bridge.   London: School of Slavonic and East
European Studies, University of London, 1967. 82p.

This is a valuable source book, accepting the limitations of date, which is divided
into a general section, one on diplomacy and military matters, and one for
biographies and memoirs.

954 **European immigration and ethnicity in the United States and
Canada: a historical bibliography.**
Edited by David L. Brye.   Oxford; Santa Barbara, California:
ABC-Clio, 1983. 458p. (Clio Bibliography Series, no. 7).

A wide-ranging annotated bibliography of articles from countless periodicals, well
indexed for ready access to materials on the Czech and Slovak (and Ruthenian)
immigrants in North America.

955 **Bohemian (Čech) bibliography: a finding list of writings in English
relating to Bohemia and the Čechs.**
Thomas Čapek, Anna Vostrovský Čapek.   New York, Chicago,
London, Edinburgh: Fleming H. Revell, 1918. 256p.

A worthy and fascinating predecessor to the present volume, although conceived
on slightly different lines. The entries mostly relate to partly forgotten 19th-
century materials and are not annotated, but this is, to some extent, compensated

by the sectional annotations contained in the introduction. Although inevitably outdated in many respects, some of the sections still provide an illuminating guide to early English work on, for example, Comenius or Hus. The particular curiosity of the work is its section 34 entitled 'Bohemia in British State Papers' with its earliest entry dated 1302 and going up to 1639.

956 **Newspapers of East Central and Southeastern Europe.**
Edited by Robert G. Carlton. Washington, DC: Library of Congress, Slavic and Central European Division, Reference Department, 1965. 204p.

This listing of all the Library of Congress holdings is not just a useful guide to the collection as such, but a valuable source of titles especially of some of the more minor regional and local papers, some of them defunct. Czechoslovak holdings are on p. 35-69. A bibliography of relevant bibliographies is included.

957 **A subject bibliography of the Second World War: books in English 1939-1974.**
A. G. S. Enser. Boulder, Colorado: Westview Press, 1977. 592p.

Three sections have a relevance to the present bibliography: 'Czechoslovakia' (p. 122-23); 'Heydrich', the assassinated Reichsprotektor of Bohemia and Moravia (p. 198); and 'Lidice', the most famous of the Czech villages obliterated by the Germans in response to Heydrich's assassination in 1942 (p. 247).

958 **Legal sources and bibliography of Czechoslovakia.**
Edited by Vladimír Gsovski. New York: Praeger, for the Free Europe Committee, 1959. 180p.

A useful, if dated, reference work which includes a list of all the legislative acts for the period 1945-57.

959 **Czechoslovakia 1968-1969: chronology, bibliography, annotation.**
Zdeněk Hejzlar, Vladimír V. Kusin. New York, London: Garland, 1975. 316p.

Although the events of 1968-69 in Czechoslovakia continue to invite considerable attention from political and social historians, the greatest output was obviously in the years immediately following. This extensive bibliography is usefully divided into several sections, starting with a 'where-to-find-them guide' to English translations of the main documents. This is followed by a bibliography of speeches and works by Alexander Dubček during the period, a selected list of newspapers and periodicals published in Czechoslovakia during these two years, many since defunct, and a selected bibliography of Czech and Slovak articles from, and relevant to, the period. The book is framed by a month-by-month chronicle of events at the beginning, and a bibliography of books published world-wide in various languages, including some from Czechoslovakia itself selected as symptomatic. The brief introduction gives the compilers' interpretation of events preceding, during, and since this critical period of Czechoslovakia's recent past.

Bibliographies

960 **Russia, the USSR and Eastern Europe 1975-1980.**
Stephan M. Horak.   Littleton, Colorado: Libraries Unlimited,
1982. 278p.

A bibliography of limited scope which lists some of the major book publications
on the area in the period in question. The section on Czechoslovakia (p. 210-12)
is brief enough to make recourse to the otherwise useful index almost
unnecessary.

961 **East Central Europe: a guide to basic publications.**
Edited by Paul L. Horecký.   Chicago, London: University of
Chicago Press, 1969. 956p.

This extremely useful annotated bibliography contains a mass of titles in both the
extensive general section (p. 3-134) and the special Czechoslovak section (p. 137-
358). It includes items on all topics, in many languages and from various origins,
East and West.

962 **Czechs and Slovaks in North America: a bibliography.**
Esther Jerabek.   New York: Czechoslovak Society of Arts and
Sciences in America; Chicago: Czechoslovak National Council of
America, 1976. 448p.

The very complete list of 7,609 entries is ordered by subject, from 'agriculture' to
'travel', while such exclusions as might be detected are defended in the
introduction. Any item listed in one section which could be equally expected in
another can be readily traced through the comprehensive index. The book is an
invaluable research tool for anyone interested in any aspect of the history of
immigration and the present distribution, artistic and scientific endeavour, or the
daily life of Czechs and Slovaks in America. Relevant periodicals are also listed.

963 **Soviet and East European foreign policy: a bibliography of English
and Russian language publications, 1967-1971.**
Roger E. Kanet.   Santa Barbara, California; Oxford: ABC-Clio,
1974. 208p.

A number of the books and articles cited here deal specifically, or generally, with
Czechoslovakia's foreign policy.

964 **American bibliography of Slavic and East European Studies for
1981.**
Compiled and edited by Zenon E. Kohut.   Stanford, California:
American Association for the Advancement of Slavic Studies,
1984. 214p.

This all-discipline annual bibliography has appeared since 1956, with some
changes of scope and publisher, and almost inevitably it is somewhat in arrears. It
records all US and Canadian publications, including works on the immigrant
communities, and is ordered by topic, sub-ordered by country. Czechoslovakia is
always well represented.

965 **Czech and Slovak literature in English: a bibliography.**
George J. Kovtun. Washington, DC: Library of Congress,
European Division, 1984. 132p.

From this copious bibliography, despite its sporadic inaccuracies and omissions, it
is plain that there is already a respectable corpus of Czech and Slovak literature
available in English. Many of the titles emanate from Czechoslovakia and are, *eo
ipso*, not easy to come by, and many are the inevitable product of the large Czech
and Slovak minorities in North America; such works are also less easy to obtain
outside the United States except in specialist libraries. Nevertheless, especially for
Slovak literature in translation, this will be the only source. The book runs to 220
separate entries, divided into literary anthologies, folklore anthologies and works
of history and criticism. Two further sections give additional titles, author by
author and separately for Czech and Slovak, with cross-references to the first
three sections where relevant. A total of 214 Czech and ninety-three Slovak
authors are represented, with such as Kollár and Šafařík appearing in both the
Czech and Slovak listings.

966 **Tomáš G. Masaryk, 1850-1937: a selective list of reading materials
in English.**
George J. Kovtun. Washington, DC: Library of Congress,
European Division, 1981. 26p.

A tripartite bibliography containing: 1, English translations of Masaryk's writings,
many of which have gone into reprints in the 1970s; 2, books and articles about
Masaryk in English; and 3, articles in the American press about Masaryk during
his stay in the United States in 1918. Masaryk has been written about as a
sociologist, philosopher, diplomat and above all as a politician, and this
bibliography covers just over 200 quite varied titles.

967 **Slovak bibliography abroad, 1945-1965.**
Michael Lacko. Cleveland, Ohio: Slovak Institute, 1967. 336p.
(Slovak Studies, no. 7).

This volume should be consulted in conjunction with Lacko's *Slovak bibliography
abroad, 1966-1975* (Cleveland, Ohio: Slovak Institute, 1977. 436p. – Slovak
Studies, no. 17). Taken together they provide a near-complete bibliography of
articles, books and periodicals in Slovak, or in English, by or about the Slovaks,
published by the various émigré bodies. Classification is by country of publication.

968 **A bibliography of Slavic dictionaries.**
Compiled by R. C. Lewański. Bologna, Italy: Editrice
Compositori, 1973. 2nd rev. enl. ed. 4 vols. (World Bibliography of
Dictionaries).

The work encompasses, language by language, all Slavonic dictionaries, wherever
published, classifying them as monolingual, bilingual, technical or special
purpose. It is excellently indexed for ready orientation.

Bibliographies

969 **A comprehensive bibliography for the study of ethnic minorities.**
Wayne Charles Miller, Faye Neil Vowell (et al.). New York:
New York University Press. 2 vols. 1976.

Published in 1976 this bibliography supersedes all earlier ones both in lay-out and comprehensiveness. The works listed are in English and deal with minorities in America. The relevant sections on the Czechs and Slovaks are on p. 631-36 and 637-44, respectively, with some more general works available in the 'American Slavs' section (p. 603-30). Sections are preceded by historical bibliographical essays to pinpoint some of the more significant works, and these have been published separately as *A handbook of American minorities* by the same author and publisher (1976, 225p.).

970 **25 Jahre Collegium Carolinum München 1956-1981.** (Twenty-five years of the Collegium Carolinum, Munich, 1956-81.)
Compiled and edited by Michael Neumüller. Munich: Collegium Carolinum, 1982. 109p. bibliog.

The Collegium Carolinum is a research institute solely concerned with the study of the Czech Lands. It has been praised for avoiding the nationalist ideologizing which besets so much work by, and about, Sudeten Germans, though these are by no means the only contributors to the Collegium's publications. The volume contains an account of the institute's beginnings, its publishing activities and financing, and a selection of extracts from reviews of its publications. More importantly, it contains a complete list of all the institute's publications, in periodicals, in series or out of series, which is complete in the sense that details of all the papers in the annual *Bohemia* and in collections of papers are provided in full. Topics covered are mostly historical and/or political, with much emphasis on the German dimension. There is also a ten-volume topographical lexicon, *Ortslexikon der Böhmischen Länder 1910-1965*, two series dealing with historical biography, a series on Sudeten German cultural history and others. Most titles are in German, with occasional articles in English in some of the collections of papers.

971 **Katalog des Schrifttums über die Tschechoslowakei.** (Catalogue of literature on Czechoslovakia.)
Niedersächsische Landesbibliothek. Hannover, GFR:
Niedersächsische Landesbibliothek, 1977-78. 2 vols.

This is a major source of bibliographical references on the towns and regions of Czechoslovakia (volume 1) and on individual persons or families (volume 2), although the contents are limited to the holdings of the Lower Saxony State Library. All place-names are listed in their German versions, but there is a Czech/Slovak concordance appended to volume 2. For obvious reasons there is a disproportionately large coverage of the Sudetenland but a vast amount of other references are also included, some of considerable antiquity.

972   **The 1968 Czechoslovak crisis: a bibliography 1968-1970.**
Michael Parrish.   Santa Barbara, California: ABC-Clio, 1971.
41p. (Bibliographical and Reference Series, no. 12).
Many analyses of the crisis have been published since this bibliography appeared,
but its own particular value is that it includes many of the books, pamphlets,
documents and articles published at the time, including what might be described
as 'immediate response' press items from both East and West. There is also a list
of European newspapers which carried articles on the events, but the manner of
its compilation is not entirely plain, since, for example, neither the *Guardian* nor
the *Morning Star* are mentioned. The latter omission is the more surprising in that
as an organ of the Communist Party of Great Britain it is the one newspaper
customarily available from Britain on Prague news-stands, yet its coverage of
events in Czechoslovakia during the crisis led to its not infrequent non-
distribution.

973   **Price list of Czech newspapers and journals from the Czechoslovak
Socialist Republic.**
Prague: [no publisher]; Wellingborough, England: Collet's
Holdings. annual.
This is a nearly full list of periodical publications of all types, languages and
periodicity in two sections, general and academic. A similar list for Slovak
periodicals marketed through Slovart is also available. Unfortunately, neither
provide translations for the Czech or Slovak titles, but there is hardly a subject
not covered, from alcoholism to pigeon-fancying. A less complete listing, but with
more information on individual titles is included in the annual *Europa Yearbook*
(London: Europa Publications, 1926-. annual) so widely available in public and
other libraries as to make separate listing of many newspaper and periodical titles
a luxury.

974   **Czechoslovakia and its arts and sciences: a selective bibliography in
the Western European languages.**
Miloslav Rechcígl, Jr.   In: *The Czechoslovak contribution to world
culture*. Edited by Miloslav Rechcígl, Jr. The Hague, London,
Paris: Mouton, 1964, p. 555-634.
A classified but annotated bibliography of some 1,318 entries, mostly 20th-
century, but with some from the 19th century. The range of contents is explicit
from the title and the period best represented is the First Republic, although
there are many entries also relevant to both earlier and more recent times.

975   **The international relations of Eastern Europe.**
Edited by Robin Alison Remington.   Detroit: Gale, 1979. 273p.
The first section of this annotated bibliography covers titles concerning the area as
a whole, and the second section provides a country-by-country treatment, with
separate attention being paid to Czechoslovakia (p. 111-31), including many titles
on the events of 1968 and the aftermath.

976 **Foreign affairs bibliography: a selected and annotated list of books on international relations 1952-1962.**
Edited by H. L. Roberts. New York: Bowker, 1964. 752p.
Czechoslovakia's foreign contacts are the subject of a number of important publications (p. 478-83).

977 **Aktuelle Bibliographie deutsch-, englisch- und französischsprachiger Arbeiten zur Geographie Osteuropas.**
(Topical bibliography of German-, English- and French-language works on the geography of Eastern Europe.) Edited by (vol. 1)
P. Rostankowski, B. Degenhardt, C. C. Liebman; (vol. 2)
P. Rostankowski, S. Luber, D. Krüger. West Berlin: Osteuropa-Institut an der Freien Universität, 1978, 1982. 2 vols.
(Bibliographische Mitteilungen der Osteuropa-Institut an der Freien Universität).
One of the most valuable source-works for the study of all aspects of East-European geography, it is classified by country and sub-classified by discipline, and includes some English titles from less familiar sources.

978 **East European peasantries: social relations; an annotated bibliography of periodical articles.**
Compiled by Irwin T. Saunders, Roger Whitaker, Walter C.
Bisselle. Boston, Massachusetts: G. K. Hall, 1976. 179p.
The section on Czechoslovakia (p. 17-25) is valuable since it contains abstracts in English of many articles in Czech and Slovak periodicals that would otherwise be practically inaccessible.

979 **Bibliografie literatury vydané českými a slovenskými autory v zahraničí 1948-1972 (s dodatkem do srpna 1978).** (Bibliography of works by Czech and Slovak authors published abroad 1948-1972; with an appendix to August 1978).
Ludmila Šeflová. Cologne, GFR: Index; Paris: Svědectví, 1978.
371p.
The three waves of emigration from Czechoslovakia, in 1938-39, 1945-48 and the years since 1968 have included writers and scholars in many fields and this bibliography seeks to give recognition to the size of the Czech and Slovak contribution to arts, letters and learning outside Czechoslovakia. It contains 2,618 entries and an introduction, in Czech, German and English, which explains the limitations and exclusions (for example articles are not included). For a supplementary bibliography by the same authoress see *Svědectví*, vol. 17, no. 68 (1983), p. 821-27.

980　Periodicals on the socialist countries and on Marxism: a new annotated index of English-language publications.
Harry G. Shaffer. New York, Washington, DC, London: Praeger, 1977. 135p.
This work contains a separate section on Czechoslovakia, covering periodicals published inside and outside the country. It is a useful source of linguistically accessible background reading.

981　**Slavonic and East European accessions.**
Oxford: Bodleian Library. 1967-81. quarterly.
Lists, with full bibliographical data, all new accessions, including those relating to Czechoslovakia, acquired by the Bodleian Library. Unfortunately it ceased publication in 1981.

982　**Slovenská národná bibliografia. Knihy.** (Slovak national bibliography. Books.)
Martin, Czechoslovakia: Matica slovenská. 1922-. monthly.
This is the Slovak counterpart of item no. 951, and it also has a companion series, *Články* (Articles), published by Matica slovenská, the national cultural foundation, since 1954.

983　**Grammars and dictionaries of the Slavic languages from the Middle Ages up to 1850: an annotated bibliography.**
Edward Stankiewicz. Berlin, New York, Amsterdam: Mouton, 1984. 190p.
A vital tool for the study of the early language works on Czech and Slovak, with few minor oversights; the material is arranged century by century. Czech grammars go back to Hus's *De Orthographia Bohemica* of around 1410, to which Czech (and other languages with similar diacritics) largely owes its modern conventions of spelling. Czech dictionaries go back to Master Claretus's *Bohemarius Major, Glossarius* and *Vokabulář grammatický*, three Latin-Czech dictionaries in verse, which sought to equip Czech with equivalents to the Latin terminology of the day; some of their neologisms have survived to the present. The Slovak grammars go back to Masník's *Zpráva písma slovenského* . . . of 1696, which still represents a Slovak local mutation of Czech, and the dictionaries go back to the Trnava Latin-Hungarian-Slovak dictionary of 1648 by Emanuel Alvarez. The Czech sections are on p. 3-24 and the Slovak on p. 25-28.

984　**Bibliografie českého knihovnictví, bibliografie a VTI: ČSR 1977 s doplňky 1975-76.** (Bibliography of Czech library science, bibliography and documentation: Czech Socialist Republic 1977 with addenda for 1975-76.)
Compiled by J. Straka. Prague: Státní knihovna, 1982. 447p.
The major complete Czech bibliography for the areas concerned, containing, in this issue, the impressive total of 4,258 entries.

Bibliographies

985 **Bibliografie českého knihovnictví, bibliografie a VTI 1981.**
(Bibliography of Czech library science, bibliography and
information science 1981.)
Compiled by O. Bezděková. Prague: Státní knihovna, 1984.
400p.

Published three years in arrears, this is the latest volume of the serial which
contains amongst other things a bibliography of bibliographies, from all
disciplines. It is also a useful source of information about Czech libraries. This
issue contains a total of 3,001 titles.

986 **Czechoslovakia: a bibliographic guide.**
Rudolf Sturm. Washington, DC: Library of Congress, 1967.
157p.

Although now dated, this guide still provides in its running text information on a
number of important items which, even if no longer in print, are still worth
consulting in libraries.

987 **Subject and name index to articles on the Slavonic and East
European languages and literatures, music and theatre, libraries
and the press contained in English-language journals, 1920-1975.**
Garth M. Terry. Nottingham, England: Nottingham University
Library, 1976. 198p.

Garth Terry is also the author of two related works: *East European languages and*
literatures: a subject and name index to articles in English-language journals, 1900-
1977 (Oxford; Santa Barbara, California: Clio Press, 1978. 275p.) and *East*
European languages and literatures II: a subject and name index to articles in
Festschriften, conference proceedings and collected papers in the English language,
1900-1981, and including articles in journals, 1978-1981 (Nottingham, England:
Astra Press, 1982. 214p.). Together all three bibliographical works represent a
near-comprehensive source for background and more specialist reading in the
areas stated and from the sources indicated, including corresponding sections on
Czechoslovakia. They do not include items from English-language journals in
Eastern Europe itself, nor do they contain articles in English in multilingual
periodicals.

988 **Books on communism and the communist countries: a selected
bibliography.**
Edited by P. H. Vigor. London: Ampersand, 1971. 3rd ed. 448p.

A useful annotated bibliography which covers Czechoslovakia (p. 279-85) and
contains entries for some earlier relevant titles which have not been included in
the present bibliography.

318

989 **Official publications of the Soviet Union and Eastern Europe 1945-1980; a select annotated bibliography.**
Edited by Gregory Walker. London: Mansell Publishing, 1982. Distributed in the United States and Canada by H. W. Wilson, New York, 620p.

Czechoslovak official documents of various kinds – legal, economic and statistical – along with diagrams of the structure of the government and its agencies, is covered in this work (p. 43-64).

990 **The year's work in modern language studies, vol. 45, 1983.**
Edited by Glanville Price, David A. Wells. London: Modern Humanities Research Association, 1984. 1,168p.

This is the standard British annual annotated bibliography of new work in most of the European languages. Czech and Slovak are represented traditionally by two sections each, language and literature separately, and editorship and authorship of the relevant sections may change from time to time.

991 **The Hussite movement and the Reformation in Bohemia, Moravia and Slovakia (1350-1650): a bibliographical study guide (with particular reference to resources in North America).**
Jarold K. Zeman. Ann Arbor, Michigan: Michigan Slavic Publications, 1977. 390p.

The 3,867 titles gathered here are divided into three main sections: part 1 (1-1,531) the development of the reform movement; part 2 (1,532-2,194) biography; and part 3 (2,195-3,853) topics, for example, alchemy and Jews. The small remainder are addenda. The book is partly in response to the recent revival of interest in the study of Hussitism. Of the total number of entries no less than 565 are in English. The work is well-indexed and contains a detailed explanation of the editorial conventions applied. Things to note are the non-listing of relevant editions of the Bible, the deliberately limited number of entries on Comenius and Hus himself, which can be traced in other sources, and the indications given in part 1 of where in North American libraries the particular items are to be found. This does not limit the work's usefulness in Europe since many of the listed items can be found elsewhere, indeed not everything mentioned is accorded a North American location.

Document
Collections

992   **Documentary history of Eastern Europe.**
      Alfred Bannan, Achilles Edelenyi.   New York: Twayne, 1970.
      392p.

Though it covers the whole of Eastern Europe this interesting collection of
documents intended as source materials does contain a number of items relevant
to Czechoslovak history over the last 1,000 years. The documents include
chronicles, codes of law, constitutions, treaties and travelogues.

993   **Czechoslovakia.**
      Nendeln, Liechtenstein: Kraus Reprint, 1973. maps. (Seeds of
      Conflict Series: Irredentist and National Questions in Central
      Europe, 1913-39).

This volume contains reprints of seventeen important documents (books and
pamphlets) in German, French or English pertinent to the theme of the series of
which it is a part. It begins with an Austrian publication questioning
Czechoslovakia's need to include non-Czecho-Slovak areas for its economic well-
being (1919) and ends with a Slovak document in French pointing to the menace
of a Soviet presence in Slovakia (1936). The vast majority of documents are
ultimately connected with the minorities problem. Each reprinted item retains its
own pagination, which perhaps explains the somewhat arbitrary ordering, which
does not match that of the contents page. The materials selected for reprinting
reflect an anti-Czech and anti-Soviet bias from various quarters or lines of
Czechoslovak thinking which equally highlight the dangers of conflict. The
compilation is entirely anonymous.

994 **The letters of John Hus.**
Translated from Latin and Czech by Matthew Spinka.
Manchester, England: Manchester University Press, 1972. 233p.
bibliog.
Contains the texts of 101 letters to various addressees inside and outside
Bohemia, some more intimate than others, providing an insight into Hus's
character which does not emerge in his theoretical writings.

995 **Documents on the expulsion of the Sudeten Germans.**
Compiled and introduced by Wilhelm K. Turnwald, foreword to
the English edition by F. A. Voigt, translated by Gerda
Johannsen. Munich: Association for the Protection of Sudeten
German Interests, 1953. 308p.
There is no doubt that the Czechs reacted with some violence towards the
Sudeten Germans at the end of the Second World War, but the tone of injured
innocence behind these documents and the commentary is hardly properly
adopted by the nation which had just lost that war and whose own atrocities were
practically unheard of in modern history. The volume contains, in addition to
'eye-witness' accounts of Czech excesses, texts of various memoranda and
Czechoslovak post-war legislation as it affected the German minority. It is
included here primarily for the latter documentary material.

996 **Germany and Czechoslovakia, 1918-1945: documents on German
policies.**
Compiled, with an introduction and notes, by Koloman Gajan,
Robert Kvaček. Prague: Orbis, 1965. 173p.
A collection of sixty-six archival documents, many previously unpublished, which
seeks to show the inevitability of German hostility to Czechoslovakia and
Germany's eventual occupation of the country in 1939 once French and British
indifference and appeasement created the conditions. The introduction (p. 9-41)
is a left-wing slanted political history of Germany up to 1945, including the
creation of the puppet Slovak State and the Protectorate of Bohemia and
Moravia.

997 **Eastern Europe since Stalin.**
Compiled and edited by Jonathan Steele. Newton Abbot,
England; London; Vancouver, Canada: David & Charles, 1974.
215p. bibliog. (David & Charles Sources for Contemporary Issues
Series).
This is a miscellaneous collection of documents and informal writings in English
translation intended to reflect 'from the horse's mouth' some of the trends in
recent Eastern European society, especially those which represent reform, or a
distancing from the Soviet Union. A total of ten of the fifty-four documents relate
to Czechoslovakia from the thaw to the Soviet intervention in 1968.

Document Collections

998 **Winter in Prague: documents on Czechoslovak communism in crisis.**

Edited by Robin Alison Remington, translated by Michael Berman, introduction by William E. Griffith. Cambridge, Massachusetts; London: MIT Press, 1969. 473p. bibliog.

Another important collection of seventy-two documents relating to the events before and during the 'Prague Spring' of 1968 and its immediate aftermath (the latest being excerpts from Husák's 17 April 1969 speech to the Party plenum in which he summarizes what he takes to be recent errors and sets out the targets of consolidation). Most of the documents are preceded by a useful background note to the conditions at the time when they originated. The introduction pinpoints the five core factors underlying the whole chain of events.

999 **Voices of Czechoslovak socialists.**

Edited by Tamara Deutscher (et al.). [London]: Merlin Press, for the Committee to Defend Czechoslovak Socialists, 1977. 134p.

A collection of documents by, and about, a disparate array of figures who were active in 1968, were deprived of their positions, authority and the right to publish in the years that followed, and who are now part of the unofficial 'socialist opposition'. They include both the respected playwright Václav Havel (famous for his open letter to Dr. Husák) and the pop-group known as the Plastic People of the Universe, as well as academics, politicians and student activists. The accompanying notes seek to explain to the English labour movement, the intended readership, the nature of the opposition these varied figures represent and the features of the Czech system of government to which they are opposed. Among the documents are texts of five of the offending songs by the Plastic People.

1000 **Communist affairs: documents and analysis.**

Sevenoaks, England; Woburn, Massachusetts; North Ryde, New South Wales; Wellington; Durban, South Africa: Butterworths, 1982-. quarterly.

A new venture which seeks to plug the gap caused by the inaccessibility of source documents on communist régimes and movements world-wide. A separate section is devoted to the Soviet Union and Eastern Europe, with occasional items from Czechoslovakia. The kinds of documents incorporated, in English translation, are protocols, official reports, diplomatic notes, open letters and editorials.

Index

The index is a single alphabetical sequence of authors (personal and corporate), titles of publications and subjects. Index entries refer both to the main items and to other works mentioned in the notes to each item. Title entries are in italics. Numeration refers to the items as numbered.

329

331

340

341

Dvořák *contd.*
American dimension to his career
818
biographies 815-816, 818-819
English dimension to his career 818
letters & memoirs 818
orchestral works 817
symphonies & concertos 821
Worcester Festival, Massachusetts
820
Dvořák, his life and music 819
Dvořák, I. 326, 470
Dvořák, Max 673
Dvořák symphonies and concertos 821
Dvořáková, V. 779
Dvornik, F. 123
Dwyer, J. D. 927
Dyje Dam and reservoir 595
Dyje, River 595

E

E12 route through Czechoslovakia 72
Eagle, H. J. 699
*Eagle and the small birds. Crisis in the
Soviet Empire: from Yalta to
Solidarity* 459
*East Central and Southeast Europe: a
handbook of library and archival
resources in North America* 923
*East Central Europe between the two
World Wars* 171
*East Central Europe: a guide to basic
publications* 961
*East-Central Europe in transition from
the fourteenth to the seventeenth
century* 125
East Central Europe since 1939 126
*East Central Europe: yesterday – today
– tomorrow* 407
*East European and Soviet data
handbook: political, social and
developmental indicators,
1945-1975* 388
*East European and Soviet economic
affairs: a bibliography (1965-1973)*
952
East European economic handbook 498
East European Economies in the 1970s
497
East European energy and East–West

trade in energy 542
East European government and politics
475
*East European languages and
literatures: a subject and name
index to articles in
English-language journals,
1900-1977* 987
*East European languages and
literatures II: a subject and name
index to articles in Festschriften,
conference proceedings and
collected papers in the English
language, 1900-1981, and
including articles in journals,
1978-1981* 987
*East European peasantries: social
relations; an annotated
bibliography of periodical articles*
978
East European poets 715
*East European predicament: changing
patterns in Poland,
Czechoslovakia and Romania* 412
East European Quarterly 909
East European revolution 200
*East European rules of the validity of
international commercial
arbitration agreements* 466
*East European transport: regions and
modes* 551
East of Prague 56
*East-West relations and the future of
Eastern Europe: politics and
economics* 415, 446
*East-West trade and finance in the
world economy: a new look for the
1980s* 564
*East-West trade and the technology
gap: a political and economic
appraisal* 562
*East-West trade, industrial co-operation
and technology transfer: the British
experience* 563
Easter
customs 317
story in mediaeval drama 676
*Eastern and Western Europe in the
Middle Ages* 131
Eastern Europe *see* Europe, Eastern.
Eastern Europe 26
Eastern Europe and European security:

344

346

349

F

Faber, B. L. 312, 348
Fabulous Englishman 763
Facts on Czechoslovak foreign trade
   565
Fairy tales *see* Folk-tales.
Fallenbuchl, Z. M. 562
Family 62, 371-372
   role of grandmothers 357
   size 358-359
   structure 347
Farebný atlas rastlín 79
Farkaš, A. 471
Farm policies in socialist countries 525
Farmer, K. C. 307
Farský, Karel
   biography 334
Fashion trade 886
   periodicals 890
Fauna 25, 84-92, 393
   bark beetles 88
   birdlife on spoil heaps,
      North-Western Bohemia 87
   birds 84-90
   birds of prey 84
   butterflies 92
   carp 21
   chamois 9
   fish 21, 90-91, 606
   fishpond regions 21, 89-90
   Krkonoše (Giant Mountains)
      National Park 597
   legislation protecting birds 86
   mammals 90
   moths 88, 92
   muskrat 90
   skylark 87
   songbirds 85
   Tatra Mountains region 14
   tawny pipit 87
   thrips 90
   Třeboň Basin 89-90
   trout 21
   wheatear 87
   wildfowl – fishpond regions 89
Federal Ministry of Labour and Social
   Affairs 373
Federal Office of Statistics 390
Federalization 218, 260, 403, 471
Feierabend, I. K. 181
Feiwel, G. R. 490

Fejtö, F. 207
Ferdinand I (Holy Roman Emperor)
   150
Ferenčík, J. 674
Fertility 358-359
Feudalism 127, 151-152
Feuilleton 730
Fez-making industry 531
Fibich, Zdeněk 804, 809
Fic, W. M. 163, 165
Fiction and drama in Eastern and
   Southeastern Europe: evolution
   and experiment in the postwar
   period; proceedings of the 1978
   UCLA conference 690
Field, M. G. 362
Field guide in colour to butterflies and
   moths 92
Filip, J. 99, 103
Filipec, J. 619
Films *see* Cinema and films.
Finance 493, 504-505, 509, 556, 560,
   564, 929
   Europe, Eastern 506
   in 16th century 150
   position in 1920s 58
   statistics 389
   USSR 506
Finance of Czechoslovakia in the new
   scheme of management 504
Fine, M. 277
Finkielkraut, A. 908
Finland
   ice-hockey 607
Finlayson-Samsour, R. 779
Finn, S. 567
Fireflies 707
Firsoff, V. A. 14
First Republic (1918-38) 7, 12, 172,
   175, 245, 974
   constitution 173
   cultural development 174
   Czechoslovak-Hungarian relations
      437
   democracy 394
   economy 174, 479-481
   education 174, 387, 579
   education in Slovakia 378
   election laws 462
   film industry 836, 838
   foreign relations 173-174
   German grievances 173

350

France 142, 772, 782, 823
  foreign policy 439
  literature 673
  memoirs of Czechoslovak airmen
    (1939-42) 193
  relations with Czechoslovakia 12,
    178, 205
  Slovaks 302
Francisco, R. A. 523-524
Franck, C. 831
Franz Kafka of Prague 749
Free communism: a Czech experiment
  212
Freeman, J. W. 846
Frejka, T. 358
Frekvencia slov v slovenčine 635
*Frekvence slov, slovních druhů a tvarů
  v českém jazyce* 623
French, A. 684, 728
French, R. A. 580, 587
Freshwater fishes 91
Freudenberger, H. 251
Fridrich, J. 94-95
Frinta, M. S. 777, 780
*From Dubček to Charter 77: a study of
  'normalisation' in Czechoslovakia,
  1968-1978* 223
*From Prague after Munich: diplomatic
  papers 1938-1940* 179
From a terrace in Prague 54
*From Trianon to the First Vienna
  Arbitral Award: the Hungarian
  minority in the First Czechoslovak
  Republic 1918-1938* 273
Frontiers 257, 262
  dispute with Hungary (1938) 273
Fryščak, M. 632
Fügedis, E. 125
Fuks, Ladislav 690, 716
Fulla, Ľudovít 322
Fuller, R. J. 88
*25 Jahre Collegium Carolinum
  München 1956-1981* 970
Fungi 82
Furdek: Jednota Annual 898
Furniture
  Baroque 770
  Cubist 772
Furtmüller, L. 525
Fyleman, R. 707

G

Gagnaire, J. 657
Gajan, K. 996
Galleries
  Prague 47
Garden party 723
Gardner, J. 395
Gardovský, Č. 808
Garrett, E. V. 833
Garver, B. M. 7, 157
Gas 557
  pipelines 552
  statistics (consumption) 542, 557
Gašparíková, Ž. 644
Gati, C. 351, 445, 494
Gazetteers
  Prague 47
Gellner, J. 291
Genet, J. 845
Genetics 567
Genocide (World War II) 197-198,
  277, 280, 285, 288, 290
*Gentlemen of a company: English
  players in Central and Eastern
  Europe 1590-1660* 841
Geografický potenciál průmyslu v ČSR
  36
Geography 3, 6, 8-9, 25-51, 66, 173,
  326
  bibliographies 26, 949, 977
  biogeography 28
  Dobšiná ice cave 31
  economic 25-26, 28
  encyclopaedia 935
  geographic potential of Czech
    industry 36
  historical 26, 29
  industrial 536
  maps & atlases 37-51
  mineral springs 34
  Moravia 33
  Moravian limestone cliffs & caves 30
  physical 25-26, 46
  political 25-26, 46
  regional 27, 30, 33, 35
  Slovakia 378
  statistics 68
  urban 581
Geography of Czechoslovakia 28
Geology
  Dobšiná ice cave 31

353

list of government officers 403
management of the news 856-857
national committees 477
official publications (bibliography)
989
officials 932
policy towards Slovaks 238, 260
presidency 477
traditional obedience to 454
Government Committee for Tourism
of the Czech Socialist Republic
606
Government-in-exile
World War II 191, 196, 198, 248
*Government, law and courts in the
Soviet Union and Eastern Europe*
463
*Government tort liability in the Soviet
Union, Bulgaria, Czechoslovakia,
Hungary, Poland, Romania and
Yugoslavia* 472
Government Troops (Vládní vojsko)
during World War II 199
Gower, Sir R. 274
Graham, Sylvester 333
Grammaire de la langue tchèque 646,
657
Grammaire de la langue slovaque 657
Grammar 646-661
bibliographies 983
Czech 614, 617, 644, 646-654
Slavonic 653
Slovak 617, 655-661
West Slavonic 617
Grammar of contemporary Slovak 655
*Grammar of the Bohemian or Čech
language* 667
*Grammars and dictionaries of the
Slavic languages from the Middle
Ages up to 1850: an annotated
bibliography* 983
Gramotzki, H.-E. 512
Grandmothers
role in family 357
Granny: scenes from country life 705
Grant, N. 380
Graus, F. 131
Gray, J. 414
*Great Moravia: the archaeology of
ninth-century Czechoslovakia* 114
Great Moravian Empire 113-114, 242,
250, 339

Great Powers
relations with Czechoslovakia 12
Great Soviet Encyclopaedia 936
Greek Catholic Church 336, 896
Greeks 258, 262
Green International 176
Griffith, W. E. 206, 411, 998
Groseclose, J. S. 800
Gross, J. 126
Gross National Product 389, 479, 483,
485, 494
statistics 397
Growing up in Europe 195
Grund, Antonín 678
*Grundzüge der Völkerwanderungszeit
in Mähren* 112
Gruša, J. 685, 749
Grzybowski, K. 463
Gsovski, V. 341, 463, 958
Guardian 972
*Guide to the West Slavonic languages
(Guide to the Slavonic languages,
part 2)* 617
Guidebooks *see* Travel guides.
Guinness Book of Records 393
Guth, Jiří 601
Gutkind, E. A. 584
Gütter, N. 844
Gymnastics *see* Sokol movement.
Gyorgy, A. 397, 475
Gypsies 258, 260, 262-263, 290
Romania 312

H

Habel, F. P. 265
Háberová, I. 79
Habovštiak, A. 117
Habsburg Empire 126-127, 153,
155-156, 158, 233, 292, 394
agricultural reform (18th century)
152
bibliography 953
Bohemia 149-158
demise 158, 161-163, 166, 168, 188,
257, 334, 431, 695
diplomacy 156
folk-art 325
genealogy 153
industrialization – role of banks 503
intellectual developments 156

355

Hružik, L. 78
Hubáček, J. 666
Hudec, K. 86, 89-90
Hughes, G. 819
Hujer, K. 568
Human face of socialism: the political economy of change in Czechoslovakia 215
Human rights 395, 416, 423, 425-427
Humanitarianism 330
L'Humanité 883
Humanitism *see also* Humanitarianism and Masaryk, Tomáš G. 182, 184
Humanity: the political and social philosophy of Thomas G. Masaryk 184
Hummel, Johann Nepomuk 803
Hungarian minorities in the succession states 274
Hungarians 243, 262-263, 271-276, 336, 454, 470
   First Czechoslovak Republic (1918-38) 273-274, 579
   folk-music 328
   literature (in Czechoslovakia) 756
   Romania 312
   Ruthenia 308
   Slovakia 258, 308
Hungarians in Czechoslovakia 272
Hungary 180, 225, 237, 241, 263, 273, 325, 337, 375, 439, 454, 578, 584
   annexation of Ruthenia (1939) 180
   art, Renaissance 768
   banks & banking 505
   Czechs 307
   consumption 491
   economy 415, 491
   Jews (1936-39) 278
   law 461
   occupation of Carpatho-Ukraine (1939) 253-254
   occupation of Slovakia (1919) 168
   political strategies 415
   racial problems 242
   relations with Czechoslovakia 12, 437
   relations with USSR 457
   Ruthenians 269
   Slovaks 242, 302, 307-308
   social structure 312, 348
   tourist road-map 41
   uprising (1956) 437, 457

wages 511
Hungary and her successors: the treaty of Trianon and its consequences 1919-1937 308
Hungary, Czechoslovakia, Poland 41
Hunt, J. 14
Hunters, fishers and farmers of Eastern Europe, 6000-3000 B.C. 96
Hus, Jan *see also* Hussitism and Hussite Wars 7, 134, 136-138, 983
   bibliographies 955, 991
   biographies 136-138
   letters 994
   precursors & successors 138
   trial 137
Husák, Gustav 206, 223, 403-404, 410, 416, 998
   open letter from Havel, Václav 999
Huss, John *see* Hus, Jan.
Hussite King: Bohemia in European affairs 1440-1471 142
Hussite movement and the Reformation in Bohemia, Moravia and Slovakia (1350-1650): a bibliographical study guide (with particular reference to resources in North America) 991
Hussitism and Hussite Wars *see also* Hus, Jan 7, 58, 134-148, 331, 669
   bibliographies 136, 991
   Prague 139
   role of Bohemian cities 148
   role of nobility 141, 148
   Taborite movement, 135, 139-140
Huszczo, A. 368
Hviezdoslav, Pavol Orságh 738-739
Hviezdoslav: a national and world poet 738
Hydro-electric power
   disputes with Austria & Hungary 535
   Slapy Reservoir 575
Hydrology and hydroengineering 28, 575
   Dyje Dam & reservoir 595
   Krkonoše (Giant Mountains) National Park 597
   Slovak Socialist Republic 46
   Tatra National Park 598

J

Mácha, Karel Hynek 679
  biography 704
Machek, V. 620
Machine-tools industry 574
McIntyre, R. J. 358
Mackerras, C. 826-827, 829
McKinley, H. 754
Macku, J. 372
Mackworth, C. 430
Macleod, A. 322
McMillan, C. H. 559, 562
Macocha chasm 30, 321
Macourek, Miloš 672, 714
Mačtu, P. 271
Mączak, A. 125
Maďarská literatúra v ČSSR 756
Magocsi, P. R. 252, 269-270, 306, 926
Máj 704
Máj: zweisprachige Ausgabe 704
*Making of a new Europe: R. W. Seton-
  Watson and the last years of
  Austria-Hungary* 158
*Making of the Habsburg Monarchy,
  1550-1700: an interpretation* 153
Malá československá encyklopedie 934
Małowist, M. 125
Malý, J. 91
Malý, P. 385
Malý synonymický slovník 645
Mamatey, V. S. 172, 431
Mammoth hunting
  Dolní Věstonice encampment 97
*Man of stars: the Slovakian national
  poet Hviezdoslav: an illustrated
  summary* 738
*Management problems of Slapy
  Reservoir, Bohemia,
  Czechoslovakia* 575
Managers 350
Mann, S. E. 615
Mannheim 833
Mannheim school 810
*Manuel de slovaque à l'usage des
  slavisants* 658
*Manuel statistique de la République
  Tchécoslovaque 1920-1922* 392
Mapa kulturních památek ČSSR 69
Maps and atlases 37-51, 66, 592
  Bohemia 37, 72
  Bratislava 49
  Brno 48
  camp sites 45, 47, 72

  conservation areas 50, 589
  cultural monuments 69
  Czechs in USA 293, 297
  geology 51
  German Democratic Republic 40
  Hungary 41
  leisure map of Europe 39
  national parks 39, 50, 590, 592
  nuclear power stations 534
  plants 79
  Poland 40-41
  Prague 38-39, 47
  railways 38, 42
  roads 40-44, 47, 72, 592
  rivers 42, 592
  Slovak Socialist Republic 46
  touring maps 40, 43, 66
March of the seventy thousand 164
Marczewski, J. 493
Marer, P. 397, 495
Mareš, J. 36
Margolius, I. 772
Maria Theresa (Empress) 152
Markomanni
  defeated by Romans (179 AD) 107
Marriage 358-359
Marshall Plan 204, 442
Martin, G. 713
Martin, P. 851
Martinů, Bohuslav 803, 822-824
  biographies 813, 823-824
  dramatist 822
  symphonies & chamber music 822
Martinů, C. 823
Marxism 372, 382, 409, 490, 980
  industrial location 539
Marxist governments: a world survey
  409
Maryland 300
Masaryk, Alice 190
  biography 190
Masaryk, Jan
  biographies 188-189
Masaryk, Tomáš G. 160, 162, 182-188,
  256, 334, 372, 394, 679, 939
  bibliographies 966
  biographies 182, 188, 234, 939
  early academic career 185
  interpretation of Czech history 134,
    186
  philosophy 134, 182-184, 190, 334,
    679

Minařík, Pavel 856
Minerals
output statistics 390
Mining 6, 498, 566
coal 33, 87
copper 125
gold 125, 566
metals 540, 566
science & technology 566
silver 125
Slavs 122
Slovakia (14th-17th centuries) 125
statistics 498
Ministry of Agriculture and Food
newspaper 870
Ministry of Education, Czech Socialist
Republic 382
Minorities 1-2, 5, 171, 256-290, 304,
308, 331, 364, 408, 458, 470-471
attitude of Slovak state 243
after World War I 168
bibliographies 256, 261-262, 303,
949, 969
constitutional provision 470
Croats 258
Czechs 256, 263, 289
documents 273, 993
Europe, Eastern 260-261, 277, 307
First Republic (1918-38) 173-174,
176, 308
Germans 172, 258-260, 262-263,
265-268, 317, 331, 434-436, 470
Greeks 258, 262
gypsies 258, 260, 262, 290, 312
Hungarians 243, 262-263, 271-276,
308, 454, 470
incorporation into new state of
Czechoslovakia 257
Jews 258, 260, 262-263, 268,
277-288
nationalism (1920s) 176
Poles 243, 258, 262-263, 289, 470
problem in Habsburg Empire 256
Romania 311-312
Romanians in Ruthenia 59
Russians 262
Ruthenians 258, 269-271, 470, 926
Slovaks 237, 243, 271
Sudeten Germans 167, 178, 265-267,
434-436
Ukrainians 243, 258, 262-263, 269,
271, 470

World War II 258-259, 261
Mint (at Kremnica) 566
Mirvaldová, H. 685
Missions and missionaries
Irish 129
Jesuits in Latin America 292
Mistrík, J. 612, 635-636, 655, 660
Mitchell, R. C. 190
Mitchell Beazley pocket guide to cheese
850
Mittelalterliche Glasmalerei in der
Tschechoslowakei 785
Mladá fronta 869
z Mladoňovic, Petr 137, 211
Mladý svět 881
Mlynář, Zdeněk 221, 371, 477
Mňačko, L. 211, 741
Mne soudila noc 725
Modern Czech grammar 649, 651
Modern Slavic literatures. Vol. 2.
Bulgarian, Czechoslovak, Polish,
Ukrainian and Yugoslav literatures
670
Moldanová, D. 694
Moley, R. 298
Monasteries
St. George, at Prague Castle 115
Sázava 117
Money 485, 504-506
hard & soft currency 397, 495, 504
mint (at Kremnica) 566
stabilization of the currency
(1918-38) 480, 492
Money, banking & credit in the Soviet
Union & Eastern Europe 506
Monuments 393
atlas 69
cultural & historical 10
map 39
Prague 47
Moods, impressions and memoirs 809
Morava na sklonku antiky 111
Moravčík, I. 328
Moravec, General F. 192
memoirs 192
Moravia 614
agriculture 33
anabaptists 147
archaeological finds & sites 112, 120
art, Gothic 779
art, Romanesque 767
bibliography 991

374

Slovak 240, 242, 740, 803
National science information systems: a
  guide to science information
  systems in Bulgaria,
  Czechoslovakia, Hungary,
  Rumania and Yugoslavia 578
National security 4
National Theatre 806, 849
National Theatre movement
  Czech (1845-83) 231
Nationalism 1-2, 181, 264, 488
  among minorities (1920s) 176
  Czech 224-236, 264
  Europe, East-Central 240
  Europe, Eastern 264, 397
  history 13, 176, 181
  Masaryk, Tomáš G. 184
  Ruthenians 270
  Slovak 158, 225, 237-249, 264, 291,
    305, 903
Nationalism in Eastern Europe 264
Nationalities *see* Minorities.
Native literature of Bohemia in the
  fourteenth century 675
NATO, Economics Directorate and
  Information Directorate 501
Natural resources 537
  statistics 540
Nature conservation *see* Conservation,
  Environment and National parks.
Nature reserves and parks 393
Naughton, J. D. 667, 694, 710
Navrátilová, Martina 610
  autobiography 610
Nazis 435, 746
  foreign policy 435
Nečas, C. 290
Nechvátal, B. 19
Nedělní hlasatel 861
Nelson, D. 421
Němcová, B. 705
Němcová, J. W. 751
Němec, F. 255
Němec, J. 460
Němec, L. 335, 338-340
Nemejovský, J. 383, 819
Neo-Slavism
  Czechs 232
Neo-Slavism and the Czechs 1898-1914
  232
Neprebudený 740
Neruda, J. 706

Nesměrák, I. 575
Neruda, Pablo (Neftalí Ricardo Reyes)
  706
Netherlands 375-376
Nettl, B. 328
Nettl, P. 810
Neubert, K. 16, 18
Neubert, L. 783
Neumüller, M. 970
Neustupný, E. 93
Neustupný, J. 93, 104
New Amsterdam 300
New economic patterns in
  Czechoslovakia: impact of growth,
  planning and the market 490
New economic systems of Eastern
  Europe 489, 501
New Grove Dictionary of Music and
  Musicians 830
Newall, V. 317
Newmarch, R. 802
Newspapers 859, 865-883
  agriculture & food 870
  bibliographies 951, 956, 972-973, 987
  bibliography (Czech) 951
  Bratislava 875
  Brno 875
  Catholic 872
  Communist Party, Czechoslovak
    865
  Communist Party, Slovak 866
  Czech 868-870, 874, 877, 879, 882,
    951
  Czechoslovak People's Party 872
  Czechoslovak Socialist Party 871
  during events of 1968-69 959, 972
  Europe, East 956
  foreign press digest 883
  German minority 876
  Hungarian-language 867, 882
  Košice 875
  new books 878
  Prague 875
  satirical 877
  Slovak 866, 868-874, 877, 879, 882
  Slovak (USA) 864
  Slovak Freedom Party 871
  Slovak Party of Reconstruction 873
  sport 874
  trade union 868
  women's 882
  youth 869

377

383

Review of socialist law 472
Revolutionary war for independence
    and the Russian question:
    Czechoslovak army in Russia
    1914-18 163
Revolutions 1848 127, 225, 230
    Russian (1917) 163-164, 166
    Slovak National Uprising 192, 248,
    288
Revue d'Études Comparatives Est
    Ouest: Economie, Planification,
    Organisation 915
Rezek, A.
    biography 234
Rice, C. 418, 451
Rice, M. P. 669
Richard, M. 242
Richard II, King of England 778
Richter, B. 526
Richter, František Xaver 833
Richter, L. 733
Riders in the Sky 193, 720
Riese, H-P. 426
Rilke, Rainer Maria 908
Riordan, J. 600
Rivers 585, 594, 606
    maps 42, 592
    Dyje 595
    Punkva 30, 321
Road to World War II: a documentary
    history 177
Roads and motoring 552
    E12 road 72
    E85 road 72
    maps 40-44, 47, 72, 592
    regulations & insurance
        requirements 67
Roberts, A. 448
Roberts, H. L. 976
Robertson, R. 748
Robson, E. I. 57
Rococo
    architecture 801
Rodinov
    collectivization of agriculture
        520
Rogačová, M. 10, 796
Roháč 877
Roldán, E. 10
Roľnícke noviny 870
Roman bronze vessels from Slovakia
    107

Roman cemetery at Gerulata Rusovce
    108
Roman imports in Bohemia 106
Romania 412, 578
    Czech language 665
    Czechs 310-312
    economic change 412
    Gypsies 312
    Jews 312
    Jews (1936-39) 278
    minorities 311-312
    political change 412
    relations with Czechoslovakia 12,
        438
    Slovaks 302, 307, 310-312
    social structure 312, 348
Romanians 59, 438
Romans 93, 106-111
    Bohemia 106
    cemetery at Gerulata Rusovce 108
    collapse of the Empire 111, 113
    Moravia 111, 113
    Slovakia 107-111
    victory over Markomanni (179AD)
        107
Románské umění v Čechách a na
    Moravě 767
Romanticism 693, 736
Römische und germanische Kunst in
    der Slowakei 109
Rondocubism
    Bohemia 772
Rood, W. 376
La rose de Bratislava 760
Rosenbaum, K. 735, 756
Rosická, M. 852
Rostankowski, P. 977
Rothe, D. 908
Rothschild, J. 126, 171
Rotundas, Romanesque 117
Roucek, J. S. 234, 295
Round, D. 711
Rousseau, J. J. 833
Roy, J. A. 289
Royal Air Force 205, 720
    memoirs of Czechoslovak airmen
        (1939-42) 193
Royal Scientific Society of Bohemia
    667
Rožmberk estates
    in 16th century 151
Rudé právo 865, 871

389

Speleology *see* Caves & Caving.
Spies and spying *see* Intelligence
   service.
Spinka, M. 136-138, 375, 703, 994
Spirit of Bohemia: a survey of
   Czechoslovak history, music and
   literature 128
Spiš 440
Spisar, A. 334
Šport 874
Sport under communism: The USSR,
   Czechoslovakia, the GDR, China,
   Cuba 600
Sports and recreation 8, 67, 346, 592,
   599-610, 886, 895
   athletics 608
   chalupa 13, 500, 609
   chata 13, 500, 609
   chess 602
   China 600
   Cuba 600
   facilities in Prague 47
   fishing 606
   football 607
   German Democratic Republic 600
   ice-hockey 607
   in the 1930s 59
   Krkonoše (Giant Mountains)
      National Park 597
   newspaper 874
   Olympic Games 601
   Prague 586
   skiing 605
   Sokol movement 58-59, 268, 331,
      599, 601, 603
   Spartakiads 599, 603-604
   tennis 610
   USSR 600
   water sports – Slapy Reservoir 575
   weekend homes 13, 500, 609
Šprunk, K. 654
Srch, A. 16
Staar, R. F. 478
Stacho, Ján 672
Stalin, Joseph and Stalinism 127,
   207-208, 211-212, 398, 402, 404,
   449, 459, 502
   de-Stalinization 214
   rehabilitation of victims of Stalinism
      218
Stalinism. Essays in historical
   interpretation 404

Stalinism in Prague: the Loebl story
   208
Stambuk, G. 475
Stamic, Jan Václav 810, 832-833
Stamitz, Johann *see* Stamic, Jan
   Václav.
Standard of living 348, 485
   statistics 389
Staněk, V. J. 92
Stanislav ze Znojma 136
Stanislavsky, K. S. 846
Stankiewicz, E. 611, 983
Stankovský, J. 563
Stará Boleslav 763
Staré Hradisko
   Celtic oppidum 105
Starobin, H. 208
Starý, F. 544
Šťastný, K. 85, 88-90
State Jewish Musuem (Prague) 285
State Jewish Museum in Prague 285
State of sociology in Eastern Europe
   today 372
State Scientific Library 945
Statistical survey of Czechoslovakia 390
Statistická ročenka Československé
   socialistické republiky 1957-1970
   392
Statistics 1-2, 5-6, 348, 388-393, 476,
   478, 498, 884
   agriculture 389-390, 498, 520, 522,
      525
   arms exports 397
   balance of payments 389
   banking 498
   bibliography of official documents
      989
   birds 86
   censuses 388, 391
   coal consumption 542
   Comecon trade 389
   Communist Party, Czechoslovak
      (membership) 388
   consumption 498
   crime 362, 476
   culture 388
   Czechs in USA 293
   economic 68, 446, 479-480, 481-484,
      490, 494-495, 497-498, 508, 540
   education 388-390
   electricity 542
   employment 389

398

400

Třísov, a Celtic oppidum in South
Bohemia 104
Trnka, Jiří 319, 707-708, 775
Truth will prevail 405
Tschechische Erzählkunst im 20.
Jahrhundert 682
Tuck, K. P. 329
Tucker, R. C. 404
Turkey
interwar period 170
Turkish Wars (16th century) 148, 150
Turner-Kadečková, J. 15, 285, 795
Turnock, D. 536
Turnwald, W. K. 995
Turska, K. 320
Twentieth century Czechoslovakia: the
meaning of its history 160
Two widows 813
Tybor, M. M. 22
Tyrner, P. 87
Tyrrell, J. 830
Tyrš, Miroslav 599, 601

U

Učebnik slovatskogo jazyka dlja
slavistov 658
Uhde, Milan 843
Uhlíř, L. 10
Új szó 867
Ukraine
encyclopaedia 938
evacuation in 1918 163
literature 670, 752
Ukraine: a concise encyclopaedia 938
Ukrainian National Association 938
Ukrainians 243, 258, 262-263, 269, 271,
470, 752
Prague 753
Ulč, O. 220, 397, 419, 421, 465, 494
Ullmann, W. 205, 442
Umbrella from Picadilly 717
Uniate Church 337
impact of reforms of 1960s 217
Union of Czech Writers 894
Union of Slovak Writers 894
Union of Women 355
Union of Writers
4th Congress 428
Unitarianism 330, 334
United Agricultural Cooperatives *see*

also Collectivization and collective
farms. 515
United States and East Central Europe,
1914-1918: a study in Wilsonian
diplomacy and propaganda 431
United States in Prague, 1945-1948 442
Unity of Czech Brethren 146-148, 343
Universal peace organization of King
George of Bohemia: a fifteenth
century plan for world peace 1462-
1464 143
Universities 382-386
Buda 612
Prague 234, 268, 384-385
Slovakía 22
Unwin, I. 779
Urban, R. 379
Urban development in East-Central
Europe: Poland, Czechoslovakia
and Hungary 584
Urbanization 494, 579-588
Bohemia 579
history 13, 15, 579
intellectuals 579
Prague 585-587
Urbanization in socialist countries 580
Urbanization under socialism: the case
of Czechoslovakia 581
USA 342, 823
colleges, libraries & archives with a
Czech or Slovak connection 861
Czech engineering 570
Czech intelligence activities 164
Czech journalism 294
Czech language 662, 665
Czech linguistics 293
Czechoslovak Society of Arts &
Sciences in America 295
Czechs 12, 293-300, 302, 432, 570,
702, 954, 962, 969
Czechs in Cleveland, Ohio 298
Czechs in Texas 299
ethnic groups in Wisconsin 293
folk-music 328
foreign policy towards Eastern
Europe (1943-47) 443
ice-hockey 607
Kennan, George F. (diplomatic
papers) 179
library, museum & archive holdings
on USSR & Eastern Europe 923,
925-926

pollution 590-591
thermal waters & mineral springs 34
Slapy Reservoir 575
Watney, H. 327
Wayfarer in Czecho-Slovakia 57
Weather *see* Climate and meteorology.
Weatherall, M. 330
Weatherall, R. 330
Webb, W. L. 428
Weekend homes 13, 500, 609
Weinerman, E. R. 365
Weinerman, S. B. 365
Weinryb, B. D. 277
Weir, A. R. 193
Weissbort, D. 207
Weist, W. B. 185
*Welcome to Czechoslovakia: Tourist
    Review* 895
Welfare *see also* Social services 419
    Jews 282
    Slovak Socialist Republic 46
Wellek, R. 186, 190, 673, 679, 686, 728
Wells, D. A. 990
Wenceslas, Saint 339
    crown 799
Wenceslas IV, King 138
Werich, Jan 908
Werner, Jan 668
Westböhmen in der späten Bronzezeit
    101
*West- und Sudböhmische Funde in
    Wien* 120
Wheatear 87
Wheeler, G. S. 215
Whitaker, R. 978
White, G. 770
White, P. T. 589
White, S. 395, 400, 421
White, W. 52
White-collar workers
    increase in numbers 510
White Mountain, Battle (1620) 132,
    154, 300
White Paper on Czechoslovakia
    425-426
*White stones and fir trees: an anthology
    of contemporary Slavic literature*
    672
Who is Josef Svoboda 846
Wiatr, J. J. 372
Wightman, G. 352, 414
Wien und seine Tschechen: Integration

*und Assimilation einer Minderheit
    im 20. Jahrhundert* 309
Die Wiener Tschechen um 1900 309
Wilbraham, M. 846
Wilczynski, J. 509, 551, 560
Wiley, R. J. 820
Williams, R. A. 166
Williams, William Carlos 699
Williamson, S. R. Jr. 166
Wilson, P. 221, 724
Wilson, President Woodrow 164, 172,
    431
Winch, M. 253
Windsor, P. 448
Wine 853
    map of wine centres 39
*Wings in exile: life and work of the
    Czechoslovak airmen in France
    and Great Britain* 193
Winner, T. G. 687, 690
Winter, K. 214
Winter in Czechoslovakia 605
*Winter in Prague: documents on
    Czechoslovak communism in crisis*
    998
*Winter into Spring: the Czechoslovak
    press and the reform movement
    1963-1968* 858
Winters, S. B. 156
Wisconsin
    ethnic groups 293
Wiskemann, E. 58, 433
Wojatsek, C. 273
Wolchik, S. L. 356, 420, 444
Wolker, Jiří 700
Women 353-355
    child-care 353-355
    communism 352-356, 358
    education 380
    employment 353-355, 512, 540
    everyday life 354-355
    housework 355
    legislation 354
    membership of the Czechoslovak
        Communist Party 352
    newspapers 882
    position in society (ca. 15th-20th
        centuries) 58
    Slovak in Pennsylvania (1875-1914)
        303
    social services 353
    status 347, 352-356, 358, 419

Women contd.
  suicide rate 353
Women and state socialism: sex
    inequality in the Soviet Union and
    Czechoslovakia 355
Women and world change: equity issues
    in development 354
Women under Communism 354
Woodings, R. B. 939
World of a child 744
World of Franz Kafka 747
Wood, Sir Henry 827
Wood, R. 320
Wood-carving
  ladles 793
Wooden buildings 773-774
Woodcraft movement 333
Wooden churches of Eastern Europe:
    an introductory survey 773
Woollen industry 251
  Brno (18th century) 251
Worcester Festival, Massachusetts
  Dvořák, Antonín 820
Workerism 417
Workers' councils 514
Workers' councils in Czechoslovakia
    1968-69: documents and essays 514
Working Saturdays 510
World Bank 389
World guide to beer 853
World War I 156, 158, 161, 163-164,
    166-168, 188, 434
  Britain's relations with Czechs &
    Slovaks 431
  Czech & Slovak prisoners in Italy
    166
  Czech & Slovak prisoners in Russia
    166
  Czech legion in Italy 166
  Czechs & Slovaks in Cleveland,
    Ohio 298
  novels 695
  poetry 739
World War II 7, 12, 172, 174-175, 177,
    179-181, 188, 191-199, 254, 418,
    479, 720, 721, 724, 751, 873
  activities of Zpravodajská agentúra
    Slovenska (press agency) 855
  bibliography 957
  Czech-Slovak hostility 179
  documents 996
  film industry 838

genocide 277, 280, 285, 288, 290
German occupation 172, 191, 194,
    716
Government-in-exile 191, 196, 198,
    248
'Government Troops' (Vládní
    vojsko) 199
Heydrich, Reinhard (assassination,
    1942) 192, 194, 196-198, 957
Kennan, George F. (diplomatic
    papers) 179
Krasňa massacre 197
Ležáky massacre 197
liberation 63, 185, 238, 442
Lidice massacre (1942) 197-198
memoirs of Czechoslovak airmen in
    Britain & France 193
memoirs of Kay Sun 195
minorities 258-259, 261-263, 267
proposed Czechoslovak-Polish
    Confederation 441
Protectorate of Bohemia & Moravia
    199, 258, 957
resistance movement 172, 194-196,
    199
Slovak independent state 180, 238,
    258
Slovak National Uprising 192, 248,
    288
Slovak People's Party 243, 247
Soviet seizure of Subcarpathian
    Ruthenia (1944) 255
Worth, D. 612
Wortley, B. A. 466
Wratislaw, A. H. 675, 726
Wright, K. A. 829
Wright, M. 417
Wright, W. E. 152
Writers
  during 'Prague Spring' 218
Writers against rulers 428, 857
Writing on the wall: an anthology of
    contemporary Czech literature 719,
    730
Wurm, K. 792
Wyatt, K. D. 244
Wyclif, John 135, 331
Wynar, L. R. 925
Wynnyczuk, A. 483

408

Map of Czechoslovakia

This map shows the more important towns and other features.

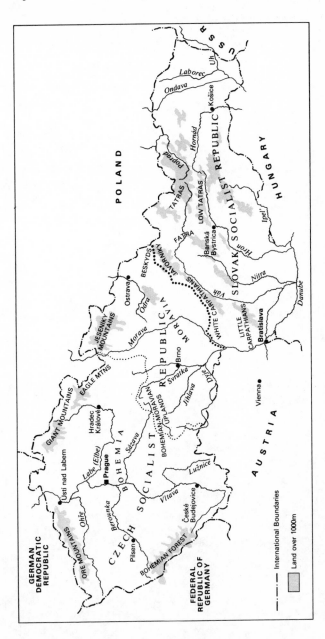